The End of Strife

The End of Strife

Understanding Why the World is at War with Itself; and the Path Back to True Peace

by Leland Johnson

WESTBOW®
PRESS
A DIVISION OF THOMAS NELSON
& ZONDERVAN

WestBow Press books may be ordered through booksellers or by contacting:

WestBow Press
A Division of Thomas Nelson & Zondervan
1663 Liberty Drive
Bloomington, IN 47403
www.westbowpress.com
1 (866) 928-1240

ISBN: 978-1-4497-4073-3 (sc)
ISBN: 978-1-4497-4074-0 (hc)
ISBN: 978-1-4497-4072-6 (e)

Library of Congress Control Number: 2012902838

Printed in the United States of America.

WestBow Press rev. date: 09/05/2014

Contents

Preface ix

A Common Understanding of Critically Important Moral Principles 1

    Evil 2

    Good 6

    Love 8

    Hate 8

    Peace 9

    Justice 12

How These Moral Principles Are Being Perverted in Today's World 14

    Good and Evil 16

    Love 17

    Hate 18

    Peace 19

    Justice 19

How the Perversion of These Moral Principles Is Being Used to
Induce the Suicidal Self-Destruction of Societies All Over the World 21

    Evil 21

    Good 23

    Love 25

    Hate 32

    Peace 33

    Justice 36

Why Is There So Much Strife in the World, or in Other Words, "Why
Can't We All Just Get Along"? 40

How We Regressed to Our Current, Sad, State 54

    Affective Reasoning vs. Cognitive Reasoning 66

    The Real-World Chronicle of Regression to Our Current State of
    Cultural Barbarism 76

    Why a Traditional Social Order and Morality Is Superior to
    Narcissistic Anarchy 91

        Faith vs. Atheism 91

        Patriarchy vs. Feminism 98

        Traditional Sexual Morality vs. Promiscuity 112

        Reproduction vs. Contraception and Abortion 113

        Heterosexuality vs. Homosexuality 114

        Sobriety vs. Drug Abuse 114

    The Device(s) Used to Regress Us to Our Current State of Cultural
    Barbarism 116

Why We Have Regressed to Our Current, Sad State? 133
How Do We Rise Above Our Current, Sad, State and Achieve True
Peace? 145
    Which Religion is the True Religion? 179
    What Is The True Path to Peace and Freedom? 185
    Why Does the Human Race So Despise God and His Moral Precepts;
    Even to the Point of Denying His Existence!? 200
    For Catholics 210
        For Priests 249
        For Laypeople 271
    A Call to Return to the Faith and a Correction of Common
    Protestant Errors and Misunderstandings 284
    Coming To a Choice and Making a Stand 299
    The Consequences of Our Choice 330
Concluding Remarks 344
Appendix A Declaration of the Rights of Man and of the Citizen 349
Appendix B Suggested Reading Material 353
Appendix C Miracles Within Christianity 361
    The Raising of the Dead: St. Stanislaus 361
        St. Stanislaus 361
    The Incorruptibility of the Saints: The Absence of Decay or
    Deterioration in Their Deceased Bodies 363
        St. Rose of Viterbo (d. 1252) 363
        Saint Sperandia (d. 1276) 363
        Saint Zita (d. 1278) 364
        Blessed Margaret of Metola (d. 1320) 364
        St. Catherine of Bologna (d. 1463) 364
        Blessed Margaret of Savoy (d. 1464) 365
        Blessed Eustochia Calafato (d. 1485) 365
        Blessed Bernard Scammacca (d. 1486) 365
        Saint Catherine of Genoa (d. 1510) 365
        St. Catherine Dei Ricci (d. 1590) 366
        Venerable Maria Vela (d. 1617) 366
        Venerable Mary of Ágreda (d. 1665) 366
        St. Lucy Filippini (d. 1732) 367
        St. Teresa Margaret of the Sacred Heart (d. 1770) 367
        St. Catherine Labouré (d. 1876) 367
        St. Bernadette Soubirous (d. 1879) 368

Eucharistic Miracles: The Miraculous Transformation or Preservation
of Consecrated Hosts 369
  Lanciano, Italy (700 A.D.) 369
  Ferrara, Italy (1171 A.D.) 370
  Santarem, Portugal (Early 13th Century) 370
  Bolsena-Orvieto, Italy (1263 A.D.) 371
  Siena, Italy (1330 A.D.) 371
  Siena, Italy (1730 A.D.) 371

Preface

As the reader must certainly acknowledge, the world today is really becoming quite a horrifying mess in an astonishingly short amount of time. Wars are being fought all over the globe on almost every populated continent, and in other places where there are not active wars it seems likely that they will inevitably come to pass in the future if humanity does not turn away from its current, suicidal tendencies and behavior. Although the immediate causative factors are primarily due to the egomaniacal nature of a great many economic "power-brokers" and political "leaders" currently holding the reins of power in nations all over the world—who see themselves as combatants in a "noble" (in their minds) struggle to seize power so that they may literally rule the world—the contributing factors that led to such dangerous creatures being able to ascend to the highest seats of power in the world are truly the root cause of the world's ills.

It is most certainly true, and an honest reader will admit, that never before in the history of the human race have so few held so much power over so many. However, with only a few exceptions, the current order of the world has come about via the consent of the governed. In many third world countries it is common to find a tyrant who rose to power at the point of a gun and who imposes his will on the people under his control through both deceit and the force of arms. However, within the developed nations of the world, and especially within Western civilization, the citizens therein have not the excuse of persecution to fall upon. The citizens of these nations have willfully chosen to subject themselves to today's odious political and economic "leaders" through their own consent.

The purpose of this book is to explain both the causes for the social and cultural breakdown(s) in today's world, as well as the solutions to our societal regression. The causes come from multiple fronts and did not develop in a matter of days, weeks, months, years, decades, or even generations. The degenerative process that has led humanity to the suicidal path it is currently embarked upon has taken several centuries of *progressive* corruption to reach this point. However, there is a way to reverse course and heal our society again; returning it to its former strength and health. The way in which a true peace can be realized in this world will be explained. It must be admitted that what it takes to achieve a more universal peace is difficult and burdensome on people for many and various reasons. However, when the reader looks at the state of the world today, it is hopeful that they will choose the difficult and burdensome road required in order to maintain a peaceful civilization rather than the bloody chaos and anarchy transpiring in today's world.

Before we begin, the reader must be properly advised regarding how to approach this work. It is of critical importance that the reader leaves their emotions "at the door" while considering the things explained in this book. There are many things presented within that contradict modern "wisdom," and as such will be found highly offensive to many people if they are not able to put their emotions aside and address what is presented here through the eyes of objective reality alone. Although many people may be offended by the content, it must be clearly stated that the purpose of this work is not to offend, but rather to inform the reader as to the true root cause(s) of the problems in this world. It is my hope that the reader will be able to push past any bruised feelings or injured sensibilities in order to understand the larger points being presented.

A Common Understanding of Critically Important Moral Principles

Before we can understand how the world has come to be in such an increasingly anarchistic state, it is absolutely necessary that the reader possess a true understanding of some vitally important moral principles. The confusion caused by the erroneous understanding of these important principles is the primary contributing factor that is driving whole civilizations down their current, suicidal path. Moreover, it is necessary to clarify and more precisely define these moral principles so that the reader will understand what is to follow; both within the proper context and in the intended, charitable spirit. These principles are commonly perverted and abused today by politicians in their self-serving political rhetoric, ignorantly (or deliberately) propagated for public consumption by the media, and as a result are almost universally misunderstood by the general public due to their constant immersion in false, childish, and shallow representations of these principles. They are: (1) evil, (2) good, (3) love, (4) hate, (5) peace, and (6) justice.

The discussion of these principles will pertain to their moral nature only; not to any of the other connotations that are often attributed to these words. For example, people will speak of an "evil" stench, a "good" book, the fact that they "love" their new car, or that they "hate" sardines on their pizza, desire world "peace," and "justice" for the working man. These, and other instances of these words that are used in similar contexts, refer to the use of these words to describe a subjective, human assignment of relative perception or value, which is different for each person in this world. The first four moral principles have their foundation in religion and theology. An attempt will be made to avoid sounding unduly "preachy"; as I am fully aware that, due to the advances of socialism and communism (through the vehicles of atheism and humanism) throughout Western civilization, the discussion of religious and theological topics are as appealing to a great many people as garlic, Holy Water, and stakes are to vampires; but to really see and understand these principles properly, and at a deeper level, people must have a solid understanding of their basis: what they are, and how they are propagated in the world. This can only be done by returning to the original foundations of these principles. Moreover, understanding

1

these principles properly is absolutely necessary for all people if they are to keep themselves from being deceived by this world's ambitious, cunning, and manipulative creatures: a.k.a. politicians, lawyers, social activists, "community organizers," etc.

The various and numerous social diseases currently plaguing the world find their cause in the spiritual realm and, more appropriately stated, they can be said to germinate from the almost complete lack of morality and the near universal abdication of self-control and personal responsibility that has engulfed the modern world. This is the reason why it is so crucial to properly understand these principles. Let's first look to the proper understanding of these moral principles individually. After that, we can then notice how they are being perverted in today's world. Finally, we will then be able to discern how the perversions of these principles are being used to usher in our suicidal self-destruction.

Evil

At its deepest level, evil is a quality, act, or state of being that opposes God's will and offends Him: "sin" being the word we use to describe the act of doing or propagating evil. The first reaction to such a broad definition is often a sarcastic, "Thanks a lot, buddy. That really makes things clear to me now"! The definition of evil may sound too broad to have any practical applicability in recognizing it in the world, but when one looks to the attributes of God it is much easier to recognize it. From numerous religious sources all throughout recorded history (saints, mystics, the Bible, prophecy, etc.) mankind has come to understand several of the attributes of God. To begin with, He is the source and creator of all things: mankind, irrational animals, trees, dirt . . . *everything.* Moreover, God is also recognized as the only being that is capable of creating something from nothing.

His greatest glory and "claim to fame," if you will, comes from being the sole creator of all things; as well as His ability to impart life to living creatures, which is another thing that only God can do. He is also known to be eternal, meaning that He has always been and will always be. But in order to be eternal, He must also be perfect; for if there were any imperfection in God, corruptibility would exist within His essence and being; which would ultimately lead to His death, just as the corruptible nature of human beings leads to their ultimate end in this world. But, since He is eternal, this is not possible. Moreover, as a consequence of God's eternal nature, it is impossible for Him to lie;[1] as a lie would signify a corruption or imperfection in His essence, which has been established by various sources throughout history to be an impossibility.[2]

We also understand from classical theology that God has a principal enemy, and self-styled competitor, for dominion over Creation: the Devil. The Devil is diametrically opposed to God in both purpose and act. The Devil's sole desire, and self-assigned purpose, is to be as resolutely opposed to God in every way and quality, so as to be the most effective at actively opposing and undermining God's will; as well as to simultaneously recruit others to join him in his spiteful hatred of, and opposition to, God: his spite being the product of his rejection and punishment by God for attempting to make himself God's equal: such insanity being the byproduct of his enflamed pride[3] and sentiment(s) of self-importance. With the above understanding, we can see that the Devil is both the complete, polar opposite of God, as well as the most pure incarnation and personification of evil, which is why he is referred to as "evil incarnate." From this, in combination with the recollection that evil is a quality, act, or state of being that opposes God's will, we can see that the Devil is not only evil by his nature, he *is* evil itself.

Whereas God is always truthful, the Devil is always deceitful.[4] Whereas God is the universal source of life, the Devil is the universal source of death. Whereas God is the universal Creator, the Devil is the universal destroyer. We can now grasp a more practical, functional recognition of how evil manifests

---

[1] This reality is explicitly stated in the Bible: "That by two immutable things, in which it is impossible for God to lie, we may have the strongest comfort, who have fled for refuge to hold fast the hope set before us." (Heb. 6:18).

[2] These facts simply cannot be fully explained or proved here. To begin with, it would distract from the main purpose of this book. Additionally, the proofs in reason and in mathematics are too long and involved to present here. If the reader is interested in investigating the various proofs of the existence of God and His attributes, Aristotle (*Physics* and *Metaphysics*) and St. Thomas Aquinas (*Summa Contra Gentiles* and *Summa Theologica*) are suggested for the proofs based in reason, and Peter Stoner (*Science Speaks*) for the mathematical, statistical proof of the existence of God.

[3] Pride is the ultimate source of all human contention. This reality is the central point that will be explained and discussed in more detail within this book.

[4] Ironically, the Devil (evil) often achieves his greatest success in deceitfulness when he slips in a single lie at a critical point, regarding an important concept or idea, amongst a thousand other truths regarding concepts and ideas of lesser importance.

itself by combining the understanding of the above stated principles. Since the Devil *is* evil itself, we can say that **evil is any quality, act, or state of being that either causes or gravitates toward destruction: especially the destruction of life (death)**. Moreover, it most often works toward, and achieves, its destructive ends through the use of deceit. In some cases there are those people who know that the things they do are evil; yet they choose to do them because, for some perversely insane reason, they enjoy being evil. These are the people who work toward evil ends without being deceived regarding the dangerous, and most often deadly, final ends that will follow as a consequence of their efforts.

Having arrived at a functional, practical way to recognize evil; we then must look to how it propagates itself throughout the world so that we can put a stop to the deception, death, and destruction that evil always leads to when not checked and abated. Since the goals and ends of evil are death and destruction, it must work toward its desired end in a manner consistent with its nature. Remembering that God is perfect and incorruptible, evil will then work toward destruction by introducing corruption into whatever it is that it is trying to destroy. The manner of corruption (moral or physical) is not as important as the introduction of a corruptive element, because once a little corruption reaches into a person it most always grows and spreads to include other forms;[5] requiring a conscious act of will to reverse the degenerative process. The corruptive element, whatever it is, attaches itself to the affected person until it either destroys them by consuming and depleting their life energy, or the person overcomes the corruption. In this way **evil can be more easily observed to propagate itself in a manner that is comparable to that of a parasite that attaches itself to a host**. It works toward destruction by depleting its host, to the point that ultimately both the host and the parasite are destroyed.

An excellent exemplification of the propagation of evil is addiction; regardless of whether the object of addiction (the corruptive element) is an illicit drug or any other craving. After a short period of time the addict, most times unaware of how or when it happened, realizes that they have become psychologically or physically dependent upon the corruptive element; whether it is cocaine, marijuana, heroin, alcohol, any other unhealthy substance; or, in the cases of socialism and communism . . . the maniacal, envious craving for other people's wealth. The addiction, introduced into a person's personality by the corruptive element, then becomes the parasite that begins to feed on

---

[5] "Know you not that a little leaven corrupteth the whole lump?" (1 Cor. 5:6).

4

its host: the addict. As time passes the parasitic addiction grows stronger by consuming the host's energy, while the addict becomes weaker in their ability to resist the addiction and just live a "normal," daily life. Eventually, the addiction either depletes the host to such a degree that the strength and will to resist is insufficient for the addict to overcome it, and as a consequence the addiction consumes both the host and itself to the point of death; or, the addict recovers their strength and force of will at a point in time that is sufficient enough to overcome and exorcise their addiction.

Good

The moral sense of the principle of good, because it also has its foundation in religion and theology, can then be understood to be the absolute opposite of evil. Therefore, at its deepest level, **being good is a quality, act, or state of being that conforms to God's will and pleases Him;**[6] "virtuous" being the word we use to describe the quality of being morally good. Looking again to the attributes of God, and realizing that good is the complete opposite of evil, we can then recognize it. God, being perfect and without error, a necessary attribute in order to ensure His eternal nature, can Himself only desire and promote those things that conform to His will: perfection (of which truth is a necessary component) and eternal life. Being that God is the universal Creator, the universal source of life, and always truthful; we are able to grasp a more practical, functional recognition of what good is by combining the understanding of the above stated principles. We can say that **good is any quality, act, or state of being that gravitates toward the accomplishment of the perfection of God's will; which manifests itself through the promotion, maintenance, and love of truth and life; and is facilitated by the propagation of virtue (fortitude, temperance, justice, etc.).**

Not coincidentally, the Ten Commandments[7] are a succinct encapsulation of behavior that conforms to moral goodness, because they come directly

---

[6] From the purely moral sense this is explained in Matthew 19:17: "Why askest thou me concerning good? **One is good, God**. But if thou wilt enter into life, keep the commandments." From this explanation, it can be seen that morally, there can only be one good; and that is God. This comes from the fact that God, being the only creator of all things, is by necessity the ultimate judge of all things regarding whether they are good or evil because He is the most knowledgeable regarding what it takes to sustain and propagate Creation, and all of the constituent elements within it. In combination with the fact that God is eternal and incorruptible, this leads one to the understanding that God must, of necessity, be the only morally pure "good." Keep in mind that within the realms of religion, theology, and morality these are territories of absolute distinctions. As a result, ideas or forces that are opposed to each other are *completely* opposed to each other at all times and in all circumstances. Recalling from the previous section that the Devil *is* evil itself; we can then understand that God *is* good itself. All others, especially people of today's world, are so full of imperfections that none of us can approach a state of being morally good in the strictest sense of the principle.

[7] Exodus 20:2-17 and Deuteronomy 5:6-21.

from God; fulfilling the primary definition of what it means to be good, as well as keeping humanity pointed in the direction of the moral good. Moreover, conforming one's behavior to the Ten Commandments is a means of avoiding the evils that manifest themselves in the world as a consequence of not following them: ingratitude, adultery, murder, lying, cheating, stealing, etc. From this, the advantage of following codified religious moral principles can be easily seen and appreciated from a non-religious perspective. It is infinitely better for the health and cohesiveness of society if its members are composed of people who are grateful rather than ungrateful; faithful rather than unfaithful to their word; defenders of life rather than murderers; honest people rather than liars, cheats, and thieves; etc.

Having arrived at a functional understanding of good, and a practical way to recognize it, we must then look to how it propagates itself throughout the world so that we can encourage the love of life that good always leads to. Since the goals and ends of good are the defense and propagation of life, it must also work toward its desired end in a manner consistent with its nature. Remembering that God is perfect and incorruptible, good will then work toward life by mitigating, and sometimes removing, the corrupted tendencies that mankind is naturally inclined to. Human beings, as a result of our perverse natural inclinations, tend to find pleasure in practically everything that is unhealthy for us: drugs, greed for money and power, unrestrained sensuality (food, sex, luxury, etc.), and just about every other unhealthy habit one could imagine. With this understanding of our own reprobated natural tendencies, **good can be more easily observed to propagate itself only by a conscious act of will within each one of us; with the intention of denying and countering our known, self-destructive tendencies**. It works toward the propagation of life by evading destructive behaviors and habits (for example: addiction, promiscuity, homosexuality, and transgenderism), so that life may proceed with diminished tendencies toward self-destructive behavior; suffered at our own hands when we indulge our natural inclinations.

An excellent exemplification of the propagation of good is abstinence, regardless of the object being abstained from. By abstaining from any particular pleasure, the human mind becomes conditioned (however painfully slow the process may be) to do without the object that a person is denying themselves: sex, luxury, alcohol, tobacco, illicit drugs, etc. Over an extended period of time, the person who abstains from any particular item slowly realizes that they are becoming psychologically or physically less dependent on, or desirous of, their object of abstinence. All human cravings and desires, no matter their object, serve to enslave the minds of mankind; because the more a person becomes "hooked" on their "little pleasures" in life, whether they are simple idiosyncrasies or deviant perversions, the greater extent a person will be willing to go to in order to preserve the availability of their particular pleasure of choice. By abstaining from any particular item, we willfully subdue the natural inclinations that direct us toward desires of things that are ultimately unhealthy for us; freeing ourselves from the grip of our psychological dependence on the object, whatever it may be. Additionally, as good is the morally opposing force of evil, we likewise see that abstinence is the opposing force of addiction and indulgence.

Love

Love can best be seen as having its foundation in a spirit of self-sacrifice. John 15:13 gives an obtuse definition of love, from which a better understanding of the principle can be derived: "Greater love than this no man hath, that a man lay down his life for his friends." The one thing most valuable to all human beings are their very lives. If the greatest love is the sacrifice of the most valuable thing a person possesses, for the sake of another, it can then be seen that **love is a desire that compels the person who loves to place the well-being of the object of their love in a position of relative importance that is superior to their own self-interest, and it manifests itself in a willingness to sacrifice one's self-interest for the interests of another**. Unlike the perception commonly propagated throughout today's "popular culture," the true meaning of the moral principle of love is unrelated to sexual gratification. The hyper-sexuality seen in today's world is actually a manifestation of hatred, both of oneself and of others, because it places a person's selfish desires for sexual gratification in a position of relative importance that is superior to the consideration of the well-being of others.

Hate

The opposing moral principle to love is hate. Due to its opposing character and nature to that of love, hate can best be seen as having its foundation in a spirit of narcissistic self-indulgence. The best way to view hatred so that it is more clearly recognizable is to view it as the exact opposite of love: **an impulse that compels the person who hates to place their** own desires in a position of relative importance that is superior to the well-being of others, and it manifests itself in a willingness to sacrifice others for one's selfish desires. Hatred is a universal sentiment in socialistic and communistic societies. Being materialistic ideologies, socialism and communism are founded on the incessant desire for material 'equality'; most specifically, taking from those who possess more material wealth, and then distributing the stolen goods and wealth among those who do not possess as much. But when someone takes something that does not belong to them, it is theft.

They use the pretext that their thievery is for the "common good" or for "the good of society," but they actually adhere to and support socialism or communism for one of two reasons: (1) because it gives its adherents hope of being able to advance their own material self-interests at the expense of others; placing the materialistic self-interest of the socialist or communist in a position of relative importance that is superior to the interests of those they are stealing from, as well as violating and discarding honest justice; or (2) because the socialist or communist wishes to convince themselves, and others, that they are morally superior to those who do not condone their perverted self-justifications. The hateful socialist or communist is willing and eager to sacrifice justice, and in so doing demonstrates a willingness to sacrifice the interests of others for their selfish desire for material wealth or to feel morally superior to others.

Peace

The principle of peace is terribly abused and misunderstood today, but one thing must be made absolutely clear: *peace is not the absence of violence*. An absence of violence is a beneficial, consequential result of peace, but it is *not*, of itself, peace. **Peace can best be considered a manifestation of harmony that is created by people who share both a common, unified mind (common beliefs), as well as the mutual intention of maintaining their unity and harmony**. Peace is not something that just happens. It must be worked for, and it must be the common purpose of a society to work for and maintain it; otherwise, it will not be found or sustained. World peace, while possible, is not likely to transpire in the near future; because what would be required is that all people, all throughout the world, come to share a common mind and beliefs, as well as placing their desire for peace above their desires to satisfy self-serving inclinations and ambitions; especially the common impulses for more money and political power: greed.

Peace will not be found in this world as long as it continues to be run, as it is today, by avaricious politicians who are greedy for more power; enabled by lawyers and social activists of all stripes who can only ply their trade by propagating hatred and ensuring that as many people as possible remain in a constant state of agitation, fear, enmity, and discord. A necessary requirement for a large and universal peace to take hold would be a very sharp increase in the common level of education and intelligence among the average person, as well as a simultaneous and commensurate decrease in their evident levels of pride and narcissism. True world peace would only be possible in a world of humiliated philosophers: all people seeking the truth, while realizing both their inability to grasp it in its totality, as well as a conscious realization of their personal shortcomings and insignificance in relation to the whole of humanity. These humble, self-effacing attitudes are not "what makes the world go 'round" today, and they never have been in all of recorded history. What can realistically be hoped for is that peace may be achieved regionally. This has happened in the past, and it is the cause of modern nations and societies: a group of people from a particular region who shared common interests, views, and goals banded together for self-protection and friendship.

There is no peace in the world today because there really are no nations and societies in the world today where the peoples within the society share common beliefs and have the intention of maintaining unity and harmony within society; and there will be no peace in the world until such time as people come to a common, unified mind. The lack of peace in today's world is due to the fact that the people who run the governments, and this is true of practically all governments today, are not the least bit interested in finding or obtaining true peace. The sole object of most all politicians today is in finding, obtaining, and maintaining political power. The most expedient way for a politician to make himself needed in office is to continually manufacture crises, find a person or abstract demographic group to blame for the crises they created in order to foster the perception in the public eye that they are personally indispensable, and then claim to be the savior of society from the crises they have created and fomented in order to secure their grasp on political power. It would be almost comical if it weren't for the fact that almost everyone today falls for most all these ploys and is seduced into hating some person or abstract group at the behest of their psychological masters: cynical, arrogant politicians who are motivated by an "electorate be damned, so long as I'm elected" attitude.

In today's world, the average "anti-war" activist uses the phrase, "All I want is world peace." These poor, pitiable people may very well be sincere, but they are also undeniably, and frighteningly, ignorant regarding what peace is and how it is achieved. Unfortunately, they have been seduced by the childishly shallow view that peace is an absence of armed conflict. Sadly, these poor people see no further than this. Any absence, or cessation, of conflict in a world full of people determined to force themselves on others—for example, socialists, communists, and now Islamic fundamentalists—is nothing more than a strategic or tactical ploy in the larger war for the hearts and minds of people all over the world. *It is not peace!* Any cessation of hostility is being used by factions the world over to forward their propaganda and gather strength for the next round of anticipated battles.

Peace activists, due to their frightening ignorance, actually work to increase the level of death and suffering in the world by large orders of magnitude. Moreover, this is a certain consequence of their actions and it is due to our perverted human nature. In any conflict there is an aggressive party and an enemy that is the object of aggression. The modern peace activist—while the sincere ones are certainly very well-intentioned, and whether they realize it or not—is perceived to be a fool and a coward in the eyes of both their enemies and the people they believe they are trying to help; because instead of standing up to an aggressor, and defending oneself from violent aggression, they attempt to appease their enemy; which is seen by the enemy as an act of cowardice. This only emboldens an aggressor and ensures more violence on a much larger scale in the future. The insanity typically plays out along the following lines:

1. An aggressor attacks their enemy.
2. The peace activist, sincerely desiring to stop any further bloodshed, steps in to try and prevent an escalation of violence.
3. For whatever misguided reason (fear of their attacker, self-righteousness, etc.), the peace activist works to pacify the attacked party and prevent them from defending themselves against an aggressive force with a military response by making apologies for the violent behavior of the aggressor. This type of pathology is referred to as the "blame the victim" mentality. It is commonly seen among abused women, and is almost always evident in those who are physically or psychologically weaker and more vulnerable than their attackers:

"I forgot to pick up his dry cleaning for a very important meeting . . . I deserved it."

"I dropped dinner on the floor and ruined everyone's meal . . . I deserved it."

"I did [this | that | the other thing] wrong . . . I deserved it."

4. The aggressor, witnessing the internal dissension and weakness among their enemy, is emboldened and increases their attacks; through the use of both more violent physical attacks where possible, and at all times through propaganda:

"The September 11 hijackers were freedom fighters, similar to America's colonial patriots . . . You deserved it."

"The United States (specifically) and Western civilization (generally) is the 'Great Satan' . . . You deserved it."

"You [do | did] [this | that | the other thing] wrong . . . You deserved it."

5. The peace activists, in a curiously insane display of self-hatred, absorb the propaganda and actually take up their enemy's cause by spreading and reinforcing their enemy's propaganda among their fellow citizens.

6. This only further aids and encourages an aggressor by assisting them from two different directions. From one direction, the peace activist actively aids the aggressor by promoting their propaganda, and then from another direction they actively work to bind the attacked party and work to prevent their own self-defense; which can only serve to greatly increase both the bloodshed and the duration of the conflict.

Justice

The principle of justice, while being a fairly easy principle to understand by most all people, seems to be one of the most difficult for the vast majority of the people of this world to actually observe and practice. Very simply, **justice is when every person receives exactly what they have earned, and rightly deserve, for their actions or labors**. The potentially unpleasant caveat concerning justice results from the fact that the principle applies in all instances of human interaction and affairs. A world where justice prevailed would be one in which everyone got what they deserved, and this would apply in both advantageous and punitive circumstances.

From the perspective of materialistic wealth, a laborer would receive an honest day's pay that is capable of supporting a small family. In our civil judicial system, it would mean that the most poor and destitute person would receive the same consideration under the law as a celebrity or wealthy person. In our criminal justice system it would mean that those who commit crimes would be punished with a level of severity that is commensurate with the crime: murderers, drug dealers, kidnappers, rapists, child molesters, etc. would be subject to the death penalty; and all people who receive sentences of a limited duration would be subject to a disciplined and punitive incarceration as part of their punishment. Sadly, due to the effeminate, cowardly, and self-righteous inclinations currently prevailing among the great bulk of humanity today, the absolutely necessary pursuit of honest justice is very rarely achieved, or even desired, any longer. As a result, societies all over the world are now being aided in their collapse because the citizens within no longer have the fortitude to sternly punish and rebuke internal predators within their own society. This sad reality is especially noticeable within Western civilization and the industrialized world.

How These Moral Principles Are Being Perverted in Today's World

Before observing how these moral principles have been perverted in today's world, the reader's attention must first be recalled to the attributes of a child; both in relation to their psychology and to their behavior. This is an unfortunate necessity because, as unpleasant of a realization as it is, the perversion of the above moral principles, and most all other things in the modern world, is due to the infantilization of the human intellect; in which a very large majority of the human race has regressed to a child's psychology and behavior.

As bold and insulting as this assertion may appear to be, the reader's indulgence is desired in order to explain why this is true. Moreover, this claim is not made for the purpose of insult. It is done with the intention of bringing people to the understanding of how they have been seduced and corrupted. To begin with, the mind of the child predominantly revolves around itself: narcissism. From birth, and throughout their early, formative years, a child is cared for by their parents or other adult authority figure. The parents assume the responsibilities of providing for their child's needs: clothing, housing, food, etc.; as well as for most all their wants. Being sheltered and protected from the concerns related to fulfilling the responsibilities of supplying their needs and wants, the child's attention is naturally drawn inward toward itself; not possessing the life experience, nor the empathy, to understand what is required of a person to live morally, ethically, and responsibly as a self-sufficient, autonomous individual in a much larger society. Moreover, while the child is aware of a larger world around them—this fact being inescapable in the course of human existence—they do not perceive an immediate, necessary reason that compels them to consider the needs, wants, dreams, and desires of other human beings.

Having no real responsibilities to burden their minds, all their thoughts and actions are directed toward meeting the demands and discipline of their parents in order to either avoid punishment or obtain a reward offered to them for their good behavior. Any other remaining time is spent contemplating what they may want (toys, video games, hobbies, entertainment, and other recreational diversions) and devising plans for obtaining what they want.

14

Being mostly unaware, and uncaring, of the burdens and responsibilities of providing for a family's material needs, or even for oneself, a child's psychological demands likewise gravitate around the satisfaction of their desires, which manifests itself in self-serving attitudes and behavior. All behaviors and actions become filtered through the child's selfish perspective of, "Will this behavior move me closer to obtaining what I want"? When demands are placed on the child by their parents, or other authority figure(s), that do not move them toward the fulfillment of their desires, the child often becomes perturbed and offers up resistance through a variety of infantile behaviors and tactics (temper tantrums, petulant and defiant attitudes, belligerent behavior and language, self-indulgent "reasoning," etc.) that are designed to avoid the distracting demands placed on them and maneuver themselves, and their parents or authority figures, back toward a course of action that serves to meet their selfish desires.

This results in a mental outlook that is dangerously narcissistic and ignorant of the larger considerations of the forces at work in the larger world; as well as a behavior that is contrary to both the greater, long-term needs of the child and the desires of the parent to raise a child that is psychologically and emotionally suited to morally and ethically assume the burden(s) of responsibility for their own life, in concert with the corresponding decisions and choices that accompany personal responsibility, as they grow toward adulthood. Consequently, the child and the parent are destined to be opposed to each other in their desires and pursuits; as the motivation for, and object(s) of, their desires are mutually opposed. The infant is born into the world in a state of selfish ignorance that understands no bounds on its desires. The parent, having the benefit of life experience, is more understanding of the necessary restraint, spirit of cooperation, and self-control that is necessary to live a productive, useful, and happier life. In their shallow ignorance, the child only perceives what it wants. In their deeper understanding, the parent knows what the child needs.

Understanding, and recalling, the psychological and behavioral attributes of a child, it is then easier to understand the psychological and behavioral attributes most responsible for the perversion of the moral principles discussed here, because they exactly mimic the attributes of a childish psychology; aping the tendencies of children to view the world through an exclusively egocentric prism: measuring life experiences against a psychological filter tuned to the fulfillment of desires rather than to the meeting of responsibilities, or even an overriding concern for individual or social survival. If an unpleasant reality or life experience does not meet with the approval and satisfaction of an infantilized mind, constantly moving that person toward the gratification of their instinctual urges and desires, they will rebel and react against it in a cunning manner that, in its effect, is meant to achieve the same ends as a temper tantrum; redirecting the attitudes and behaviors of others toward the fulfillment of the infantilized person's desires.

The cunning, infantilized mind—having the benefit of life experience and a greater understanding of human nature, as well as how to manipulate the psyches of others—understands that overtly childish behavior will most often meet with rejection. Understanding this, they devise much more subtle and sophisticated methods of coercion; most always achieved by perverting and confusing language by redefining words and principles in such a way that it suits their self-interested purposes, such as the ones we are discussing here. Common tactics include attempts to misdirect others and conceal opposing views through the use of yelling and screaming, mockery, linguistic misdirection,[1] belligerent behavior and language, self-indulgent "reasoning," etc. Let's look to how the moral principles we are discussing have come to be understood due to their infantilized interpretation in today's world.

Good and Evil

The principles of good and evil have been corrupted in today's world so that they have assumed a character in the public eye that insinuates their meaning to be anything that can be found pleasing (good) or offensive (evil) to human sensibilities. The infantilization of these principles can be seen in the egocentrically self-indulgent "reasoning" that transforms them from concrete moral absolutes to amorally relativistic, morally inert and sterile concepts. Good and evil can *never* be properly considered to be anything that pleases or offends the feelings or sensibilities of human beings. The use of these words in such a context departs from the moral sense, and instead describes an amoral context that is a subjective, human assignment of relative personal perception or value.

To use the principles of good and evil in a humanistically relative context—in such a way that they are confused with the moral context of

---

[1] Avoiding a discussion regarding a topic or line of reasoning that exposes their foolishness, selfishness, or infantile thought processes: a.k.a. changing the subject. Another common tactic is to constantly interrupt and talk over others who are trying to debate a point and counter the propagation of an immature idea.

good and evil—is a childishly simplistic error that, properly understanding the principles, elevates oneself to a level of self-importance equal to that of God;[2] aping the original error that earned the Devil his punishment, and by aping the behavior and sentiments of the Devil, making oneself evil in the process. As evidence of the infantile insanity of such a confusion of principles, consider what would be the consequence if good and evil were defined by people as those things that either pleased (good) or offended (evil) their sensibilities or feelings. The concepts of good and evil would then become completely subjective and absolutely indefinable! As there are over six billion people in the world, there would be just about that many definitions of good and evil; as every person is pleased or offended, and perceives joy or injury, to different degrees, and in relation to different objects!

Love

The concept of love has been infantilized by becoming egocentrically and self-indulgently redefined to be interpreted as being synonymous with physical, sexual arousal or gratification. This disturbing debasement of the principle of love does a gross disservice to this otherwise noble sentiment, most notably demonstrated through a spirit of self-sacrifice for the sake of others, by purposely confusing it with instinctual, animalistic urges. This debasement of the principle of love has been primarily accomplished through the commensurate debasement of the understanding of the common man, which has been underway for several generations,[3] in concert with the glorification of evil in "popular culture" outlets; such as ultra-violent and sexually explicit "art" (predominantly movies and "music") that constantly refers to "love" in both a pictorial and linguistic context that is synonymous with sexual activity; and in the worst cases sexually deviant predation.

Amazingly, modern culture has become so insanely perverted and debased that the term "love" is being used today to try and legitimize suicidal sexual deviancy and predation, such as homosexuality (especially the militant variety) and pedophilic child molestation (North American Man-Boy Love

---

[2] This is true regardless of whether a person realizes it or not.

[3] This has been accomplished via the debasement of "education" in our public schools; by changing them from institutions where facts are learned and internalized, to institutions where psychological and emotional conditioning are the desired goal.

Association (NAMBLA)); completely reversing the proper understanding of love as a manifestation of self-sacrifice for the well-being of another, and instead misrepresenting it as a manifestation of self-indulgent sexual license or predation for the purpose of animalistic self-gratification, which is actually a manifestation of hatred.

Hate

The principle of hate has been perversely redefined in the modern world, by people who are themselves full of hatred, for the sake of political advantage and the psychological enslavement and manipulation of the populace. Politicians and social activists use the term "hate" as a vehicle to propagate calumnious misrepresentations of their political opposition in an attempt to psychologically bully anyone who would dare to oppose them. In effect, hate has been perverted to mean any idea that contradicts liberal, humanistic political orthodoxy; more commonly known as "Political Correctness." The rhetoric typically falls along the lines of, "My opponents [want | don't want] to pass this new law because they *hate* [Blacks | Women | Latinos | Children | Elderly | homosexuals | etc.]." Whichever demographic group a politician or social activist is pandering to will be the group that their opposition is accused of hating. Sadly, it works all too well on a politically naïve populace, which is why it is so often used as a psycho-political weapon.

One can see that the true hatred emanates from those who use these tactics; because they use calumny to besmirch the character and intentions of their political opposition for the intended purpose of forwarding their self-interested political agenda and personal power. The infantile attributes are discernible because such accusations, impossible to prove or determine, are merely a manifestation of belligerent language and behavior directed at any who would dare to oppose the liberal orthodoxy currently being forcefully propagated throughout the world, as well as a much more sublime form of temper tantrum. The selfish child cries, "You *hate* me! You don't want me to have any fun"! In like manner, the selfish politician or social activist cries, "You *hate* [fill in the blank (any demographic group, as appropriate to the circumstance)]! You want to deprive them of [whatever the particular audience desires the most]"!

Peace

The principle of peace has been perverted by reducing it to an infantile and cowardly concept; where a beneficial effect of peace (a lack of violence and bloodshed) has been shortsightedly mistaken for the principle itself; and an understanding of the cause(s) of peace are actually not only misunderstood, but held in contempt by modern, so-called "intellectuals" and the moral relativism that the great majority of them propound. The further perversion and destruction of peace then comes from those who act on the idea that peace is, of itself, a cessation of violence.

It's an insane manifestation of sticking one's head in the sand, but leaving the body exposed to attack; or through another analogy, hiding behind Mommy's skirt for protection, and then once behind her binding her hands and feet so she is not able to protect you. Peace activism in a nation that has been violently attacked betrays both moral and physical cowardice, as well as the infantile behavior of trying to misdirect a people from tending to their duties of self-defense; so that those with an infantilized mind can then return their attention, as well as that of their fellow citizen, to the pursuit of their selfish and hedonistic pleasures: those things that had fixated the populace's attention before they were attacked.

Justice

The infantilization of the principle of justice in the modern world is more easily discernible because the abuse of this principle has resulted in behavior that more closely resembles an overt display of a temper tantrum. It has been sadly reduced to the intellectual equivalent of a child's plaything; calls for "justice" being used freely, unabashedly, and indiscriminately by any and every malcontent who isn't happy with their life's circumstance; and among those accustomed to forcing themselves on others, but are stopped short of getting their way. If someone doesn't receive a court ruling to their liking they present themselves before the public and stir up discontent among other like-minded people by claiming that "justice" was not done; for no greater reason than because they didn't get their way. If someone isn't happy with their income they cry that there is no "justice" because they aren't receiving the kind of income or benefits they believe themselves entitled to.[4]

In the hyper-politicized culture that has taken shape over the last several decades (all over the world), if a politician or social activist is unsuccessful in achieving their aims, which includes disgracing their political opposition, they are one of the first—among a larger backdrop of compatriot "drama queens"—to complain of "injustice." In most circumstances today where the word justice—or conversely, injustice—is used, the reader should perk their ears and finely discern the context within which it is invoked; because sadly, most people today who invoke the principle of justice do so for self-interested and self-serving reasons that have nothing to do with the honest receipt of what one deserves for their actions (whether for good or for ill): the true meaning of the principle of justice.

---

[4] This argument is very popular, and effective, amongst labor unions and their associated spokesmen; even to the self-destructive point of bankrupting whole businesses and putting everyone out of business and out of a job. Do any of the readers remember a company called Eastern Airlines? Of course, in such situations the union doesn't go out of business. The union employees who pretended to represent the interests of Eastern Airlines employees never lost their jobs. Only those poor souls foolish enough to stand by union counsel lost their jobs.

How the Perversion of These Moral Principles Is Being Used to Induce the Suicidal Self-Destruction of Societies All Over the World

Finally, as we move to the further examination and observation of how most of humanity is being reduced to a state of anarchy and self-willed slavery—via humanistic attitudes and mental processes—we must first explain how the confusion that has resulted from the erroneous understanding of these important moral principles is being used to induce social and cultural suicide all over the world.

Evil

The perversion of the understanding of what evil is has caused a situation that, by its nature, directs the mind toward narcissistic psychological processes that gravitate around arrogance, belligerence, and conflict; ultimately concluding with mass violence as its natural consequence and end. We are witnessing the early effects of this perversion of the understanding today, and it is going to become *much* worse unless people quickly begin to understand how their understanding has been corrupted. By redefining what evil is, based on a "liberal," morally relativistic model; mankind has both elevated himself to a level equivalent to that of God, and simultaneously put in place an ideological construct that can only lead to mass violence. By believing that evil is a humanly subjective and morally relativistic measure of the human perception of those things that offend people, the whole concept of evil has been turned upside down from a singly-defined, common understanding of behavior that all people could understand, and accordingly modify their behavior so as to avoid it, to an indefinable concept with almost as many different "definitions" as there are people in the world.

For the many people who subscribe to the modernly perverted understanding of evil, a new scenario presents itself. By believing that they can define evil within a moral context that "works for them," the moral relativist assigns themselves the authority of God. Additionally, when someone defines good and evil based on a personal, individually internalized moral code that applies solely to oneself, a person then puts themselves in a position where the "moral" positions upon which they make their "principled stands" are based solely on a "morality" composed of nothing more than their own musings. Meanwhile, every other moral relativist in the world, of which there are literally *billions*, is simultaneously laboring under the same delusion.

Consider what happens next when one person or group's definition of morality clashes and contradicts another person or group's definition of morality. One side says, "My 'morality' is right, and yours is wrong"! The other side says, "No! My 'morality' is right, and yours is wrong"! These contrary views may start out as simple disagreements; but as time wears on, and the perceived importance of the issues involved become larger and larger in scale, the anger and resolve on both sides of the issue harden and grow to the point of open violence, and in the worst cases bloodshed and warfare; as we are seeing with greater frequency today. Additionally, while the arguments continue on unresolved, those people on both sides of a moral argument are constantly trying to recruit new adherents to their position either through debate (politicians, lawyers, social activists, etc.) or through force (socialists, communists and Islamic fundamentalists); so as to numerically overwhelm their opposition through strength of numbers.

As the reader can see, both from an understanding of basic human nature as well as the nightly news, the morally relativistic definition of good and evil, which has largely taken up residence in the minds of a very large majority and percentage of the people of the world today, is a guaranteed path toward anarchy, chaos, and massive bloodshed. Moreover, the correct recognition of what evil is—any quality, act, or state of being that gravitates toward destruction; especially the destruction of life—will lead us to an understanding that the sensate, sensual component of our human nature naturally compels us toward evil tendencies if our appetites are not held in check by our reason; because it is natural and common for people to desire those things in life that are truly evil and lead to our corruption and dissolution (drug addiction, sexual licentiousness, greed for money and power, etc.).

This reality leads many insane and perverted people in today's world to conclude that those people who oppose their dissolute choices, attitudes, and lives—homosexuality, abortion, pornography, sexual license and predation, drug addiction, etc.—are the evil ones because, in an attempt to reach and dissuade those who have made poor and suicidal choices from their chosen path of self-destruction and dissipation, both individually and as a society; they offend the profligate sensibilities of those who have succumbed to their evil, and often suicidal, desires. As a result of the perceived injury to their feelings and sensibilities, the infantilized moral relativist regards any who would dare oppose or rebuke their dangerous behavior as being evil themselves.

Good

The perversion of the understanding of what good is has caused a situation that, by its nature, channels the mind toward suicidal behavior; immediately causing the "softening" of society, and ultimately concluding with mass suicidal death as its natural consequence and end. Recalling that human beings tend to find pleasure in practically everything that is unhealthy for them, it is easy to understand why the modern, morally relativistic definition of good can only lead to the dissolution of society as a whole, and of its members individually. By confusing the moral principle of good with the morally relativistic perception of what is good—those things that please the sensibilities and feelings of people—a great many have set themselves upon a suicidal road. This is most succinctly symbolized in the irresponsible and hedonistic mantra, "If it feels good, do it"!

Living one's life chasing after fleeting and ultimately useless distractions or pleasures, as if life were a constant party, may *feel* good in the moment, but the consequences of the momentary pleasure aren't so pleasant: obesity (overeating), sexually-transmitted diseases and unwanted pregnancies (homosexuality and sexual licentiousness), effeminate laziness (hedonism and luxuriousness), hangovers and vomiting (drug use), etc.; in the best cases leading to a premature death, and in the worst cases leading to an immediate death. Moreover, a routine capitulation to our hedonistic nature leads to addiction, which again ultimately leads to a premature death.

The desire for unrestrained sensuality in excesses of food, sexuality, and luxury all serve to take the mind away from the necessarily unpleasant nature associated with the duties of daily living. The desire for sensate satisfaction works through the same means as an addiction to illicit drugs. It causes a person's mind and life efforts to gravitate around the object of their sensate desire(s); directing the mind to a constant want for more of whatever object is perceived to bring a person pleasure. This causes a softening of the internal character and disposition (the "guts" or "grit") of the individual who succumbs to their appetites for sensual gratification, and a commensurate revulsion for the necessary, and often unpleasant, responsibilities of life. It is also the source of very many other evils that cause social dissolution, and may also result in a premature death:

1. Adultery — A slighted spouse may never regain the ability to trust their spouse. It may also lead to the dissolution of a marriage, and in the harshest circumstances may result in the offended party killing their spouse or the spouse's lover to satisfy their desire for retribution.

2. Abortion — A baby is murdered as a result of a couple's lack of self-control and restraint.

3. Unwanted children — Choosing not to abort a child, a couple's lack of self-control and restraint results in the greater likelihood that the child will be born to either biological parents who do not love or want them in their lives, leading to emotional or physical abuse, or being given up for adoption, which often leaves a lifelong emotional scar on the child.

4. Obesity — Overindulgence in food causes a myriad of medical and psychological problems. The medical problems and complications of obesity are responsible for more premature deaths than just about any other "natural" cause of death.

In truth, the majority of evils in life have their root cause in a desire to satisfy a sensate pleasure: those briefly listed above, drug addiction and greed for money and power,[1] and just about any other thing the reader can think of. As a result, the humanistic moral relativist, who subscribes to the belief that something is good if it makes them *feel* good, is actually setting themselves up for a multitude of evils that will most likely lead to their dissolution: morally, ethically, or physically.

It's important to note that the perversion of the concept of good is being further used to corrupt the human race by facilitating people's natural greed

---

[1] Most people are greedy for money and power for two primal reasons: in order to have the means to freely satiate their sensate desires in abundance and ease, or to satisfy their enflamed, narcissistically self-glorifying pride.

for money and power. Greed causes a narrowing of mental, interior vision that eventually leads to suicidal lapses in judgment. This is most evident today in the field of politics; where politicians have become so disgustingly enamored with positioning themselves for votes, and manipulating the perception of the average citizen, that they apparently neither care, nor understand, the consequences of the things they do. Frighteningly, a great number of today's politicians have become so completely enthralled with their desire for power and wealth that most of them don't even possess the basic common sense needed to understand how dangerous their ignorant greed and party-politics positioning is to the rest of us: those they are *supposed* to be serving. As a result, many initiatives and laws that are *perceived* to be good (from a shallow, narcissistically self-righteous perspective) on the surface are actually destructive to society when their consequences, both intended and unintended, are more thoroughly examined (for example, government entitlement programs).

Love

The common perception today that love is to be considered a synonym for sexual activity or gratification has been one of the most influential driving forces that has put the world on a quicker path toward dissolution; primarily for two reasons: the regression of humanity into irrational, instinctual animals, and the fatal consequences that accrue from such a barbaric and narcissistic psychology. By having established a false association between love and sexual activity, many people have been turned into the psychological equivalent of irrational animals in perpetual heat; thoughtless and ignorant of the ultimate consequences of their actions. The young people of any age are the most susceptible to this infantile confusion of principles because the youth of a society are most always more impetuous and unwise in relation to those with more life experience. But regardless of who has fallen prey to this hateful, homicidal, and self-indulgent error, the consequences have been socially cataclysmic: exponential increases over the last several decades in the incidences of abortion, sexually-transmitted diseases (herpes, AIDS, and others), unwed mothers, unwanted pregnancies, homosexuality, transsexuality, etc.

It is the natural tendency of human beings to pursue ease and pleasure, and likewise avoid difficulties and pain. When this behavior is combined with the understanding that physical, sensate pleasures work through the same means as addiction, it is easy to envision and understand the natural consequences that we are seeing in today's world. The mind of the person who falls to this debased level gravitates around their constant desire for sexual gratification and the incessant pursuit of the same. The combination of the two factors (the natural desire for sensate gratification and the tendency toward addiction to gratifying objects) renders people almost completely blind to any and all consequences of their behavior. As the "mind's eye" is drawn toward, and gravitates around, the satisfaction of sensate pleasures, the actions and events of the larger world around a person will pass by mostly unnoticed unless they also serve to satiate the pleasures and desires of the individual(s) in question. Consequently, this gives rise to a dangerously self-indulgent, blind ignorance among those who have been reduced to the animalistic level of associating love with sexual gratification; because they excuse, justify, and propagate their dissipating, licentious behavior and perverted moral attitudes by calling it "love," rather than understanding that what they are experiencing are actually forms of lust, addiction, or infatuation.

The dangers inherent in such promiscuous behavior can be seen at both the individual and the societal level. It is damaging to the individual both physically and emotionally. The physical dangers of promiscuity are evident in the increased incidences of sexually-transmitted diseases and unwanted pregnancies. The emotional damage comes from the shallow nature of such relationships. The sole purpose of promiscuous behavior is to satisfy an instinctual, animalistic desire to gratify a sexual impulse. However, succumbing to such impulses leads the affected individual into a relationship that will never proceed beyond the superficial and self-serving gratification of a physical passion; retarding the development of deeper, emotional relationships and rendering it impossible to develop a more permanent and intimate connection with the other person.

The social damage from promiscuity accrues from the consequences of the behavior. The increased incidences of sexually-transmitted diseases associated with promiscuity drives up the social burden of having to deal with the medical problems that result from licentiousness. More importantly, however, is the destruction that such behavior brings to the innocent: the children within a licentious society. Increased sexual activity results in increased pregnancies, despite any "precautions" that may be taken. The consequent effect of such self-indulgence has been the propagation and expansion of the social acceptance of the neglect, abandonment, or murder of children within society. If these pregnancies occur outside of marriage, the consequences will accrue to the detriment of the newly conceived children. If the child is not murdered through abortion, they will most likely be neglected when born.

Children have always been, and will always be, the weakest members within any society; and the younger they are, the weaker they are. As societies have moved toward a greater, materialistic ethos of instant self-gratification over roughly the past two centuries, the considerations of responsibility and duty (both to others and to oneself) in the average person's mind have been so greatly abandoned that sentiments of rights and entitlements have superseded and replaced them within the minds of a dangerously large segment of society. This reversal of proper priorities has caused self-indulgence to flourish while the proper attention that should be afforded to the fulfillment of one's responsibilities has been mostly discarded and abandoned.

This sad circumstance corrupts and damages children in several ways. Firstly, because such a large number of "adults" have succumbed to a hedonistic, self-indulgent way of life; a dangerous and poor example is being displayed for them to imitate as they grow up, which only further accelerates the dissolution of society with the passage of time by inculcating the idea within the young that there are no serious consequences for the selfish abandonment of self-control. Additionally, as many of today's adults are abandoning their burdensome responsibilities in deference to their pleasures, a great number of children are being neglected and abandoned by self-indulgent "parents." Not being desired by their parents, most children who are brought into the world as a result of promiscuity are ultimately abandoned to a lifetime of emotional neglect and scarring; either by being given up for adoption or by direct neglect at the hands of their biological parents. As more and more "parents" come to revolve around the gratification of their selfish desires, their children are abandoned to their own devices; left to be raised by the television or their peers in the absence of the parents who have abandoned their duties as parents because such difficult duties interfere with the pursuit of their self-gratification.

As is often the case, the pernicious products of promiscuity take a generation or more to show their bitter fruit. Many of these children grow to adulthood with emotional scars and a narcissistic egoism that guides their world view (Barack Obama, for example: neglected and abandoned by both his father and mother as a child); further dissipating society by inculcating an ethos of utilitarianism within the society at large. Children are the greatest responsibility, as well as the greatest psychological, emotional, and financial burden that a person will ever undertake. This is not to say that this is the child's fault. It is simply a fact of life, and the nature of human development. Those of us that are adults today were just as onerous and burdensome on our parents during our youth, due to the ignorance of youth. We simply didn't realize it at the time due to the naturally narcissistic tendencies that children embody. When conceived in promiscuity, it is most always the case that the biological mother and father of the child will not have the energy, desire, will, or wisdom to set a good and healthy example for the child to emulate as they grow into adulthood.

Finally, the false association of love with sex is also the primary force behind the "hypersexualization" of society, and can be attributed as being the underlying cause behind several moral evils and socially suicidal practices: abortion, homosexuality, and transsexuality. Because licentiousness has caused an exponential rise in the number of unwanted pregnancies, it has naturally led to a rapid increase in the number of abortions: the murdering and discarding of the most helpless within our society in order to avoid the responsibilities that a person's willful actions have brought about; so that these same self-indulgent people are able to continue on unabated in the gratification of their naturally hedonistic inclinations.

Considering the consequences of abortion on the individual, it needs to be clearly understood that abortion is an act of murder; in that it is the willful destruction of a human life. Is it a debatable point whether a human fetus or embryo is truly a human being? For those who are honest, this is not a point of legitimate contention. Let us understand why by answering the most fundamental of questions . . . "When does anything begin"? Obviously, the beginning of anything, regardless of its nature, occurs at its inception. The beginning of plant life occurs at its germination. The beginning of human endeavors occurs when the idea(s) are conceived in the human mind. And naturally, the beginning of human life begins at its conception: the fertilization of the embryo being the "germination" of a new human being. Clearly, although in its earliest stage of development, abortion is the destruction of a newly conceived human life.

To understand this on a more personal level, just consider when your own life began and whether you would consider it murder if your life were exterminated. For those of us living today, we *should* be able to understand that the beginning of our lives began at the beginning of our existence: our conception. Any denial of this most fundamental reality devalues all human life to a mere intellectual abstraction; for if humanity is willing to accept the idea that life does not begin at conception, then the next natural question must be answered . . . "Well then, when does life really begin"? If humanity refuses to recognize that life begins at its beginning (conception), they must then determine at what point it actually does begin; opening up a veritable "Pandora's Box" of contention for those who wish to deny the obvious in order to suit their own passions and desires. By denying that human life begins at its beginning, humanity has become entrenched in an amoral morass of justifying the destruction of human life in order to suit the unrestrained passions of the living. And like all things related to human passions, they are issues that are never settled and always vacillate according to the charisma of their protagonists, which is always in flux and never conclusive; leading to perpetual, social antagonisms. As a result, it can be seen that the act of abortion, in itself, is both an instance of murder as well as a primary cause of rancorous, pointless, and socially destructive animosity.

Considering the consequences of abortion on the social body, it can be seen that it is ultimately as damaging to the society that tolerates it as the act is to the person being murdered; in that at the larger level of human civilizations abortion can only accrue to the dissolution of the civilization due to the willingness of the living to destroy those who would ultimately grow into the people who would sustain and perpetuate their society in the future. The natural question that arises when one reaches the end of their life or career is, "Who will take my place"? When a newly conceived human life is destroyed they will subsequently not be alive at some point in the future to take the place of those who are passing away; for they will have been destroyed through abortion; contributing to the diminution of society as a whole.

As a natural consequence of the "sexual revolution" (licentious dissipation) that has swept through Western civilization over the past century, there have also been dramatic increases in the prevalence of two forms of sexually-based insanity: homosexuality and transsexuality. The suicidal nature of these practices is readily apparent to any person who observes their objectively real consequences. It is necessary for the reader(s) to understand with certainty why they are clearly unacceptable forms of sexual deviancy that cannot be tolerated within a society or culture that desires self-preservation and perpetuation.

Homosexuality and transsexuality are directly related; in that they are two manifestations of the same dysfunction: gender/sexual confusion. Homosexuality results as a consequence of a person's inability to establish and maintain a healthy, procreative relationship with a member of the opposite gender. Transsexuality results as a consequence of a person's inability to accept themselves as they are; with both disorders gravitating around sexuality.

The reason these aberrant behaviors are intolerable is due to the very nature of the concept of tolerance and what it implies. Toleration of any behavior or idea suggests an implicit acceptance of the behavior or idea in question; as if to say, "I may not agree with your behavior, but it's OK if you want to do it." In the case of such severe disorders as transsexuality and homosexuality, it is definitely *not* acceptable if people feel like doing it. The reason why they are not acceptable is due to the ultimate, severely adverse consequences of the acts on both the people involved and on society as a whole.

How do these disorders adversely affect society? At the most fundamental level, a society can only sustain and perpetuate itself via a definite, particular process: reproduction and transmission. The reproduction of new members to replace those who pass away, followed by the transmission of the principal ideas and philosophies that form the foundation of the society into which the newly reproduced members are born into; so that they may in turn sustain society in their era, reproduce in the future, and continue to transmit to following generations the same ideas and philosophies that sustained society during their lives. Homosexuality and transsexuality completely destroys this process, because these two psycho-sexual disorders negate the absolutely necessary function of reproduction, and by so doing demonstrate themselves to be two forms of societal suicide. Transsexuality, due to the destruction of the reproductive organs, renders reproduction a biological impossibility. Homosexuality, due to the repudiation of the opposite sex, renders the homosexual reproductively inert.

Is it true that there have always been, and will always be within humanity, those who succumb to the disorders of homosexuality and transsexuality? The honest answer is, "Absolutely, yes." However, the critical point of corruption and breakdown within Western civilization in this era is that such easily demonstrated, suicidal disorders have come to be considered as tolerable within society. But, as has just been observed, the concept of tolerance of these two disorders carries with it much greater threats to society than the original disorders themselves, because tolerance implies a tacit acceptance. The ultimate consequence of toleration and acceptance of homosexuality and transsexuality—or any other harmful or deviant type of behavior (sexual or otherwise)—is the transmission of tolerance and acceptance of societal suicide to current and future generations; so that the disorders of transsexuality and homosexuality will then be empowered to dissipate society at an exponentially greater rate in the future than they already are today. This initially occurs as a consequence of introducing these psychoses into society as socially acceptable, and then secondarily by tacitly encouraging them as a direct consequence of their social acceptance and tolerance.

Moreover, if there is any remaining doubt within the minds of the readers regarding the unacceptability of these practices, then simply extend their consequences to their logical extremes. This particular technique of intellectual investigation is the best way of determining whether any specific idea or action is good or evil; beneficial or harmful. Additionally, we can then compare the consequences of these disorders to the consequences of encouraging the traditional family; extended to their logical extremes. In the cases of homosexuality and transsexuality, what would be the consequence to a society if all within it were to practice one of these disordered behaviors? . . . The death of the society in less than a single generation due to the absence of reproduction; because after the population grows older and becomes unable to care for or defend itself, a foreign power would then move in to conquer it.

On the other hand, what would be the consequence to society if all within the society were to grow up and raise families? . . . The eternal perpetuation of that society. Is either prospect a realistic expectation? No, but that's not the point. The purpose of the exercise is to evaluate and contrast the beneficence or maleficence of the opposing practices; and by so doing it is easy to see the beneficence and strength to be drawn from a society built upon the traditional family, and the opposing maleficence and degeneration that society suffers as a consequence of the toleration of socially suicidal, sexually deviant practices: a social degeneration that is being actualized in the modern world.

Beyond the severely destructive consequences to society posed by homosexuality and transsexuality, there are the suicidal consequences to the homosexual. Several different studies have documented the average life expectancy of the homosexual to be in the forties. The incidence of HIV/ AIDS—introduced into the world via the homosexual community—and all other sexually-transmitted diseases (herpes, anal warts, genital warts, etc.) is dramatically higher within the homosexual community than among the general population. The incidence of promiscuity is higher within the homosexual community than among the general population. The incidence of domestic violence is higher among homosexuals than within married families. The rate of alcoholism, drug use, and depression are all higher among homosexuals than among the general population. The propensity toward suicide is greater among homosexuals than it is within the general population. All things considered, the homosexual "lifestyle" is extremely dangerous to one's health and well-being, both psychologically and physically.

All these manifestations of individually and socially suicidal behaviors have arisen as the ultimate consequence of the debasement of the understanding of the principle of love; by synonymously associating "love" with sexual gratification. Too many pitiable people now draw the perverse social equation within their consciences—sex = love; so that more sex = more love—while remaining completely ignorant of, or willfully denying, the homicidal and suicidal consequences of their reprobated moral attitudes and behaviors.

Hate

What makes the abuse and ignorance of the principle of hate so dangerous today is that it is effectively being used as a political tool to subdue and punish political opposition. A major vehicle for this type of political persecution is already in place via the institution of "hate-crime" laws all over the world. The greatest injustice with hate-crime legislation is that it is impossible to determine; because there is no way for any human being to know what is in another person's heart and mind. With the institution of hate-crime legislation, the way has been paved to institute mass campaigns of political persecution against an ambitious politician's (or political party's) ideological opposition. The same methodology was used by Lenin and Stalin to solidify both their personal hold on power, and that of the Communist Party, in the early days of Soviet Russia; concluding in the Russian "show trials" of the 1930's Stalinist purges. What's worse, it is quickly becoming possible for a cunning politician, lawyer, or political party operative to imprison his opposition without a real crime being committed. All that is necessary is for public opinion to be made to believe that someone acted from sentiments of hatred. Whether they actually did, or did not, act out of hatred is both impossible to determine and not necessary to establish as long as a majority of the public (and in the courtroom, a jury) can be convinced of the accusation.

Ultimately, this will lead to the criminalization of "unorthodox" thought and mass persecution of a large segment of the population without the necessary requirement of proving a crime.[2] This is how aspiring tyrants operate . . . Make an allegation. If enough people can be convinced of the accusation, a person could be sent to jail or executed; regardless of the [impossible to establish] truth of the accusation. All that is needed is for public

---

[2] Offending a person's profligate sensibilities is *not* a crime.

perception to be manipulated in favor of the accuser. *That is true hatred*: when a person or organization would manipulate public perception for the purpose of self-interestedly securing their hold on political power; at the expense of the freedom, and in some cases the lives, of others who may be guilty of nothing more than opposing the objectives of a politician or political party. This is a common, trademark operational tactic and overarching strategy within modern politics and social activism.

A tremendous example is the cultural debate over homosexuality. The militant homosexual accuses any who would dare oppose them of bigotry ("homophobia") and subscribes motives of hatred as being the basis for the opposition to their behavior. In truth, this is completely false. The militant homosexual uses their opposition as a reflection of their own hatred for those who do not debase themselves in such a manner. As we just discussed, homosexuality must be forcefully opposed due to its suicidal consequences, both on the homosexual and upon society. Those who oppose homosexuality, and all other manner(s) of suicidal behavior, do so out of a sincere concern and desire to help others: primarily to defend those who may be more susceptible to corruption (primarily children); but secondarily to the reprobate as well, who may be reformed and once again regain their sanity if they could only comprehend the destructiveness, both to themselves and others, of their behavior(s) and choices. This scenario is also an excellent exemplification of the perversion of the principle of evil that we have just discussed; because in this situation, and others like it, it is the evil person who decries the sane man as evil for no greater reason than the offense that is rendered against their profligate sensibilities.

In all cases, simply recall the proper understanding of hatred—**a desire that compels the person who hates to place their own self-interest in a position of relative importance that is superior to the well-being of others, and it manifests itself in a willingness to sacrifice others for one's selfish interests**—in order to see the true source of hatred in any point of social or cultural contention.

Peace

Understanding that the true cause of peace is a common belief system and a unified mind, it can be seen that the modern-day, elitist "intellectual" and "opinion-maker," through the moral relativism that most of them promote, actually works against the cause of peace by promoting personal codes of ethics and morality that are different for each individual in a society. Moral relativism sets the stage for massive confrontations between not only cultures and nations, but between people and groups within a society; because once a culture has been infected with the deadly virus of moral relativism, the people within the society then turn to struggling against one another to assert their personal definitions of right and wrong on others, which can only lead to violence when disagreements are not reconciled while emotions are simultaneously agitated past a "breaking point." Deviously cunning people understand this inherent danger in moral relativism and use it to their political advantage; intentionally pitting people and groups against one another.

The purpose of the strategy is to psychologically align as many people as possible into an allegiance to the deviously cunning politician or political party; abusing those people who trust blindly in the promises of ambitious men and women, and who are likewise ignorant of the types of psychological tricks that are being used against them. In Soviet Russia, Lenin and Stalin both referred to these types of sycophantic people as "useful idiots." The ultimate aim is for the devious politician to propel themselves forward to higher seats of political power and control over others; psychologically at first, and with the ultimate goal being the physical subjugation of any possible political opposition (political prisoners and perpetrators of "thought crimes," such as those charged with "hate crimes"); in a more overt form of slavery. In actuality, peace is neither intended nor desired by these people; because if peace were ever to come about within society the public clamoring for the self-appointed, ambitious, and deviously cunning "white knights" and "saviors of society" would evaporate overnight, as people would no longer need a savior if they have themselves come to a state of peace with their fellow man.

Understanding the childishly simplistic minds of those who believe that peace is merely an absence of violence, the violently aggressive then use this delusion to forward the idea that it is the fault of the victims of violent aggression that there is no peace. An aggressor attacks, and then follows up their attack(s) with claims that all violence and bloodshed would end if the attacked party would simply relent and give in to the demands of the attacker. The cowardly (of which there are, sadly, entirely too many in today's world) grasp for an end to the violence at all costs; preferring their enslavement, and the enslavement of their fellow citizens as well, to the prospect of possibly losing their life in an armed conflict. This type of behavior is most clearly evident among the modern incarnations of "peace activists." The modern-

34

day peace activist is doomed to failure because, as explained earlier, these poor people don't possess a true sense, and a deeper understanding, of what peace is and how it is achieved.

Thinking with an immature mind, they look at the world from a shallow view of only what is placed before their eyes; either not understanding, or willfully choosing to ignore, how their frightful simplicity of mind is being used to prolong conflict, violence, and bloodshed by themselves choosing sides in a conflict and, predictably, choosing the side of the aggressor by trying to restrain the attacked party from exercising a forceful defense. Instead of looking at the justification for violence given by the attacker, and then making a decision to fight or relent based on principle, they choose to cower in the face of a threat; believing that capitulating to a violent aggressor will somehow make them non-violent and non-aggressive. Sadly, such a thing has never been, and it will never be! The only way that peace, and the consequent absence of violence and bloodshed, will be achieved in this world is when mankind comes to adhere to a common understanding and perspective; which, regretfully, doesn't appear to be on the horizon in the immediate future.

If the reader desires peace then let them embrace the *original, foundational* American ideal: each person within society must manage their own lives and provide for themselves and their family. It's simple! By embracing the responsibility for the outcome of one's life, peace is more readily achieved when the citizens within such a society look to themselves and their family for the support of their lives, rather than blaming nameless, faceless "others" when one's life hits a snag, which it always does for every one of us at one point in life or another. In today's world a spirit of cowardice is most responsible for destroying peace among mankind by leading people to blame and scapegoat others when something goes wrong in their life that causes them to feel disaffection for any reason. This is also what makes peace so hard to find in the world and allows social conflict(s) to so easily build, because it takes courage to live one's life in peace. It is difficult and emotionally distressing to face up to the fact that each of us is responsible for our lot in life; especially when beset with a painful and arduous difficulty. It is so much easier to simply look to blame others for our life's difficulties, which is why so many people find it so hard to be at peace with one another and even themselves; because they are so easily encouraged—primarily by politicians, lawyers, and social activists—to blame others for the problems and disaffection that they experience in their lives.

Justice

The perversion of the principle of justice is contributing to the dissolution of society because it is most commonly used to perpetrate an injustice. By associating justice with the satisfaction of one's desires, especially the desire for retribution, injustice is both promoted and propagated at an alarming rate. Clear examples of this sad truth are freely available, and are sadly becoming more and more common every day: cigarette smokers sue tobacco companies when they get cancer, overweight people sue fast food restaurants because they are fat, crime victims sue gun manufacturers when a criminal uses a gun to harm them or a family member, consumers sue product manufacturers when they hurt themselves using a product improperly, etc. Recalling the true understanding of the principle of justice—that one earns what they deserve for their labors and actions; nothing more and nothing less—it is easy to see the injustice in the situations noted here.

Smokers know the dangers of smoking, and have known it for more than forty years. If they become sick they have nobody to blame but themselves for their lack of self-control. Obese people know their excess consumption of food is the cause of their overweight condition, and that fast food is the least healthy of foods. When they become obese they have nobody to blame but themselves for their lack of self-control. When a criminal uses a firearm to harm someone, the manufacturer of the firearm cannot justly be held responsible for the actions of the person who committed the crime. It is completely unjust and ludicrous for a firearms manufacturer to be held responsible for the irresponsibility or criminal intent of an individual. Such factors are completely out of their (or any third party's) control. The responsible party is the criminal. If a person, through their own negligence or stupidity, uses a product in a dangerous manner, or that it was not designed for, they have nobody to blame but themselves for their lack of judgment. A product manufacturer cannot justly be expected to foresee all the outrageously stupid, and potentially dangerous, things that many people will do while using their products in a manner they were not originally designed or intended for.

The examples noted here are very brief, and the reader is probably able to note many more. The "dirty little secret" that is really no secret at all, and which most everybody simultaneously realizes and self-interestedly or conveniently ignores, is that the main cause of most all the cases of injustice related to product or service liability lawsuits are due to greed on the part of opportunistic lawyers and defendants who see the prospect of making an easy financial gain through the willful perversion of justice by blaming others for their faults, or holding a party responsible for factors beyond their control; for no other reason than the party being sued has "deep pockets": a.k.a the "legal lottery." Such perversions of justice have been noticed in previous ages, with contempt and disgust:

> And as licentiousness and disease breed in the city, aren't many law courts and hospitals opened? And don't the crafts of medicine and judging give themselves solemn airs when even large numbers of free men take them very seriously?
>
> How could it be otherwise?
>
> Yet could you find a greater sign of bad and shameful education in a city than that the need for skilled doctors and lawyers is felt not only by inferior people and craftsmen but by those who claim to have been brought up in the manner of free men? **Don't you think it's shameful and a great sign of vulgarity to be forced to make use of a justice imposed by others, as masters and judges, because you are unable to deal with the situation yourself?**
>
> I think that's the most shameful thing of all.
>
> Yet isn't it even more shameful when someone not only spends a good part of his life in court defending himself or prosecuting someone else but, through inexperience of what is fine, is persuaded to take pride in being clever at doing injustice and then exploiting every loophole and trick to escape conviction—and all for the sake of little worthless things and because he's ignorant of how much better and finer it is to arrange one's own life so as to have no need of finding a sleepy or inattentive judge?
>
> This case is even more shameful than the other.[3]
>
> — Plato, from *Republic*, written around 380 – 360 B.C.

This type of behavior, whether on a great or small scale, causes a coarsening within society that leads to an atmosphere of perpetual mistrust between both individuals and businesses; with all parties trying to

---

[3] Plato, *Republic*, trans. G.M.A. Grube, 2nd ed., revised by C.D.C. Greeve (Indianapolis, IN: Hackett Publishing Company, Inc., 1992), 81-82, 404e-405c.

outmaneuver one another for either the ability to protect themselves against all claims (business interest) or the ability to exploit a potential oversight (consumer). It inculcates a predatory mentality into the average citizen and a combative, defensive mentality into the average business interest; which can only lead to an increasing frequency of social conflict and an unsupportable economic burden on society as business interests amass great costs in pursuit of protecting themselves against predatory lawyers and consumers: ultimately doing great harm to the economic infrastructure of any society.

This behavior is also commonly used by today's racial bigots and social activists: Jesse Jackson, Al Sharpton, white supremacists, La Raza (NCLR), et al. Such people and organizations attempt to blame the living for the sins of the dead. When the living have the audacity to defend their innocence and decry the injustice of today's true racial bigots they are viciously, and calumniously, attacked by today's perpetuators of racial bigotry and hatred. Regardless of race, a careful observer to the racial activism scene will notice a predictable *modus operandi* among the modern race hustler(s). Anyone who "knuckles under" and gives in to the demands of the bigoted racial activist is pretty much left alone in return for their acquiescence and compliance with the demands made on them; but those who dare to stand up to the racial bigot are themselves viciously demonized and calumniously accused of just about every evil imaginable: typically of being a "racist" for not complying with the bigot's demands. Sadly, it's always the same with these evil people; for there really is no other play in their playbook:

1. Make demands on a person or group, and threaten retribution if demands are not met: extortion.
2. If the object of the extortionary demands complies; leave them alone and "milk" them for as long as they are useful.
3. If the object of the demands resists attempts at extortion; defame them publicly until either they relent and acquiesce to the demands made of them, or until such time as an easier "mark" is found.
4. When the object of extortion is either no longer useful, or another "mark" is found, return to step 1. and begin the process again.

It is truly that simple. The saddest part is that there are so many ignorant, self-pitying people in the world that this type of abuse of justice often works, because the race hustlers are fully aware of the extremely high level of ignorant greed that exists within humanity today, and they are more than happy to use it to their advantage; both in terms of financial gain and a gain in celebrity, name recognition, and political power:

> There is another class of colored people who make a business of keeping the troubles, the wrongs, and the hardships of the Negro race before the public. Having learned that they are able to make a living out of their troubles, they have grown into the settled habit of advertising their wrongs, partly because they want sympathy and partly because it pays. Some of these people do not want the Negro to lose his grievances, because they do not want to lose their jobs. . . I am afraid that there is a certain class of race problem solvers who don't want the patient to get well, because as long as the disease holds out they have not only an easy means of making a living, but also an easy medium through which to make themselves prominent before the public.[4]
> — Booker T. Washington

---

[4] http://www.btwsociety.org/library/books/My_Larger_Education/05.php, accessed November 30, 2011.

Why Is There So Much Strife in the World, or in Other Words, "Why Can't We All Just Get Along"?

The answer to this question is quite a paradox in the modern world because it will simultaneously enkindle within each one of us both a sense of great hope and one of great consternation. While it is very simple to understand intellectually, which will give rise to great hope; the consternation comes from the realization that the only way we will be able to transcend the current difficulties in this world is to—as much as each one of us is individually able—conquer ourselves by both first noticing, and then attempting to eradicate, the faults within our own behavior and attitudes that are contributing to the current levels of social strife that are spiraling into an ever-increasing crescendo of combativeness; for it is a perverse component of our human nature to ever so easily find fault in others while excusing, or not even noticing, those that exist within ourselves. Directly to the point, the primary reason we can't all get along in this world is due to the great cultural battle(s) that have erupted all over the world—primarily within the past several centuries—that, when traced back to their ultimate cause(s), can be seen as a violent eruption of insane rage in opposition to sanity.

To understand this reality, the reader has to understand what is sane and what is insane. Considering the age we live in, the situation of the world today demonstrates a classic philosophical observation: "In a world of insanity, the sane are considered insane." The attempt will be made to demonstrate the insanity of today's world, and then in turn shine a light down the path that returns mankind to sanity. We must first come to possess a clear understanding of what constitutes sanity and what constitutes insanity. To discern between the two we must all refer to the only proven and impartial judge that humanity has ever known . . . objective reality: those articles in life that can be demonstrably shown to be true and real. In our case consider it the application of the scientific method to social phenomena. Objective reality is the most astute judge in these matters precisely because of its impartial nature. Very simply, it is what it is: a true state of affairs completely devoid of any consideration of human desires and passions. Black is black and white is white; regardless of whether any of us like it. A deprivation of oxygen in the human body will lead to death, fire will burn, extreme cold will freeze, etc. These are simple realities that no sensible human being can deny.

From this we can then clarify that sanity is the process of recognizing objective reality and conforming one's behavior to that which is healthy and productive. Conversely, insanity is the process of repudiating and denying objective reality. How then does the unstable and disconcerting influence of insanity so easily inject itself into the world and, rather than providing the stability and consolation of sanity, instead cause so much confusion and doubt? This degenerative process will be referred to as the "lawyering" of reality. To understand this process I will attempt to demonstrate, and hopefully make clearly understandable, the reality of today's insanity and the pernicious products that have followed as a result.

We will begin by using some anecdotal life experiences as a vehicle to illustrate some important points. Several decades ago, as a young Naval-Officer-in-training at the U.S. Naval Academy (Annapolis), it was routine to witness episodes that transpired between our instructors and those of us who were aspiring to someday become commissioned officers in the U.S. Navy. The turn of events always followed a certain behavioral template.

To understand this social transaction the reader must first understand some of the basic, rudimentary foundations of leadership training within the U.S. military that should, but all too sadly does not, embed itself within the psychological and philosophical disposition of responsible adults. From the first days of our training as future leaders there were two dispositions that were *constantly* pounded into our heads, and they were reflected by two automatic responses that were required of us whenever we were either found to be wanting of information or in the performance of our assigned duties. The first was, "I'll find out, sir." This was the expected response when we were asked to produce information that we did not know. The second was, "No excuse, sir," when we failed to perform a task assigned to us. In most instances the two responses were seemingly conjoined, because it was the purposefully intended nature of our training to weigh us down with such a heavy burden of information and learning that only those with apparently photographic memories could ever absorb it all; and in most all cases it was a certainty that no matter how intellectually gifted a particular person was, we would all get "caught with our pants down" at one time or another; lacking in either knowledge or the duties assigned to us.

41

The scenario usually played out as follows . . . "Mr. Johnson, what is the maximum rate of climb for an F-14 Tomcat"? Either having failed to learn this information, or not remembering it due to information overload from the multitude of subjects being studied, the unpleasant but inevitable answer would follow . . . "I'll find out, sir." Having been assigned the duty to learn this information previously, the inquisitor would then begin to dig the claws in: "Why don't you know this information, Mister! This is basic information that you should have learned a week ago"! These inquisitions were usually given in rather animated language and in a most severe demeanor. Those of us who were quicker to understand the routine simply spent more time devoted to the information requested of us. If you said, "I'll find out, sir," you catalogued in your mind what was requested of you and subsequently went and learned the necessary information: self-assured that the requested information would again be demanded in short order . . . and it most always was.

This was a sublime game of psychological warfare and everybody within the situation knew it, whether they liked it or not. What was the purpose of such harsh and rigorous treatment? The sole purpose was to transform people who showed up at the institution as those who thought as children into those who thought as responsible adults; in the full knowledge that such a psychological disposition was what was required of those who would be leading others in the future; possibly to their very deaths! In one sense it was sort of a "game," but in its greater part the lesson to be learned was one of actions vs. consequences; and that there were severe reprisals for failure in one's duties. In short, it was a crucible designed to firmly impress a serious sense of responsibility on those subjected to the ordeal.

During the normal course of things there were roughly nine instructors (seniors at Annapolis charged with the administration of our version of boot camp; known as "plebe summer") grilling a group of about one hundred bewildered freshmen (a.k.a. "plebes"): a ratio of 11 or 12 plebes per instructor. The plebes would be lined up against a wall as an upper-classman would work his way down the line "asking" (oftentimes barking) various questions. If the plebe knew what was asked of him and was performing as desired the inquisitor moved on to the next plebe in line and began the same treatment; seeking out a fault that he could capitalize on. This evolution was extremely psychologically stressful for the plebes; both when undergoing the inquisition, as well as when they were awaiting their turn for questioning. In some cases, depending on the imagination of the plebe, the waiting could be worse than the actual questioning; like a condemned prisoner awaiting his turn at the guillotine.

However, early on in the "game" there were a few people who didn't quite have an intuitive understanding of the rules. Although they were taught from the beginning the proper responses of "I'll find out, sir," and "No excuse, sir," they still had the natural, human tendency of excuse-making and blame-shifting embedded within their psyche. When probed for information that they didn't know, or when questioned regarding their failure to perform an assigned task, they would supply an excuse intended to deflect the blame for their failure in knowledge or performance. When such events came to pass, it seemed that everyone within earshot had the same impression and foreboding of what was to immediately transpire; because it wasn't going to be pretty for the one trying to make excuses. The reaction was immediate and merciless. The particular instructor who was the first to hear excuses being offered for any particular failing—instead of "I'll find out, sir," or "No excuse, sir"—was quick to call the sharks to the feeding frenzy. As we were at the Naval Academy, the particular call to arms had to have an obligatory nautical flavor to it . . . "Ohhh! We've got a sea-lawyer over here"! As soon as the call went out it seemed as if time dragged to a near standstill.

The particular "sea-lawyer" who failed to provide the proper response was immediately besieged by a multitude of instructors who began to pick apart his excuse, mock him for his attempt to make excuses, and assault him with an intense degree of questioning exponentially greater than would have otherwise transpired if he had simply regurgitated the expected automatic response(s). This treatment would most always produce severe sweating and trembling in the sea-lawyering plebe; occasionally accompanied by crying, depending on the intensity of the treatment and the psychological strength of the plebe in question. What this meant for the rest of us plebes was that there was a good chance that our inquisition would be suspended so that our inquisitor could devote his attention to the newly-found sea-lawyer. Although we didn't realize it at the time, this chain of events was equally as instructive to the audience as it was to the unfortunate center of attention; because the emotions and thoughts that developed within us taught us invaluable lessons about human nature and psychology that we would have never learned so directly and deeply were we not immersed in such an intense environment.

The primary emotions and thoughts imparted to the bystanders of such merciless onslaughts were sentiments of joy, pity, and guilt. The joy arose from the greatly heightened prospect that our immediate, personal trial was going to be immediately suspended so that our inquisitor could devote his undivided attention to the sea-lawyer. The pity arose, naturally, from the certain understanding of the awful trial that was about to be delivered to our fellow plebe. And finally, to bring the mind full circle upon itself, the guilt arose from our sense of joy at being relieved of our intense questioning; because it was clearly understood that in finding our relief someone else was going to suffer more greatly in our stead, and he was the one whom we felt intense pity for, which only served to "tweak" the sense of guilt even further. The end result of such psychological trials is to incapacitate the mind's rational ability when it is subjected to the "weight" of intense emotions; and as the intensity of the scene increased, the force of the emotional elements caused the mind to "implode" on itself. A comparable analogy in the physical world is that of an astrophysical black hole. As the mass of matter increases, the force of gravity causes the large mass to compress itself; so that eventually the force is so overwhelming that not even light can escape. In a psychological sense, as the mass of intense emotions increases, this emotional mass compresses the mind in upon itself and becomes so overwhelming that the light of rational thought cannot escape from it.

How does this anecdotal story relate to the problems facing the world today? Very simply, the mass of emotion and emotionally-based psychological constructs (humanistic "liberalism") that have been increasingly inculcated within the human race over the past several generations and centuries is reaching its "critical mass": the point at which human reason is no longer able to overcome the force of human emotions, desires, and passions. Why is this so and how did it come to pass? This change in the human psyche from that of sane, rationally-based mental processes to those of insane, emotionally-based mental processes has occurred primarily via the corruption of educational institutions—from the elementary through the university level—throughout the world, and has been further compounded by the natural difficulties that burden all human beings who reach adulthood and feel the pressure of meeting and overcoming everyday difficulties and responsibilities; especially among those who face the burdens of being responsible for others as well as themselves: particularly parents, but others as well.

There are several important points to observe in the above sea-lawyer scenario that are important for all people to understand, because the application of the principles discovered through such an event are universally applicable to the human condition. The first thing to notice is both the futility, and ultimately negative consequences that accrue, from making excuses for one's failings in life instead of facing up to them and making the best efforts to amend and overcome them. Honest people will admit to themselves that human beings are both greatly flawed and highly limited in their individual capacities. This is simply a product of our human nature; in that the human mind can only attend to one task and thought process at a time. This is an absolute truth, regardless of how some people attempt to delude themselves and others with their supposed ability to "multi-task." In truth, the accomplished "multi-tasker" is no more able to process thoughts simultaneously than any other person. At best, they are simply able to shift the focus of their attention from one task to another with greater speed, precision, and coherence than others; which is a great talent unto itself. However, they are still limited to the same mental constraints as the rest of us; only possessing the capability to process one particular progression of thought or reasoning at a time.

Understanding this reality, it then becomes obvious that none of us can become all things to all people; taking upon ourselves responsibilities and duties that exceed our capabilities to perform. Moreover, there are a great many people in this world who—through either sloth or poor character—are slow, or obstinately refuse, to be responsible for themselves or those they are legitimately responsible for (for example, a parent who is rightly responsible for their child's welfare). As a result, when somebody fails to meet their responsibilities—due to incapacity, imperfection, or negligence—it should be clearly understood that the fault lies with the one who failed to meet their responsibility. Each and every human being on the face of this earth is subject to this universal truth, and in the increasingly frenetic pace of the world it should be clearly understood that *all* of us (myself included), at one time or another, fail in our duties or responsibilities to ourselves, others, or both.

As parents, maybe we forgot to sign our child's report card or didn't pay into their lunch account at school before it ran dry. As employees, maybe we didn't finish that important report in time for the expected deadline. As debtors, maybe we didn't pay our mortgage or car payment on time. From articles in life that are mere trifles to those substantially more consequential, we all "drop the ball" in one form or another on an almost daily basis, while trying to mitigate and manage our failings as best we can: internally prioritizing and attending to the more consequential items before moving on to the smaller considerations.

Realizing this sad state of our imperfect nature brings us to the second point to notice in the sea-lawyer scenario: that facing up to our failings—as discomforting as it may be—is substantially less difficult, and is attended by much less severe consequences, than if we simply admit to our failing(s) and make a sincere attempt to modify our behavior and attitudes so as to improve ourselves as we move forward into the future. Why is it easier to admit our failings, and why are the consequences of excuse-making always more severe than if we had forthrightly admitted to our shortcomings? The simple answer is that admitting to our failings as human beings is nothing more than an acknowledgment of the frailty and incapacity inherent within human nature; while trying to make excuses for our failings erodes the trust and confidence of those around us who witness the blame-shifting, excuse-making behavior. Consider the above examples as cases in point.

The forthright person who admits to their children that they honestly forgot to sign their report card or fill up their lunch account, apologizes for the oversight, promises to correct it, and subsequently signs the report card and funds the lunch account will demonstrate to their child that they are just as human as everybody else. While the child may be a little disappointed with their parent for their failing in the circumstance, they wouldn't justly doubt their parent's sincerity or honesty; especially if the parent takes immediate steps to correct their fault. If instead the parent made an excuse; blaming the oversight on an obligation at work that required their undivided attention, or some other similar deflection of fault; the trust and confidence in the parent, which the child may have previously felt, would most certainly be eroded; and as such episodes increase over time the child will quickly come to view their parent(s) as unreliable and untrustworthy. Knowing that there will always be something "important" for the parent to attend to, the child will be left with the impression that they are not apparently important enough to command their parent's attention: leaving the impression on the child that they are not a priority in their parent's lives and considerations.

As an employee, if we admit our fault and devote ourselves to correcting our time management skills or attention to our responsibilities, the employer will feel let down in the particular circumstance; but if we are making visible efforts to improve our performance they will at least be satisfied with a conscientious effort to improve in the future. However, if we instead offer up an excuse for our failing the employer will become more greatly annoyed with us; coming to view us as unreliable in the workplace as such events repeat themselves over time, which could ultimately cost us our jobs. And finally, as everyone is aware, excuses fall on deaf ears and are not tolerated when it comes to paying our financial obligations. If we take steps to cut our expenses—while organizing and disciplining ourselves to pay the bills on time—we will subsequently incur less debt in the future as we pay off our existing debts in a timelier manner, which will more speedily relieve ourselves of existing debt as we increase our credit worthiness; reflected by an improved credit rating that will consequently improve our chances of receiving credit in the future. On the other hand, making excuses for failing to meet one's financial obligations, as reflected when one's debts are not paid on time, only results in a greatly diminished credit rating that will make it much harder to purchase items in the future.

These examples demonstrate the universal applicability of the principle that taking personal responsibility for our inevitable failings will likely cause us some temporary discomfort, embarrassment, or humiliation. However, the consequences that result will ultimately serve to improve both our character and our esteem in the eyes of others as we move forward into the future; because those who recognize their flaws are then able to take steps to mitigate and correct them in the future. Contrarily, those who make excuses for their failings—or even worse, blame other people ("My debtors didn't pay me on time," "My wife/husband has been too demanding," etc.) or abstract ideas ("It's 'society's' fault that I can't get ahead," "Everybody's letting me down," etc.)—will never see their flaws and failings in any situation; always finding fault in others while never seeing any in themselves. Like an alcoholic or drug addict, if the excuse-makers and blame-shifters of the world never come to see fault in their own behavior they will never take any steps toward improving themselves or their life situation, which ultimately leads to a person who continually debases their character to lower and lower degrees as time passes and the excuses pile up.

Why don't people realize their imperfect nature and human limitations any longer; but instead busy themselves contriving elaborate excuses for their failings? The answer to this question is similar in nature to the original question posed in the title to this chapter; in that it is quite a paradox for modern humanity because it is both easy to understand while being extraordinarily difficult to correct and overcome for almost all human beings. *At the foundational level, all the world's ills in this age can be traced back to a single, primary source . . . simple, human PRIDE!* Human pride is the single most corrosive and destructive element that injects itself into all social relations. It matters not which socially degenerating problem is under consideration. When traced back to their root cause(s), it can be seen that the seed from which they all germinate is human pride. It is so extraordinarily and potently deceiving because it is an inherent quality of pride—for those who fall victim to it—to not notice the self-deception that so strongly affects the person who succumbs to it.

An honest, disinterested observer will be quick to notice that the deeper a person falls into sentiments of human pride, the more difficult it is for them to recognize their self-delusion. Pride, a sentiment that is inherently natural to all of us, is a downward, psychological spiral that, if not checked by the faculties of rationality and reason, leads all those who fall victim to it into a state that becomes increasingly difficult to overcome as its victims fall further into its self-admiring snare. The more "puffed up" and haughty a person becomes regarding their own self-asserted perfections, abilities, and "greatness"; the harder it becomes to realize, and freely admit to, their failings. In the worst cases the psychological disposition of those overcome by pride becomes so severe that in a great many cases it becomes psychologically impossible for the affected person to correct; as their psyches become so fragile and self-glorifying that they are not able to face their faults, imperfections, and failings without suffering something equivalent to a psychological collapse.

This reality is a difficult thing to digest for most all people due to the implications that emanate from it. Let's take a hard look at the most prominent manifestation of human pride and source of strife in the modern world—narcissism—to exemplify the point. Narcissism can be properly understood as a mental disposition that places one's desires and passions as the center upon which one's life gravitates. Why is narcissism such a supremely dangerous and self-deluding frame of reference? The important thing to understand is that the dangers of narcissism, in most instances, lie not only in its immediate effects—the satisfaction of an individual's immediate passions—but also from the consequence(s) that accrue from such a disposition; socio-psychological blindness: a lack of understanding regarding the consequences of one's self-oriented passions and actions on the larger society in which one lives.

We can only understand this truth if we have a common understanding of some basic realities regarding the human condition. The most important point of understanding is the environment within which we live; for if we are ignorant of our environment we will suffer the fatal consequences of our ignorance. Astronauts who are ignorant of the environment outside their spacecraft will certainly explode if subjected to the vacuum of outer space without the protection of a space suit; scuba divers who are ignorant of the environment around them will certainly drown if their depth exceeds the physiological limitations of their body; and firemen will certainly be consumed if they are ignorant of the dangers accompanying a raging inferno and enter the conflagration without their protective gear.

There are two fundamental questions that must be considered and answered if we are to truly overcome the social collapse into cultural barbarism that the modern world is falling into: (1) "What kind of social environment does humanity live within"?, and (2) "Why is the overwhelming ignorance of our true social environment endangering humanity"? The answer to the first question is that we simultaneously exist as both autonomous individuals and as members of a larger society. Just as a human being is composed of conjoined body and soul; on a social level the individual is both a member unique to themselves within the world while participating as a constituent member of the larger society within which they live. There is a constant, dualistic dependence of one upon the other: body and soul; the individual and the society. One cannot properly survive, and certainly not live well, without the sustenance of the other.

From the individual perspective we can all understand the necessity to attend to our personal development; for if we fail in that most basic responsibility to ourselves we quickly grow into stale and apathetic automatons: empty shells of humanity lacking depth and substance; and as a result becoming bitter, unproductive, and hateful creatures: burdens on the society we should be fortifying and building up. Within the larger social context, while retaining our individual identity, we are also dependent on the greater society within which we live in order to further our personal development.

> No man is an island, entire of itself; every man is a piece of the Continent, a part of the main; if a clod be washed away by the sea, Europe is the less, as well as if a promontory were, as well as if a manor of thy friends or of thine own were; any man's death diminishes me, because I am involved in Mankind; And therefore never send to know for whom the bell tolls; It tolls for thee.[1]
> — John Donne, English clergyman and poet

No person can make it through this world without the aid of others. The butcher cannot make it through life without the services of the clothier who makes his clothes, or the manufacturer of cutlery; who makes the implements that the butcher needs to cut his meat. The consumer of the butcher's products needs the plumber and the garbage man to carry away the waste products of the meats they consume. The public utility worker, who processes the consumer's aggregate waste products; brought to the waste treatment facility by the plumber's implements or to the landfill by the

---

[1] http://www.poemhunter.com/poem/no-man-is-an-island/, accessed November 22, 2011.

garbage man, requires the services of the butcher to sustain their lives so that they can then continue on in their work of processing the community's waste products.

Through a multitude of almost innumerable, circuitous paths we all rely on one another to provide the things we need in this world that we cannot otherwise provide for ourselves. These are the realities of the environment within which we live. The important point to understand is that our relationship to both spheres of interaction—the individual and the society— must be nurtured and balanced; for if either element is neglected it will ultimately damage the other. If the individual abdicates their individuality to the greater needs of society, forgetting their responsibility to their own personal development, they subsequently forfeit their own identity and individuality. If the individual indulges their desires and passions devoid of a proper and healthy sense of self-restraint, forgetting their responsibility to the larger society within which they live, then the society begins to break down into a narcissistic collapse, which is what we are witnessing in this age.

This reality encompasses the answer to the second question ("Why is the overwhelming ignorance of our true social environment endangering humanity"?). The overwhelming narcissism of this age has led most all human beings to place the primary focus of their existence on their selfish desires, while remaining willfully ignorant of the damaging consequences that the indulgence of many of their self-willed passions causes to the greater social body. By allowing ourselves to gratify our passions without responsible and healthy social restraints (heterosexual licentiousness, homosexuality, transgenderism, drug addiction, etc.), we have started down a path of societal murder/suicide!

Human civilizations have been around for roughly five thousand years and they will continue to exist, in some form or another, until the end of time. Human beings live, typically, less than one hundred years. Understanding this reality, we can then see that within the larger sphere of humanity our time on this earth is relatively short. Moreover, understanding our place within the larger body of humanity, it then becomes easier to see that for the short span of time that we walk this earth we are burdened with the responsibility of leaving this world a better place than we found it when we came into it. The operative word here is *responsibility!* Although each one of us is an individual within a larger society—searching for our own place within it so that we "fit in" more comfortably—our primary *responsibility* is to maintain and uplift our society or civilization so that those who come after us are not burdened with cleaning up any social "messes" we may leave behind as a result of our narcissistic selfishness.

This is simply a reality of the human condition. Nobody asked any of us whether we like this reality or not; and let me be the first one to commiserate with you when you feel that this reality isn't pleasant or "fair." Moreover, although it is not my desire to appear callous, I feel compelled to remind the readers of the age-old axiom, "Life isn't fair." However, it's not all your fault. It's not all my fault. Every one of us contributes to the imperfection of the world in one small part or another due to our own human imperfections. This is simply the reality of life, and we must *all* endeavor to make the best of it as we can . . . in the most *responsible* way we can.

Looking at the behavior of the human race today—most specifically those within Western civilization—it can be seen that most of us are not behaving in a responsible manner that is sufficient to sustain our respective civilizations. Let's briefly recap the primary points of dissipation in order to clearly recognize our manifest irresponsibility. Promiscuity and licentiousness has led to a large increase in the number of pregnancies and the incidences of sexually-transmitted diseases. Increased pregnancies have driven an increase in abortions among those pregnancies that were unplanned or undesired; murdering those who would otherwise take their place within society as its heirs and perpetuators. For those children who are unplanned or undesired, but not aborted, a great many of them suffer neglect at the hands of their "parents" due to the increasingly narcissistic nature of modern humanity. The result of such neglect leads to emotionally and psychologically wounded children who grow up embittered, confused, and spiteful; and who then, all too often, participate in all manners of socially destructive and degenerative behavior, which further accelerates the dissipation of human civilization(s). The combination of unchecked narcissism and rampant promiscuity has fueled a historically unheard of militancy among homosexuals and transsexuals—demanding that they be respected and celebrated—even when their behavior retards the propagation of human civilization(s); as these disorders are suicidal both to themselves as well as to the societies they are attacking.

Sadly, these social and moral problems have become articles of severe and unhealthy dispute in the modern era, and this is only the case because the perception of the average person today has become so confused that they cannot see these issues in their proper, rational context. Instead, they are debated and argued from an emotional, narcissistic perspective: "I want what I want and you have no right to tell me that I can't have what I want. You're a 'hater' for trying to deprive me of what I want"! It's important to note that nothing presented here is forwarded from motives of "hate" or a spiteful disposition. The ideas presented here are sincerely meant to encourage human life and preserve our respective civilizations. That abortion, homosexuality, transsexuality, and licentiousness promiscuity are fatally destructive to human civilization(s) is clearly evident when one looks to that eternally impartial judge: objective reality. By evaluating these problems from a rational (actions vs. consequences) perspective their intolerable dangers can be easily grasped without resorting to a contentious or "hateful" disposition. Moreover, we must remember our [small] place in the order of time and within the context of our relationship to the greater society, and of human civilization(s) at large. In the end, what is important in our lives are our efforts and actions to fortify and strengthen human civilization(s); not the extent to which we were able to gratify our passions and egos while we lived. The former pursuit is more noble and selfless, while the latter is more degenerate and selfish.

All socially destructive behaviors stem from, in one form or another, mankind's instinctual appetites—especially those that are sexual in nature—and it is of especial note that, on whole as a species, the human race is destroying itself because it can no longer control its barbaric, animalistic passions. This fact is especially tragic and heartbreaking when one considers that of all the species on Earth, the human species is the only one capable of reason; so that we have the gift and ability to understand the consequences of our actions. All other creatures in the animal kingdom simply exist from one day to the next; driven to action by whatever their instinctual passions dictate: sex, food, sleep, etc. This is a difficult reality to face, but it must be faced up to if we are going to save ourselves from our own reprobation. By allowing themselves to succumb to their passions, a great number of the human species have abdicated their humanity by refusing to acknowledge, through the use of their reason, the dangers that they bring upon both themselves and our respective societies; having instead regressed to an existence as mere instinctual animals. What's even worse is that those within Western civilization are now being conditioned to this dangerous and undignified state by the public education systems and through the bad influences they are being exposed to in the debauched world of "entertainment": TV, movies, music, etc.

Finally, recalling the proper understanding of what hate is—**a desire that compels the person who hates to place their own self-interest in a position of relative importance that is superior to the well-being of others, and it manifests itself in a willingness to sacrifice another for**

one's selfish interests—it can then be understood that all these aberrant disorders are true instances of hatred; both of oneself and of the human race as a whole. When we are aware of the damaging consequences to ourselves and others due to our lack of self-control; yet we still engage in, and indeed encourage, such suicidal behavior; those behaving in such a manner are demonstrating that they believe their own selfish desires are superior to the needs of others, which exactly fits the proper understanding of the principle of hatred.

How We Regressed to Our Current, Sad, State

As stated previously, humanity has come to its current, sad state due to the "lawyering" of reality. The term "lawyering" is used because of the way in which lawyers ply their trade: argumentation and debate; otherwise known as dialectics. The corruption of the modern world did not happen overnight. It has been a process of slow, but deliberate, degeneration that has been taking place over the past several centuries, and it has been facilitated by people who deliberately inject corruptive ideas and philosophies into the social body in order to serve their own self-serving agendas. The use of dialectics in order to change the perception of humanity has always been the tool used to persuade others. However, as it applies to the corruption of the modern world, the use of this technique made a significant rupture from previous eras in the latter half of the Eighteenth Century, during the period known as the "Age of Enlightenment," with the introduction of the philosophy of rationalism that, as a natural consequence of the philosophy, resulted in the self-deification of man in the minds of those who subscribed to the philosophy.

It is a philosophical belief that all truth can be discovered by reason and factual analysis. The greatest problem with rationalism is that people who use rationalistic techniques—those who claim to use strict reason applied to known facts—have very rarely used both sound and consistent reason or applied their "reason" to *all* the known facts. Most every politician in the Western world today uses rationalism to mislead both themselves and the public. It is an extremely effective tool of misdirection, because the rationalist intends to appear, and in most cases actually believes themselves to be, intellectually superior to those they are contesting. A demonstration of enormous pride and self-conceit. The typical approach is to state the "facts" as they see them—or wish them to be—and then extend a line of reasoning based on their purported "facts."

What makes the rationalistic approach so dangerous is that if the purported facts that form the foundation of the rationalist's line of reasoning are not absolutely correct, then the supposed truths that are built up over successive iterations of false reasoning become more and more flawed; to the point that there is no basis in truth or reality at the end of a "reasoning" process that is built on the false foundations of erroneous beliefs. Plato spoke of the dangers of rationalism and its accompanying technique, dialectics, in his classic work, *Republic*. He describes how easily it was, and still is, abused and misused to the discredit of honest philosophy and the application of sound and consistent reason:

> I don't suppose that it has escaped your notice that, when young people get their first taste of arguments, they misuse it by treating it as a kind of game of contradiction. They imitate those who've refuted them by refuting others themselves, and, like puppies, they enjoy dragging and tearing those around them with their arguments.
>
> They're excessively fond of it.
>
> Then, when they've refuted many and been refuted by them in turn, they forcefully and quickly fall into disbelieving what they believed before. And, as a result, they themselves and the whole of philosophy are discredited in the eyes of others.
>
> That's very true.
>
> But an older person won't want to take part in such madness. He'll imitate someone who is willing to engage in discussion in order to look for the truth, rather than someone who plays at contradiction for sport.[1] He'll be more sensible himself and will bring honor rather than discredit to the philosophical way of life.[2]
>
> — Plato

In today's world, the formulaic system of dialectics that is most widely used by politicians, lawyers, social activists, and others, in order to confuse and misdirect the public, is termed the "Hegelian Dialectic"; named after an early-Nineteenth Century, German philosopher: Georg Wilhelm Friedrich Hegel. Although Mr. Hegel didn't explicitly refer to this process, he used several forms of "triadic"[3] philosophical constructs, which probably led to

---

[1] "lawyering"

[2] Plato, *Republic*, 211.

[3] A philosophical construct composed of three components; where an idea (first component) gives rise to its opposing idea (second component), and from these two opposites commonalities are sought to form a reconciliation (third component) between the opposing ideas: for example, being-nothingness-becoming, immediate-mediate-concrete, and thesis-antithesis-synthesis.

him being infamously associated with the system. It is composed of three distinct components: Thesis, Antithesis, and Synthesis. The thesis is an original, stated belief or ideological position on any particular subject matter. The antithesis is a view that is contrary to the stated thesis. The two opposing positions, because they cannot both be simultaneously true, represent a clear contradiction of each other. In order to resolve the contradiction between opposing views, it is proposed that the two opposites must be melded into a single view at a "higher level" than the two constituent and opposing views, so that any contradictions or inconsistencies may then be addressed and resolved in the newly synthesized view.

Those fond of using this technique are like Plato's puppies: psychologically or emotionally immature individuals who "enjoy dragging and tearing those around them with their arguments." The Hegelian Dialectic has proved to be a horrific disgrace to the field of philosophy and reason; especially because—due to the very nature of the processes employed—it is not meant to arrive at the truth as its final destination, which is the true aim of honest philosophy and debate: discovery of the truth. Due to the very nature, process, and methodology of the Hegelian Dialectic, *it is not possible* to reach the truth and can only result in the propagation of erroneous ideas and "philosophies."

Why is this the case? Because the functional methodology of the process, at its foundation, is utterly and completely dishonest and erroneous. If we look to the nature of reality and truth it will become immediately apparent. Within the context of what is demonstrably real, both the functional and intellectual processes of reconciling or synthesizing two completely opposing, contradictory opposites into a new philosophical or ideological "truth" is a clearly impossible task. It supposes that two incongruous ideas, or realities, can somehow be fused together to form a new perception of reality that contains components of both constituent ideas that result in the elimination of contradictions between the two opposites. Moreover, it assumes that this process can be applied to all things perceptible to human cognition.

From this perspective, those who use this dialectic system would have the world believe that resolving opposing views is like mixing paint; where they can be melded together like black (thesis) and white (antithesis) in order to make a new, homogenous product: gray (synthesis). Common sense and common human experience expose such beliefs to be the height of folly. There are some things that are simply absolutes incapable of admixture with other things, which is what is required in the synthesis process: that two opposing things be "mixed" to form a new one that transcends both of the original, opposing things. For instance, there are the opposing perspectives of religious faith vs. atheism, or the state of being pregnant vs. that of not being pregnant, and the most definitive of all . . . the state of being alive or of being dead. These are just three examples of polar opposites that cannot be fused or synthesized in order to establish a new perception that resolves all contradictions between the two opposites.

There are certainly a multitude of other examples of absolutes incapable of admixture that also occur to the reader. The existence of absolutes clearly clarifies that there are some things in life that either are, or are not, and there is no middle ground between them. As is intuitively obvious to all, there is no such thing as being "a little bit pregnant" or "a little bit dead." In such instances of absolutes that are complete opposites it is instead a situation of trying to mix oil (thesis) and water (antithesis) and expecting to be able to synthesize a homogenous composite from the two. It is not possible in the real world to produce a synthesized medium from two absolute opposites. In the ideological and philosophical sphere, such a pursuit is like trying to mix an absolute falsehood with an absolute truth. Of course, when such a thing is attempted the only product that can possibly occur is for the truth to be corrupted, which is exactly what has been happening over the past several centuries since the Hegelian Dialectic has been codified into a formulaic, dialectical system.

Within the context of the nature of truth, the Hegelian Dialectic is clearly seen as fallacious. The truth, in any situation, is analogous in the ideological realm to a journey's destination in the physical world. When one is trying to find their way to the truth it is like starting out from a position of ignorance or curiosity, consulting a roadmap of known and established facts along the way to the truth, and then finally arriving at the truth if, *and only if*, the roadmap of established facts is itself completely accurate and unflawed; because each "fact" along the way to the truth is like a new road, or a widening of an existing road, of reasoning. If one of the necessary factual roads is an erroneous, false turn, one will never come to their desired final destination of truth unless they backtrack, find the point where they were diverted onto a false road of reasoning, discover the correct road of reasoning, and then continue on to the truth. The most important element to take from the understanding of the nature of truth, and how to arrive at it, is that the truth is a fixed, immovable destination at the end of the road(s) of sound reason; just as a city is a fixed destination in the physical world at the end of equally fixed roads.

Black is black; white is white; pregnant is pregnant; and dead is dead. There is no deviation from the fixed position of such absolutes. With this understanding in mind, it is easy to see how the Hegelian Dialectic is used to mislead and confuse people; especially the uneducated and weak-minded. The dialectic proposes two opposing views to every circumstance or idea, but in the knowledge that truth is a fixed destination it is now easy to understand that there is only one right way to the truth. Generally, either the thesis or the antithesis puts a person's mind on the right road to the truth, while the other is used to direct a person's mind away from the truth and toward either a subtly erroneous error or an absolute lie. Let's consider what happens to those who try to use the Hegelian Dialectic as their roadmap to the truth.

To begin with, when faced with two opposing ideas on the way to the truth, only one road of reason will be true and correct; so that with every branch in the road(s) of reason the mind is actually faced with a choice between a turn to the truth or a turn toward falsehood. Following the Hegelian Dialectic, one will never come to the truth because they will never make a firm choice to follow the right road to the truth. They will eternally choose to try and synthesize a new perception—a new reality and "road" to the truth, if you will—by somehow fusing a lie with the truth; resulting in the person's acceptance of a half-truth (at best) as their new perception of *the* truth, and then continuing down such false roads of reasoning; erroneously believing themselves to be on the right road to the truth. The following illustration is meant to visually demonstrate how Hegelian synthesis will take a person's mind farther from the truth and closer to the acceptance of a lie with every subsequent iteration of the dialectic process:

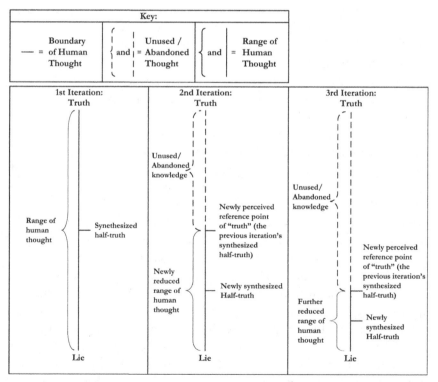

Figure 1. How the Hegelian Dialectic Corrupts Truth

Following the 1st iteration, the newly synthesized half-truth then becomes a person's *perception* of the truth, but it is a false perception. Next, we notice that the absolute positions of the truth and of a lie are unchanged, but the person's perception of the truth is changed to now establish the newly synthesized half-truth as their perceived "baseline" of truth. As a consequence, several damaging things result. First, the mind now accepts a half-truth as the full truth, which is a lie in itself. Secondly, in order to accept this newly synthesized half-truth as the full truth, one's mind must willfully lose sight of absolute truth and circumscribe their internal, mental vision within a narrower range of thought; so as to completely obscure their vision of the truth (that which they have either rejected or have been deceived into abandoning) while simultaneously allowing a person to abandon truth without being subjected to the contradictions of the half-truth(s) constantly nagging at their conscience. The dotted line between the newly perceived, synthesized "truth" and the absolute truth represents the muddled mental vision of the path back to the truth. Thirdly, it's important to observe that each time that the mind moves through one of these iterations, the range of human thought is incrementally narrowed.

In the above illustration, the graphical distance between the absolute truth and a lie represents the depth and breadth of human thought. As a new perception is synthesized from two opposing views, the newly synthesized perception of "truth" simultaneously takes the mind further from the actual truth and closer to the acceptance of a falsehood, while narrowing the range of human thought and discourse at the same time. The effects of a poor, purposefully misleading education, and the acceptance of false perceptions of truth over an extended period of time, eventually lead to a situation where following generations have no true reference point for, or path back to, absolute truth; and all their perceived truths are actually half-truths that are daily approaching lies and narrowing their range of thought. George Orwell warned of the use of such tactics to reduce the range of thought in his book *1984*; as he described the purpose of the newly evolving language, termed "Newspeak," which today we refer to as "political correctness."

> Don't you see that the whole aim of Newspeak is to narrow the range of thought? In the end we shall make thoughtcrime[4] literally impossible, because there will be

---

[4] Thoughts that ran contrary to the approved orthodoxy of the Party of Big Brother were criminally punishable. In the real world of today we call it "hate crime" legislation.

no words in which to express it. **Every concept that can ever be needed will be expressed by exactly one word, with its meaning rigidly defined and all its subsidiary meanings rubbed out and forgotten**. Already, in the Eleventh Edition,[5] we're not far from that point. But the process will still be continuing long after you and I are dead. Every year fewer and fewer words, and the range of consciousness always a little smaller. Even now, of course, there's no reason or excuse for committing thoughtcrime. It's merely a question of self-discipline, reality-control. But in the end there won't be any need even for that. The Revolution will be complete when the language is perfect. Newspeak is Ingsoc[6] and Ingsoc is Newspeak," he added with a sort of mystical satisfaction. "Has it ever occurred to you, Winston, that by the year 2050, at the very latest, not a single human being will be alive who could understand such a conversation as we are having now?[7]

Over an extended period of time, whole societies can be, and have been, propagandized into believing that abject falsehoods are absolute truths; as the same process of thesis > antithesis > synthesis is repeated through

---

[5] The character is speaking of the Eleventh Edition of the Newspeak Dictionary, which he is currently working on.

[6] Ingsoc is the Newspeak word for English Socialism in the dystopian world of *1984*. Briefly, Newspeak endeavored to limit what people were able to think by both eliminating words and concatenating multiple words into a single word that represented a complete idea, rather than using a collection of words to convey a more detailed and nuanced expression of a thought. In so doing, the Party of Big Brother, an allegory for communist rule, is able to literally control what people think by limiting what they would be *able* to think. If language could be debased to the point of eliminating the words that would be used to express a desire to resist the rule of Big Brother, then people could never even conceive of resisting their slavery. That, in combination with a multitude of concatenated words that were specifically defined regarding their exact meaning—all redounding to the glory of the benevolent rule of Big Brother, of course—would eventually make the conception of a reality apart from their slavery completely unthinkable; because there would be no words to express the thoughts!

[7] George Orwell, *1984* (New York, NY: New American Library, a division of Penguin Putnam, Inc.), 46-47.

subsequent iterations, and then delivered up for public consumption via print and television media, as well as within the government "education" system. Following from the above illustration, one may ask themself the question, "Can the synthesis of ideas ever move toward the truth, or rather must it always move away from the truth and toward falsehoods"? The answer is that it must always move away from the truth, and this is again due to the nature of truth in relation to opposing falsehoods. Remember, when dealing with absolute truths they are analogous to fixed points. Absolute truths cannot be moved or changed just because some (or most all) people wish that they could be moved or changed. Believing such ridiculous notions is contrary to observed reality and dangerous to the sanity of those who attempt it.

We refer to such mental processes as delusional thinking. As a mind leaves the fixed point of an absolute truth the only possible direction of movement is away from the fixed point of truth; just as departing the fixed point of a city takes a traveler away from the city, regardless of the direction of motion. The severity of a falsehood depends on how far away from the truth one travels, as the analogous separation from a city depends on the distance traveled away from it. Figure 1 showed a one-dimensional view of the relationship between truth and falsehoods; how the Hegelian Dialectic, and the dialectical process in general, is used to take people's minds away from the truth. Figure 2 shows a two-dimensional view of the same relationships, which makes it even more obvious why the Hegelian Dialectic will *always* lead a mind away from the truth; because any synthesis involving a truth will only lead to a departure from the truth.

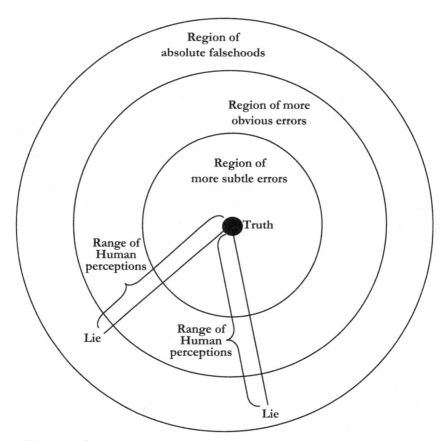

Figure 2. Graphical representation of the truth in relation to errors and falsehoods (2-dimensional).

Consider the analogy of colors, where white represents absolute truth (thesis) and black represents its complete opposite: absolute falsehood (antithesis). From a one-dimensional point of view, if the falsehood of black is introduced to white it will immediately corrupt the truth of white, lead the mind away from the truth, and turn it toward a "gray area"; depending on how much black (the severity of the lie) is introduced. This example is also instructive to illustrate how the cleverest liars operate when attempting to purposefully corrupt the truth.

In Figure 1, for the sake of illustration, we supposed that each iteration brought us to a halfway point between the thesis of an absolute truth and the antithesis of its opposite: an absolute lie. In reality, if someone were to try and synthesize a new perception of the truth by so dramatically tainting it with a clearly recognizable falsehood, the average person would most likely immediately notice that they were not being presented with the truth, avoid the person who was trying to implant a falsehood within their minds, attempt to increase their mental grasp on the truth so as to maintain it, while guarding themselves against further attempts of manipulation and deception.

It is analogous to mixing one part white paint with one part black paint. The product will immediately be recognized as being corrupted. However, the very best, most cunning, patient, and consequently most effective liars corrupt the truth by very small bits; chipping away here and there at the most easily corrupted parts. They will tell you a hundred or a thousand truths in order to slip in a single lie concerning a critical idea that they believe will corrupt the reasoning of those who hear their arguments. By operating in this fashion they are able to build up people's trust in their veracity, thereby putting people off their psychological guard for the introduction of a falsehood. It takes much longer to corrupt the truth in this manner, but the likelihood that a single falsehood will be accepted as truth when it is hidden among hundreds or thousands of known, or verifiable, truths is much higher than if a person tried to introduce a larger falsehood immediately, within a single iteration.

The slow and steady approach to corrupting the truth is like mixing a drop at a time of black in a gallon of white. The newly synthesized product would be so close to the original that the difference is imperceptible. Later, after the public eye has adjusted to the newly corrupted color and accepted it as pure, the liar introduces another lie in addition to the one already accepted; adding another minute degree of black to the already corrupted white and slowly and imperceptibly making it darker with every iteration of the process. The liar waits an appropriate amount of time, then starts another iteration to introduce a new lie, etc. In this manner public perception is perverted over time. After many years of corrupting the pure white of truth, there is not a single person left who can accurately remember what the truth looked like in its original, uncorrupted form. Moreover, if a liar is ever caught in their deception, they can always claim ignorance and move on to corrupt the truth at a different point than where they were discovered. Good liars are extraordinarily patient, because they also understand the nature of truth. If they have trouble corrupting people's understanding on one point they simply move on to another point and wait for a future opportunity to attempt to corrupt the previous "trouble spot" that, in a previous day and time, resisted their falsehood.

To add more complexity, consider the multi-dimensional case. Allegorically, not only is our pure white truth being corrupted by black, but other people are also trying to corrupt it with yellow, blue, green, orange, red, purple, and thousands of other different colors; each of these different colors representing a falsehood of a different nature or subject matter than the others. One can see that as an extra dimension is added, the resulting potential for confusion is increased exponentially; to the point that it is not possible for any person to keep the truth straight when they live in a world where people are constantly trying to introduce false perceptions into their consciousness so as to serve their own self-interest, which is also indicative of how many deceptions we undoubtedly take in unseen every day while never realizing or understanding their damaging effects on our consciousness.

As an illustration of how a falsehood or error in reasoning compounds in damage over time, consider a cruise ship sailing from a coastal city to a small island named Truth in the middle of the ocean some three thousand miles away. The ship's captain has the finest charts available and he knows the course he must steer to reach the island of Truth. The voyage (reasoning process) is begun, and from the beginning the seas and environment (false arguments) work against the ship (human mind) and push it off course a mere one-half of one degree (a subtle error is accepted into the reasoning processes) and nobody knows any better; the deviation in course (error in reason) being so slight. In the beginning the deviation from the necessary course is small and the danger(s) are not readily apparent. For every mile traveled, the deviation from the desired course is a ridiculously small forty-six feet.

At first, the effects of the error in course are not of great concern, but we have a three thousand mile journey ahead of us! After that first mile we would only be forty-six feet off course, but after one hundred miles we are approaching a mile off course. After a thousand miles we are almost nine miles off course. Finally, after we have traveled the three thousand miles and are expecting to arrive at Truth, what started out as a contemptibly small deviation from Truth has put us over twenty-six miles off course! At that distance, Truth would be beyond our visible horizon, we would have no idea where we went wrong, and would likewise be ignorant of the direction we should turn in order to try and seek out Truth.

In modern political jargon, having been applied and "fine-tuned" over several hundred years of rationalism, the application of the Hegelian Dialectic is today referred to as "coming to a consensus." For those who know what they are doing and understand the nature of absolute truth, this approach has offered, and still continues to offer, a guaranteed, built-in advantage for the dishonest and self-serving people over the honest and truthful people; because while the truth only lies in one particular place, falsehoods are everywhere else that the truth is not, and in varying degrees (like the "bull's-eye" in Fig. 2). The dishonest and self-serving politician knows that it matters not whether the public will accept their errors and lies today. Because the public is always clamoring for "change," which requires the synthesis of a new consensus, they are fully aware that any newly synthesized consensus will result in a deviation away from the truth.

All the clever politician has to be able to do is notice the direction of movement of a fallacious line of reasoning and place themselves in the path of the false road of reason in order to take credit for the change, assign blame to their political opponents for opposing their "wisdom," and personally benefit from the deviation away from the truth; no matter how this deviation manifests itself in the world. As a result, the most atrocious, self-defeating, and suicidal errors and evils have been, and are still being, forced upon humanity daily. It is most critical to be aware that in the realm of politics and government the only possible direction that the application of the Hegelian Dialectic can move a society toward is slavery to the political class: the self-conceited masters of humanity.

While the Hegelian Dialectic delineates the overarching methodology to be used to corrupt a truthful and coherent understanding of reality, there must be a means to implement the Hegelian methodology so as to deceive the public, take them away from an understanding of the truth, and incrementally walk them into their own slavery. That means of implementation is referred to as "affective reasoning." Let's discuss affective reasoning so as to demonstrate how it is used to obtain Hegelian synthesis and pervert human understanding.

Affective Reasoning vs. Cognitive Reasoning

> Mankind are governed more by their feelings than by reason.[1]
>
> — Samuel Adams, American politician and Founding Father of the United States

Description of Orwellian "doublethink":

To know and not to know, to be conscious of complete truthfulness while telling carefully constructed lies, to hold simultaneously two opinions which cancelled out, knowing them to be contradictory and believing in both of them, to use logic against logic, to repudiate morality while laying claim to it, to believe that democracy was impossible and that the Party was the guardian of democracy, to forget, whatever it was necessary to forget, then to draw it back into memory again at the moment when it was needed, and then promptly forget it again, and above all, to apply the same process to the process itself—that was the ultimate subtlety: consciously to induce unconsciousness, and then, once again, to become unconscious of the act of hypnosis you had just performed. Even to understand the word "doublethink" involved the use of doublethink.[2]

Far and away the most monumental and important achievement of those who are tirelessly at work enslaving humanity—while getting the great bulk of humanity to simultaneously beg their masters for their slavery—was to successfully induce a wholesale shift among humanity regarding how the average person processes information and experiences in their daily life; for it isn't important or necessary to instruct people regarding *what* they should think if it is instead possible to teach them *how* they should think; and then subsequently manipulate their thought processes so that they think *how* one wants them to think. The ultimate goal is to manipulate and direct the minds

---

[1] http://www.quotedb.com/quotes/3575, accessed March 20, 2008.
[2] Orwell, *1984*, 32-33.

of the average human being into processing information in such a way that it works in favor of the interests of our aspiring masters and against our own best interests. There are two examples that make this principle more understandable. The first example is directly analogous to the axiom, "Give a man a fish; feed him for a day. Teach a man to fish; feed him for life." Trying to instruct a person in *what* to think is comparable to giving a man a fish and instructing him to, "Chew on this idea for a while. It will feed you for now, which is enough to get you through today." Of course, once the particular idea has been digested by the person in question they must then return to their instructor/master for their new ideological food to get them through the following day's obstacles.

Training up a person in *how* to think is comparable to teaching them to fish; so that they can then feed themselves ideologically without constant direction from their instructor/master. By instructing a person in a particular process of thinking, the person becomes self-sufficient in that particular method; through both repetitions of examples by those instructing them, and real-life experiences. In this manner, the person trained to think in a particular fashion is then able to come to their own conclusions, which naturally conform themselves to the conclusions and modes of thinking of those who originally tutored them. This is how the natural process of learning works. A student mimics their teacher. As the student becomes more adept at applying the processes and lessons learned at the hands of their original teacher, they in turn mimic and propagate the same processes and lessons to others; eventually becoming teachers themselves and passing their learned behavior on to subsequent generations of students.

The second example is analogous to taking a path in life. Those who are told what to think are like blindfolded travelers who must be taken by the hand and led by a guide so that they do not stumble on unseen obstacles. Every step they take must be directed by a guide external to themselves; rendering them completely reliant on their chosen guide(s). Teaching a person how to think is analogous to removing the blindfold from the traveler and instead having the guide direct them toward a particular path. Being able to see the path, the person instructed in a particular mode of thought is then able to see it, as well as the surrounding environs. They can visualize their next step for themselves and will walk as they have been instructed by their trusted guide. The great danger here lies in choosing a person's guide through life. If one chooses poorly they will be put on a path that serves the self-interest of the deceitful, and that most often leads to an unforeseen cliff and ruination. If they choose well they will be put on a path of their own enlightened self-interest.

The reader must quickly come to realize, and learn well, that there are two diametrically opposed foundations of perceptual reality that exist in this world, and that these two opposing foundations of human thought and perception cannot be reconciled with each other. In keeping with the analogy of different paths through life, they are complete opposites; 180 degrees out of phase with each other in both direction and final outcome. One is true, and the other is false. One is sane, and the other is insane. One is orderly, and the other is chaotic and anarchistic. One is rational, and the other is irrational. These two opposing foundations of human thought are constantly at war within the hearts and minds of mankind. As a result, the origins of all ideas and opinions spring forth from these two opposing foundations, which ultimately break down to the eternal battle between the emotion and the intellect: the "heart" vs. the "head."

Those that "think with their hearts" use emotion as the foundation of their reasoning and logic: morals, ethics, and rationality based on feelings and intentions—devoid of any cognitively observable basis—and not on facts or consequences. This is termed "affective" reasoning. Affective reasoning drives the individual toward satisfying their wants and desires of the moment, while leaving a person's needs for their life either as a weak, secondary consideration or even a completely ignored factor. This is a shortsighted, narcissistic reasoning construct; drawing those who use it into a cycle of constantly seeking the satisfaction of their immediate desires and passions. Affective reasoning is the process of thinking and acting instinctually, and it reduces those who use it to the same intellectual level as that of an irrational animal. The affective thinker is subjected to constant, delusional mental processes that induce emotional instability and hostility, which also leaves them easy prey for those who wish to psychologically manipulate them.[3] They become effeminately sensitized to rely on their emotions to process life experiences and make decisions; as opposed to using logic and reason applied to objectively observed reality.

Essentially, it's easier to "push their buttons" in order to push and pull their minds in the direction that the manipulative and deceitful people of this world want to direct them toward. The delusional aspect of this mental

---

[3] The "elitists" of this world: those who have purposefully induced this debased manner of delusional thinking amongst humanity in order to enslave humanity to their self-interested ends.

process stems from the fact that affective thinkers base their worldview, actions, and reactions to life and world events based on the emotional response of, "How does it make me feel"?, rather than a deliberate and logical reflection of causes and effects of life and world events based on demonstrable facts. Because it is a natural, human tendency to seek avoidance of pain, either psychological or physical, affective thinkers will adjust their worldview in whatever manner is necessary to make them feel better about themselves and the larger world around them. This manner of emotional and psychological gymnastics is what induces constant delusions among affective thinkers.

In order to make one's understanding of the world, and their respective lives', fit a particular worldview that is the least emotionally disturbing and painful requires that the affective thinker must deny many critical facts and details on a daily basis, or even deny the existence of demonstrable facts. Ultimately, the affective thinker transforms themself into a person whose worldview is a conglomeration of half-truths and outright lies, and therein lies the source of delusion. **The affective thinker views the world and themselves as they wish they would be, rather than seeing the world and themselves as they really are.** To mitigate and minimize emotional stress, affective thinkers will deliberately lie to themselves—and believe the lies—for the purpose of maintaining emotional tranquility.

The irony and paradox of affective thinking, and the personalities who employ it, is that the actual consequences of this type of mental gymnastics are exactly opposite of those desired; as is always the case when people live their lives lying to themselves. Affective thinkers are in a perpetually disturbed emotional state that leads them toward anger and hostility directed at those who don't view the world and reality through their dishonest and delusional viewpoint. This reaction stems from their dishonest approach to reality. They attempt to force the world outside their minds to conform to their perception of reality, rather than adjusting their view of the world to fit reality. Forcing the world to come to them, rather than going out to face the world on its terms. Because affective reasoning is intended to make people feel good about themselves and their worldview; when affective thinkers are presented with demonstrable or documented facts that contradict their beliefs they become very angry and hostile because they are presented with a truth that invalidates their "feel good" worldview. This is a result of the psychotic, Orwellian "doublethink" construct working within their minds:

1. Affective thinkers hold a false opinion or position that makes them more comfortable with themselves and the world around them.

2. They are presented with verifiable, documented evidence that their opinion or position is false.

3. They are forced to face the reality that they are wrong and that their reasoning process(es) are flawed.

4. Their minds "snap" because they are confronted with irreconcilable positions that they are psychologically too weak to face. When proved wrong, they are forced to the knowledge that they are wrong; but facing the truth and admitting to themselves or others that they are wrong would injure their pride and seriously disrupt their delicate emotional equilibrium. Therefore, they will discard the truth and cling to their delusion(s) because they are either just too weak-minded or proud to face the truth.

5. Even though they may try and discard an uncomfortable truth in deference to a comfortable lie, a part of their psyche still recognizes that they are lying to themselves, which creates an inescapable trap that tortures the affective thinker; thereby negating the original, desired intent of affective reasoning: emotional tranquility.

6. Anger and hostility develops when they realize within themselves that they are either too weak or too proud to face reality. The subconscious recognition of their weakness drives them toward sentiments of self-loathing. Because they are fighting themselves to keep their "feel good" emotional equilibrium, they direct their anger away from themselves and toward whomever confronted them with the truth; a "kill the messenger" mentality. They are genuinely angry, spiteful, and hateful toward those who present them with the truth because they are being forced into a situation that they intentionally strive to avoid. In their own minds they become a house turned against itself, and they despise those who confront them with the truth because they see those who present them with the truth as the cause of their torment; not having the requisite courage to face the fact that the true source of their unhappiness and displeasure is their own lack of either courage or humility to face the truth forthrightly.

This type of behavior is especially evident in politics, and has been observed in ancient times as well as the modern day:

A young man is not equipped to be a student of politics; for
he has no experience in the actions which life demands of
him, and these actions form the basis and subject matter of
the discussion. Moreover, **since he follows his emotions,
his study will be pointless and unprofitable, for the
end of this kind of study is not knowledge but action.**
*Whether he is young in years or immature in character
makes no difference*; **for his deficiency is not a matter
of time but of living and of pursuing all his interests
under the influence of his emotions.** Knowledge brings
no benefit to this kind of person, just as it brings none to
the morally weak. But those who regulate their desires and
actions by a rational principle will greatly benefit from a
knowledge of this subject.[4]

— Aristotle

As the people of the United States and the rest of the world become
increasingly, slavishly dependent upon politicians, and others, to serve as
their masters, affective (emotionally driven) thinkers will only continue
further down the mad, irrational road toward increased anger and hatred;
brought about by their frightful delusion(s). Ultimately, if the insanity of
affective reasoning isn't stopped and corrected, it will end in increasingly
violent confrontations.

Affective reasoning is natural to the narcissistic personality, as its
underlying objective is to satisfy a person's desires and ego. Their first
thought is to their self-interested wants and desires. They are generally
angry and hostile people; especially in the modern world, where things are
finally coming to a climactic point. True to the character and nature of their
psychosis, they blame a multitude of people—anyone but themselves—for
the sad and dangerous state of the world; not understanding the causes or
true nature of the threat(s) facing them: mass immorality, sexual license and
deviancy, militant Islam, socialism, and communism.

If confronted with a truth that they don't like, they can become quite
hostile. They don't like to face reality and have their worldview proved
invalid. It's too upsetting to their emotional equilibrium. They are constantly
trying to change the world in order to bring the world in line with their

---

[4] Aristotle, *Nicomachean Ethics*, trans. Martin Ostwald (Upper Saddle River, NJ:
Prentice Hall, 1999), 5-6.

delusional worldview. When they hear what they want to be told they become sycophantically slavish and compliant to the messenger, which makes them easy to manipulate. Because they cling to a "feel good" ideology and message, they generally won't investigate, ponder, or look to the deeper consequences of ideas that give them emotional tranquility, regardless of how bad or dangerous the ideas may be. Many, if not most, of them are completely sincere regarding their self-righteous intentions, but their delusional thought processes never lead them to the path of actually *doing* good.

On the other hand, those who "think with their heads" use their minds and the record of history as the foundation of their reasoning and logic—ethics and rationality based on facts and observed consequences to contemplated actions—rather than on feelings. This process is referred to as "cognitive" reasoning. Cognitive reasoning drives the individual toward satisfying their life's needs, while delaying or sometimes overlooking their wants or desires in deference to life's necessities. This is a long-term, humbling reasoning construct; drawing those who use cognitive reasoning into a cycle of constantly seeking the attainment of their long-term needs; shaping and determining a person's current life-course in order to direct them to the best course of action for their future. The ability to use cognitive reasoning is only available to human beings. The only tool that places humanity above all other animals in this world is reason, as expressed and communicated by language.

Language gives humans the ability to formulate ideas and plans, and directly share thoughts and experiences between one another at the present moment; as well as the concurrent ability to record those thoughts and experiences in order to serve those who will come into the world at a future time. A perfect example of this reality is in the use of the ancient Greek philosopher's (Plato and Aristotle) observations throughout this work. The tool of language is the only thing that enables us to record history and bind human experience into a continuous and unbroken endeavor; from the past, to the present, and into the future. The greatest thing about the existence of history, and the tool of language that enables it, is that we are able to learn from the mistakes of others who came before us. By noting the mistakes of previous generations, we are able to avoid them and make wiser decisions for our future; thereby refining and raising the common level of knowledge and wisdom of humanity as our species progresses through time. The cognitive reasoning process is the process of placing reason above emotional instinct; with our reason being instructed by lessons learned from both one's own life as well as those passed down by our predecessors.

The cognitive reasoning process applies a pseudo-scientific process to decision making. Facts are checked against history and the current state of affairs in order to form a decision regarding how to proceed. The reliance on facts and history is what makes it much more difficult to manipulate cognitive thinkers. The same arguments used to manipulate affective thinkers usually don't work against cognitive thinkers, because the first reaction to any argument or idea is a rational evaluation of the consequences of pursuing any proposed course of action. As history has shown us, almost nothing is how it appears on the surface. When the cognitive reasoning process is used to evaluate ideas that more easily manipulate affective thinkers, the errors in judgment and reasoning, or deliberate deceptions, of the underlying details become more readily apparent. As the saying goes, "The devil is in the details."

The sane and rational aspect of cognitive thinkers comes from the pursuit of truth, knowledge, and an understanding of the world around them; so that they may make informed decisions that will ultimately prove to be beneficial to their lives. In direct opposition to the mentality of affective thinkers, cognitive thinkers develop and adjust their worldview based on the realities of life rather than seeing things the way they would like them to be. This approach to thought and reason is almost always more emotionally disturbing to those who apply it to real-life situations and problems, but it is more honest and provides solutions to problems that affectively reasoned "solutions" either do not provide or that cause a greater aggravation of the original problem. **The cognitive thinker views the world and themselves as they really are, rather than seeing the world and themselves as they wish they would be**. To more successfully administer their lives, cognitive thinkers search for the truth, regardless of how uncomfortable their conclusions may make them.

Ironically, cognitive thinkers are more emotionally stable and calm than affective thinkers. While cognitive thinkers may find the world emotionally troubling, they accept it as it is because they know that they cannot change it simply because they don't like what they see. They resign themselves to the facts they are faced with, and then make a decision on a course of action for the future that will better the lives of themselves, their families, and others; in consideration of the current situation they are faced with. The calmness comes from the understanding that they are not responsible for all the troubling problems in this world. They will change for the better those things they can control. They will not take responsibility or blame for those things that are out of their control.

Cognitive thinkers have very definite tendencies. Their first thought is to their needs. If confronted with a truth they don't like, they either set out to rectify the situation or accept it as it is if they are not able to control or effect a change regarding the problems they see. When they are told something that is too good to be true, they begin analyzing the possible consequences and results of what they are being told, which makes them a much more difficult person to manipulate. Cognitive thinkers do good things by acting in the reasoned best interests of all involved.

Finally, upon comparing the two reasoning processes, take note of what they engender in the human psyche. Affective reasoning seeks to mitigate emotional distress and enhance the individual's comfort; both psychologically and physically. Therefore, every time a person is in expectation or fear of confronting an unpleasant reality they will run from it or attempt to obfuscate reality. Affective reasoning encourages moral weakness and cowardice. Cognitive reasoning seeks to understand the truths of the world so that one can plan wisely for the future. Some of this world's truths are pretty disconcerting, but cognitive thinkers prefer an uncomfortable truth that can help them successfully navigate their life, rather than a comfortable lie that will badly mislead them. Cognitive reasoning encourages moral strength and fortitude.

Converting people to a narcissistic, affective perceptual context is how the Hegelian Dialectic has been successfully implemented over time. By directing a person's vision and perception toward a more self-oriented perspective, it is then easier to push the human mind into narcissistic thought processes, which necessarily restricts the person's understanding of the larger world around them and their relationship to it. When faced with an unpleasant truth, it only takes persistence to corrupt people's understanding by offering them an alternate interpretation of reality that appeases their discomfort. Applying this technique constantly over the past several centuries has been the primary methodology for corrupting the human race.

It is highly evident that a majority of people in this world have either complete, or extremely strong, tendencies toward affective, emotionally-based thinking (as evidenced by the criminals that the citizens of "free" countries are electing to office; via their own, willful choices), which is the single greatest poison that is grinding our world down to a slow and painful death. Correcting the degeneration of the modern human mind and spirit is directly comparable to an "intervention" in behalf of a drug-addict who refuses to admit their addiction, which is exactly what this work intends. The realization of how humanity is being misled is one of the beginning steps to fixing the problems we face and overcoming the suicidal manipulation foisted on the backs of humanity by extraordinarily egomaniacal and evil people. Moreover, it should be noted that affective thinking draws the human psyche toward the psychological attributes of a small child—refusing to recognize those things in life that do not move the affective thinker toward the realization of their wants and desires: exhibiting temper tantrums, petulance, and belligerence when their desires are either thwarted or not met—which serves to further exemplify the infantilization of the human intellect. Let's look at how this process has regressed Western civilization into a state of cultural barbarism over the past few centuries.

The Real-World Chronicle of Regression to Our Current State of Cultural Barbarism

Before the common acceptance of rationalism took hold, the human race mostly lived their lives by a code of moral and social absolutes passed down to man by God, which compelled mankind to live by His commandments and centered the focus of their existence on the accomplishment of His will, or risk facing the possibility of eternal damnation. These moral and social absolutes were those as expressed by the Christian faith, as what is known today as Western civilization was once referred to throughout the world as Christendom. However, after the acceptance of rationalism took hold, the philosophy functionally elevated man into the position of becoming his own god; because if *all* things could be discovered through human reason or factual analysis alone it would make obsolete any "absolute truths" that were formerly dictated by God's commandments and the common religion. These previously accepted truths of the Faith were then called into question and denigrated by the "factual analysis" and "reason" of the rationalist.

As a consequence, man's "reason" dethroned God's wisdom and decrees; slowly replacing God's laws with mankind's own inventions; thereby shifting the focus of all human endeavors away from the accomplishment of God's will, and instead toward the pursuit of mankind's own ambitious and self-serving egos. The deadliness of such a philosophy was first demonstrated during the French Revolution; where men murdered and imprisoned one another in the name of "Liberté, égalité, fraternité" (in English: liberty, equality, fraternity; the "brotherhood of mankind"): those sad, foolish souls never attaining to the understanding of the contradiction between their stated aims and their own, barbaric behavior. The French Revolution was the point of departure between man and God in the modern world; because it codified rationalism—a manifestation of practical atheism—into law via the *Declaration of the Rights of Man and of the Citizen* (Appendix A).

This pivotal document within the history of Western civilization compromised faith by supplanting mankind's previous psychological reliance on the Creator for their care; in its place installing reliance on human intellect and laws, as well as a foolishly presumed fraternal instinct among mankind. This singular document crowned the legislative body of the nation as the highest authority in all things, which effectually declared religious faith and an adherence to higher principles as subordinate to the national government and human law; ambitious politicians then taking up their place as mankind's new god(s). It is just such a mentality that ushered in the age of government, law, and politics as the new secular "religions" of Western civilization; the bitter fruits of which we are suffered to be living through: a nihilistically narcissistic, self-destructive paradigm that is plainly evident in today's world.

The inhabitants of the West most certainly didn't realize it at the time of the French Revolution; but their new, secularist philosophy laid the groundwork for the introduction of anarchy within human civilization by holding to the position that if men pass laws declaring that any particular thing shall be true, it shall be made true by force of the supreme power of human laws; even if a legislative proclamation repudiates an objectively observed reality. By assigning ultimate authority to the nation and its legal system, a mechanism was put in place by which legislators could declare that good is evil and that evil is good, and that it must be true because the legislature has declared it to be so; an insanely delusional socio-political construct that tacitly allows the repudiation of objective reality and immutable truths if those who constitute the particular legal system of the affected nation—legislators, lawyers, and judges—believe that adhering to a position that repudiates objective reality is politically expedient.

Under this new way of thinking, objectively observed principles of right and wrong—as dictated by the observance of actions taken and the consequences that arise from those actions; both negative and positive—no longer stood by themselves as a guide to human action. Instead, it was now asserted that what was right and good, or contrarily wrong and evil, were solely dependent upon how the laws of the nation determine to define right and wrong; a functional description of both insanity and practical atheism. Under such a social construction the new gods and arbiters of right and wrong then become whoever controls the levers of political power.

Naturally, bitter struggles to control those levers of power ensue as a result, as disparate factions compete for the ability to define right and wrong by codifying their interpretations into law and forcing their position(s) on the rest of society; even when such laws contradict objective reality. It is just such a bitter struggle for power that the world is witnessing today via Party factions and identity politics: Democrat vs. Republican, liberal vs.

conservative, Black vs. White, young vs. old, rich vs. poor, homosexual vs. heterosexual, etc. The factions develop their own agendas, and then compete for control over their respective governments and societies as a whole; many people and factions basing their belief systems solely upon considerations of self-serving political expediency.

This sickening paradigm completely, and purposefully, disregards the larger considerations of immutable truths and the observance of objective reality; with lawmakers crowning themselves as our new gods by pretending to be the sole arbiters of what is right and what is wrong; what is good and what is evil; placing themselves outside of the consideration(s) of the real consequences of their actions; without regard for how foolish and dangerous they may be to the rest of the society. The modern politician knows very well that most all people in today's world don't really care about what is truly right and good, or understand why it is so important to fight for what is good and against what is evil. The modern citizen wants whatever it is they want; led by the nose by their fickle emotions and passions. Modern politicians engage in a constant, fevered competition to try and pander to the populace so as to win their favor; completely disregarding such pedestrian (in their minds) considerations of what is in the best interest of the nation; because their true goal is instead the seizure of political power for their own self-serving ends rather than for the maintenance and benefit of their nation and of its citizens.

It is a simple, albeit sad, reality that our human nature, unchecked by any restraining force, naturally leads the individual to seek after the gratification of their own desires and sensate passions; regardless of how perverse or self-destructive their desires may be. Ordering whole societies upon such a paradigm equates to the functional description of anarchy; being that the pursuit of self-interested desires among the citizens of a society will naturally lead to violence, as the passions of the human heart are both multitudinous and extraordinarily diverse; both for good, and especially for evil. Within such a society, which Western civilization is daily becoming in the modern era, a natural competition would erupt between good and evil; with both sides pressing their demands for absolute "freedom" to express themselves in the public square. Such a circumstance can only end in bloody violence; as evil people would possess the same expectation of autonomy and rule as the good people within society, and they would likewise be willing and eager to force their evils on society.

As it is inherent within human nature to want whatever it is a particular person may desire, the force(s) of anarchy are always working from an advantageous position within the hearts and minds of mankind. Figure 3 illustrates this principle, in that the "high ground" is always the easiest to defend and the most advantageous position from which to launch an attack on one's enemy. Several other points are also evident from this illustration. To begin with, the primary line of defense is always the closest to the point of initial attack; making the first line of defense the most important for two reasons. Firstly, the initial line of defense is the most heavily fortified; giving the inhabitants within the fortifications an added sense of confidence in it. Secondly, because the initial line of defense is closest to the attacking forces, the enemy has less room to gather momentum for their initial attack. As long as the bulwark of Faith was intact, the other defensive works that were encompassed by it (patriarchy, sexual morality, family, sobriety, etc.) were safe from the attacks of the common enemy of human civilization: anarchy.

The destruction of the fortification of Faith, and the subsequent descent into a state of culturally barbarous anarchy began in earnest with rationalism, but it has increased in speed and destructive potency both within the secular and the spiritual realms. Within the secular realm, the natural outgrowth of rationalism has been socialism and communism; as the stated aims of the communist revolution were exactly identical to those of the French Revolution: Liberty, Equality, and Fraternity; as these principles have come to be understood through the lens of atheistic rationalism.

Through such an immature and imprudent philosophical construct, "liberty" has come to be understood from the narcissistically humanistic perspective of roughly, "I can do as I please and nobody has a right to contradict my desires or actions"; rather than the moral understanding of liberty in which the use of governmental force or coercion is rendered unnecessary due to the common understanding among the people of what it takes to lead a productive, responsible, and virtuous life. "Equality" has taken on a materialistic connotation of, "Everybody should have the same amount of 'stuff' as everybody else"; rather than the moral understanding of equality in which everybody is afforded the same consideration under the law; regardless of whether they are rich or poor, celebrity or unknown. And finally, "fraternity" has come to be understood as, "Everyone will get along congenially, or else those who hurt another's feelings will be harshly punished via the force of punitive laws"; rather than the moral understanding of fraternity in which everyone actually viewed their fellow man as true brothers and sisters, and was likewise as solicitous of their fellow man's interests as they were of their own. This is a natural consequence of the repudiation of Faith; for if a society disdains God by abandoning their Faith, then that society will likewise abandon any morality or moral norms that were derived from that Faith, as we are seeing very plainly in the modern world, even among a great number of self-described Christians.

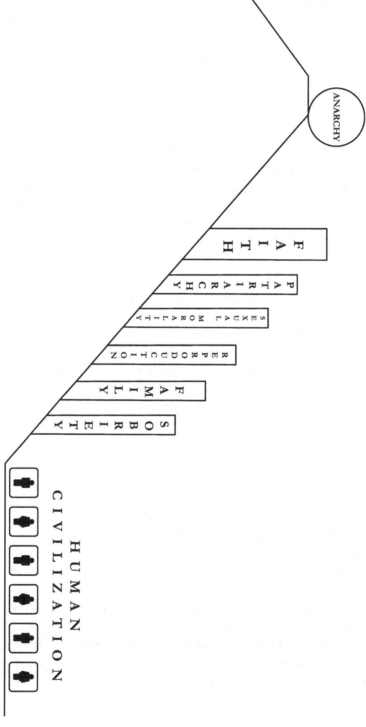

Figure 3. The Bulwarks of Social Order: The Sliding Slope

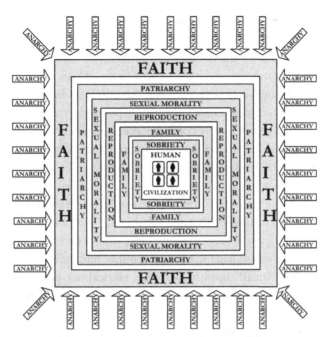

Figure 4. The Bulwarks of Social Order: The Fortress

Within the spiritual realm, the destruction of the fortification of the Christian faith within Western civilization was followed by the introduction of an alternative religious philosophy in the early Twentieth Century known as "Thelema": introduced in 1904 by a well-known occultist named Aleister Crowley. According to his own account, a spirit, who allegedly spoke through his wife, dictated the text of a new "holy book" that he was to write and serve as prophet for the new Aeon[1] (the Aeon of Horus) that mankind was entering. The book was titled *Liber AL vel Legis*: in English, *The Book of the Law*. The key principle within *The Book of the Law* and the foundation of Thelema was, and still is, "Do what thou wilt shall be the whole of the law": a 'religious'

---

[1] In Thelema, history is separated into Aeons, which are ordered around pagan lines; as they were named after ancient Egyptian, pagan gods. The first aeon was the Aeon of Isis, in which it was considered that the feminine nature predominated amongst humanity; resulting in a matriarchal society. The second aeon was the Aeon of Osiris, in which it was considered that the masculine nature predominated amongst humanity; resulting in a patriarchal society. The current aeon that (according to Crowley) began in 1904 with the publication of *The Book of the Law* is called the Aeon of Horus, in which it is considered that the nature of the child (the infantilization of the intellect) predominates amongst humanity.

philosophy that translates into pure narcissism. The reader will hopefully notice that this is the same spirit that animates modern liberalism in today's world, as exemplified by the liberal catch-phrase, "If it feels good, do it."

After the compromise of the bulwark of Faith, at least among the greater part of those within Western civilization, the strongest fortification against anarchy was breached, which simultaneously exposed the weaker fortifications within to an open attack by the common enemy. The compromise of Faith accomplished two things that practically ensured that the remaining defenses would eventually be broken down. Initially, because the inhabitants living within the fortification of Faith (Western civilization) had placed such confidence in their strongest line of defense; once that fortification was compromised the confidence that the inhabitants had once placed in it was struck a devastating psychological blow. The primary defense of civilization, once thought by its inhabitants to be impenetrable, had indeed been breached. Secondarily, and critically important from a tactical perspective, as anarchy broke through the first line of defense the subsequent defensive positions were seen to be inherently weaker than the initial defensive bulwark. Moreover, they were rendered more ineffectual by the absence of Faith as an assisting, defensive barrier.

As Figure 3 illustrates, once the initial line of defense was broken down the enemy enjoyed a greater latitude of motion; so as to increase its forward momentum as it attacked the other secondary defenses. As each defensive bulwark fell, the others that followed were attacked by a greater force than the preceding lines of defense were faced with. Referring to Figure 4, such a circumstance is also, in principle, equivalent to an enemy making their way within the outer walls of a fort. Once an enemy is able to force its way through the main gates of a fortress by penetrating the strongest, initial defenses, they are then able to freely move about within the fortress; probing the interior defenses for its weakest points, and then massing and applying its greatest force against the weakest points within the interior defenses when they are subsequently discovered. This methodology is exactly how Western civilization has been broken down.

Once the human race abandoned their true God, and instead crowned human intellect and "reason" as their new gods, mankind's current descent into cultural barbarism began, and its first manifestation was the abolishment of the patriarchal society. Without a true God, who compels a patriarchal social structure for humanity through the force of His laws—for He is God the *Father*—there was then no intellectual justification nor any compelling impediment to an ascendancy and "equality" of the feminine nature with that of the masculine; excepting the objections of mere men, which were characterized and ridiculed as petty, selfish, misogynistic, and "oppressive" by the strident feminist. It was this very same idea (equality) that was extended to encompass all things, and as a result of that philosophical ignorance of simple, objective reality mankind decided that the human intellect would simply figure out how to make everybody equal as humanity progressed to a more *enlightened* stage of human existence; even if such a pursuit meant attempting to remake the very essence of human nature.

This has proved to be a foolish and dangerous pursuit; our ancestors never fully understanding the ensuing insanity, as well as the breadth and scope of evil consequences, that would naturally erupt as a result. Blindly following the narcissistic impulses of their shortsighted and immature minds, they thought that all that was needed to remake human nature was the "simple" desire to reprogram human nature and the human mind. Can the reader appreciate the grossly insane, narcissistic vanity of such arrogant conceit: thinking themselves equal or superior to God by believing that they could reconstitute the composition of human nature according to their wills? Figures 3 and 4 are meant to demonstrate the descent into anarchy that has naturally resulted as a consequence of the tearing down of a successfully developed social structure that was previously built up by almost *five thousand* years of human civilization.

It took almost seventy years after the conclusion of the French Revolution for this radically new way of thinking to establish itself within the West as a whole, via feminism's roots taking hold politically within the West upon the 1868 founding of the *National Society for Women's Suffrage* in the United Kingdom; due to the fact that the bulwark of Faith had not been torn down as completely as it has been in our time. It took the peoples within Western civilization longer to adjust to the new socio-psychological construct of rationalistic atheism: what is known as "secularism" in the modern world.

After Faith and a patriarchal social structure were undermined, anarchy then made its way to the next line of social defense: sexual morality. A byproduct of the 'Siren's song' of feminism within Western civilization was an unraveling of previously established norms of morality; especially sexual morality. As vocal feminists came forward proclaiming the "liberation" of women from the "oppression" of a patriarchal social order, the natural consequence was a libertine form of "liberation" from the sexual morality that previously dominated under the patriarchal social order; as any form of self-restraint and self-denial of mankind's animalistic urges by feminists, and their liberal compatriots, were characterized as attempts to "repress" women. Faith, having already been greatly disparaged, was additionally bypassed as a reason to exercise self-discipline and restraint.

Accordingly, without a conception of accountability for one's actions, sexual promiscuity began to flourish with the rise of feminism. As is only natural, as more and more people began to engage in sexually licentious behavior, there arose a large number of unwanted pregnancies. Due to the pressing demands of rationalistically humanistic voices within the political structure(s) of Western civilization, the response to the objectively obvious consequences of sexual "liberation" was not a return to sanity and a moral code of behavior that had proved to be successful via thousands of years of previous human existence: a moral code that prevented the creation of unwanted children. Instead, the proposed *solution* to the rising number of unwanted pregnancies was the murder of the innocents created as a result of the profligate and degenerate dissolution that had swept through Western civilization.[2]

The acceptance of the destruction of human life, when such lives are seen as an impediment to an individual's ambitions or desires, was directly caused by the destruction of sexual morality within the West, which then continued on to give rise to homosexuality, transsexuality, and all other forms of sexual deviancy within the West; as it was a natural outgrowth of the psychology of a narcissistically self-gratifying "liberation," which arose as a byproduct of feminism; which itself arose as a byproduct of rationalistic atheism. The direct cause(s) of the social chaos being witnessed in today's world sprang forth as a direct consequence of the paradigm shift in the worldview of the average citizen within Western civilization; away from a sense of ultimate accountability and responsibility for one's choices and actions in this life, and toward a perspective of self-actualization and the pursuit of one's self-important desires over and above the consideration of one's obligations to sustain the health of their families and their society.

---

[2] It's important to notice the identical psychology and justification process used by the Nazi Party of WWII Germany and the modern abortionist. During World War II, Nazi Party officials openly debated, "What is to be done regarding the 'Jewish *question*'"? As we all know, they finally decided on the "Final Solution": the murder of those deemed to be undesirable by that government. The abortionist asks an analogous question, "What is to be done regarding the 'unwanted child *question*'"? As we all know, they have adopted the same moral position: murdering the children who are considered undesirable by those who are in a position of power over them.

Under a psychological construct of Faith and ultimate accountability, the individual's conscience is formed in such a way that they first attend to their duties and responsibilities before looking to the gratification of personal desires. Conversely, under a rationalistic psychological construct, a person's conscience is either not formed at all or is retarded to such a great degree that the rationalist never progresses beyond the conscience and understanding of an ignorant child; seeing their purpose in life as one of gratifying self-serving desires, whatever they may be, and without consideration of the consequences that will always, and naturally, arise as a result of their nihilistically narcissistic, self-absorbed perspective.

Finally, due to the repudiation of the objectively observed consequences of the moral dissipation of the West, many people have sought shelter and comfort through the use of pharmaceutical agents, both legal and illegal, in an attempt to temporarily escape the anarchistic "hell on earth" that rationalism (liberalism) has created in this world. Make no mistake about it. Rationalistic liberalism has declared that mankind can do whatever it pleases to do, and that there are no ultimate consequences for one's behavior as a result; at least none that man's *reason* can't solve. However, merely proclaiming through the legislative process that good is evil and evil is good cannot contravene objective reality. Such a belief is grossly ignorant and suicidally insane! This is like saying that in ten years all modes of transportation will run on either water or banana peels, for no greater reason than because Congress has decreed it to be so. Sadly, however, this is the world we live in today.

Legislative bodies all throughout Western civilization pass laws that deny observable reality, and then actively punish those who notice reality and call their neighbor's attention to it. People notice the sick consequences that have accrued as a result of rationalistic liberalism and, whether they are consciously aware of it or not, rebel interiorly against the insanity forced on them by the insane creatures within their society by attempting to alter their consciousness through drug use; hoping that they will either be able to escape the insanity through the use of drugs—so as to distract their minds away from the incessant assault on their consciousness—or to alter their consciousness to the point that they will be able to conform their minds to an acceptance of insanity: a perverse actualization of the old adage, "If you can't beat 'em, join 'em."

Let us now combine the application of the Hegelian Dialectic (Figure 1) with the bulwarks of social order (Figures 3 and 4) to visually understand how the West has been almost universally seduced into a nihilistic, self-hating, and self-destructive psychology (Figure 5, next page).

85

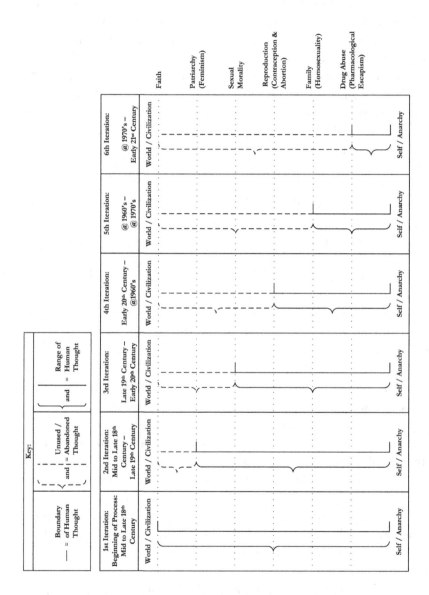

Figure 5. Psychological/Intellectual Corruption of the West

Figure 5 is meant to draw a visual representation of the West's dissolution into its current, barbaric state. The first thing to notice is how the intellect and understanding of the average person has become "compressed" with the passage of time. Previously held, proven tenets of morality and social construction have been incrementally "pressed" out of the human psyche. This type of intellectual compression is a trademark consequence of the corruption of the human psyche when the methodology of the Hegelian Dialectic is applied; where the newly synthesized perception forces out previously held ideas and compresses the human understanding so that the range of thought of the human mind no longer perceives the previous, dynamic range of thought that once existed in the human consciousness. This "compression" of human understanding is the same methodology that is used to accomplish the "pressing out" of human minds into a psychological paradigm of slaves and masters, which will be further explained in the following section.

Secondly, as the Hegelian Dialectic has been applied to modern, Western civilization it is critical to notice that the central focus of human perception—that which the human mind gravitates around in the formation of their psyches and characters—has likewise been altered. Several hundred years ago, as illustrated by the first iteration of Figure 5, the vast majority of mankind used to view their lives from a perspective of religious faith. The psychological center that mankind gravitated around was one of a whole and complete worldview, where men perceived their infinitesimally small place within the world from a perspective of how their actions and beliefs effected the greater world around them; for when mankind once believed in God and an ultimate accountability for their actions they used to contemplate, and understand, the restrictions placed on their animalistic urges. They understood the negative consequences that would accrue as a result of violating the moral norms established by religious doctrine. In short, at that time (late Eighteenth Century) people once understood how their attitudes, and the consequent behaviors that manifested themselves as a result of those attitudes, filtered down through the rest of society to either build it up or tear it down. This is what is signified by the captions "World/Civilization" and "Self/Anarchy" at the extremes of human understanding in Figure 5.

In the mid-Eighteenth Century and earlier, a greater number of people used to see their place within the world and understand how their tiny little part in it affected the greater whole. As a consequence of this expansive worldview they attempted to live by higher, moral ideals that served the greater good of their respective societies. With each passing iteration of the

Hegelian Dialectic within Western civilization—the advent of Feminism, the abandonment of sexual morality, the tolerance of contraception and abortion, the toleration of homosexuality, etc.—two things were simultaneously accomplished. Primarily, the intellect and understanding of the average person was incrementally reduced over time. As a result, many people in following generations could no longer grasp those ideas and philosophies that previous generations once took for granted as universally understood truths.

Secondarily, the central focal point of human contemplation was drawn away from a consideration and understanding of the effects of one's attitudes and behaviors on their larger societies; having been drawn inward upon itself, and toward the gratification of personal desires: narcissism. The third article to note is the acceleration of the West's dissolution as previous bulwarks of social order and construction were torn down. This principle conforms to the analogy of social fortifications in Figures 3 & 4. As previous social defenses were torn down, the subsequent fortifications were torn down in a more rapid succession as the common enemy (anarchy) of mankind made its way within Western culture and broke down the social fortifications at their weakest points; primarily through the weakness of the vacillating and compromising tendencies inherent within the feminine nature.

After the original dissolution of faith (late 18th Century), the beginnings of feminism (1868, with founding of the *National Society for Women's Suffrage*) took roughly seventy years to accomplish. After the advent of feminism, the beginnings of the wholesale dissolution of sexual morality followed only a few decades later (late 19th to early 20th Century): culminating in the "sexual revolution" of the 1960's. After the fortification of sexual morality fell, the cry for "reproductive rights" (contraception and abortion) followed by only four or five decades (mid-20th Century). After abortion and contraception were socially normalized, homosexuality and a sharp increase in the rate of divorce ascended to a position of social tolerance within only one to two decades (1970's). And finally, after homosexuality and divorce became socially normalized the rapid increase in drug use as a means of psychological escapism followed up in another, single decade (1980's).

Observing the historical, accelerating dissolution of Western civilization; it can be seen that it took a full century for feminism and the rising dissolution of sexual morality to eclipse religious faith. After these initial iterations of the Hegelian Dialectic within the West, the other socially destructive iterations of the dialectic were accomplished within less than a single century, with the last three (abortion/contraception, homosexuality, and rampant drug abuse) ascending to a level of social tolerance within only a few decades time (early

1960s – early 1980s)! Moreover, Western culture has become so reprobated that there are some nations who have legalized psychotropic drugs; while in the U.S. and Canada there is a large constituency of people who are clamoring for the legalization of many, if not all, of the currently illicit psychotropic drugs—most especially marijuana—and even encouraging their use among the general population via the socially revered professions of medicine and psychiatry; including the use of psychotropic prescription drugs (Ritalin, Prozac, etc.) as an alternative to parental discipline.

Finally, as it relates to where Western civilization stands now (in the early 21st Century), it is important to note how "flattened out" the intellect and understanding of the average Westerner is; so that they are literally unable to conceive of a great many ideas and principles that were once universally understood and accepted by most all people.[3] After several hundred years of the accelerating corruption of the West by the application of the Hegelian Dialectic, which is essentially the compromising of principles in order to "get along," most people are simply intellectually unable to understand what has been done to their civilization and why it is in such peril; because after a whole lifetime of subjection to fallacious propaganda within the government school systems, within the television and print media, and even among personal acquaintances; a great majority of people are no longer able to formulate ideas that can coherently explain reality and make it understandable. Moreover, the most pathetic part of this whole scenario is that for the most part it is nobody's fault, at least among the currently living generations, as those who started the corruption of Western civilization are long dead; with those who are alive today and knowingly continuing to corrupt the world being numbered in the tiniest fraction (probably no more than a few thousand in all the world).

Those who are suffered to be born into a reprobated world aren't aware of how perverted it is, as they are raised to believe that what modern man considers good, normal, and tolerable has always been the perversion we live in today, which understandably perverts human understanding from the moment of a person's birth! Such a circumstance of multiple generations and centuries of people who have had their minds warped via false principles inculcated into the "public" mind makes the current world circumstance(s) more understandable; when people clearly see the world slipping away before

---

[3] This corresponds to George Orwell's description of *Newspeak* and how language has been corrupted via sophistical, dialectical tactics that have been used to achieve this end.

their very eyes, yet don't understand how it has come to this dangerous point or see a way out of it. Sadly, the intellect and understanding of the average person has become so "flattened out" that they are actually no longer able to conceive of the causes and effects that have brought us to this point!

The good and hopeful news is that, as bad as the intellect and understanding of the average, modern person has been corrupted, there are *clear* remedies to this situation that are able to, almost overnight, solve the problems we are currently suffered to be burdened with, which we will explore in the final section that addresses how we reverse course in order to achieve true peace among humanity. However, we have several more items to discuss before we address the solutions to our current state. It is first necessary to understand why a traditional social order and morality is superior to the anarchy we are ushering in via our collective descent into mass narcissism. After this discussion, the devices used to "lawyer" our civilization into its present state of anarchistic reprobation will be explained; so that the reader will be aware of, and hopefully guard against, their continued psychological manipulation via these techniques; both now and into the future.

Why a Traditional Social Order and Morality Is Superior to Narcissistic Anarchy

Having chronicled our descent into cultural barbarism over the past several centuries, and explaining the devices used to facilitate our dissolution, it is necessary for us to discuss why a civilization constructed around a traditional social order and moral code is far superior to the barbarism and anarchy of a society built on narcissism and a humanistic moral-relativism. The articles to be examined here are those delineated in Figure 5—the visual representation of the corruption of Western civilization—and comparing them to their opposites: (1) faith vs. atheism, (2) patriarchy vs. feminism, (3) sexual morality vs. promiscuity, (4) reproduction vs. contraception/abortion, (5) heterosexuality vs. homosexuality, and (6) sobriety vs. drug abuse.

Faith vs. Atheism

When we compare the natural consequences and implications of religious faith to those of atheism the great beneficence to humanity that results from religious faith are readily apparent. To begin with, let's consider what lies at the foundation of the worldview of those who adhere to a religious belief system. First and foremost is the belief that there is a greater power that created the physical world, and that He (God) is watching everything that we do and think. Several beneficial implications result from this primary belief; the most important being that when each one of us dies we will be held accountable, and either given an eternal reward that is too wonderful to comprehend or an eternal punishment that is too horrible for the mind to fathom; with all judgment being based on our thoughts and actions during our life. Secondly, religious faith attributes a universal belief that God is perfect while people are horribly perverse and evil by their very nature (the doctrine of original sin), and that due to our corrupt nature we must constantly struggle against our own natural impulses and inclinations. Thirdly, regarding the circumstances that people encounter in their lives, the religious generally believe that all good things come through the providence and inspiration of God; not through the power of men and governments. Conversely, the evils that befall the religious are generally believed to come

91

from either men or governments corrupted by man's natural inclinations, by God as a test of faith or virtue, or some combination of both. With this understanding of the religious perspective, those with a spiritual consciousness constantly struggle against their own natural inclinations and try to form their thoughts and actions around theological principles called virtues; some of which are humility, gratitude, justice, charity, hope, courage, and perseverance.

Humility is meant to remind people that in the bigger picture of the world they are small and insignificant in relation to the greater whole; just one little, replaceable cog in the larger machine of life, and that there is nothing that makes any individual more important or "special" than any other on this earth: all human beings being equally "special" in God's eyes; regardless of whether they are rich or poor, old or young, black or white, etc. Humility opens up the mental vision of the religious by inculcating a reality-based world view. Each one of us is just one out of over *six billion* in the world. When one of us dies, although it may bring a permanent and deep sadness to our friends and immediate family members, the rest of the world continues to move on. The person is replaced by another at their work and life keeps moving forward. A subordinate, consequential quality that grows from humility is gratitude. Gratitude is the spirit of thankfulness for the benefits and gifts one has received. It also fills the mind with an appreciation of, and satisfaction with, the things that one possesses, even if one's possessions are meager; as in the case of the poor.

Justice teaches the ageless maxim known as the 'Golden Rule': "Do unto others as you would have them do unto you." It establishes a mental framework of behavior whereby people expect from life what they put into it. A just person expects to work for everything they gain, and does not try to take from others what does not belong to them. It shields against irresponsibility and superimposes an empathetic mentality on the minds of those who strive for and desire honest justice; so that just people, when considering their actions in life, look beyond the easy and simple consideration of, "What's in it for me"?, and consider the consequences of their actions on others as well. Additionally, a just person demands the same consideration from others within society.

Charity is an accompanying virtue of justice, in that charitable people— in consideration of the charity they show to others—hope to receive the same treatment in return from those they encounter in their lives. Moreover, charitable people understand that nothing good can come from an uncharitable disposition. Hope can be a bit more complex, but it is meant to sustain people during difficult and burdensome trials in a person's life. Hope has several different facets. The simplest aspect of hope is a desire and belief that you will see better days than those being experienced in the present day if you will exercise perseverance in the face of difficulties. The more difficult part of hope, but certainly encouraged in the religious, is the belief that as bad as things may seem today relief *will* eventually come; even if that relief has to be delayed until your departure from this world. Courage and perseverance manifest themselves as byproducts of hope. As hope instructs the religious to not capitulate to despair, it instills a sense of courage in the person to continue facing their problems with a patient, perseverant resignation, in the hope that things will improve. Perseverance imparts a spirit and attitude of not giving up in the face of life's hardships regardless of how hopeless the adversity *appears*, while courage provides the strength necessary to persevere. Courage and perseverance build "toughness" into the human character.

Now, let's consider the consequences and implications of atheism. First and foremost, atheism is the belief that there is no God or "higher power" responsible for the creation of the world, and who likewise records everything that we do and think. Several maleficent implications result from this primary belief; the most important being the conviction that when each one of us dies it will simply be the end of our existence and consciousness. As a consequence of this primary belief, a powerful tool of self-control is removed; as the atheist does not have any fear of ultimate, divine accountability for their actions in life. Moreover, if there is only this life to be lived, the justification to struggle against our natural, evil impulses and inclinations is greatly undermined.

Such a belief system drives the mind toward sentiments of nihilism, narcissism and hedonistic self-indulgence. Regarding the circumstances that people encounter in their lives, the atheist generally believes that all things, both good and bad, come through the providence of men and governments; using their applied intellect to divine solutions to worldly problems. With this understanding of the atheistic perspective, those with an atheistic consciousness constantly struggle against their fellow man in order to indulge their passions and desires; in the mental conviction that they must live for themselves, and in the moment, because after they die there will be nothing more to hope for. Such a psychological disposition results in serious character faults that militate against religious virtues, as well as an ordered, civil society.

Now, compare the differences between these two world views side-by-side. As you consider the complete, polar differences between the two opposing psychologies, it is hopeful that the reader will fully appreciate why religious faith is beneficent and supportive of human civilizations, and conversely why atheism is maleficent and destructive to them. Ask yourself, "Which one is more conducive to sustaining whole societies, and an even larger world full of billions of people"?:

Atheism	Religion / Spirituality
Atheism: Removes all incentives to maintain self-restraint and act in an honest and straightforward manner; due to the repudiation of divine accountability. The only restraining force in society is that which can be achieved through physical force.	*Religion*: Enforces a mental construct of self-restraint via a fear of ultimate accountability for all of our actions throughout our lives. Consequently, this belief in accountability encourages justice, truth, and honesty in one's life.
Materialism: Teaches people to value material goods and the immediate self-gratification of temporary things (honors, money, fame, etc.) as the most important pursuit in this life.	*Spirituality*: Teaches people to value the virtues as the most important pursuit in this life. It also fosters the belief that all other good things will come as a consequence of exercising virtue.
Pride: Encourages a narcissistic, delusional self-absorption and conceit; whereby people order their priorities around their selfish desires.	*Humility*: Encourages a reality-based conception of one's life and their place in the world; as only one of more than six billion people on earth: no more important or "special" than any other human being; regardless of one's position or function within the world.
Ingratitude, Jealousy, and Envy: Materialism causes a perpetual lack of satisfaction with life. Ingratitude for benefits received alienates people from their benefactors, and humanity at large. As someone will always have more of something than another person, jealousy and envy can never be satiated.	*Gratitude*: Causes a perpetual satisfaction with life. Being grateful for benefits received ingratiates people with their benefactors, and humanity at large. As someone will always have more of something than another person, the grateful resign themselves to being appreciative for what they have.

Atheism	Religion / Spirituality
Injustice: Causes perpetual social turmoil. As self-absorbed people remember an injury at the hands of another, injustice fuels anger, bitterness, and the desire for reprisals. It also militates toward social chaos and anarchy. Because narcissistic/egoistic people act upon personal prejudices rather than a predefined code of conduct or rules, the result is constant inconsistency and confusion within society when people fail to exercise uniform standards of behavior throughout their society. Additionally, when people are dealt with in an unjust manner they are provided with legitimate grounds for disaffection and complaint.	*Justice:* Facilitates peace and order within a society. Because a just society lives by a predetermined set of rules and standards (morality), those within that society know and understand the rules and standards that they are expected to conform to, and choose to live by them for the benefit of all and for themselves. As the underlying foundation of justice is that everyone gets what they earn—nothing more and nothing less—within a just society, there are no legitimate grounds for complaint when someone becomes ungrateful or disaffected with life for whatever reason.
Contentiousness: A contentious and uncharitable disposition, which naturally develops as a consequence of a narcissistic disposition, nourishes constant bitterness and dissatisfaction with life. As people tend to respond to others in a reciprocal manner to the way in which they are treated, a contentious spirit only perpetuates more of the same; to the point that such behavior becomes the expected norm within society: spawning many other undesirable consequences, which include cynicism, apathy, distrust, fear, and hatred.	*Charity:* Charity makes life, amidst all of the problems that we face every day, a little more endurable, and occasionally pleasant. As people tend to respond to others in a reciprocal manner to the way in which they are treated by others, charity tends to build a friendly disposition within society; spawning many other desirable consequences, which include a spirit of cooperation and mutual assistance.

Atheism	Religion / Spirituality
Despair. The foundation for an innumerable number of evils within society; especially the other evils of cowardice and capitulation. A person who has fallen into despair, for whatever reason, is much more susceptible to psychological manipulation at the hands of cunning and ambitious people, because once a person has reached the point of despair, they begin to seek *any* means to rescue themselves from their situation; no matter how illegitimate, immoral, or deceitful they may be.	*Hope.* The foundation for the other virtues of courage and perseverance. People who hold out hope for a better day to come than today wait patiently for that better day to come. Hope fortifies the mind against psychological manipulation at the hands of cunning and ambitious people, because those who have hope do not succumb to the desperate desire to resort to any measure, especially immoral or deceitful measures, in order to extract themselves from an unpleasant circumstance.
Cowardice. Cowardice is a manifestation of moral weakness. Those who demonstrate a cowardly disposition refuse to accept their life circumstances with courageous resignation. Individuals display their cowardice by refusing to accept what befalls them in their lives with uncomplaining resignation and fortitude; blaming others for their particular life's difficulties and attempting to force others to solve their problems rather than facing the responsibility for their own lives. A society demonstrates cowardice when it refuses to face life as free people. Such a civilization manifests its cowardice by begging government to take care of them (socialism and communism); thereby encouraging their own enslavement.	*Courage.* Courage is a manifestation of moral strength. At the very least, for those who show the qualities of courage, it is a resignation with one's life and circumstances, as well as an aversion to burdening others with one's particular problems. Individuals within a society display their courage by accepting what befalls them in their lives with uncomplaining resignation and fortitude—unwilling to burden others with their particular life's difficulties—in the knowledge that other people are suffering their own difficulties and do not need to be further burdened by a stranger's complaints.

Atheism	Religion / Spirituality
Capitulation: Capitulation is a product of cowardice: giving up when things "just get too hard." Societies make themselves ripe for the slavery of socialism or communism when the population capitulates under the burdens of real life by willfully evading their responsibility to face their own life's problems when they clamor to be saved from themselves by their government.	*Perseverance*: Perseverance is a product of courage: gutting out the difficulties in one's life when real life throws hardship and disappointment at your feet, which always happens in practically everyone's life. A society of perseverant people would never face enslavement by their government, because they would have too much dignity and self-respect to be cowards. Moreover, the perseverant do not wish to encourage capitulation and cowardice amongst their fellow citizens by themselves setting a poor example.

Patriarchy vs. Feminism

There are people in Europe who, confounding the various attributes of the sexes, claim to make man and woman into creatures not only equal but alike. They ascribe the same functions to both, assign them the same duties, and grant them the same rights. They mix them in all things: work, pleasure, affairs. It is easy to see how trying in this way to make one sex equal to the other degrades them both and how the only thing that can ever come of such a crude mixture of nature's works is weak men and disreputable women.[1]

— Alexis de Tocqueville, French diplomat, politician,
and author of *Democracy In America*

In today's world, feminism has progressed to such an extent that feminist dogma has become engrained within the public conscience as a point of morality; meaning that feminist ideology (primarily "equality" of the genders) is considered by most all people to be inherently morally good, while patriarchy is contrarily considered to be inherently morally evil. Sadly, this is an absolutely false perception, and I will attempt to explain why the patriarchal social order is the best and strongest basis for society, and as well to illustrate the insanity of feminism.

To begin to understand this, we must first look to the opposing characteristics of the feminine and masculine natures; recognizing the physical, emotional, and psychological differences between men and women, and noting the proper relationship between the genders in order to provide for a strong and stable society. At the most fundamental level, it must be understood and admitted that men and women, rather than being equals, are instead *interdependent* and *complementary*. It is exactly this traditional, symbiotic relationship between the feminine and masculine natures that make society sustainable; for without a balance between the extremes of the feminine and the masculine natures, society would destroy itself; the rate of destruction being dependent on how far the society had deviated to either of the extremes. An effeminate society would be destroyed by its inability to defend itself due to its inhering weaknesses: for example, the modern United

---

[1] Alexis De Tocqueville, *Democracy In America*, trans. Arthur Goldhammer (New York, NY: The Library of America, 2004), 705.

States and Western civilization. On the other hand, an excessively masculine society (tyrannical or despotic) would consume itself due to its predominantly brutish and predatory nature: the Soviet Union, Nazi Germany, Cambodia, and other communistic, or otherwise tyrannical, societies; to include the militant Islamists attempting to impose themselves on the world. Men and women possess innate, natural tendencies that we are born with, and these tendencies counter each other. The below table illustrates a few of the more obvious differences between the masculine and feminine natures. The reader can probably think of others not mentioned here.

Opposing Characteristics	
Masculine Nature	**Feminine Nature**
Firmness	Softness
Resolute	Indecisive
Bold	Timid
Logically Centered. Cognitive Thinker. Predominantly Influenced By Reason	Emotionally Centered. Affective Thinker. Predominantly Influenced By Emotions
More Difficult To Threaten/Intimidate	Easier To Threaten/Intimidate
Stronger	Weaker
Grounded/Fundamental	Vain

Opposing Masculine/Feminine Characteristics of Human Nature

Within a healthy society these opposing tendencies serve to temper and complement each other, so as to create an overall balance within society:

1. The softness of the feminine nature tempers the firmness of the masculine nature, so that men would not be firm to the point of being excessively harsh; while the firmness of the masculine nature tempers the softness of the feminine nature, so that women would not become unduly flaccid.

2. The resoluteness of the masculine nature tempers the indecisiveness of the feminine nature, so that women are not indecisive to the point of being unable to reach a decision; while the indecisiveness of the feminine nature tempers the resolution of the masculine nature, so that men are not resolute to the point of unwarranted obstinacy.

3. The timidity of the feminine nature tempers the boldness of the masculine nature, so that men are not bold to the point of boorish obtrusiveness; while the boldness of the masculine nature tempers the timidity of the feminine nature, so that women are not unduly sheepish.

4. The reader undoubtedly understands the principle(s) at work, and can extrapolate the interactions of other opposing, innate tendencies of the masculine and feminine natures.

Where do the fundamental differences between the masculine and feminine nature originate from? There are undoubtedly many factors that account for the differences, but the foundation can be found in the relative disparity of physical and psychological strength that exists between the two genders. While it is certainly true that there have always been, and will always be, women who are born with masculine tendencies, as well as men who are born with effeminate tendencies, we will be discussing the overwhelmingly predominant rule of nature, as its effect is of much greater influence within society than is the exception.

With that said, generally, women are both physically and psychologically weaker than men. The psychological weakness occurs as a natural consequence of the feminine nature's emotional center. Conversely, the rational center of the masculine nature provides the man with a psychological advantage; as a man will generally accept an unpleasant reality in a more resolute and stoic fashion, while a woman will generally not accept an unpleasant reality; attempting to either alter reality, or their perception of it, in order to appease their emotional discomfort, which ultimately leads a person down the dangerous path of affective reasoning. Moreover, the difference between the sexes in relation to physical strength contributes to this condition; because, being aware of their innate physical disadvantage in relation to men, women must use opposing tactics and techniques of persuasion to neutralize or dissuade the masculine nature from realizing its unrestrained expression. Hence, the more sublime aspects of the feminine nature are used to temper and civilize the masculine nature.

It is for just this reason that a patriarchal social order is the most beneficial and stable basis from which to build and maintain a civilization; due to the stronger characteristics of the masculine nature as compared to those of the feminine nature. The stronger, masculine nature is better suited to sustain civilizations because there are two requirements that must be met for any nation or society to perpetuate itself. First, it must be able to administer its own affairs during times of relative peace; and second, it must be able to defend itself when it is attacked by an enemy. From the standpoint of administering its own affairs, a nation is sustained and best served when it is led by people who are emotionally and psychologically grounded to the fundamental principles that built their nation; an adherence to tradition and first principles that have proved to be prudent and wise. From a foundation built upon first principles they continue into the future to perpetuate those same principles with a resolute firmness. Their decision-making processes regarding the questions of their day should be based on a rational examination of the probable consequences of the decisions they make, which are best made by referencing the historical record regarding similar problems from the past; how they were addressed and the consequences that accrued as a result. Moreover, when a good leader is challenged by self-interested opposition they must possess the psychological strength to oppose the challenge in order to do what is truly in the nation's best interest.

On the other hand a nation is ill served, and led into regression and degeneration, when its leaders are not grounded upon first principles; but rather animated by vain, emotional, or self-serving motives. Not having a foundation built upon traditional values that have proved to be prudent and wise for the sustenance of civilization, such leaders will often steer a nation down the blind alleys of innovation in order to appease the prejudices of the ignorant majority. Their decision-making processes regarding the questions of their day are not guided by any rational sentiment, but rather by a desire to appease the majority so as to perpetuate their hold on power. Being animated by such vain and self-serving motives, they will be much more easily intimidated and indecisive; often demonstrating great weakness, especially in matters of great importance.

From the standpoint of defending one's society, it is natural that this duty should fall to men; as the defense of a nation is ultimately resolved through combat (both physical and psychological), of which the masculine nature is more naturally suited and inclined.

Before we leave this point, it is necessary to clarify something that is most often confused in the modern world; where the pursuit of pleasure and personal gratification has become the paramount priority in the lives of the great majority of the people. It has been stated that the patriarchal social order is the most beneficial and stable basis from which to build and maintain a civilization; and it is certainly true. However, it must be admitted that such a social order is not the most "fun." Why? For exactly the same reasons that make a patriarchal society so strong: it's adherence to first principles and an unwillingness to compromise those principles in order to placate undisciplined voluptuaries. By necessity, a patriarchal social order requires self-discipline from those who compose the society, because it requires a certain level of self-denial and fortitude on the part of both men and women; a level of discipline among the women to accept being socially subject to the men in their lives (husbands, fathers, etc.), and a level of discipline among the men to accept the responsibility placed on them while refraining from abusing their authority for self-serving motives: using their position within the lives of their female relations (wives, daughters, etc.) to act in the best interests of all, in the true spirit of love, rather than from egoistic or selfish intentions.

Let's now look to the insanity inherent within feminism. Feminism is a political movement and ideology, with the stated goal of making women the "equals" of men. The routine demands are for "equal rights," "equal opportunity," and just about anything else where it is believed that men are in possession of some type of perceived advantage over women, such as exclusively male organizations (country clubs, fraternal organizations, etc.). At first glance, and using nothing more than affective reasoning processes designed to make the reader feel good about themselves, this may appear to be a noble goal. However, when one critically analyzes the situation using cognitive reasoning processes based on objective reality, it will be immediately recognized that the great problem with feminism is that it is predicated on a dangerously delusional, false premise: that men and women are indeed alike.

This is a patently false supposition. The reader may recall a very popular book published in 1992, and which is still popular today: *Men are From Mars, Women are from Venus*. The author, Dr. John Gray, noted numerous ways in which men and women were different in very many fundamental and consequential ways. Dr. Gray summed up the situation in the introduction to his book: "Not only do men and women communicate differently but they think, feel, perceive, react, respond, love, need, and appreciate differently."[2] This is a reality that honest people, both men and women, understand intuitively from common experience. They see it both in themselves and in those of the opposite gender.

It is important to notice how the feminist exemplifies Orwellian doublethink. They must admit that men and women are different—as this reality is impossible to ignore: biologically, emotionally, and psychologically—while simultaneously demanding that women be treated as if they were the same as men. For the feminist to demand equality between men and women is to willfully deny the obvious reality that men and women *are* different, simply because the feminist does not like her relatively weaker position in society in

---

[2] Dr. John Gray, *Men are From Mars, Women are From Venus*, (New York, NY: HarperCollins Publishers, 1992), 5.

relation to men. It's like holding up a pencil directly in front of a person's face and asking, "Do you see the pencil in my hand"?; and in response the person claims, "You aren't holding anything in your hands." The person makes this outrageous statement because they don't like the reality they are presented with and refuse to acknowledge it, even though they clearly see it directly in front of them. In like manner, an obvious reality is held up to the feminist. Yet, because they despise reality, they rebel and try to manufacture a counterfeit reality, and likewise force their false delusions on the rest of the world.

This being the case, it is then clear to see that feminism is a manifestation of delusional insanity. It attempts to overthrow either the will of God (for the faithful) or nature (for the faithless) by sheer force of the feminist's will alone; as if complaining loud enough and long enough will be able to effect a change in the immutability of human nature, which is itself another insane belief; because in order to be able to change human nature one would have to be God. Why? Consider that if someone is determined to make a change in the design of any article—whether it be a manufactured item or a human being—that person would need access to the design level of the article being redesigned: the "blueprints" of the article in question. Therefore, if one is determined to redesign mankind and our very nature it would require the ability to access and modify the nature of mankind at the design level. Something only the Creator of mankind could do . . . God.

In the beginning of this section, Alexis de Tocqueville noted, "It is easy to see how trying in this way to make one sex equal to the other degrades them both and how the only thing that can ever come of such a crude mixture of nature's works is weak men and disreputable women." This is the only natural consequence that can result from feminism, because to make men and women perceived "equals" requires the application of unnatural cultural and psychological pressure and force to both men and women. Men must be forcibly feminized, and women must be forcibly made more masculine.

> Many men have denied some of their masculine attributes in order to become more loving and nurturing. Likewise many women have denied some of their feminine attributes in order to earn a living in a work force that rewards masculine attributes.[3]
> — Dr. John Gray, author of *Men are From Mars, Women are From Venus*

---

[3] Ibid., 7.

Either way, the critical point to observe is that the great majority of both men and women are being subjected to intense, unnatural psychological and cultural pressure by a small, but *very vocal*, bullying minority of disaffected and self-loathing people;[4] so as to persuade the vast majority of people to forcibly deny their very nature in order to accommodate the insane delusions of the disaffected and self-loathing. As the feminist desires to remake the nature of humanity, it is only fitting to apply a manufacturing analogy to this situation. Just as a sheet of metal, no matter how strong and resilient, is warped when subjected to constant external forces over an extended period of time; the human mind, no matter how strong and resilient, will become warped when subjected to constant cultural and psychological forces over the course of their entire lifetime. The entire psychosis of feminism has resulted in a culture and society of people who are psychologically at war with themselves.

The direct consequence of the past several generations of people trying to forcibly deny their very nature has been an explosion in other gender-confusion psychoses among the most weak-minded and vulnerable within society, whereby those poor people who have succumbed to the psychological warfare being waged against society by militant feminism have become alienated from members of the opposite gender (homosexuality); or, even worse, some have even become militantly alienated against their own gender and even their own person (transsexuality). Having been psychologically broken, they then resort to repudiating their own nature or irreparably mutilating themselves.

But let no person mistake or misrepresent my intentions regarding the modern manifestation of these behaviors. These poor people are to be pitied, and offered help whenever they choose to seek it; for they are the victims and casualties of unnatural socio-cultural pressures that they have been subjected to for all their lives; having been subjected to such enormous pressure that it has warped their minds to the point that they truly believe that such unnatural disorders are acceptable, or even "normal." This is a clearly observable exemplification of the immutability of human nature. Not being able to change their nature, a great many people have instead succumbed to the insanity of self-loathing, social suicide. Feminism has not been able to change the basic nature of humanity. It has instead psychologically broken a great deal of its weakest members. It has certainly recast modern societies in its own image, but it has not been able to remake the essence of human nature.

---

4 Women who despise femininity and their existence as a woman, as well as men who despise masculinity and their existence as a man.

By seeking to make women the perceived equals of men, feminism has destroyed the cooperative, complementary relationship that once existed between men and women. Instead of being partners in society, each gender assuming their respective roles and playing to their natural strengths in order to forward either a family unit or society as a whole; most women have been pushed toward more masculine characteristics while most men have been rendered more effeminate in order to meet at some undefined, androgynous "twilight zone" between the masculine and feminine natures. Under this radically altered social paradigm, when the "new man" (emasculated) and "new woman" (masculinized) meet on the modern field of society they no longer identify themselves as cooperative agents in a common goal or cause: the perpetuation of either family or society.

They now more closely identify themselves as competitors for an individual goal or cause: the self-indulgent gratification of personal passions; commonly referred to today as the "Battle of the Sexes." But we should not be fighting each other! We should be helping each other; the members of each gender playing to their strengths, while the members of the opposing gender compensate for the opposite gender's weaknesses, because our weakness is most often the opposing gender's strength. In the process, each other's strengths and weaknesses are held in check, so as to create a more stable and balanced society.

Naturally, the social consequences of feminism to families, individual men and women, children, and society as a whole has been pitiful and heartbreaking to behold: an excessive rate of divorce and infidelity; increases in the incidences of violence (both domestically and within society more generally); and atrociously poor examples of personal irresponsibility being displayed for our children's consumption by irresponsible and selfish parents who are themselves too emotionally immature to be parenting children, but who are also unaware of their incapacity and emotional retardation due to a lifetime of delusional psychological conditioning that has resulted in their particular, perverted frame of reference as a predominantly androgynous "new man" or "new woman" of the new millennium.

Additionally, feminism has caused an astounding dissipation in the strength and vigor of the various societies and cultures within Western civilization via the effeminate tendency to maintain a non-confrontational disposition; by extolling physical weakness, moral weakness, and cowardice as "virtuous"; while castigating physical strength, moral strength, and courage as being "belligerent." Of course, when the article(s) of contention in question are petty—the subject or object of simple, human pride—one should search for a means of avoiding confrontation on such points. However, when first principles are involved—those articles of contention that involve matters of right vs. wrong or good vs. evil—a masculine firmness is an absolute necessity in order to defend what is good and right and overcome what is wrong and evil. Yet, as a consequence of the feminization of Western culture, the citizens therein have become much more pliable and yielding in practically all cultural matters; rendering most citizens either amoral or morally impotent, which has allowed all manner of moral evils to overtake the society: feminism itself, homosexuality, transsexuality, atheism, socialism, pornography, abortion, adultery, the depraved licentiousness of "popular culture," etc.

Antagonistic cultures (most specifically, militant Islam) have observed this effeminate disposition within Western civilization and are now using it to their advantage to force themselves on the West. It is also this disposition that is at the foundation of the West's steadily-encroaching physical weakness. Lacking either the desire or the requisite courage (excepting the actual soldier) to undertake a physical confrontation with any adversary(s), an alarming number of Westerners are choosing the route of trying to appease their enemies; demonstrating a frightful disposition of moral and physical cowardice that will only embolden our enemies rather than placating them; ignoring the lessons of history regarding the suicidal consequences of cowardice and appeasement in the face of evil.

Feminism will *always* gravitate toward the dissipation of the social order within any society due to the emotionally-centered aspect of the feminine nature. An excellent exemplification of the great danger of this reality, as it is making itself manifest in today's world, is within the judicial system: both civilly and criminally. The characteristics of the feminine nature that are destroying our judicial system are: (1) the feminine tendency to filter ideas or thoughts through an emotional prism: affective thinking (civil and criminal); (2) nurturing instinct: a desire to be comforting or accommodating and non-confrontational (civil and criminal); and (3) a weaker and more easily intimidated nature (criminal).

Let's first consider the corruption of civil justice: product liability lawsuits. A great many product liability lawsuits are deplorably unjust; especially among industries where the product is used irresponsibly, in full knowledge of the user, only to result in damage to themselves or another: firearms, fast food, etc. In these situations the proper response to these lawsuits is, "They harmed themselves or another through their own irresponsibility or evil intent. We aren't going to reward them for their irresponsibility and punish the manufacturer, who had no part to play in the irresponsible use of their product." However, what has been happening with much greater frequency is that the effeminate observe the same situation, and they unjustly respond to the situation via an emotional reaction. As a result, the effeminate person, regardless of their biological gender, "reasons" within themselves, "Oh, that poor person. They are suffering because of the particular product that was [mis]used. They deserve to be compensated for their suffering by the company that made the product."

By ignoring the fact that the use of the product, whatever it may be, was willfully entered into by the person in question, the effeminate jurist displays a terrible example for those who view the outcome of these lawsuits. These examples of effeminate, affective thinking actually work to rapidly accelerate the dissolution of society, and the people within it, by rewarding irresponsibility or criminality while (unintentionally) encouraging dishonest people to assume the undignified role of the perpetual "victim" in pursuit of compensation for an "injustice" that they fabricate in order to "work the system" and extort money from various business interests; having witnessed the example of effeminate jurists in the past who ignore the fault of the "victim," thereby giving the dishonest person an avenue to extort business interests via the civil legal system. The natural, nurturing instinct and softness of the feminine nature desires to be comforting and accommodating regarding any person who is suffering; but in the cases of those who are rightly suffering as a consequence of their own irresponsibility, the excessive softness of the feminine nature misguides the thought processes and actions of the effeminate and renders a judicial result that is completely contrary to what is responsible and just.

The corruption of the criminal justice system works along the same lines, and it has worked to encourage criminality and predation within society by manifesting itself as a morally bankrupt "sympathy for the devil" mentality. The best cases to exemplify this "sympathy for the devil" psychosis, which *always* results in a miscarriage of justice, are criminal defendants who have themselves suffered abuse in the past. A rational view of the situation would lead an observer to the perspective of, "That person was raised in an evil and abusive environment. Knowing how miserable and destructive it was, he should have been more aware of the evil(s) he was committing, and henceforth been more vigilant to avoid perpetrating the same evil acts against others." However, an effeminate jurist views the same situation through an affective, emotional prism and arrives at an opposing conclusion: "Oh, that poor creature. They only became evil and violent because their upbringing was evil and violently abusive. They just don't know any better because they have never been shown a better example in their life. I will take pity on them."

In some obscene cases the jurist may even hold the criminal blameless, and instead blame another person, or even worse, an abstract idea, for the evil act(s) that many criminals decide to commit: "It's [their parent's | society's] fault that this criminal turned out to be the person that he is."

In cases where jurists are more readily accessible to the public, a defendant may resort to threatening the life of the juror, or their family members, if they are not acquitted of the charges; a threat that has a much greater probability of success when used against the natural weakness of the feminine nature than when used against the stronger masculine nature. The consequences of effeminate, emotional dispositions when applied to the criminal justice system are even more dangerous than within the civil justice system; because leniency regarding criminality, especially violent criminality and predation, also works toward the dissolution of society, and the individuals within it, by displaying an example of moral weakness to the rest of society. Other criminals who view the weakness of society in relation to their behavior are not dissuaded from their evil intentions when they witness the ease and leniency that they expect will await them; even if they are caught in their misdeeds. By showing softness and weakness in the face of criminality and predation within an effeminate society, the society actually encourages more criminality and predation; because the evil, criminal mind despises the weakness of such a society and is emboldened to victimize their fellow man with an even greater vindictiveness and savagery than if they had lived in a morally accountable society. In effect, they despise their society all the more because of its weakness; seeing potential victims as "low hanging fruit" to be plucked with impunity.

We should now look to why feminism will always gravitate toward socialism and communism: socially and culturally degenerative ideologies that Western civilization is falling prey to. The primary reason is because feminism *artificially* "empowers" women; so that it inculcates a mentality of gender equality with men via political fiat. However, such self-deceiving political proclamations do not impart a commensurate change, or promotion, within the inner strength of the woman. The feminine nature still remains unchanged within most all women, despite the feminist's ardent desire to be just about anything other than what she actually is: a woman. The aspect of the feminine nature that exposes itself to victimization by socialistic and communistic propaganda is the natural, feminine desire for safety and security. Whether women are consciously aware of it or not, the feminine nature desires to be taken care of: physically and materially. This natural, feminine tendency makes the average woman easy psychological prey for communists and socialists because the underlying premise behind these ideologies is a promise that government is going to take care of them; thereby satisfying their craving for safety and security.

Unfortunately, very few feminine minds come to understand that the foolish pursuit of their safety and security by political proclamation requires the abdication of their physical security: the slavery they are selling themselves (and their families) into in order to acquire their fallaciously promised security.

> They who can give up essential liberty to obtain a little temporary safety deserve neither liberty nor safety.[5]
> — Benjamin Franklin

Even worse, fewer still are historically aware of the proven inability of socialistic and communistic governments to fulfill their promises to provide for the needs of its citizens; or of the forcible, violent, and bloody nature of communism. The exact opposite result of those promised by socialist and communist propagandists. Moreover, the natural inclination of the feminine nature toward vain sentiments and habits leads the feminine mind toward mental processes that are more egocentric and self-involved than the masculine nature, which tends to render the feminine mind much more inattentive regarding the dissipating consequences that subvert a society when it assumes the weakness of the feminine nature; rendering a feminized society much more vulnerable to subversion and attack from both domestic enemies and foreign intrigue.[6] Additionally, the "equalization" of men and women, via political declaration and cultural pressure, has proved to be one of the primary engines behind the dissolution of the family in modern times.

At its foundation, the delusion of gender equality has set up a social paradigm whereby men and women have become psychologically conditioned to act as "co-equal" competitors rather than cooperative partners in the family enterprise, which immediately provides a framework for constant friction within the family as man and wife disagree on particular matters that daily affect a family; each of them believing that their views are equal, and oftentimes superior, to those of their spouse; a certain source of constant

---

[5] http://www.brainyquote.com/quotes/quotes/b/benjaminfr136955.html, accessed 26 October, 2012.

[6] For example, the current "War on Terror" and the diluted will of the American people to stand and fight back firmly against the Islamic fundamentalists and their supporters and enablers within America: most of the print and television media.

pettiness and argumentativeness. Secondarily, the natural tendency of the feminine nature to pursue material and physical security offers up an implicit—however unintended it may be—vote of "no confidence" regarding the husband's ability to provide for the needs of the family; because by pursuing socialistic and communistic governmental policies and programs, the wife, by her actions, betrays an attitude of, "Just in case you can't care for us, it will be nice to have a 'safety net' in place to catch us if we fall." As a consequence of these factors, the rates of infidelity and divorce have commensurately increased with the acceleration of feminism and socialism within the prevailing cultures of Western civilization.

The existence of government programs to "take care of" (enslave) the average citizen has provided a perverted, corrupting "justification" for both men and women to abandon the sometimes unpleasant responsibilities associated with family life. Before socialistic and communistic governmental policies and programs became the norm within Western culture, the great majority of men and women persevered through difficult lives and marriages during periods in which family life sometimes became oppressive; not desiring the shame, self-loathing, or social castigation that would accompany the stigma of abandoning one's family, as well as potentially leaving them destitute. However, since the institution of Social Security, Welfare, Medicaid, Medicare, and all other similar programs; a new excuse has been provided to the morally weak within society. In their own minds, if a marriage and family become "too difficult" to continue on they can now abandon their families in the expectation that the government will take care of them; providing a ready-made outlet for the quicker, and easier, dissolution of families as the government is now available to step in as the family provider if one of the spouses decides to abandon their family.

To conclude, it is necessary to address a primary argument that has been used by feminists to forward their cause since the beginning of feminism . . . that fulfilling the role of a traditional woman—devoted wife and mother—is somehow "degrading" to women. This complaint is an unjustified attack on femininity and their own feminine nature: a demonstration of the self-hatred of the feminist. To consider any particular act or circumstance as degrading, two elements must be satisfied. The first element is that of willful and intentional humiliation. The particular act or circumstance must be purposefully designed by one person to diminish the dignity of another. The second element is that of consent. The party that is on the receiving end of a purposeful humiliation must consent to their humiliation. Without both elements being satisfied, a person cannot be made to forfeit their dignity, and hence, be degraded. The willful humiliation and degradation of another is a form of extremely malicious bullying.

If one party intentionally tries to humiliate another (for instance, when a feminist attempts to belittle and denigrate traditional women), but the intended target of humiliation refuses to consent to their degradation by conducting themselves in a dignified manner that exemplifies self-respect, the tables are actually turned on those who are attempting to degrade others; because when a person endures an unjustified attack and refuses to surrender their self-respect and dignity, the malicious intent of the accuser becomes much more readily apparent to impartial observers. In this manner, an unjust accuser is often exposed as the malicious bully that they truly are; while the intended target of humiliation preserves, and often times enhances, their aura of self-respect and personal dignity. Hence, by refusing consent to a false and unjust humiliation, the malicious person is exposed as a manipulative bully and actually degrades themselves via their undignified behavior.

The claim of feminists that the traditional role of women in society is "degrading" is an exemplification of consenting to a supposed humiliation, but in the absence of an identifiable party that is attempting to humiliate her; a very sad manifestation of self-hatred.[7] Before the advent of feminism, men and women for thousands of years both understood their respective, interdependent and complementary roles within society; and the members of each gender "played their part" in the propagation of the human race and the continuation of their particular society, more specifically. However, the advent of feminism brought forth a particular, socio-psychologically aberrant segment within society that decided—solely on the basis of their self-hatred—that the traditional, proven role of the female within society was "degrading"; thereby consenting to a humiliation that the feminist creates within her own mind!

The feminine nature *is not* degrading to women. It is only *apparently* degrading to the self-important pride and worldly ambitions of feminists; who despise their own gender and their traditional role within society. The feminine nature, as embodied by feminine women, *is* absolutely necessary in order to sustain civilization; as it is necessary for the feminine nature to temper many characteristics of the masculine nature, which would push civilization

---

[7] It is true that the feminist blames men specifically, and the masculine nature more generally, for their supposed humiliation and degradation; but this too can be seen as a false accusation. Men did not provide the female, or the feminine nature, with their relative weakness in relation to the masculine nature. This readily observed reality is a product of God's decree, or of nature, and no man can be held responsible for an objective reality that they had no participation in, or responsibility for, creating.

toward its own self-destruction if left unchecked. Moreover, the falsely derived complaints of feminists further demonstrate the infantilization of the human intellect. Just as small children complain to, and blame, their parents regarding unpleasant realities of life that the parents are not responsible for creating; the feminist complains to, and blames, men regarding unpleasant realities of life that men are not responsible for creating.

Traditional Sexual Morality vs. Promiscuity

A society that encourages traditional sexual morality is far superior to a promiscuous society; due to both what it encourages, as well as to what it suppresses. Having previously discussed the evil consequences of promiscuity, we'll instead focus on the beneficial consequences of adhering to traditional sexual morality: abstaining from sexual relations outside of marriage. The primary article to be most greatly encouraged in society is the family. The family unit is the foundational building block of any civilization. Participation in a family gives all within it both a sense of belonging to an enterprise greater than oneself, as well as teaching a sense of social responsibility to those within it; two articles that are beneficial to emotional health and instructive regarding how to live one's life responsibly and successfully; contributing to the propagation of both the individual family and the larger society within which one lives.

By abstaining from sexual relations outside of marriage it guarantees that all children are conceived within a traditional, nuclear family. This does not necessarily mean that all conceived children are planned and intended; as "accidents" still happen, even among married couples. It simply means that when the child is born, it is born into a family unit with both a mother and a father; providing the most advantageous environment for the development of the child. Moreover, a tremendous incidental advantage that is learned and reinforced from traditional sexual morality is fidelity to the spoken word. The marriage vows are meant to be taken seriously and for life. If people are able to persevere in faithfulness to their spouse during the course of their adult life, these same people will be much more likely to exercise that same faithfulness to their promises when dealing with other people outside the family; fostering trust, friendship, and unity within the society while providing for a sense of security and confidence. Additionally, it should also be understood that while a traditional code of sexual morality is constructive for society; it, by necessary implication, also suppresses the evils that result as a consequence of promiscuity: unwanted pregnancies, sexually transmitted diseases, etc.

Reproduction vs. Contraception and Abortion

The primary reason that artificial or pharmacological contraception should not be used is due to the perversion of understanding that it produces regarding the purpose of the sex act. Sexual relations have a purpose: the propagation of the human race. However, when contraception is used the person who uses it is directly attempting to circumvent the very purpose of the act they are engaging in. It's like people who plant a tree, but then as soon as they are finished with the planting process, dig up that tree and burn it. Within a rational context, this is completely irrational, but within an affective (emotional) context it can be seen that the purpose of the sex act has been largely forgotten or abandoned by the human race in deference to more profligate motives, and this reality has been greatly exacerbated by the profusion of contraception. Instead of viewing the sex act in its proper context and function, people in this age have been seduced into pursuing sexual relations for purely sensual motives: merely as a pursuit to satiate a physical urge, and as a form of diversionary entertainment, rather than as a purposeful act intended for the propagation of the human race.

Look to the great damage this does to both individuals and our society. By replacing the true purpose of the sex act (reproduction) with a counterfeit purpose (sensual gratification) we are only greatly encouraging the socially dissolute consequences that result—promiscuity, marital infidelity, homosexuality, and all other aberrant behaviors of a sexually motivated nature—and the cascading chain of evil consequences that arise from licentiousness. Contraception, including abortion, is a catalyst that promotes loose morals and irresponsible behavior; because when it is used it gives those who use it a false sense of safety: the belief that because they are using contraception any limits on their behavior are thereby lifted and they can engage in sexual relations as often as they like, and with whomever they like, without any fear of unwanted consequences, such as pregnancy or disease; many ignorant people believing that contraceptive techniques will also protect them against sexually-transmitted diseases. Of course, this is a completely false sense of security, and it has only accrued to the creation of large numbers of illegitimate children and the propagation of all manners of sexually-transmitted diseases. Sadly, the most vulnerable to this type of warped understanding are children—especially teens—who are young enough in years and understanding to be ignorant of the real-life consequences of their irresponsible behavior, while thinking themselves wise and invulnerable.

And finally, consider this. The human race is rapidly descending into a mentality of chasing after the hedonistic gratification of sensual pleasures without an understanding or appreciation of the damaging and evil consequences that result. This being the case, how can we then discern any difference between the mentality of the modern human race and that of irrational animals? They also run about blindly, in pursuit of gratifying instinctual passions without contemplating the consequences of their actions. However, the irrational animals are not at fault for their situation. They are not able to reason and understand the consequences of their instinctual impulses. Human beings, on the other hand, do possess the gift of reason and are able to understand the consequences of the things they do. With this being the case, what does it say about the human race if we understand the damage we are doing to ourselves, yet continue to choose doing them anyway? It is nothing less than mass insanity: a form of willful, social suicide.

Heterosexuality vs. Homosexuality

Having already discussed the dangers of homosexuality to both the homosexual as well as to the larger society; the primary point to emphasize, as it relates to the propagation and maintenance of human civilizations, is that of the dissolute effect of homosexuality on the society. As homosexuality increases within a society, the rate of reproduction will begin to decline; eventually being unable to sustain or defend itself, especially when coming under attack from a foreign aggressor. This same effect is currently being witnessed in today's Western Europe; as immigrant populations from antagonistic—primarily Islamic—cultures have taken up residence within it and have begun to overtake the Western European nations through reproduction rather than through the force of arms. The end result will be that the refusal or inability of the population to mature and reproduce will lead to their own self-destruction by a foreign, conquering power.

Sobriety vs. Drug Abuse

The dangers of drug abuse to society are readily manifest, as both the guilty and the innocent are destroyed by it every day. The most visible indicator is the large numbers of people who use some form of drug, either legal or illegal, and then proceed to operate an automobile or some other form of dangerous equipment. Predictably, this behavior concludes in numerous, otherwise innocent people, losing their life due to the impaired mental faculties caused by the drugs. Another manifestation lies in the emergency rooms of just about every urban hospital, especially in the late evenings, as "partiers" are brought in for treatment due to an overdose of some type of drug. The most pitiable and heart-breaking cases die in solitude; looking for just a little "fix" to get them through their difficulties, while not realizing that this particular time they took just a little too much of their chosen palliative. These are the direct and immediate dangers from drug abuse.

The secondary danger from drug abuse, which is almost completely overlooked by most all people (especially the users), is the unknown secondary effects of their reaction within the brain, which are just as damaging to society over time as the immediate effects. This is most especially the case with any type of psychoactive drug (legal or illicit), as these drugs have the effect of changing human behavior by altering human perception. Within the past generation, it has become increasingly popular for modern parents to drug their children into docility as an alternative to discipline. The extraordinary danger of drugging our children into submission is that nobody truly understands the long-term physiological and psychological effects that these drugs have on the human mind. It has been reported that many children have suffered increases in the incidence and intensity of homicidal and suicidal thoughts after beginning their use, and likewise experience a reduction after discontinuing their use. Moreover, this type of side effect is not limited to children, but adults as well.

Every person's physical constitution is different. This makes the long-term effects of drug use impossible to predict; as their effect on the brain of the user will be unique within each individual. However, one thing is certain about their use that cannot be forgotten. The use of psychotropic drugs will change the consciousness and perception of the user. If that person had been somewhat sane when they began using drugs, it is an absolute certainty that their drug use will fundamentally alter their brain; perverting their perception away from a cognitively sane state and leaving them in a more psychotic condition. Moreover, the more drugs a person uses, and for a greater amount of time, the greater the likelihood is that they will descend into a more severely psychotic condition, even while not experiencing the immediate effects (i.e. being high), due to the unknown long-term changes that psychotropic drugs cause within the human brain.

The Device(s) Used to Regress Us to Our Current State of Cultural Barbarism

How is it that so many people are allowing themselves to be subjugated and manipulated toward their own ruination? Sadly, the easily understood (albeit unpleasant) answer is that they have been psychologically conditioned to their prevailing life circumstances for all their lives! They simply cannot conceive of any other existence than the one they are living today; not having any experience or frame of reference from which to conceive of an alternate reality or way of life. Very few people have ever known anything different from what they are today and what they see on the surface of their everyday lives. They either do not, or cannot, conceive of a better way of life, and a better world, because the great majority of people in today's world have been rendered suicidally confused and ignorant via the combined effects of a multitude of factors; the most damaging being the intentional corruption of minds that has been taking place in the various manifestations of "public education"—courtesy of the National Education Association (NEA): the teacher's union that steers and defines the curriculum being taught in modern government schools—for the past several generations.

Having chronicled our regression to the sad state we are suffered to live in today, and so that the average person can defend themselves against the techniques that have been, and are still being, used to corrupt humanity to its current, narcissistically depraved level; it is important to understand the primary technique used to facilitate the corruption of human understanding: the deliberate corruption and manipulation of language, which returns us to the principle of the "lawyering" of reality: compromising principles through the use of dialectics in order to manipulate and change human perception.

> Abuse of words has been the great instrument of sophistry and chicanery, of party, faction, and division of society.[1]
> — John Adams

---

[1] http://www.brainyquote.com/quotes/quotes/j/johnadams134172.html, accessed November 24, 2007.

> Great ambition, the desire of real superiority, of leading
> and directing, seems to be altogether peculiar to man, and
> speech is the great instrument of ambition.[2]
> — Adam Smith, Scottish economist and author of *The
> Wealth of Nations*

It is even more certain of a truth in today's world than it was in John Adams' day. The corruption of language in order to manipulate the understanding of the citizen is the primary means by which people can be turned against others, and even their own self-interest. The great success of this tactic is evident by the numerous people in today's world who have been deceived into feeling guilt for things they are not guilty of and even turning people against one another and the best interests of their own families and the larger society. Furthermore, modern Western civilization has been manipulated into not only tolerating, but gladly accepting and complying with, ideas and behaviors directly opposed to the interests of the citizen, their families, and the larger family of their society via this deceitful tactic. To understand how language can, and in a great many cases is, used as a manipulative element requires an understanding of the nature of language: what it is, and how it is possible to manipulate it in order to facilitate a destructive, self-serving end.

At its core, language is the *only* vehicle by which a person can communicate to others their internal thoughts and share ideas among one another. It is the most efficient and commonly used means to transport ideas from one mind to another. Since language is the primary vehicle used to transmit ideas, it is then necessary to corrupt the language in order to corrupt the ideas transmitted to others via language. This is the methodology Mr. Orwell was trying to warn humanity about through his fictional allegory: "Every concept that can ever be needed will be expressed by exactly *one* word, with its meaning rigidly defined and all its subsidiary meanings rubbed out and forgotten . . . Every year fewer and fewer words, and the range of consciousness always a little smaller . . . The Revolution will be complete when the language is perfect."

This process of corrupting language and ideas is directly analogous to the transmission of viral agents between people. A sick person transmits a virus to a healthy person through the exchange of a common article; such as a glass of water or the air they breathe in proximity to each other. Once the virus is transmitted to the healthy person it then causes the healthy person

---

[2] http://iperceptive.com/quote/73.html, accessed January 8, 2014.

to become diseased, as well as making him an agent of transmission for the particular disease he is infected with. Likewise, a mentally ill person with a diseased mind transmits a corruptive idea to others through the exchange of the common vehicle of language. Once the sick and corruptive idea is passed on, it infects the mind of the recipient and causes their mind to become diseased, as well as making them an agent of transmission for the corruptive idea.

The ability of the self-servingly clever to mislead so many people is a consequence of the very *inexact* nature of language. Many words have more than one meaning. The manipulation of the public is effectively played out when a person's words are either taken out of context or the meaning implied is purposefully misrepresented by their ideological opponents in order to imply a more sinister connotation than was intended by the original author or speaker.

When someone uses any particular word—let's call it *"The Word"*—to explain their ideas and beliefs to others they intend to convey their ideas to the public under a particular definition of *The Word*. Their ideological opponents hear the use of *The Word* and immediately try to discredit them by applying a different definition or connotation of *The Word* than was actually intended by the person who spoke.

> If you can bear to hear the truth you've spoken twisted by
> knaves to make a trap for fools . . .
> — Rudyard Kipling, from his poem *If*

To understand the purpose and ability of language is to understand that language can and will be used to either lift humanity up or beat it down under the boot of the malevolent and self-servingly clever. People who strive to lift humanity up from their current level of ignorance will always be attacked and vilified because those with a vested interest in keeping humanity ignorant (the great majority of politicians, lawyers, social activists and agitators, numerous "journalists," "educators" administering the government school systems, etc.) are threatened with both the loss of their revenue source and their stature within society if the truth of the situation were to be understood by the greater population.

Let's now look at some of the most flagrant and intentional abuses of language currently being used to propagate suicidal perversions throughout our culture. The public is often lectured to that we need to show more tolerance, less discrimination, and strive for equality for all peoples. That sounds idealistically altruistic on the surface, doesn't it? However, when the implications of such propaganda are examined the danger of accepting such ideas will become apparent. When words are bent, broken, and misused to the point that they are made to imply something they should not—more precisely, when they are used to browbeat the listeners by those who wish to reduce their audience to a slavish, dependent, and self-loathing state—they take on an entirely different connotation. To understand what the creatures who propagate such insanity are truly trying to do to our nation and society requires that we look to what the concepts of tolerance, discrimination, and equality actually mean; and then demonstrate how these words are purposefully misused to propagate a corrupted understanding throughout our society.

Let's look at the definitions of tolerance, discrimination, discriminate, equality, and equal[3] to demonstrate the corruption:

1) Tolerance: **1**: capacity to endure pain or hardship : ENDURANCE, FORTITUDE, STAMINA
   2 a : sympathy or indulgence for beliefs or practices differing from or conflicting with one's own **b** : the act of allowing something : TOLERATION
   3 : the allowable deviation from a standard; *esp* : the range of variation permitted in maintaining a specified dimension in machining a piece
   4 a (1) : the capacity of the body to endure or become less responsive to a substance (as a drug) or a physiological insult esp. with repeated use or exposure <developed a ~ to painkillers>; *also* : the immunological state marked by unresponsiveness to a specific antigen (2) : relative capacity of an organism to grow or thrive when subjected to an unfavorable environmental factor **b** : the maximum amount of a pesticide residue that may lawfully remain on or in food

2) Discrimination: **1 a** : the act of discriminating **b** : the process by which two stimuli differing in some aspect are responded to differently
   2 : the quality or power of finely distinguishing
   3 a : the act, practice, or an instance of discriminating categorically rather than individually **b** : prejudiced or prejudicial outlook, action, or treatment <racial ~>
   syn see DISCERNMENT

---

3   Merriam-Webster's Collegiate Dictionary. 11th Ed. Versailles, Kentucky, 2012.

3) Discriminate: *transitive verb*

1 a : to mark or perceive the distinguishing or peculiar features of **b** : **DISTINGUISH, DIFFERENTIATE** <~ hundreds of colors>
2 : to distinguish by discerning or exposing differences; *esp* : to distinguish from another like object
intransitive verb
1 a : to make a distinction <~ among historical sources> **b :** to use good judgment
2 : to make a difference in treatment or favor on a basis other than individual merit <~ in favor of your friends>
<~ against a certain nationality>

4) Equality: **1 :** the quality or state of being equal
2 : EQUATION 2a

5) Equal: **1 a** (1) : of the same measure, quantity, amount, or number as another (2) : identical in mathematical value or logical denotation : EQUIVALENT **b :** like in quality, nature, or status **c :** like for each member of a group, class, or society <provide ~ employment opportunities>
2 : regarding or affecting all objects in the same way : IMPARTIAL
3 : free from extremes: as **a :** tranquil in mind or mood **b :** not showing variation in appearance, structure, or proportion
4 a : capable of meeting the requirements of a situation or a task **b :** SUITABLE <bored with work not ~ to his abilities>
syn see SAME

Modern politicians and social agitators tell us, "We have to be tolerant of our differences." When they speak in such a manner they are trying to imply that the definition of the word tolerance, as they use it, is according to definition '2 a': *sympathy or indulgence for beliefs or practices differing from or conflicting with one's own.* This may be true to a certain, limited extent; but there must be limits to the things any nation and its people will tolerate: tolerating cosmetically different practices while rejecting demonstrably evil and self-destructive ones. Moreover, the reality that this world is constantly undergoing a battle between good and evil—this singular truth being abundantly demonstrated throughout human history, and being especially self-evident in today's world—must always be kept at the forefront of human consciousness while attempting to *discriminate* (under definition '2' of discrimination: *the quality or power of finely distinguishing*) between what may be tolerated and what must not be tolerated. To say that people must be universally tolerant of other's differences imposes a social paradigm of absolute amorality: a tacit toleration and acceptance of evil as well as of good, as if good and evil were morally equivalent and had an equal right of acceptance within society: an insane idea.

This is exactly how so many evil, dissolute, and suicidal practices and ideas have crept into the fabric of our culture (homosexuality, abortion, promiscuity, and others). Moreover, such an idea is not only patently false, it is the moral obligation of the sane members of society to actively work to extirpate the evils and promote the good within our culture; in the interests of the health and long-term viability of our society, and of those who compose it; which requires the citizens within a society to *discriminate* (finely distinguish and discern) between good and evil by honestly assessing the objective consequences of any idea or behavior and actively oppose those that are harmful, while promoting those that are healthy to the sustenance of the society. Notice also definition '1' of tolerance: *capacity to endure pain or hardship.*

The reader should note that as a greater level of perversion and reprobation is being propagated throughout our culture, the tolerance of the sane within society (under definition '1') is being sorely, and unnecessarily, tested. The narcissistically seditious, revolutionary element within the U.S. is fond of pontificating that if one isn't tolerant of the wholesale destruction of American culture that is taking place from within, that they are intolerant; and they make this assertion implying a negative connotation. Again, they use the word tolerance and attempt (with great success to date) to make the public believe that any resistance to their perversion(s) and the bending and breaking of our heritage of individual freedom, personal responsibility, liberty, and Judeo-Christian principles is "intolerant," under the implication that those who are "intolerant" of perversion and insanity are not accepting of simple differences and a "diversity" of viewpoints; but for this to be a true characterization of the case, which it most certainly is not, would require a situation of moral and consequential equivalence between the ideas and behaviors in question. Let the reader answer the question for themselves. Are the objective consequences of patriarchy as opposed to feminism, or promiscuity as opposed to abstinence, identical? What about between abortion and birth . . . the homosexual and the heterosexual . . . the drug user and the sober?

The consequences of these ideas and behaviors are objectively opposed to each other; such that some tend toward the construction and sustenance of a civilization (good: patriarchy, abstinence, birth, heterosexuality, and sobriety) while the others work toward the objective destruction of a civilization (evil: feminism, promiscuity, abortion, homosexuality, and drug abuse). Contrary to the manner in which the modern liberal mocks the culturally intolerant, it is just such an intolerance of self-destructively suicidal ideas and practices that is not only healthy and necessary for the sustenance of our civilization; but is also the moral duty of every sane human being: to oppose everything objectively evil and self-destructive while promoting everything objectively constructive to society.

Naturally, if we are to determine what we should, or should not, tolerate as a society, it becomes necessary for us to be able to discern the objective consequences between two opposing ideas or practices. In short, we must be *discriminating*, in the sense of definition '1 b' of the intransitive verb *discriminate* (to use good judgment). We must use good judgment and distinguish between the maleficent or beneficent consequences of opposing ideas and practices. The manipulation of the words discrimination and discriminate demonstrate the nature of the deception. Any time that any political pressure group believes they can forward their self-serving political agenda by inciting and enflaming emotions to their benefit they will invoke the word *discrimination* for a two-fold purpose. First, they use it as a call-to-arms to the ignorant and uneducated masses they are addressing: those who are myopically tuned to forwarding their own self-serving agendas while ignoring the greater good of the whole of society. Second, they use this sophistical tactic to confuse and psychologically bind their political and ideological opposition. It has thus far proved to be a very effective tactic, which is why it is so commonly used today. However, let's look to some easily understood examples to understand why it is absolutely necessary for people to discriminate; in the sense of discerning and distinguishing between different articles under examination.

Consider the case of several beverages presented to a person for consumption that contain the following: (1) hemlock, (2) cyanide, (3) arsenic, and (4) orange juice. Only one of the drinks offered supports human health and life. The other three are deadly toxins. The danger to the individual presented with these beverages is readily apparent by the objective consequences that follow as a result of consuming either of the four: three of them leading to death, and only one leading to sustained or improved health. To ensure their continued health, the person presented with these four choices must *discriminate* between them: accepting the only healthy choice while positively rejecting the other fatal choices. In the current age, the word discriminate is abused by professional social agitators to impart a perception among the public of definition '2' of the intransitive verb (*to make a difference in treatment or favor on a basis other than individual merit*); purposefully implying an unjustified foundation for discrimination based on an inherent bigotry. These self-interested creatures make it their business to force themselves on society for no greater reason than because they want preferential treatment and protection within society, which is itself a perverted irony; because those people or groups who complain about discrimination are themselves asking—even demanding—that people discriminate against others in their favor.

Applying the principle of discrimination to the above example, let's extend it and consider a scenario that bears a closer resemblance to reality. A school board is charged with determining what food products can be offered within their school district. At first, the obvious, simple choice is made and orange juice is allowed to be included in the school menu, while beverages laced with Hemlock, Cyanide, and Arsenic are dismissed out-of-hand due to their toxicity. One would think that the end of an easy decision process had been reached. However, members of the Hemlock Society allege discrimination during the selection process when their offering to the school menu is rejected. They hire the American Civil Liberties Union (ACLU) and file a civil rights lawsuit against the school board for discrimination; insinuating definition '2' of the intransitive verb: *to make a difference in treatment or favor on a basis other than individual merit*.

During the court proceedings, the school board administrators are deposed under oath and asked the direct question by an ACLU attorney, "Did you knowingly discriminate against my client's submission (Hemlock) to the school menu"? Being under oath, the administrator answers truthfully, "Of course we discriminated against Hemlock"; intending that the word discriminate would be understood within the context of definition '1 a' of the transitive verb: *to mark or perceive the distinguishing or peculiar features of.* The ACLU however, having successfully perverted and confused the meaning of the word *discriminate*, then returns to the court and claims, "The school board openly admits that they discriminated against my client. Therefore, your honor, we request a $50 million judgment against them: $20 million to be distributed to the ACLU as compensation for their legal representation of the Hemlock Society, $5 million to the Hemlock Society for the psychological pain and suffering caused by the school board's callous disregard for their feelings, and $25 million to establish an educational fund that will be used to raise public awareness regarding the evils of Hemlock discrimination by developing curricula within the public school systems and empowering our children to eradicate Hemlock discrimination from within our society." Does this scenario sound ludicrous or comical to the reader? It is not. This is exactly what has been transpiring within our society for the last several decades. Let's change the names in the preceding example so as to more easily recognize the guilty.

Under the guise of "diversity," the deviant and dissolute, socially suicidal evils of promiscuity, abortion, homosexuality, and transsexuality are being taught to our nation's children as optional "lifestyle choices." Through sex education curricula, young school children are taught just about all the mechanical and biological aspects of human reproduction. After their immersion in this material, the culture within the schools, as well as at home via a television culture that markets most everything through sexual references and innuendo, encourages children to "explore their sexuality" and experiment with sex (including homosexuality) in order to give the child the basis of experience necessary to make an "informed" choice regarding their sexual preferences. The false representation is that choosing between a life as a homosexual or as a heterosexual family person results in similar consequences to both the individual and society; and is as morally and consequentially relevant as deciding between fish or chicken for dinner. "Responsible" instruction in sex-ed naturally includes information on contraceptive techniques: how to obtain and use oral contraception, how to use condoms, and how to procure an abortion if the child becomes pregnant.

Those people who decry and oppose the abject perversion that is taking over our society through the indoctrination and corruption of our children in the government school systems, under the cover of sex-ed curricula, are derided as being "bigoted" because they desire to abolish this point of entry within the schools for all manners of perversion that are turning the nation's children into little more than sexual animals; especially when such curricula is only used as a cover for the encouragement of practically every type of dangerous and sexually deviant behavior that is individually dissolute, suicidal to the child, and self-destructive to the greater society as a whole. Additionally, in order to combat the "discriminatory bigotry" within society, as the proponents of perverting our children would characterize it, school-sponsored clubs are beginning to emerge as support groups for homosexual and transgendered schoolchildren and to "raise awareness" of homosexual and transgendered children; an obvious attempt to pervert young and impressionable minds at as early an age as possible.

The reader must reconcile the following question in their minds and consciences, "In principle, how are any of the above scenarios different from one another"? The specific details of the scenario may vary from case to case, but at the foundation of each scenario lays a basic choice between choosing behaviors and practices that lead to health and life, and those that lead to dissolution and death. With each progressive scenario, all that has changed are the details of the example. This was done as a method of transitioning from the hypothetical to the real, while demonstrating a consistent principle: the conscious choice between life and death. As the examples progressed from the purely hypothetical to the real it is important to note that the availability of healthy options was impeded, and then removed entirely. In the original, hypothetical scenario orange juice was offered as an option that was healthy. In the subsequent, hypothetical scenario the healthy option was originally considered the only acceptable offering, but a suicidal option was forced on the schools, and the rest of society, by the ACLU and a complicit legal system. In the final, real scenario, there are no longer any healthy options being taught or encouraged within our society; a self-destructive reality taking place all throughout the country every day and in very many schools. Most all the "options" being presented to our society today by way of our popular media culture, and especially to our children through our government school systems, are dissolute and deadly to both the citizens and the society as a whole.

All the individually and socially healthy options—abstinence, a family-centered society, and the necessity to choose life over murder in the event of an unwanted pregnancy—are mocked by modern society's reprobated culture. As a society, we began treading this road toward materialistic and nihilistic corruption several generations ago; when the progressive corruption of the nation's children was instituted by perverse reprobates who began corrupting the society by corrupting the children in the public school systems of the nation. These insane creatures hate those life choices that lead to health and life of the individual and society because such choices require the citizens to exercise self-control, self-denial, and personal responsibility for their actions; principles that are completely contrary to the undisciplined, voluptuous culture that the West has been progressively seduced into becoming. As a result of the encroaching corruption over the last century or more, there is rarely an analogical equivalent of orange juice being promoted within modern America (and the rest of the West): a cultural promotion of ideas and practices that lead to the maintenance and health of both the whole of society and the individuals who constitute it.

The final concept to examine regarding the abuse of language is that of equality.

> Democracy and socialism have nothing in common but one word, equality. But notice the difference: while democracy seeks equality in liberty, socialism seeks equality in restraint and servitude.[4]
> — Alexis de Tocqueville

> There is in fact a manly and legitimate passion for equality that spurs all men to wish to be strong and esteemed. This passion tends to elevate the lesser to the rank of the greater. But one also finds in the human heart a depraved taste for equality, which impels the weak to want to bring the strong down to their level, and which reduces men to preferring equality in servitude to inequality in freedom.[5]
> — Alexis de Tocqueville

This puts me in the very peculiar position of having to defend one idea while refuting another. The peculiarity arises from the fact that both ideas are represented by the same word: equality. The key to understanding these two very different ideas is within the way the concept of equality is applied. If we are to understand these differences we must first acknowledge the reality that amongst the human race the possibility of true equality is an absolute fallacy. No two human beings are alike. Therefore, there are no two people in this world (including identical twins) who are legitimately each other's equals, in conformance with definition '1 b' of equal: *like in quality, nature, or status.* Just consider what it means to be equal. It means that two people would not only have to be alike or similar, but *exactly* the same. In mathematics, the equation is simple; $3 + 3 = 4 + 2 = 5 + 1$, because the resultant sum of these numerical representations are not only similar, but exactly the same. This is the beauty and elegance of mathematics. There is a right and a wrong answer to every problem. It is a purely objective science, devoid of any "gray" areas that lend themselves to rhetorical manipulation.

---

[4] http://www.brainyquote.com/quotes/quotes/a/alexisdeto135752.html, accessed November 28, 2007.
[5] De Tocqueville, *Democracy In America*, 60.

There are too many innumerable differences between human beings for two to ever be the same, or equal; variances in religion, morality, language, temperament, judgment, work ethic, intelligence, life philosophy and worldview, strength (either psychological or physical), and many other manners in which people are different. With so many different variables working simultaneously within every person, with each characteristic contributing to the formation of the personality and character of each person, it should be easy to comprehend how no person can be another's equal; even in a world full of billions of people.

Understanding this reality, how then can people ever utter a word about being "equals"? The sad answer is that the vulgar (uneducated, ignorant, or indolent) masses embrace such an idea because it serves the material self-interest of the weak and unproductive to claim they are the "equals" of the strong and productive. What Alexis de Tocqueville observed was the application of equality from two opposite perspectives: that of the greater mass of society being all equally vulgar and debauched, where the vulgar attempt to drag the lofty into the ditch with them; or of the greater mass of society aspiring to improve themselves and rise above their current situation or station in life, where the lofty attempt to lift the vulgar and debauched out of their ditch.

The key to remaining free from emotional and psychological manipulation is in understanding the particular context under discussion, while refusing to allow a clever sophist to exchange, admix, pervert, and confuse the context; from one, to another of a dissimilar nature. An excellent example of the perversion of the concept(s) of equality is in the perversion of the ideas which built the United States; from a nobler conception to a base and self-serving interpretation. When discussing the idea of equality the modern basis of the discussion, in large part, often falls back to the Declaration of Independence, and its famous assertion, "We hold these truths to be self-evident: that all men are created equal: that they are endowed by their Creator with certain unalienable rights: that among these are life, liberty, and the pursuit of happiness . . ."

Thomas Jefferson conveys to the reader "that all men are *created* equal." In truth, all people are created equal; from the standpoint that we are all equally "blank pages" waiting to be filled up with life experiences and actions. What is to be noted is what happens to people after they are born. As they emerge from the womb they have no preconceived prejudices whatsoever. After they are born, the process of differentiation from others begins. This is also where the sadness begins, because depending into what family a child is born, so also their character is born.

Let's look at the extremes to demonstrate the point. A child born to parents who are members of the KKK, the NAACP, La Raza, or any other organization or ideology which inculcates within its members a separatist mentality amongst its members will undoubtedly be conditioned by their parents to propagate their particular bigotry. In short, they will be indoctrinated by their parents to be evil creatures from the moment of their birth. On the other hand, a child who grows up in a home where they are truly loved; taught personal responsibility and accountability for their actions; respect for their parents and proper, adult authority; the value of a good work ethic; who learn to differentiate between good and evil through the consistent exercise of discipline; and are taught to be self-controlled, stands to have a much greater chance of excelling in this life in both the constructive things they bring to society as well as in their personal pursuits.

Some people are born into such a situation that a decent education is not available to them. Others have the finest of teachers and opportunities to extend themselves, their learning, and their wisdom from an early age. While it may be true that all are created equal—within a moral context—it must be understood that from the day of our birth, and going forward, we begin to differentiate ourselves from others depending on the lessons we have been taught by life experience, our individual talents, and the way we choose to apply those lessons and talents; either for good or for evil.

What Mr. Jefferson asserted is a form of moral equality; that no person is better or superior to another simply by reason of their social station at birth. The child of poor, "common" parents is not inferior to that of wealthy, "noble" parents. From the context of the passage, as it directly refers to rights granted to man by God, it is easy to see that what Jefferson was discussing was a moral concept that lied within the context of natural law. What Jefferson asserted was a negation of the European, monarchical sense of nobility: that some people deserved certain privileges, and others were refused them, solely based upon their parentage or "station" in life. This can also be more clearly understood as the sentiment of the Founding Fathers when it is also observed that a similar safeguard was written in to our Constitution; in Article 1, Section 9: "No title of nobility shall be granted by the United States: and no person holding any office of profit or trust under them, shall, without the consent of the Congress, accept of any present, emolument, office, or title, of any kind whatever, from any king, prince, or foreign state."

128

The colonists of Jefferson's day were particularly sensitive on this topic, because this was one of the primary excuses used by King George III to justify his impositions on the colonies: that he was the king, and as such was superior to the colonists, who owed him obedience as lesser subjects in relation to himself; thereby self-justifying any impositions that he may choose to impose on the colonies. What the idea of moral equality, within the context of natural law, ultimately distills down to is a sense of *impartiality* under the law. The poor, anonymous beggars deserve the same consideration in justice as the wealthy or famous. It should in no way be interpreted that all men are truly "equals" or that they should in any way enjoy equal social status in society, or under the law, for the duration of their lives.

Some people choose to be mass murderers, while others choose a life of sincerely devoted service to others. Because of this reality, we do not treat the mass murderers, child molesters, and other human predators the same (equally) as the saintly and socially constructive; nor should we. While we may be created equal, the choices we make and the actions we take in life distinguish us from one another.

When today's social agitators speak of equality they frame their argument(s) so as to portray a very narrow, materialistic understanding of equality; where they forward the idea that everybody should have the same amount of material wealth, while falsely implying that definition '2' (*regarding or affecting all objects in the same way*: impartiality) of *equal* is being violated. The insinuation is that those people or groups they are advocating for are not being treated impartially because they aren't as materially successful as they believe they should be. Such arguments are meant to have such a strong emotional impact that the average, unsuspecting person will circumvent their rational faculties and be deceived by the propaganda. In the modern world, equality has primarily come to be understood as a materialistic equality of wealth distribution across the whole of society; and any socio-economic group of people falling below the average are said to be *discriminated* against and are characterized as being deprived of their *equal* rights; as if some average amount of income is somebody's right, whether they have earned it or not. Such creatures are those who are animated by the sentiments that Alexis de Tocqueville warned against: those with "a depraved taste for equality, which impels the weak to want to bring the strong down to their level . . ."

The fallacious nature of materialistic equality is in its hypocrisy and the necessity to use overtly discriminatory treatment on a massive scale to enforce it. The producers must be discriminated against in favor of the unproductive; and within the sphere of ideas, a form of moral equality must be forced on society; a manifestly clear contradiction of equality in the sense of impartiality. To illustrate the point, let's refer back to our above scenarios regarding discriminating (*marking or perceiving the distinguishing or peculiar features*) between life and death choices. The objectively real consequences of homosexuality, promiscuity, and abortion are completely opposed to those of heterosexuality, abstinence, and childbirth. As a result, they cannot be rightly described as morally, or consequentially, *equal* choices; dependent solely on personal preferences. One group leads to death, and the other leads to life; thereby demonstrating the contradiction that the modern reprobate embodies when trying to sell their deadly perversion(s) to the rest of the world by demanding *equal*, or even preferential, consideration and treatment; because demanding equal or preferential treatment in relation to their practices is to say that death is equal, or even preferable, to life: a *clearly* insane proposition! Moreover, demanding preferential consideration, a tactic the modern reprobate now pursues through legislative and political action—to the desired elimination of his ideological adversaries—clearly contradicts their demands for *equality*, when they aspire to deny it to their opposition: a situation that demonstrates the modern reprobate's extraordinary, self-contradictory hypocrisy.

Finally, it is absolutely critical to understand that the perversion of our world, and the destruction of the observance of objectively real consequences for one's actions, has been attained by perverting the understanding of the average citizen through the intentional perversion of language. This destructive reality has been actuated via the purposeful misrepresentation and confusion of the meanings of words: demonstrating the incredible power of language to control whole societies; especially when purposefully used to pervert and deceive. Moreover, what has simultaneously exacerbated our society's downward path is the steady decline in our education system. With each passing decade, as our citizenry has become less and less educated over the past century, the ability of the average citizen to discern these linguistic tricks and confusion of principles has been reduced accordingly; so that as time has passed, fewer and fewer educated and understanding people remain to warn their fellow citizens regarding how the society has been, and continues to be, corrupted; moving the society ever closer to the point of collapse, while the average citizen remains ignorant of the threat(s).

Most of the citizens of the United States are blind to both politics and human nature. Most people appear to believe that their elected representatives (including the President) actually care about serving their best interests and those of our nation. In actuality, the understanding of politics and human nature are conjoined, because politicians are—in a general sense—much more understanding and attentive to human nature than the general public. The essence of modern (early Twenty-First Century) politics, properly understood, has been debased to the point that it has now become the art of manipulating the electorate based on a particular politician's understanding of human nature; with the politicians who possess the greatest understanding rising to the top of the political pack via the most cunning use of deceitful rhetoric.

Before our culture and language was so horribly mangled, there were once words to describe political leaders; especially those holding public office who were truly animated by sentiments of acting in the public's best interest. These words were "statesman" and "statesmanship." There are practically no statesmen left in the government of the United States, nor in any other Western government for that matter. There seem to be only puppets, and their associated puppeteers, remaining who are ardently pursuing the myopic goal of winning us over to the realization of their foolishly vain "greatness." Their intellectual arrogance and vanity condemns both themselves and our society for trusting in them instead of trusting in ourselves and our own abilities and potential to actuate our own lives.

The word used today that describes the pursuit of the manipulation of the public mind is "spin." Politicians think to themselves, "How can I *spin* this turn of events"? The word spin is a euphemism for crafting a believable lie. Most modern politicians spend their nights and days ruminating over how they can manipulate language and human perception so as to turn any event in public life to their favor. They are not constrained by the pedantic and sophomoric (in their minds) considerations of good or evil. Their only care is to persuade you to: (1) see their political position as the "enlightened way," and (2) develop an allegiance to their person: a promotion of their own "cult of personality."

There is a connection between the misleading abuse of the words tolerance and discrimination that stands out to expose the horrible cruelty of those who hate the founding principles of America and the ideals of individual freedom, liberty and personal responsibility. What the citizens of the United States need to realize is that they must be selective and discriminating (i.e. discerning; in the sense of definition '1 a' of the intransitive verb discriminate: *to make a distinction*) regarding what they are willing to tolerate (according to definition '3' of tolerance: *the allowable deviation from a standard*). Yes, as difficult as the realization may be, we must use good judgment and make distinctions. What is tolerable to *our* citizens and what is not? Many people, myself among them, make the simple observation that those who champion "ultra-tolerance" are the most intolerant (according to definition '2 a' of tolerance: *sympathy or indulgence for beliefs or practices differing from or conflicting with one's own*) among us.

They have no sympathy or indulgence for those who believe in God, stand up for the higher principles of liberty and the individual, or those who denounce liberalism, socialism, and communism as degenerate ideologies and prove it through simple reason, logic, and the observance of historical examples that demonstrate their evil consequences. Most all of them have a hidden agenda to promote everything perverted. The reason why the "ultra-tolerant" are so intolerant themselves is because they wish to freely practice their perversions and degeneracy in the light of day, and are fighting for a world where anything goes and we are all "free" of the chains of self-restraint, self-discipline, morality, and objective reality. This is a recipe for anarchy and mass murder. The arrogance of the "ultra-tolerant" is breathtaking. They appoint themselves as the torchbearers of progress; referring to themselves as "progressives." However, it's up to the remaining, sane people within society to ask the following: "What are we *progressing* our society and nation toward: Utopia or a Hell on Earth"? Simply turn on the daily news and the frightening answer is evident to all.

Why We Have Regressed to Our Current, Sad State?

The answer to this question can be easily comprehended, but it will also give rise to great sadness and consternation; because, whether the reader wants to realize it or not, the average "work-a-day" man and woman of this world has allowed it to come to pass through a combination of moral cowardice, willful ignorance, and apathy; beaten into psychological submission through the application of the Hegelian Dialectic over the past several centuries. Directly to the point, we have come to this current, sad state because there are certain people in this world who expressly desire it to be so! They see themselves as superior to the common man:[1] intellectually, morally, spiritually, physically, or in all these aspects.

All people should understand that for a certain few there beats within their breast the desire to rule the world: an ever-present hunger within the heart to rule over others; believing that their personal "greatness" should command respect, awe, and obedience from the "great, unwashed masses." Such delusions of grandeur direct these creatures toward pursuing professions that will put them into a position of realizing their self-asserted "greatness." As it applies to the modern world, they are naturally attracted toward the fields of law and politics; so as to have the greatest effect on the largest number of people. These creatures are incredibly astute. They have seen that over the course of human existence it has been demonstrated time and again that people naturally rebel against direct attacks against their freedom(s) and personal autonomy. When presented with the proposition of forcible submission to a conquering force, people naturally rebel.

Understanding history and human nature, the modern conquerors of humanity have instituted a much more sophisticated and nuanced form of conquest: cajoling their subjects into desiring their subjection and slavery by fabricating all manner of crises; both real and imagined. They then use these crises, which they were primarily responsible for manufacturing, to excite and menace the public mind with all manners of fear, doubt, and uncertainty.

---

[1] Friedrich Nietzsche's nihilistic "Übermensch."

> You never want a serious crisis to go to waste. Now what I
> mean by that is an opportunity to do things that you think
> you could not do before.[2]
> — Rahm Emanuel, Chief of Staff to President Barack
> Obama

Once the public has been sufficiently imperiled and propagandized, so as to agitate and befuddle the great majority, these creatures then enter the scene forwarding all forms of promised solutions and undefined, "feel-good" rhetoric ("hope" and "change," for example) in order to save the society from the menace they, and their ideological compatriots, manufactured in order to establish the basis for the illusion that they are the public's "knights in shining armor"; eager and able to vanquish all fears and resolve all problems. After several generations of this subtle subversion of the human spirit, the great majority of the people of the world have succumbed to despair; wanting to believe in some sort of human, political savior. However, and not coincidentally, the self-proclaimed savior's "solution" to any problem, whether it be real or merely apparent, is to gather more power into their own hands; demanding more control over the public, the nation, the culture, and its laws. This is all done in the name of saving the people from themselves and the crises that were created and encouraged in order to render the public desperate enough to submit and willfully subject themselves to their own slavery; a form of slavery that renders chains on the body mostly unnecessary, as the chains on the spirits and minds of the people within the subjected society accomplish the same purpose, while circumventing an overt demonstration of physical force and violence.

How is it that whole nations and peoples could be seduced into becoming slaves to a ruling class, especially in a country like the United States; a nation built on the ideological products of rugged individualism, personal responsibility, and independence!? Why would people consent to such a grotesquely self-debasing and self-humiliating attitude and mentality of willful subjection to a ruling class of elitists? There are several aspects to the answer: primarily fear, ignorance, *self-doubt*, and cowardice. The starting point of mankind's capitulation and consent to their slavish existence began, as it always has, with fear. Life is an uncertain prospect. One can never be absolutely sure from one day to the next what tomorrow will bring. Will it rain or will it shine? Will this be Aunt Martha's last Christmas with us, or will

---

[2] http://www.youtube.com/watch?v=_mzcbXi1Tkk, accessed August 17, 2010.

she make it another year? Will I be able to pay my mortgage this month? On and on goes the parade of fears; both anticipated and real. In the minds, and especially within the *imaginations*, of human beings lurks the most horrifying future existence that any person could ever conceive of. And of course, the trepidations, pitfalls, and major calamities that potentially await each one of us in our daily lives are most always, and apparently, more serious and cataclysmic than those imagined or foreseen by our neighbors.

This is the psychological state of affairs for most human beings. This is a common component of human nature, and one can be certain that politicians are acutely aware of this; because they are constantly using fears of what *may* come to frighten the populace into obedience, or at the very least into electing them to public office so they can fight "for the people, and against the powerful." These tactics are so well known, and so overused throughout history, that people living in today's world have no good excuse for allowing themselves to be baited and manipulated by these parasitic creatures; especially since their plans and designs have been very well documented over the past several centuries by a multitude of various sources desiring to warn humanity regarding their evil intentions;[3] and in light of the fact that these plans and intentions are playing out in the real world as if the warnings were a prophetic script.

The problem is that while most all people know intuitively, in their hearts, that in today's world "something's not right" or that "something's up," they choose to remain willfully ignorant of what is being done to them because they doubt themselves and their ability to care for their own life's responsibilities: self-doubt. In a shameful display of moral cowardice, too many people today have been psychologically conditioned to let themselves be lied to and manipulated simply because it provides for the *promise* of an easier existence in the immediate term; rather than taking the "hard road" of caring for one's own interests and responsibilities; confronting life forthrightly without forcing complete strangers to compensate for one's own deficiencies and failings.

Western civilization has become so corrupted that people can no longer claim ignorance regarding its reprobation. With huge economic debts piling up at astronomical rates all throughout the U.S. and Europe, it has become odiously apparent that the path we have been taking for the past several generations—a rising spirit of subjection to centralized government; a self-imposed form of

---

[3] See Appendix B: Suggested Reading Material [New World Order (NWO) / Conspiratorial].

psychological slavery to elitist, political masters, and the "nanny state" in order to care for a citizenry that has grown too weak, flaccid, and debauched to even be responsible for their own lives—has become unsustainable.

It took several generations and centuries to reduce humanity to this dangerously suicidal point, but the "simple" answer regarding how we have come to such a poor and ominous point is that the great majority of people all over the world, in practically all nations and societies, have been psychologically decapitated. The reference to decapitation isn't merely a means of describing a method of murder. It is exactly what must be done to people, at the most fundamental psychological levels, in order to subjugate them. Modern politicians, social agitators, and self-styled "leaders" understand this reality completely, and refer to the process of psychological decapitation as "psycho-political warfare." The intended end is the *complete* removal of the ability to reason from the human species, with the singular exception of a select few within the ruling class. It is a decapitation in the sense that while humanity maintains possession of their anatomical brains, they have been so dramatically propagandized and psychologically assaulted over their entire lifetime with emotional appeals intended to excite, agitate, confuse, and disorient them that they do not know how to use their minds for the purpose that it is able, and was meant, to serve: to independently think, reason, and evaluate the world.

They have been so deluged with propaganda of an emotional, hateful, and violent nature (as part of an implementation of a multitude of psycho-political warfare tactics and strategies) that they have come to "think"—actually, to react as they have been psychologically programmed to react[4]—in ultimately self-hating platitudes; not realizing that they have become mere parrots, and that the platitudes they spout are completely nonsensical when critically evaluated; because they have not been trained, educated, and armed with the ability to critically analyze the very platitudes they spout and believe in. In that sense, today's humanity has been decapitated; because access to higher order analytical skills, and the knowledge of how to independently use and apply reason, has been slowly, purposefully, and systematically eradicated from most of humanity over the past several hundred years. That sounds like quite an accomplishment, and it truly is if one is to consider the scope of the undertaking, but it isn't as difficult as one may initially think; given the nearly inexhaustible patience and time available to those innumerable "true believers" who, through their boundless, blind faith and dogmatic determination have brought this situation into being; especially in light of all

---

[4] In principle, this is exactly the same as the conditioning of "Pavlov's dog."

the technological tools they now have at their disposal to disseminate their propaganda: TV, radio, print media, computers and the Internet, etc.

The cause(s) of the insanity, and the catalysts that have always sustained the degenerative processes that are corrupting the minds and spirits of mankind are paradoxical because they are simultaneously quite easy to understand, but very hard to confront forthrightly because it is offensive to human pride. They work from two different directions to simultaneously apply psychological pressure on the average, unsuspecting human mind. These catalysts are those psychological attributes that emanate from the master and slave mentalities. From the perspective of the 'master' there is insane, narcissistic arrogance; and from the perspective of the 'slave' there is cowardice, ignorance, and *self-doubt*. Those who fall prey to these evils are either the most obstinately and narcissistically conceited (master), or the most psychologically weak (slave) within society.

The reader should visualize these psychological types as if they comprised the top and bottom of a societal continuum. The 'master,' thinking themselves above everybody else, would be positioned at the top of the continuum; while the 'slave,' conceiving themselves to be the lowliest and neediest (self-pitying) within society, would comprise the bottom of the continuum. Additionally, they should also be viewed as comprising two ends of a socio-psychological vise; with both of these extremes (master and slave) combining forces to compress the self-sufficient "middle" of society. The ultimate goal is for the two ends of the "vise" to "compress" the psyches of the average human being until their spirit is broken and the mind succumbs to the social pressure being applied; subsequently gravitating toward the psychological attributes of either a master or a slave. Each end of this psychological vise operates from differing and opposing motivations, but the common goal is to break the will of the self-sufficient and force the average person to "fall in line" at either end of the social vise as either a master or a slave.

The motivation from the master's perspective is to force those caught within the vise of this social paradigm—everyone who hasn't taken their "proper place" within society as a slave—to "learn their place" and recognize the 'masters' as morally and intellectually superior creatures. The motivation from the slave's perspective adheres to the principle "misery loves company." Believing within their own hearts that they are the weakest, most flaccid, and helpless creatures within their society, the 'slave' personality desires to corrupt his fellow man so that the slave's conscience will not persecute him so vigorously for being so weak and cowardly. The slave takes pride in corrupting and eroding the will of others so that it is then easier to face their own countenance in the mirror by telling themselves, "See, I'm not so bad. Look how [latest victim of their corruption] fell into the same trap as I did. No, we're not weak and bad. We're just 'misunderstood.'" As the process develops over time, psychological pressure is applied and incrementally increased; because as people are psychologically broken they then join the ranks of either the master or the slave, and are then available, and subsequently put to work, increasing the pressure on those members of society who have not yet been subdued; until all humanity breaks out into the mentality of either a master or a slave (See Figures 6 through 8); with the masters dictating practically all things of even minor importance to the slaves, who dutifully hear and obey the commands of their masters.

Naturally, as the mechanism works like a vise, equal pressure must be applied from both the top (master) and the bottom (slave) of society to increase the pressure on those remaining who are still caught within, as well as to be the most efficient in breaking the will of the unwitting "middle" of society. As human psyches are broken down and redistributed to either end of the vise, it should be noted that the distribution of psyches to either the master or the slave end will follow what will be referred to here as the "First Law of Psychodynamics"; which is directly analogous to the First Law of Thermodynamics. The First Law of Thermodynamics is referred to as the "Conservation of Energy." It states that energy may be changed from one form to another, but it cannot be created or destroyed. The analogous "First Law of Psychodynamics" is comparable and will be referred to as the "Conservation of Ego." It states that human ego may be changed from one form to another,[5] but it cannot be created or destroyed. This, of course, is not entirely true and as rigid as a law of physics, but it helps to understand what happens to people when they are psychologically broken and fall into either the mentality of the master or the slave; as well as to their distribution between the masters and slaves. Examine Figure 6, representing the distribution of ego toward the beginning of this socially degenerative process, to notice several things:

1. The egos of the great bulk of humanity reside in the "middle" area of self-sufficiency.

---

[5] For instance, from an independent and self-sufficient individual and mentality, to either a master or a slave mentality, which is exactly what is intended by the spiritual and psychic compression being applied today by the existing master and slave mentalities of the world.

2. Those who comprise the master personality types are fewer in number than either the self-sufficient or the slave, and their egos are also larger than the others.

3. The combined force of wills of the masters equals the combined force of wills of the slaves, so that equal amounts of social pressure can be applied to psychologically compress the self-sufficient middle. Moreover, the force of wills of the masters and slaves will remain proportionally equal as the process progresses; so as to maximize the social pressure being applied.

4. In the beginning stages of this process the amount of social pressure that the masters and slaves are able to apply to the middle is fairly modest, as their relative numbers are much smaller than those who occupy the self-sufficient middle of society.

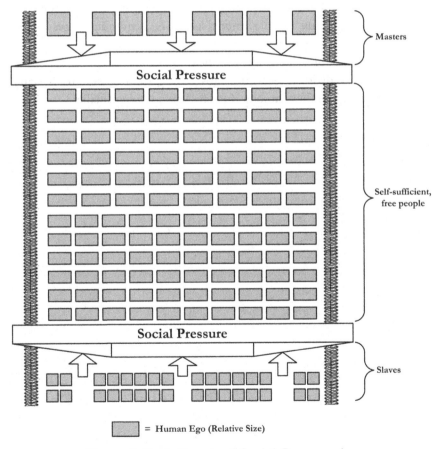

= Human Ego (Relative Size)

Figure 6. Early Stages of Social Compression

Next, examine Figure 7, which represents the distribution of ego toward the middle of this socially degenerative process, to notice several changes:

1. The egos of the great bulk of humanity are now more evenly distributed between the three groups: master, self-sufficient, and slaves; with the two extremes gaining more adherents at the expense of the self-sufficient members of society.

2. Those who comprise the master personality types are still fewer in number than either the self-sufficient or the slave, but their egos are still larger than the others, and continuing to grow, while they are likewise gaining adherents to their egomaniacal tendencies.

3. The force of wills between the masters and the slaves are still identical; but larger in terms of adherents they now claim, and the amount of social pressure that they are now able to apply to the self-sufficient. Their relative numbers, as a percentage of the society's population, are much greater than at the beginning stages of the process; causing an acceleration of the social degeneration as the amount of pressure applied to the middle increases.

4. At the individual level, the egos among the masters are growing larger, while those among the slaves are growing smaller.

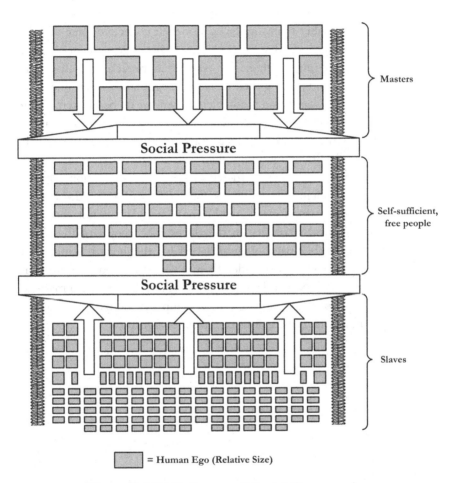

= Human Ego (Relative Size)

Figure 7. Middle Stages of Social Compression

Finally, examine Figure 8, which represents the distribution of ego at the end of this socially degenerative process, to notice the final results:

1. The egos of the self-sufficient middle of humanity have been broken and destroyed and are now distributed between the two delusional, reprobated extremes.

2. Those who comprise the master personality types are still far fewer in number than the slaves. For their collective force of wills to counterbalance that of the slaves, their egos are necessarily considerably larger than the slave's; approaching self-deistic sentiments and feeding their delusional, egomaniacal self-image.

3. The social degeneration is complete. There are no people remaining who can conceive of an existence as a self-sufficient, free human being. By the time this point is reached, any obstinate individuals who persist in maintaining their self-sufficient, freedom-loving spirit have been either murdered or sent to "re-education camps." The enslavement of humanity is concluded; with the added benefit (within the warped minds of the masters) that it is not necessary to use physical restraints on the slaves. The people of the world have chosen their psychological slavery to other human beings with enflamed egos, who consider themselves to be gods among men (Übermensch). Naturally, as good slaves dutifully obey their masters, the people of the world begin to worship and idolize their masters as if they actually were gods or messianic figures.[6]

---

[6] This has actually already begun in the modern world with many in the U.S. media and public life ascribing messianic qualities to Barack Hussein Obama, and adoring and obeying him as if he were truly a deistic figure or presence.

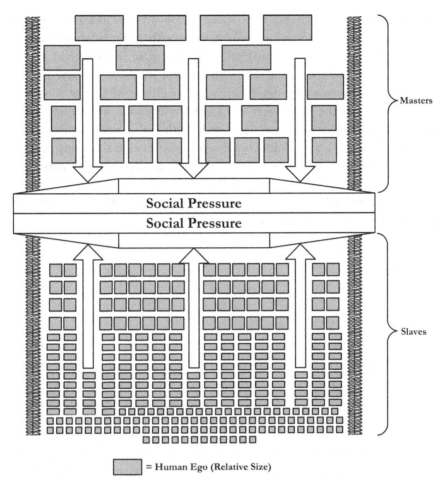

= Human Ego (Relative Size)

Figure 8. Final Goal of Social Compression

Modern Western civilization has progressed beyond the state depicted in Figure 7 and is rapidly approaching what is depicted in Figure 8. All throughout the process, as the self-sufficient, freedom-loving people are being psychologically broken down and redistributed; the great majority of them will fall into the habits and attitudes of the slave. Observing the "First Law of Psychodynamics," this is a natural consequence as the summation of the forces of will between the masters and slaves must be maintained at equilibrium in order to maintain a "functional" society. And as the total amount of ego is conserved, neither being created nor destroyed, one can see that as the self-image of twenty self-sufficient people is diminished to the level of the slave, their "egotistical quanta" does not simply evaporate into thin air. Instead, another of the self-sufficient persons who are broken and distributed to the master end of the social vise absorbs the lost self-image of the newly debased slaves, which provides the newly self-proclaimed master personality type with a delusional, self-important view of themselves.

This process is occurring continuously, and has been ongoing for all time. The clearly evident, degenerative social effects of this process are visible today via the devolution of human civilizations, as demonstrated by the rapid increase in anarchy and strife both within and between most nations of the world; a natural consequence of the master-slave paradigm; when the psychological slaves rally around the cause(s) of their masters, and the masters—emboldened by the sycophantic support of their idolatrous subjects—continually increase social pressures incrementally so as to enslave even more of humanity than they already control.

How Do We Rise Above Our Current, Sad, State and Achieve True Peace?

How can we stop the decline of Western civilization, and the rest of the world, and return it to a place of peace and true freedom? We have been laid so low in so many ways due to the relentless application of the Hegelian Dialectic in order to purposefully corrupt the public mind. Referring back to Figure 1, simply replace the descriptive extremes of human thought and perception from 'Lie' and 'Truth' to 'Self' and 'World' (respectively, as in Figure 5), so as to be able to directly transpose these concepts.

An egocentric worldview focused on the satisfaction of personal desires, independent of the consideration of the greater needs of all, is an absolute, socially self-destructive lie; because such a disposition will only lead people into narcissistic conceit. A sure recipe for conflict, as self-involved people will never come to a true unity of mind or purpose with others because they are always trying to forward their own advantage in the world at the expense of others. Contrarily, true understanding will only be achieved through a worldview that considers the needs of all. This philosophy is the true focus of human action and contemplative pursuits that leads to the strength and sustenance of a larger society; being that we are all mutually interdependent upon one another to forward human civilization.

This simple reality draws the understanding to how the Hegelian Dialectic has been used to corrupt modern Western civilization, because it is this very socio-psychological methodology that has been incrementally applied over the past several centuries to draw human perception away from a consideration of the greater needs of the respective societies within Western civilization; so as to focus human perception—to the dangerous detriment of all effected societies—on the egocentric perspective of the self: the self-absorbed, naval-gazing, "I have needs"! and "It's all about me"! mentalities. The ironic answer to how this situation has come about is that the United States and Western civilization have fallen victim to the brilliant successes of their past. As a result, the great majority of U.S. citizens in our day have completely lost a connection with the fundamentals of life; abdicating adherence to higher principles, and instead preferring vain and unproductive distractions: TV, popular music and entertainment, video games, etc.

> The things that will destroy America are prosperity-at-any-price, peace-at-any-price, safety-first instead of duty-first, ***the love of soft living***, and the get-rich-quick theory of life.[1]
> — Theodore Roosevelt, 26th President of the United States

Following upon the great successes of the past generations that built up Western civilization, the current generation(s) are now living out their lives in the modern world as if those of us who live today need not do anything to sustain and fortify our civilization; in the grotesquely arrogant presumption that today we are "untouchable" due to the successes of our ancestors. This has led most all Westerners to succumb to their naturally debased, effeminate, and hedonistic inclinations; almost unanimously ignorant of, and ungrateful for, the sacrifices our forebearers made in our behalf! To be fair to the current occupants of Western civilization, such behavior is only natural to our human nature. Most Westerners today have devolved into the psychological equivalents of spoiled children due to the prosperity and ease of life that the sacrifices of previous generations have made possible for us today. However, this simple observation should not be interpreted solely as a rebuke of the modern Westerner, but rather as a lesson to learn from, so as to correct our errors and put us back on the right path; because in the larger scale of time and human existence the world we live in today is nothing more than a culminating consequence of prior generations and the choices they made, which resulted in what we know today as the "modern world."

We who live today had very little to say about the formation of it, as the corruptive elements that have embedded themselves within our culture had their beginnings several hundred years ago! As the saying goes, all of us are a "product of our times." However, does this absolve us of our duty to correct the errors of the past when we come to understand them? No, of course not. Each one of us has a responsibility to our society to maintain and sustain it so that future generations will be able to live and thrive in true freedom.

If we are to extricate ourselves from our self-imposed societal suicide, the very first change that must take place within the hearts and minds of the modern Westerner is a sincere desire to educate themselves regarding the principles that made the U.S. and Western civilization so great in the past—because an ignorant people will not have the heart or motivation to repudiate

---

[1] http://www.brainyquote.com/quotes/quotes/t/theodorero164291.html, accessed November 30, 2007.

their evil habits without an understanding appreciation of the superiority of a different and better way of living—accompanied by a reinvigoration of the sense of responsibilities and duties that we owe to others, as well as to ourselves. Some suggestions regarding instructive material have been included in Appendix B (Suggested Reading Material), but there are certainly other materials that are not included in this brief list that would be equally instructive regarding what once made America great.

It was noted earlier that the most prominent manifestation of human pride and source of strife in the modern world is narcissism: the psychology of self-worship and the pursuit of gratifying one's passions; whatever they may be and without consideration of the totality of damaging consequences of one's actions. It is exactly this interior psychological disposition that has blinded the people of this world and retarded their maturation, as narcissism is an expression of an immature mind. If the human race either refuses, or is unable, to overcome this character defect, then there is absolutely no way to avert a major social catastrophe in the near future; because as the psychosis of narcissism progresses it proceeds from a stage where people merely try to assert themselves in the public domain, to a stage where they will attempt to force themselves on society; regardless of how dangerous their self-willed passions are to the greater society (for example, proponents of homosexual "marriage," militant socialists and communists, and Islamic terrorists). Moreover, a nation of narcissists is truly no nation at all, but rather a geographical collection of millions of sub-nations where each narcissist comprises their own personal nation, because their loyalty lies within themselves and not to any higher ideal.

How can this grave character defect be corrected? As narcissism is a manifestation of self-indulgent pride that seeks to gratify and glorify the narcissist, the antidote would then be an unselfish humility that seeks to glorify the highest ideals of one's society and culture. This change in life philosophy would be a major rupture from the current, self-oriented and depraved mindset of the great majority of people in the world today. However, if this change is not achieved soon, we will certainly consume ourselves. The approach to a horrible climax can be seen with each passing day, as cultural battles intensify and escalate on practically every contentious issue within society.

How can a person who was born into, and raised, in a materialistic and hedonistically self-indulgent world be disabused of their dangerous beliefs? The first step is for the readers to realize the dangers of narcissism to both themselves and the larger society. The effort has been made to explain these dangers in the preceding pages, but if the reader refuses to acknowledge them there is simply nothing more that can be done for that person. They will continue on wreaking havoc and destruction on human civilizations.

But, if the reader does come to appreciate the dangers of a self-indulgent, self-centered worldview, then the obvious solution to such a problem is to instead seek the highest, most noble principle to stand for instead of simply oneself. It is important here to emphasize the necessity to seek the highest, and most noble, first principle—what Aristotle referred to as the "unmoved mover": the original cause and animating force behind all things—rather than merely a higher and nobler intermediate principle.

Why, and what does that mean? Intermediate principles are things such as environmentalism, socialism, community organizing, or any other ideological system or pursuit that does not address the source of all things. The reason these intermediate principles are to be avoided is exactly because of their intermediate nature. There are a great many ideological systems and pursuits in the world today. Naturally, they are not all complementary and tolerant of one another; such that seeking for an intermediate principle to stand for would merely leave the reader at really no better of a position than if they had simply remained narcissistically self-serving, because in the end the predictable outcome of clashing ideologies will leave human civilizations at the same point of discord as they are today. Consequently, the only way to truly find peace in this world is to seek for the highest and first principle; what the philosophers of all ages have come to know as the Creator, or God.

The primary reason why such a pursuit would necessarily cause peace to break out all over the world is due to both the nature of God and the essence of peace. God is the ultimate and infinite 'singularity'; meaning that He has only *one* will. Because He is infinite, there can be no other being like Him;[2] and because He is only one, He can only have one will, which is likewise His essence.[3] This unity of will, or singular purpose, conforms to the true understanding of what peace actually is: a manifestation of social harmony founded on a people who share a common, unified belief system. If all mankind were to sincerely seek after a singular, common purpose—such as the pursuit of understanding the true will of God—the natural product of such a pursuit would necessarily be a universal peace.

This seems to be a sore and difficult topic for a great many people in today's world. For this reason, I am going to try to avoid "preaching" to the public and stick to merely making a case from a direct examination of established facts. The best part of what follows is that the items discussed

---

[2] More than a single infinite being would be a complete contradiction of the concept of the infinite.

[3] This principle is more explicitly explained by St. Thomas Aquinas in his work *Summa Contra Gentiles: Book One: God*, specifically in Chapter 73 of that work.

can be understood from a "scientific" perspective: examining and testing historical data to isolate the cause(s).

Somewhere deep inside most all of us, we realize that the direction this world is headed is completely unsustainable and is leading us all to a point where "something has to give," because "we can't keep going on like this"; whether anyone wants to face up to it or not. As everyone realizes, anyone can say, and convince themselves, of practically anything; so when someone comes to the scene and says that the world as we know it will soon be over, most people mock and laugh at them because there is no source of authority for the proclamations that they make. Many of the prognosticators apparently produce their claims out of thin air, or from a source that is not universally understood or acknowledged to be truthful. I endeavor to be an exception to this case; attempting an honest demonstration of our dire situation through an examination of historical data, in combination with a relevant situational analysis of the modern day, rather than merely human conjecture or protestations.

If people would open their eyes and minds to the world around them, they would notice that the world is devouring itself through many different mechanisms. Fortunately for us, we have the absolute truth of history to teach us; if we will only submit to being taught and learning our lesson. Of even greater benefit and fortune for humanity today, the reader will come to understand that these simple truths are understandable even to those who currently consider themselves to be an atheist. The design of the world and the lessons of human nature and history will make the cause and effect relationship between fidelity to the observance of religious principles and tenets of moral and ethical behavior understandable, even from a strictly pragmatic and non-religious perspective. The only catch is that you can't come to this understanding through affective reasoning constructs: desiring to see and understand the world in such a way that it conforms to what the reader wants to believe. Instead, the reader must submit to cognitive reasoning and see the world as it is, whether any of us may like what we see.

To begin this investigation, let's imagine ourselves as observers and analysts who are completely removed from the situation under examination. This attitude will help us to more dispassionately consider the facts from a more abstracted and less self-involved perspective. In today's world there is a lot of fascination among many with UFOs and extraterrestrial aliens: beings we perceive as coming from another world. For the purpose of investigation, let us pretend that we are just such creatures. In the course of our explorations of the universe we come upon an odd and curious world. We take an interest in these creatures, who call themselves human beings, because about fifty light-years distant from their home planet one of our exploratory probes began to receive electromagnetic transmissions from their planet of something they called *I Love Lucy*. Our interest being piqued by the strange behavior of this odd species, we decide to send an investigational team to take a detailed look into their culture and existence. As we draw nearer to their planet we notice several things.

At first, we find that these curious creatures appear to be quite goofy and backwards; from the inanity of *I Love Lucy* to their simple-minded conception of interstellar travel and the beings that live outside their solar system, as revealed by another of their electromagnetic transmissions entitled *Star Trek*. As a result, our original reaction to these creatures is one of condescending amusement. Because we first discovered these creature's transmissions about fifty light-years away from their planet, it will take us about five months of their time to travel to their home planet (Earth) in our advanced spacecraft. During this time we will have an opportunity to study the species further before arriving at their planet. As we make our way to Earth we continue monitoring their electromagnetic transmissions; realizing that what we are viewing is compressed in time, as the transmissions we were receiving when we started toward Earth began fifty years in the human's past, and are progressing to their modern day in only five of their months. While monitoring the transmissions we find one of their channels dedicated to a program called "News." We quickly realize that *I Love Lucy* and *Star Trek* were fictional accounts made strictly for the entertainment and diversion of the creatures, while the "News" was a depiction of what was actually transpiring within their world. As we draw nearer to their planet we are able to watch ten years of their civilization transpire in a month of our traveling time. Our initial amusement quickly turns into horror as we notice how rapidly their civilizations are degenerating into increasingly hostile groups attempting to destroy one another. We also noted from the human's transmissions that this species has already discovered atomic fission and has used it to create nuclear weapons.

Our frustration increases as we approach Earth, because we are still a few weeks of travel time away from their planet and the last three species we encountered had experienced the same rapid degeneration into suicidal self-destruction. Unfortunately, the previous species had consummated their self-destruction before we could arrive to investigate and intercede in their behalf. As we progress further toward Earth our frustration is only exceeded by our incredulity that the great majority of this species doesn't even seem to notice the extremely rapid escalation in violence and self-destructive behaviors that it is engaging in. It recalled to our minds an allegory we had seen discussed in one of their transmissions: the frog in the pot of boiling water. It described taking a frog and getting it to cooperate in its own death by deception. If one tried to put the frog in a pot of boiling water, the creature would immediately sense the danger and avoid the pot. However, if the frog was enticed into the pot before the heat was turned on it would be much easier to coax him into the pot and then turn up the heat slowly. By the time the water begins to get too hot, it is too late for the frog to rescue himself. Having received this transmission from Earth, we became even more incredulous as to how this species could continue to destroy itself when they had many among them who were feverishly trying to warn them of their impending self-destruction. Ultimately, it seems that the humans were having too much "fun" destroying themselves to turn away from their self-destructive practices.

As dispassionate observers, and because we truly want to help these imperiled creatures avert their own self-destruction, we gather and analyze as much information as we can regarding their competing philosophical belief systems; so that we may properly educate ourselves regarding "what makes them tick." We realize that only an understanding of the foundational philosophy of these creature's lives will allow us to intercede with them and contribute to a peaceful resolution of their current turmoil. As astute observers of their various cultures, we understand that the principal foundation of their personalities is based on something that they call "religion." Our investigation reveals that there are literally hundreds of religions on their planet, and that a great many of the creatures believe their religion to be the one, true religion; which is ultimately the primary cause of discord between them. Having analyzed all the data available to us regarding the different religious beliefs among these creatures, and in consideration of their evident behavior, our initial analysis discovers a horribly unsettling contradiction between their proclaimed religious beliefs and the application of these beliefs within their lives. The source of this contradiction seems to lie within another philosophical belief system that has risen up among them over the last several centuries of their time, and they refer to this philosophy as "humanism." This adherence to humanism has apparently developed in coordination with their understanding of the mechanisms of matter. Sadly, they have unwittingly allowed what they call "science" to supersede and overshadow their religious principles, so that they have come to the state of worshipping at the altar of science instead of at the altar of their proclaimed religion(s).

We quickly come to understand that this confusion of philosophies has led these poor creatures into worshipping themselves; most all of them remaining completely ignorant regarding this contradiction of self-worship.

How has science confounded their understanding? Before the advent of science, these creatures attributed the solicitude and sustenance of their lives to an unseen intelligence that most of their major religions referred to as God, and who was likewise believed to have been their Creator. However, after humans began to understand the more detailed composition of matter they began to more greatly admire both themselves and their fellow creatures; especially those who could explain the more complicated principles of the composition of matter. They called these people "scientists." As time progressed the continual and increasing discovery of the mechanisms of matter revealed by the scientists began to astonish the creatures, so that they began to look at scientists as their new "holy men" of science. Naturally, the human race became beguiled by the details of the construction of the material world, as the things being discovered were truly extraordinary in comparison to their previous knowledge. In their fascination, the creatures remained mostly oblivious to the fact that they were engaging in something that their major religions called "idolatry": the worship of false gods; in this case, material things. They harnessed their understanding of matter to make their lives easier to live than in previous generations of their species.

Being naturally grateful for an ease in the exertions necessary to sustain themselves, they came to focus the object of their gratitude on the facility of science rather than God. We came to understand how such a confusion of principles could come to pass when we considered their relatively short lifespan and the exigencies of their existence. As advanced beings, whose intelligence and lifespan extend to a veritable eternity in comparison to their pitifully short lives, we understood how easy it was for the humans to grasp at an immediate gratification when their lives only persisted for less than a hundred of their years. We also understood how they could become so blind to their actions and behavior when we considered their situation from a more universal perspective unconstrained by the limitations of their conception of time.

As witnesses to their shortsighted vision, we focused our efforts on making them aware of the intrusion of humanism into their religious observances and how this intrusion has led them into idolatry; especially when the poor creatures had many evidences of their Creator (God) extant among them, which they called "miracles." To help these creatures we formulated a plan of intercession. The most remarkable quality we noticed among these creatures was their intransigent nature. Their old religious texts referred to the creatures as being "stiff necked." This referred to the creatures as being obstinate in their refusal to accept any idea that contradicted their current beliefs or established way of life. Once these creatures got a particular idea

152

lodged within their mind, there were a great many of them who would not be disabused of their erroneous beliefs; even in the face of substantial and physical evidence that demonstrated their beliefs to be false! We had quite a difficult task before us, but out of pity for the creatures we endeavored to continue on and attempt to reconcile them with one another.

To bring the creatures back from the precipice of self-destruction they have approached, we must positively demonstrate the answers to several fundamental questions their lives and existence largely gravitate around. The first, and most universal, question at the heart of the matter is . . . "Is there a God"? If we attempt to demonstrate to the creatures that there is indeed a God, a superior intelligence that created and rules their material world, we must then answer a question that directly arises from such a position: "How can we know and be convinced that there is a God"? Finally, if we are sufficiently able to demonstrate the existence of God to the creatures, the final question to be answered is, "What way (religion) is the *true* way to properly worship and recognize Him"? Determined to demonstrate positive answers to these questions, we analyze the recorded history of the creatures.

Our analysis initially concludes that the existence of a creator God can be answered in the affirmative. We came to this conclusion by simultaneously considering the first two questions at hand. Likewise, we realized that the best way to demonstrate the existence of God can best be understood by an intellectual vehicle that one of the creatures (St. Thomas Aquinas) referred to as "remotion": approaching the investigation from a perspective of removing what is not possible from that which is possible.[4] The intellectual process of remotion is what is employed when answering a question on a multiple choice test when we aren't positively sure of the answer. If one is able to remove the false answers from the test, one can ultimately approach a greater certainty of arriving at the correct answer. Thus, in simplistic terms, it's like mastering the art of test-taking. In light of the creature's beliefs, we understand that the whole of the created world is similarly ordered, as the religious believers of most faiths refer to their existence on Earth as a spiritual test administered by their Creator (God).

---

[4] See St. Thomas Aquinas, *Summa Contra Gentiles: Book One: God*, trans. Anton C. Pegis, F.R.S.C. (Notre Dame, IN: University of Notre Dame Press, 1997), 96: "[2] Now, in considering the divine substance, we should especially make use of the method of remotion. For, by its immensity, the divine substance surpasses every form that our intellect reaches. Thus we are unable to apprehend it by knowing *what it is.* Yet we are able to have some knowledge of it by knowing *what it is not.* Furthermore, we approach nearer to a knowledge of God according as through our intellect we are able to remove more and more things from Him."

We determine it best to answer the positive existence of God by directly addressing the secondary question, "How can we know and be convinced that there is a God"? Humans can know and be convinced of this truth through three vehicles, in order of their greatest influence: (1) the intercession of a supernatural[5] power in the material world (miracles: He has made manifest the reality of His existence all throughout the history of the human race, in all places and in all times, via the vehicle of miracles), (2) the demonstration of supernatural events (hauntings, demonic possessions, etc.), and (3) the fulfillment of prophecy. These three factors, taken both individually and together, serve to provide undeniable evidence for the real existence of the supernatural.

We begin by examining the phenomenon of miracles and formulate our demonstration based on an analogy to their most beloved machine, which they call a "computer." A computer has a triune (three) level of hierarchy. The highest authority is the Basic Input Output System (BIOS), the intermediate authority is the Operating System (OS), and the lowest authority is the "application." Observing the hierarchy from the top down, the BIOS can be considered as the natural laws of the material world that rule physical existence: principles such as $E=mc^2$ (Energy equals mass times the speed of light squared), $p=mv$ (momentum equals mass times velocity) and $F=ma$ (force equals mass times acceleration). All transactions within the material world *must* behave according to these principles, which they call the "laws" of physics. Secondarily, the OS, which operates within the circumscribed confines that the BIOS defines, can be viewed as the political organizations and alliances the creatures determine to form among themselves (nations, states, cities, etc.). Finally, the application, which operates within the circumscribed confines that the OS (political authority) defines, can be viewed as the behavior of an individual acting within society.

Each level of authority exercises its ability to function only within the predefined constraints placed on it by that level of authority immediately superior to it within the hierarchy of control. It is simply not possible for the system (the human race) to function correctly when either the application attempts to supersede the authority of the OS (citizens attempt to circumvent the laws of their particular society), or when the OS attempts to supersede

---

[5] Etymologically, the prefix "super" denotes that which is higher in quality or degree, and "natural" meaning those things that pertain to the material world. Consequently, a supernatural power is one that exercises a higher degree of power and authority over the material, natural world.

the authority of the BIOS (nations and rulers attempt to circumvent the laws of nature, and of God). When such an event transpires it *always*, in every instance, leads to what the humans call a "crash." Depending on the level of hierarchical control at which a transgression of authority is attempted, the result of a crash has differing consequences. At the lower level of authority the consequences are of lesser influence on the whole system, but at the higher level of authority the consequences can be catastrophic.

If an application (citizen) attempts to supersede the authority of the OS (government authority), the OS recognizes the transgression. For more minor transgressions the OS causes the application to "freeze" (the citizen is arrested) in order to prevent the pernicious activity of the application from threatening the continued, orderly functionality of the system. The OS will attempt continued communication with the application to reconcile the transgression, so that the application may once again resume its functionality (the state will incarcerate and punish the criminal in order to attempt their rehabilitation, with the intention of reincorporating them back into civil society if at all possible). If the application continues to attempt further violations the OS will keep it in a "frozen" state (repeat criminal offenders are re-incarcerated). In the case of more serious transgressions (murder, treason, etc.), the OS recognizes the greater threat and "kills" the application altogether (the death penalty) to prevent the egregious transgression from corrupting the system and imperiling the continued functionality of the OS.

At the higher level of authority, transgressions are much more severe and will lead to a crash of the whole system; which likewise causes the destruction of currently operating applications, through no fault of their own, due to their subordinate and reliant position within the hierarchy of control. Within the most popular operating system used by the creatures, they call the result of such a severe breach of hierarchical control the "Blue Screen of Death" (BSOD) (man-made famines (Russia, Ethiopia, Somalia, and others), wars, etc.). When a BSOD is experienced the system must be restarted (entirely new nations and societies are established following the destruction of famines and wars—maps are redrawn and people are dislocated). If there are multiple, competing operating systems extant on a particular computer (numerous nations and societies, religions, and ideologies on Earth), each of them demanding supremacy over the others, the system may become so degraded that none of them will function properly and the computer (analogical human civilizations) will be rendered completely dysfunctional and non-operational.

In the course of our explanation we will first remind the humans that the highest level of authority in the world—the analogical BIOS—are the physical laws of nature. It is freely acknowledged by the creatures that this is the case, as *all* their inventions and science rely on this fact. If it were not so it would not be possible for them to universally apply the underlying principles of matter to harness the power of the material world. Therefore, any event that demonstrates a deviation from the physical rules of the material world *must* be acknowledged by the intellectually honest as having its cause in the supernatural: a power and authority that exists to define, control, and circumscribe the material world.

Through the vehicle of this analogy we hope to demonstrate two points to the humans. First, that the objectively real, verifiable, existence of miracles—which we will expound on later in the discussion relating to the true religion of the human race—in their world positively demonstrates the existence of God; and second, that it is exactly this type of destructive behavior (competing nations and societies, religions, and ideologies) that is grinding the humans down to their own self-destruction. The applications (citizens) no longer circumscribe their activity within the confines of their OS (the "laws of the land"), and their operating systems no longer circumscribe their activity within the confines of the BIOS (nations and leaders who arrogate to themselves the ability to rule the world).

Having demonstrated this reality, we will then address the second vehicle through which the humans can be convinced of the reality of God's existence: the demonstration of supernatural events. We notice that, just as the humans are fascinated with the existence of extraterrestrials, a whole "cottage industry" has been built up around phenomena they call "paranormal": events that cannot be explained or understood within the context of the material world. The most prevalent form of the paranormal is a phenomenon they call "hauntings." During the course of their existence numerous organizations and individuals have studied the paranormal and have documented their findings. This phenomenon has become more popularized through the vehicle of their televisions, as a show devoted to the paranormal has become quite popular among many of the creatures: *Ghost Hunters*. Moreover, various motion pictures have been made that document such events: *Amityville Horror, The Haunting in Connecticut*, and numerous others.

We will attempt to convince the creatures that such paranormal events provide positive proof of the existence of the supernatural, which confirms the real existence of God. How do such events confirm God's existence? We explain our position by referring to the fact that every effect in the world *must* proceed from a definite cause. One of their earlier scientists and mathematicians, regarded by the creatures (especially the scientists) as one of the most influential men in the history of their world (Sir Isaac Newton), incorporated this certain reality into his observations. Mr. Newton's studies began a system of physics that today is referred to as *classical mechanics* or *Newtonian physics*.[6] His third law of classical mechanics states that for every action there is an equal and opposite reaction. Such an observation marvelously exemplifies the point of cause and effect; for if there is to be an effect (reaction) there must certainly be a cause (action). We will remind the humans that the great majority of their scientific knowledge had its genesis in Mr. Newton's studies and laws of physics. Objects are not moved unless there is a mover that moves them.

This reality is critical in proving the existence of God, because in the study of paranormal events the impetus for investigation primarily gravitates around effects that have no demonstrable cause in the material world: objects move through an unseen force, apparitions appear out of nowhere, sounds and other physical effects manifest themselves without any possible cause in the material world. Applying the principle of remotion, we hold up before the humans the following choices in a multiple-choice test consisting of only two possible answers: "You have events that have transpired in your world. It is not possible for these events to have occurred within the constraints of the laws of the material world. Are these events natural or supernatural"? Removing the possibility of natural causes, we must conclude that these events transpired due to supernatural intervention, which directly affirms the existence of God.

Finally, we will address the third way humans can be convinced of the real existence of God: prophecy. The phenomenon of prophecy and how it proves the existence of God was well explained in one of the creature's books, *Science Speaks*, written by Dr. Peter W. Stoner, a man of science. He was the Chairman of the Departments of Mathematics and Astronomy at Pasadena City College until 1953; Chairman of the Science Division at Westmont College from 1953-1957; and Professor Emeritus of Science at Westmont College. *Science Speaks* was an examination of prophecy through the use of mathematical probability.

Probability is explained as follows: "If the chance of one thing happening is one in M and the chance of another, and independent, thing happening is one in N, then the chance that they shall both happen is one in M times N."[7]

---

[6] Mr. Newton's system of mechanics and physics is still recognized today as certainly valid and is one of two major fields of science: classical mechanics and quantum mechanics. A third field is emerging today that is attempting to reconcile the seemingly irreconcilable differences between the two: string theory.

[7] Peter W. Stoner, *Science Speaks* (Chicago, IL: Moody Press, 1963), 71.

The chance of any particular prophecy coming to pass due to the agency of human wisdom alone is one in M. For example, consider the flipping of a coin. If one guesses heads or tails correctly, the probability of this "prophecy" is 1 in 2; as there is only one correct conclusion from two possible outcomes. Additionally, if a person prophecies correctly ten consecutive flips of the coin, the chance of this happening is 1 in 2^{10}, or 1 in 1,024. From this, it can be seen that as the number of prophecies is increased, the probability of all these prophecies coming true through the agency of human wisdom alone becomes astronomically small at an exponential rate.

Prophecies contained in one of the human's religious texts, which they call a *Bible*, were examined. Eleven instances of prophecy were considered. Mathematical probability was applied to the prophecies, and it was determined that the possibility that all these prophecies were derived through human wisdom alone was 1 in 5.76×10^{59}. We find it best to let the original author speak for himself regarding the enormity of the situation:

> Let us try to visualize our probability of 1 in 5.76×10^{59}. Let us round this off to 5×10^{59}. Let us suppose that we had that number of silver dollars. What kind of a pile would this be?
>
> The volume of the sun is more than 1,000,000 times that of the earth, yet out of 5×10^{59} silver dollars we could make 10^{28} solid silver balls the size of the sun.
>
> Our group of stars, called our galaxy, comprises all of the stars which stay together in this one group. It is an extremely large group of at least 100,000,000,000 stars, each star averaging as large as our sun. At great distances from our galaxy are other galaxies similar to ours, containing about the same number of stars. If you were to count the 100,000,000,000 stars, counting 250 a minute, it would take you 750 years, counting day and night, and you would only have counted the stars in a single galaxy.
>
> (NOTE: All computations are only approximate and all numbers are expressed with only one or two digits.)
>
> It has been estimated that the whole universe contains about two trillion galaxies, each containing about 100 billion stars. From our 5×10^{59} dollars we could make all of the stars, in all of these galaxies, 2×10^5 times.
>
> Suppose we had marked one of these silver dollars, and had stirred it into the whole pile before we had made them into balls the size of the sun. Then suppose we had

blindfolded a man and told him to go over all of these great balls and pick up the dollar which he thinks is the right one. What chance would he have of finding the right one? It would be a very great task to look over this mass of dollars. If our blindfolded man were to travel 60 miles per hour, day and night, it would take him five years to go once around a star. This would give him a very poor chance to select what might be the marked dollar from that star, but this amount of time per star would take 500 billion years for each galaxy. Let us suppose our man were extremely speedy, able to look over all of the dollars contained in 100 billion stars each second (instead of 500 billion years), it would still take him about 3×10^9 years to look over the whole mass. This is one half the six billion years back to creation. It is absurd to think that he would have any conceivable chance of picking up the right dollar.[8]

It is our hope that the humans will recognize the impossibility that Biblical prophecy was derived from human wisdom alone; unaided by the inspiration of God. The probability for such a thing is simply too immense to be considered even remotely feasible. Having demonstrated the certain existence of God through each of these vehicles (miracles, supernatural events, and prophecy) we hope to bring the consciousness of the humans back to a realization that (1) God **IS**, and (2) in consequence of His existence there are certain behaviors that the humans must conform to if they wish to avoid an eternity of suffering that is so horrible that the human mind cannot conceive of it in this life. We will also attempt to remind them that circumscribing their lives within the confines of true religious doctrine will not only save them from eternal punishment; it will also make their lives on earth immeasurably happier than they are now; a humanistic world of their creation that has been almost completely subdued by philosophies called materialism and nihilism.

Although the evidence of God should be undeniably convincing to the rational creatures among the human race, we still notice a sad, and horribly destructive, phenomenon we must address before we can proceed any further in our intercession: various degrees of unbelief and faithlessness in the real existence of God. These genera of the human species are referred

---

[8]   Ibid., 96-98.

to as agnostics (those who are unsure of the existence of God) or atheists (those who positively deny the existence of God). This phenomenon is most prevalent among the creatures competing for adulation and worship in their world: the humanists; most of them gravitating to the fields of law, politics, and scientific pursuits. We come to understand that the primary motivation of such creatures lies in their intellectual pride, which compels them to desire to be adulated at a level that is superior to their true God: as supreme intelligences among the creatures who are worthy of the highest form of awe and respect. We see exact parallels between such creatures and the spirit their major religions refer to as Satan, or the Devil. In the human's ancient texts we see an accounting of Satan's fall due to his intellectual pride and his desire to be worshipped as God.

Such creatures recall to our understanding the analogous demonstration that was made earlier in this work, where one holds up for examination a tangible and demonstrable reality before them: "Do you recognize the reality of miracles before you"?; and in response these sorrowful creatures claim, "There are no miracles." Such a person makes this outrageous statement because they don't like miracles—as they prove the reality of a Creator God—and refuse to acknowledge their existence; even though the effects of many miracles have left behind material evidence of their supernatural cause: proof of their reality that is clearly demonstrated in an irrefutable manner!

Notwithstanding the influence of agnosticism and atheism in their world, we will endeavor to explain to the creatures that although their existence is at times intolerably frustrating, sorrowful, and burdensome—the death of loved ones (especially children), injustice, spurned ambition, etc.—the denial of a Creator God is an act of insanity when there are so many objectively real, tangibly material proofs of His existence. We are hopeful that we are able to demonstrate this point to enough of the humans that they will, however begrudgingly, admit the real existence of God and make earnest attempts to live their lives in a manner that is more subservient to His will. From an examination of the humans we understand two things. First, that such a position will be completely unacceptable to a certain segment of their race: the militant atheists. Sadly, there is very little hope for such creatures. They have become so intransigently hateful of God that many of them will deny Him with their lips to their dying breath, even if in their hearts they come to realize that He is real. Our second observation, which instills within us the highest degree of pity and sorrow for this species, is that if the humans continue to deny the real existence of God, and likewise refuse to turn away from their evil behavior(s), there will be no hope of reconciling them with one another; as they will continue on in their attempts to force themselves on one another, even at the expense of the loss of the majority of the human race.

With this understanding, we will nevertheless move forward with our examination of their religions and their relationship to God; in the hope that enough of them can be shown, and convinced of, their errors in order to avert the self-destruction of the human race. Having established that God is real, we must then move on to the third question relating to Him: "What way (religion) is the *true* way to properly worship and recognize Him"? We observe that there are really only two religions that could be viably considered as the one, true religion of the human race: Judaism or Christianity. Why only these two? This conclusion was based on two primary factors that are similar to those that prove His existence, in order of their greatest influence: (1) the miraculous manner in which the religion was revealed to the human race, and (2) miracles and supernatural events associated with the religion. To understand our reasoning we decide to first clearly explain to the creatures what religion is, and likewise what it is not. Properly understood, religion is a vehicle of worshipping the supernatural being that people believe to be the Creator.

Religion is *not* simply a way of living one's life in order to make their lifespan longer, happier, or more peaceful. Any ideological system that serves such an end is instead rightly understood as a philosophy: an ideological framework that one decides to live within. From their history, we understood that the people whom they refer to as the ancient Greeks commonly lived under such a system of competing philosophies: the stoics, the hedonists, the sophists, etc. This is not religion. Instead, religion is the worship of a being that exists outside the material world and who likewise controls and exercises authority over it: an intelligence that is indeed supernatural. For this very reason we were able to reduce our examination of viable religions to these two; due to the supernatural miracles that occurred in coordination with the revelation of the religion, and even more so in the accomplishment of supernatural phenomena by the adherents of the religion during its history.

For reasons of a more practical nature, and in light of the current situation facing the humans, we also decide to consider the Islamic faith as a potential true religion for two reasons. Primarily, because it was claimed to have been revealed to Islam's prophet (Muhammad) in a supernatural fashion;[9] and secondly, because there are such a large number of adherents to Islam within their world; many of whom are purposefully working to destroy their fellow creatures in the name of Islam.

---

[9] During the "Night of Power" Muhammad claimed that an angel, whom he identified as Gabriel, had violently attacked him while announcing his mission as the prophet of Islam.

As it relates to the miraculous revelation of the religion to mankind, we will present the humans with the following, brief comparison to exemplify the point:

Publicly Manifested Miracles Attributed To The Prophet of The Religion		
Judaism (Moses)	**Christianity (Jesus)**	**Islam (Muhammad)**
The plagues of Egypt: 1) Water turned to blood, 2) Frogs, 3) Gnats, 4) Flies, 5) Pestilence, 6) Boils, 7) Hail, 8) Locusts, 9) Darkness, and 10) Death of first born[10]	Supernatural healings: 1) The blind see,[11] 2) The lame walk,[12] 3) Lepers are cleansed,[13] 4) The deaf and dumb hear and speak[14]	None
The parting of the sea to allow the Israelites to escape Egyptian soldiers [15]	The raising of the dead: the widow's son,[16] Lazarus,[17] and the daughter of Jairus[18]	
The providence of food from the heavens: manna[19]	The multiplication of food[20]	

Having limited our initial examination to this point, the supernatural revelation of the religion to humanity, it appears that both Judaism and Christianity have a strong potential claim as the one, true religion of the

---

[10] Exodus 7:14 - 12:29.

[11] John 9:1-7.

[12] Luke 5:18-25, Mark 2:3-12.

[13] Matthew 8:2-3, Mark 1:40-42.

[14] Mark 7:32-35.

[15] Exodus 14:15-31.

[16] Luke 7:11-15.

[17] John 11:1-44.

[18] Luke 8:41-55, Mark 5:22-43.

[19] Exodus 16:4-35.

[20] Matthew 14:15-20, Mark 6:37-44, Luke 9:12-17, John 6:5-13; and on a second occasion . . . Matthew 15:32-38, Mark 8:1-9.

human race. It also appears that Islam's claim to being a true religion is unsubstantiated at this point.

We will then proceed to the secondary factor: the exemplification of the truth of the religion via the facility of miracles that were accomplished through the agency of an adherent to one of their particular religions. We understood that any example of such an event *should* be accepted as evidence of a supernatural being and intelligence working among them. We develop another comparative demonstration to exemplify a few of the miracles that have been attributed to the adherents of the three religions under consideration:

Miracles Attributed To The Adherents of The Religion		
Judaism	**Christianity**[21]	**Islam**
The raising of the faithful to heaven in their earthly form: Enoch[22] and Elias[23]	The raising of the dead: St. Stanislaus	
The raising of the dead: Elias[24]	The incorruptibility of the saints: the absence of decay or deterioration in their deceased bodies	None
The raining of fire from heaven: Sodom & Gomorrah,[25] Egypt,[26] Solomon,[27] and Elias[28]	Eucharistic Miracles: the miraculous transformation and/ or preservation of consecrated Hosts	

Having extended our initial examination to this secondary consideration, the accomplishment of miracles by adherents to the religion(s), it appears that

---

[21] See 'Appendix C: Miracles within Christianity' for greater detail of the miracles.

[22] Genesis 5:23-24.

[23] 4 Kings 2:11.

[24] 3 Kings 17:17-22.

[25] Genesis 19:24.

[26] Exodus 9:23-24.

[27] 2 Paralipomenon 7:1.

[28] 3 Kings 18:38.

both Judaism and Christianity are strengthened in their claims as the one, true religion of the human race. It also appears that the claim of Islam to even be a true religion is becoming increasingly suspect.

The purpose of noting the miracles accomplished by the prophets and adherents of Judaism and Christianity was to establish that, through the agency of supernatural miracles, Judaism and Christianity comply with the law of witness originally established within Judaism; while Islam fails this test: "[15]One witness shall not rise up against any man, whatsoever the sin or wickedness be: *but in the mouth of two or three witnesses every word shall stand.*"[29] Christ confirmed this doctrine, especially as it pertained to Himself:

> [31]If I bear witness of myself, my witness is not true. [32]There is another that beareth witness of me: and I know that the witness which he witnesseth of me is true. [33]You sent to John [the Baptist]: and he gave testimony to the truth. . . [35]He was a burning and a shining light: and you were willing for a time to rejoice in his light. [36]But I have a greater testimony than that of John: for the works which the Father hath given me to perfect, the works themselves which I do, give testimony of me, that the Father hath sent me.[30]

> [36]Do you say of him whom the Father hath sanctified and sent into the world: Thou blasphemest, because I said, I am the Son of God? [37]If I do not the works of my Father, believe me not. [38]But if I do, though you will not believe me, believe the works: that you may know and believe that the Father is in me, and I in the Father.[31]

Christ confirmed that one who testifies solely of or by himself, without the witness of another, is not true. Jesus used the witness of John the Baptist, and the miracles He worked while on Earth (most especially the raising of the dead), as testimony to the truth of His teachings and doctrine. Muhammad, however, had neither the testimony of any man, nor that of God—through miraculous works—to testify to the truth of his doctrines. Everything that is proposed for belief in Islam and the Qur'an came through the doctrines

---

[29] Deuteronomy 19:15.
[30] John 5:31-33, 35-36.
[31] John 10:36-38.

established solely on the testimony of Muhammad; even going to the point of claiming that every utterance he spoke was to be considered the word of God: "³Nor does he [Muhammad] say (anything) of (his own) Desire. ⁴It is no less than Inspiration sent down to him."³² Islam violates the law of witness previously established under Judaism and confirmed in Christianity; especially as it pertains to those proposing prophetic revelation; because Muhammad was the only witness to his own "revelations."

The law of witness is an important point, because the adherents to Islam claim it to be a continuation of Judaism and Christianity: a third and final revelation of God's will. If this is to be true, it must not contradict previously revealed doctrine established by God during the days of Judaism and Christianity. This is because God's will is singular and unchangeable: "For *I am the Lord, and I change not . . .*,"³³ and "Every best gift, and every perfect gift, is from above, coming down from the Father of lights, *with whom there is no change, nor shadow of alteration.*"³⁴

In Jesus' ministry he explicitly stated that it was not his intention to overturn the moral doctrines established within Judaism, but rather to expand on them: "Do not think that I am come to destroy the law, or the prophets. I am not come to destroy, but to fulfill."³⁵ Moreover, God related that any prophet who commanded a deviation from previously established doctrine was speaking through their own presumption, and that he would allow such men to come to pass in order to test people's faith: "¹If there rise in the midst of thee a prophet or one that saith he hath dreamed a dream, and he foretell a sign and a wonder, ²And that come to pass which he spoke, and he say to thee: Let us go and follow strange gods, which thou knowest not, and let us serve them: ³Thou shalt not hear the words of that prophet or dreamer: for the Lord your God trieth you, that it may appear whether you love him with all your heart, and with all your soul, or not."³⁶ This doctrine is also expressed within Christianity: "But though we, *or an angel from heaven*,³⁷ preach a gospel to you besides that which we have preached to you, let him be anathema.",³⁸ and,

---

³² Qur'an 53:3-4.

³³ Malachias 3:6.

³⁴ James 1:17.

³⁵ Matthew 5:17.

³⁶ Deuteronomy 13:1-3.

³⁷ This is especially applicable to Islam, as Muhammad was assaulted by what he believed to be an angel from heaven.

³⁸ Galatians 1:8.

"¹³For such false apostles are deceitful workmen, transforming themselves into the apostles of Christ. ¹⁴And no wonder: *for Satan himself transformeth himself into an angel of light.*"³⁹

These admonitions are directly applicable to Muhammad and Islam, as Muhammad directs his followers to worship a strange god (in relation to the God of Judaism and Christianity) with the same name (Allah) and iconography (crescent moon and star) as an Arabian, pagan, moon god; while trying to represent Allah as being the same deity as the God of Judaism and Christianity. We will not ascribe any intentionally evil motives to Muhammad's ministry, as he was born into a predominantly pagan society and may have been largely ignorant of Judaic and Christian doctrine. In his defense, and as it relates to the beginning of Muhammad's ministry, during the "Night of Power" it was entirely possible that Muhammad was unaware of a demon's ability to present himself as an impostor of the angel Gabriel, which would put him in a position of being more easily deceived; especially since Muhammad claimed that the event manifested itself in a supernatural fashion.

Looking back at the events Muhammad described during the "Night of Power," the manner in which the message was conveyed to him should raise suspicion regarding the true source of the spirit. Muhammad related that he was treated belligerently and attacked repeatedly, and that each attack was so distressful that he thought he might lose his life. The first thing to notice regarding these events is that its nature is incompatible with the manner in which God had theretofore, and thereafter, used to communicate a message to one of His messengers. All throughout the history of Judaism and Christianity it has been the case that when God either speaks directly to men, or sends an angelic messenger, He attempts to ease the natural, human fear at being confronted with a supernatural being rather than compounding it; often counseling the creatures to "fear not" when first addressing them. A second, more overt indicator that the religion is false is the name of Islam's god.

Al-ilah—which translates into the chief among all gods (the Arabian, pagan equivalent to Zeus in Greek mythology)—was the name of a moon god in Muhammad's day. His name was shortened by frequency of usage to Allah. Pre-Islamic archaeological remains show that Allah existed before the advent of Islam and Muhammad's ministry as its prophet. Muhammad's father was named Abd-Allah and his uncle was Obied-Allah; demonstrating

---

³⁹ 2 Corinthians 11:13-14.

that the appellative in honor of the pagan moon god was in common use well before the advent of Islam; especially within Muhammad's own family. Sincere followers of Islam today pray to Allah; envisioning that they are praying to the same monotheistic deity that the Jews and Christians worship. However, the one, true God would never share His name with a false, pagan god enjoying widespread worship among the pagan Arabs of Muhammad's day, and be worshipped as such. Names have definite meanings, for it is primarily by name that humanity is able to finely distinguish various articles. It would be both degrading to the dignity of the true God to be referred to using the same name as a false, pagan god, as well as being too open to a confusion of principles among the humans; especially the Arabs of Muhammad's day who were already familiar with Allah as a pagan moon god. Consider a similar example to properly comprehend the absurdity of naming the one, true, monotheistic God of Judaism and Christianity after a pagan god.

After Israel became an established nation, they were in constant warfare with the Philistines. One of the Philistine cities was Accaron (Ekron). The pagan god of that city was Beelzebub, who was once consulted by Ochozias, a king of Judah, and later came to be known among the Jews as the "prince of the devils." The one, true god of Judaism and Christianity would certainly never tolerate being addressed as Beelzebub, an espoused enemy of Himself. And as if that isn't enough, the primary iconography of Allah, the pagan moon god, was the crescent moon and star; the same iconography associated with Islam, which should make sincere people, Muslim or not, reflect more soberly and honestly on the true nature of the worship of Allah.

We must also examine the text of the religion (Qur'an) and the doctrines that it develops to more clearly demonstrate the false nature of Islam. We will bring to the creatures' attention several areas in which Judaic and Christian doctrines are not only slightly altered, but completely contradicted; thereby disqualifying Islam from consideration as revelation in the same line as Judaism and Christianity. Some of the most significant contradictions are: (1) the treatment of those outside the religion and the propagation of the Faith, (2) the treatment of enemies, (3) the treatment of women, (4) the treatment of marriage and divorce, (5) idolatry, and (6) the part of human nature (lower pleasures of the flesh or higher pleasures of the spirit) that the religion appeals to. Let's begin with the way in which the Faith is spread. Judaism and Christianity offer the following guidance:

Arise, and go to Ninive the great city: and preach in it the preaching that I bid thee.[40]

And going, preach, saying: The kingdom of heaven is at hand.[41]

That which I tell you in the dark, speak ye in the light: and that which you hear in the ear, preach ye upon the housetops.[42]

And he said to them: Go ye into the whole world, and preach the gospel to every creature.[43]

To whom he said: To other cities also I must preach the kingdom of God: for therefore am I sent.[44]

And he commanded us to preach to the people, and to testify that it is he who was appointed by God, to be judge of the living and of the dead.[45]

Preach the word: be instant in season, out of season: reprove, entreat, rebuke in all patience and doctrine.[46]

The chosen method of proselytization is through preaching to the people. People are not compelled to believe in the Faith, because compulsion makes void free will. On the other hand, Islam enjoins a contradictory, much more severe method of spreading the Faith:

[190]Fight in the cause of Allah those who fight with you, but do not transgress limits; for Allah does not love transgressors. [191]And slay them wherever you catch them, and turn them

---

[40] Jonas 3:2.
[41] Matthew 10:7.
[42] Matthew 10:27.
[43] Mark 16:15.
[44] Luke 4:43.
[45] Acts 10:42.
[46] 2 Timothy 4:2.

out from where they have turned you out; for tumult and oppression are worse than slaughter; but do not fight them at the Sacred Mosque, unless they (first) fight you there; but if they fight you, slay them. Such is the reward of those who suppress faith.[47]

Let those fight in the cause of Allah who sell the life of this world for the Hereafter. To him who fights in the cause of Allah, – whether he is slain or gets victory – soon shall We give him a reward of great (value).[48]

Not equal are those believers who sit (at home) and receive no hurt, and those who strive and fight in the cause of Allah with their goods and their persons. Allah has granted a grade higher to those who strive and fight with their goods and persons than to those who sit (at home). To all (in Faith) Allah has promised good: but those who strive and fight He has distinguished above those who sit (at home) by a special reward.[49]

Those who believe, and adopt exile, and fight for the Faith, in the cause of Allah, as well as those who give (them) asylum and aid, – these are (all) in very truth the Believers: for them is the forgiveness of sins and a provision most generous.[50]

But when the forbidden months are past, then fight and slay the Pagans wherever you find them, and seize them, beleaguer them, and lie in wait for them in every strategem (of war); but if they repent, and establish regular prayers and practise regular charity, then open the way for them: for Allah is Oft-forgiving, Most Merciful.[51]

---

[47] Qur'an 2:190-191.
[48] Qur'an 4:74.
[49] Qur'an 4:95.
[50] Qur'an 8:74.
[51] Qur'an 9:5.

Say: 'Can you expect for us (any fate) other than one of
two glorious things – (martyrdom or victory)? But we can
expect for you either that Allah will send His punishment
from Himself, or by our hands. So wait (expectant); we too
will wait with you.[52]

Therefore, when you meet the Unbelievers (in fight), smite
at their necks; at length, when you have thoroughly subdued
them, bind a bond firmly (on them): thereafter (is the time
for) either generosity or ransom: until the war lays down
its burdens. Thus (are you commanded): but if it had been
Allah's Will, He could certainly have exacted retribution
from them (Himself); but (He lets you fight) in order to test
you, some with others. But those who are slain in the way of
Allah, – He will never let their deeds be lost.[53]

These passages from the Qur'an exhort the followers of Islam to extreme
violence and the murder of those whom either do not believe in Islam or
refuse to convert to it; completely contradicting the previously established
method of proselytization and changing its nature from one chosen by
force of argument and gentle persuasion to one chosen by force of arms and
compulsion. Moreover, Islam establishes an internal self-contradiction on
this point; as the Qur'an forbids compulsion in religion: "Let there be no
compulsion in religion: Truth stands out clear from Error: whoever rejects
Evil and believes in Allah has grasped the most trustworthy hand-hold,
that never breaks. And Allah hears and knows all things."[54] The second
contradiction of Judeo-Christian doctrine to observe is the way in which
people are taught to treat their enemies. Judaism teaches that vengeance
is God's prerogative alone; while Christianity adds to this doctrine that of
forgiveness:

Revenge is mine, and I will repay them in *due* time, that
their foot may slide: the day of destruction is at hand, and
the time makes haste to come.[55]

---

[52] Qur'an 9:52.
[53] Qur'an 47:4.
[54] Qur'an 2:256.
[55] Deuteronomy 32:35.

[23]If therefore thou offer thy gift at the altar, and there thou remember that thy brother hath anything against thee; [24]Leave there thy offering before the altar, and go first to be reconciled to thy brother: and then coming thou shalt offer thy gift.[56]

Revenge not yourselves, my dearly beloved; but give place unto wrath, for it is written: *Revenge is mine, I will repay*, saith the Lord.[57]

And to him that striketh thee on the *one* cheek, offer also the other. And him that taketh away from thee thy cloak, forbid not to take thy coat also.[58]

But I say to you, Love your enemies: do good to them that hate you: and pray for them that persecute and calumniate you:[59]

Contrarily, Islam commands retribution and vengeance:

The prohibited month for the prohibited month, – and so for all things prohibited, – there is the law of equality. If then any one transgresses the prohibition against you, transgress you likewise against him. But fear Allah, and know that Allah is with those who restrain themselves.[60]

The third contradiction of established, Judeo-Christian doctrine lies in the way in which women are treated. The Bible states:

[25]Husbands, love your wives, as Christ also loved the church, and delivered himself up for it: [26]That he might sanctify it, cleansing it by the laver of water in the word of life: [27]That he might present it to himself a glorious church, not having

---

[56] Matthew 5:23-24.
[57] Romans 12:19.
[58] Luke 6:29.
[59] Matthew 5:44.
[60] Qur'an 2:194.

spot or wrinkle, or any such thing; but that it should be holy, and without blemish. [28]So also ought men to love their wives as their own bodies. He that loveth his wife, loveth himself.[61]

Contrarily, Islam establishes a paradigm that condones forced submission through violence:

Men are the protectors and maintainers of women, because Allah has given the one more (strength) than the other, and because they support them from their means. Therefore the righteous women are devoutly obedient, and guard in (the husband's) absence what Allah would have them guard. As to those women on whose part you fear disloyalty and ill-conduct, admonish them (first), (next), refuse to share their beds, (and last) beat them (lightly); but if they return to obedience, do not seek against them means (of annoyance): for Allah is Most High, Great (above you all).[62]

This passage from the Qur'an practically guarantees that Muslim women will be brutally subjugated by Muslim men due to the precise wording of the passage. It refers to "those women on whose part you *fear* disloyalty and ill-conduct." *Fear* is the operative word here; meaning that if a man merely suspects a woman of some misdeed he is free to beat her for her suspected misdeed, even if that misdeed is purely imaginary on the man's part. For those men with depraved imaginations, the women in their lives are guaranteed a miserable existence, because this passage does not require that any suspected misdeed be demonstrated or proved.

The fourth contradiction of established, Judeo-Christian doctrine lies in the treatment of marriage and divorce. Within Judaism it was considered allowable for a man to issue a wife a bill of divorce if he was unhappy with her for some reason:

[1]If a man take a wife, and have her, and she find not favour in his eyes, for some uncleanness: he shall write a bill of divorce, and shall give it in her hand, and send her out of

---

[61] Ephesians 5:25-28.
[62] Qur'an 4:34.

his house. [2]And when she is departed, and marrieth another husband, [3]And he also hateth her, and hath given her a bill of divorce, and hath sent her out of his house or is dead: [4]The former husband cannot take her again to wife: because she is defiled, and is become abominable before the Lord: lest thou cause thy land to sin, which the Lord thy God shall give thee to possess.[63]

Within Christianity, Christ expanded on this doctrine and taught an even more stringent enjoinder against divorce; the only exception being that of adultery. The reason for this is explained that once a man and woman become married they become as "one flesh" in the eyes of God, and that it was God's intention from the beginning that man and woman would take one spouse and remain with them for life:

[3]And there came to him[64] the Pharisees tempting him, saying: Is it lawful for a man to put away his wife for every cause? [4]Who answering, said to them: Have ye not read, that he who made man from the beginning, *Made them male and female?* And he said: *[5]For this cause shall a man leave father and mother, and shall cleave to his wife, and they two shall be in one flesh.* [6]Therefore now they are not two, but one flesh. What therefore God hath joined together, let no man put asunder. [7]They say to him: Why then did Moses command to give a bill of divorce, and to put away? [8]He saith to them: Because Moses by reason of the hardness of your heart permitted you to put away your wives: but from the beginning it was not so. [9]And I say to you, that whosoever shall put away his wife, except it be for fornication, and shall marry another, committeth adultery: and he that shall marry her that is put away, committeth adultery.[65]

Looking at what Islam prescribes on this point demonstrates an absolute contradiction of the Judaic and Christian law regarding marriage;

---

[63] Deuteronomy 24:1-4.

[64] Jesus

[65] Matthew 19:3-9.

compelling men to sin against the Judaic and Christian law in order to obey the Islamic law:

> So if a husband divorces his wife (irrevocably), he cannot, after that, re-marry her until after she has married another husband and he has divorced her. In that case there is no blame on either of them if they re-unite, provided they feel that they can keep the limits ordained by Allah, which He makes plain to those who understand.[66]

Beyond what the Qur'an establishes for marriage, a certain type of marriage called "Mut'ah" exists within Islam. Mut'ah is a marriage of a fixed duration that is agreed on by the man and woman before entering into the temporary marriage: one hour, one day, one week, etc.; whatever duration the two agree on. It is also referred to as a "pleasure marriage."

The fifth contradiction of established doctrine relates to idolatry. In Judaism and Christianity idolatry is absolutely forbidden; so much so that it is the First Commandment in the foundational laws of their religion(s): the Ten Commandments:

> [6]I am the Lord thy God, who brought thee out of the land of Egypt, out of the house of bondage. [7]Thou shalt not have strange gods in my sight. [8]Thou shalt not make to thy self a graven thing, nor the likeness of any things, that are in heaven above, or that *are* in the earth beneath, or that abide in the waters under the earth. [9]Thou shalt not adore them, and thou shalt not serve *them*. For I am the Lord thy God, a jealous God, visiting the iniquity of the fathers upon their children unto the third and fourth generation, to them that hate me, [10]And shewing mercy unto many thousands, to them that love me, and keep my commandments.[67]

However, in violation of this preeminent commandment of the Jewish and Christian faiths, Islam tolerates idolatry:

---

[66] Qur'an 2:230.
[67] Deuteronomy 5:6-10.

You do not revile those whom they call upon besides Allah, lest they out of spite revile Allah in their ignorance. Thus have We made alluring to each people its own doings. In the end will they return to their Lord, and We shall then tell them the truth of all that they did.[68]

The sixth contradiction of established doctrine lies in the different parts of human nature that Islam appeals to in contrast to Judaism and Christianity. Christianity calls for its adherents to deny themselves the sensual things "of the flesh" in order to attain to the spiritual; as well as a depiction of the afterlife that is wholly spiritual and devoid of sensual appeals:

> [11]Who said to them: All men take not this word, but they to whom it is given. [12]For there are eunuchs, who were born so from their mother's womb: and there are eunuchs, who were made so by men: and *there are eunuchs, who have made themselves eunuchs for the kingdom of heaven.*[69] He that can take, let him take *it.*[70]

> [5]For they that are according to the flesh, mind the things that are of the flesh; but they that are according to the spirit, mind the things that are of the spirit. [6]For the wisdom of the flesh is death: but the wisdom of the spirit is life and peace. [7]Because *the wisdom of the flesh is an enemy to God*; for it is not subject to the law of God, neither can it be. [8]And they who are in the flesh, cannot please God.[71]

> Adulterers, know you not that the friendship of this world is the enemy of God? *Whosoever therefore will be a friend of this world, becometh an enemy of God.*[72]

> [24]And Jesus answering, saith to them: Do ye not therefore err, because you know not the scriptures, nor the power of

---

[68] Qur'an 6:108.

[69] Priests.

[70] Matthew 19:11-12. Biblical basis for the celibacy of the priesthood.

[71] Romans 8:5-8.

[72] James 4:4.

God? ²⁵For *when they shall rise again from the dead, they shall neither marry, nor be married, but are as the angels in heaven.*[73]

Contrary to these principles, Islam appeals to humanity's carnal, sensual nature to promote devotion among its followers; as evidenced by Mut'ah marriages and the appeal of the faithful Muslim warrior's promise of seventy-two virgins for all eternity. Muhammad had multiple wives and concubines; making him a serial adulterer under the Judeo-Christian moral ethic. One of his "wives" included a seven year old child (Aisha) whom he was patient enough to wait on until her tenth year before consummating the "marriage": an act Muslims are unashamed of. Contrarily, such behavior is considered to be pedophilic child molestation within Judeo-Christian morality: two absolutely abominable, mortal sins. In the Qur'an's descriptions of the afterlife the depictions represented are those of more sensual appeals of the flesh:

But those who believe and do deeds of righteousness, We shall soon admit to Gardens, with rivers flowing beneath, – their eternal home: therein shall they have Companions pure and holy: We shall admit them to shades, cool and ever deepening.[74]

⁴⁰But the sincere (and devoted) Servants of Allah, – ⁴¹For them is a Sustenance determined, ⁴²Fruits (Delights); and they (shall enjoy) honor and dignity, ⁴³In Gardens of Felicity, ⁴⁴Facing each other on Thrones (of dignity): ⁴⁵Round will be passed to them a cup from a clear-flowing fountain, ⁴⁶Crystal-white, of a taste delicious to those who drink (thereof), ⁴⁷Free from headiness; nor will they suffer intoxication therefrom. ⁴⁸And besides them will be chaste women, restraining their glances, with big eyes (of wonder and beauty). ⁴⁹As if they were (delicate) eggs closely guarded.[75]

⁵¹As to the Righteous (they will be) in a position of security. ⁵²Among Gardens and Springs; ⁵³Dressed in fine silk and in

---

[73] Mark 12:24-25.

[74] Qur'an 4:57.

[75] Qur'an 37:40-49.

rich brocade, they will face each other; [54]So; and We shall join them to Companions with beautiful, big and lustrous eyes. [55]There can they call for every kind of fruit in peace and security;[76]

Before we leave the discussion of Islam, there is a final item that we think we should bring to the human's attention; that the behavior Islam promotes corresponds exactly to that of communism, except under the guise of religious pretext. Communist societies operate from the top down. A law-making body dictates to the affected society how they are to behave, down to the minutest detail in many instances. The purpose of such an intrusive micromanagement of the population is to exercise absolute, tyrannical control over the population. The justification for the tyranny is always that it's for "the good of the people," and it's founded on two assumptions: (1) that individual citizens are too ignorant to manage their own lives competently and responsibly; thereby necessitating an "enlightened" government bureaucracy of intellectually elite creatures to rule over the subjugated society; and (2) that tyrannical control of the society is necessary to more efficiently control the "just" redistribution of material wealth among all its members. Communism is atheistic, and therefore materialistic; seeing the greatest goal in society as being the redistribution of material wealth more uniformly throughout the population. These goals are achieved through mass murder, violence, and terroristic tactics intended to subdue the populace.

Likewise, in the case of Islamic societies, they also operate from the top down. A clerical law-making body dictates to the affected society how they are to behave, down to the minutest detail in many instances. The purpose of such an intrusive micromanagement of the population is to exercise absolute, tyrannical control over the population. The justification for the tyranny is always that it's for "the good of the people," and it's founded on two assumptions: (1) that individual citizens are too evil to manage their own lives morally and responsibly; thereby necessitating an "enlightened" clerical body of morally elite creatures to rule over the subjugated society; and (2) that tyrannical control of the society is necessary to more effectively promote the proper level of "holiness" and virtue among all its members. Islam's religious foundation sees the greatest goal in society as maintaining and propagating the Faith. These goals are achieved through mass murder, violence, and terroristic tactics intended to subdue the populace.

---

[76] Qur'an 44:51-55.

It is our hope that we will be able to sufficiently demonstrate the false nature of Islam as a religion to the humans, and that many of the world's Muslims may come to see that Islam can in no way be a further revelation of God's will in the same line as Judaism and Christianity; as most of its doctrines are completely opposed to those taught by Judaism and Christianity. Moreover, due to the nature of the development of God's revelation of Himself to mankind, there would be no need of further revelation. Under Judaism, God showed His friendship to His favored people: the Israelites. When Christ came, He then extended this fellowship to the entire human race. With all human beings having been included through Christ's revelation of how to attain to God, there would be no need for further revelation; especially one that so greatly contradicts previously established doctrines. Moreover, having extended His friendship to the entire human race through Jesus Christ, we must ask the humans, "Who else would Muhammad's revelation encompass if Jesus Christ had already expanded His friendship from the Israelites alone to the whole of the human race"?

We are certainly convinced that there will inevitably be many zealous adherents to Islam who will be so absolutely invested in their false religion that they will refuse to recognize the many glaring faults in their belief system; especially its contradiction of God's will—demonstrated through His revelations to the Jewish and Christian Faiths—and in consideration that Islam claims to be the third revelation of God's will. However, it is also our hope that we may be able to reach a great many of them; those creatures (Muslim and non-Muslim alike) who possess a desire to seek the truth and the ability to critically compare and analyze known facts.

Which Religion is the True Religion?

Through our examination of the human's history, we have come close to answering this question. Via the use of supernatural events that have transpired during the revelation and historical life of Judaism and Christianity, God has put his proverbial "stamp of approval" on these two religions. Moreover, it is important to note that He has not performed any such favor for any other religion or self-proclaimed prophet. In resolving to determine which religion is the true religion of the human race, the first question that needs to be answered is, "In light of the fact that both religions have received supernatural witness of divine approval, are both religions true and valid"? While this remains a remote possibility, we find it highly unlikely for a couple of reasons. To begin with, because God's will is singular, there can only be one way to approach to and worship Him as He desires. Secondly, if there were multiple true religions, with each one containing elements within the religion that contradicted the other(s), it would establish a situation whereby God would be contradicting Himself while simultaneously placing the human race in constant conflict regarding the contradictory elements within their respective religions.

Within both Christianity and Judaism God is referred to as "Our Father" or "The Father," which would make all human beings His spiritual children. From that perspective, we would then all be spiritual brothers and sisters to one another. Under such an understanding, maintaining multiple true religions is like having inconsistent rules and standards within the same household; one group of children is said to operate according to one set of rules, while another group of children operates under a different set of rules. Such a scenario can only work toward division and animosity within a household, as different children within the same household will ascribe their allegiances to those who worship as they do, and withhold favor from those who do not follow as they do. Moreover, such a scenario is counterproductive to God's purpose, which is the salvation of the human race. For these reasons we find it highly unlikely that there could be more than one true religion at any one time.

At this point we stand at an *almost* irreconcilable contradiction. God has shown His favor to both Judaism and Christianity via many and varied extraordinary miracles, yet it doesn't seem possible that there could be more than one true religion. The only possible way to reconcile the potential contradiction is to understand the validity and truth of these religions within the context of time. If both religions are (or were) true, yet it seems that only one can be true at any one point in the history of the human race; it then appears that the only way to reconcile both realities is that if one (Judaism) was the original true religion at one point in time, and that it was superseded by the other (Christianity) at a subsequent time in the past. This situation was foretold and expected by the ancient Israelites, and is fully supported by the sacred texts of both religions: the Tanakh (Judaism) and the Bible (Christianity), which also includes the Tanakh within its "Old Testament."

From the beginning of Judaism, Moses announced a messianic prophet[1] who would come in the future: "The Lord thy God will raise up to thee a PROPHET of thy nation and of thy brethren like unto me: him thou shalt hear:"[2] During the long history of Judaism, those prophecies related to the coming of the Messiah foretold by Moses, and other of the ancient Jewish prophets, came to be known as messianic prophecies. This type of prophecy is spread all throughout the Tanakh and is especially prevalent in the writings of the prophets. As it relates to the relationship between Judaism and Christianity, it is important to note that the details of Jesus' life have fulfilled all the prophecies, with the only exception being those prophecies that pertain to a future time. No other man has ever done this. Moreover, Christ Himself explicitly declared Himself to be the Messiah on several separate occasions:

> [61]But he held his peace, and answered nothing. Again the high priest asked him, and said to him: Art thou the Christ, the Son of the blessed God? [62]And Jesus said to him: *I am.* And you shall see the Son of man sitting on the right hand of the power of God, and coming with the clouds of heaven.[3]

> [25]The woman saith to him: I know that the Messias cometh (who is called Christ); therefore, when he is come, he will tell

---

[1] A Messianic prophet is one who delivers the faithful from their captivity. In the case of Moses, he was messianic in the sense that he delivered God's chosen people from the earthly slavery of Egypt. In Christ's case, He is messianic in the sense that he has delivered God's chosen people (the human race) from the spiritual slavery of sin, which is why Moses used the term "like unto me" . . . a Messiah.

[2] Deuteronomy 18:15.

[3] Mark 14:61-62.

us all things. [26]Jesus saith to her: *I am he*, who am speaking with thee.[4]

[24]The Jews therefore came round about him, and said to him: How long dost thou hold our souls in suspense? If thou be the Christ, tell us plainly. [25]Jesus answered them: I speak to you, and you believe not: the works that I do in the name of my Father, they give testimony of me. . . [30]*I and the Father are one*. . . [36]Do you say of him whom the Father hath sanctified and sent into the world: Thou blasphemest, because I said, *I am the Son of God?*[5]

But since any man can claim to be anything he pleases, heaven itself testified to Jesus' identity at the occasions of His baptism and during His transfiguration:

(Baptism)
[13]Then cometh Jesus from Galilee to the Jordan, unto John, to be baptized by him. [14]But John stayed him, saying: I ought to be baptized by thee, and comest thou to me? [15]And Jesus answering, said to him: Suffer it to be so now. For so it becometh us to fulfil all justice. Then he suffered him. [16]And Jesus being baptized, forthwith came out of the water: and lo, the heavens were opened to him: and he saw the Spirit of God descending as a dove, and coming upon him. [17]*And behold a voice from heaven, saying: This is my beloved Son, in whom I am well pleased.*[6]

(Transfiguration)
[1]And after six days Jesus taketh unto him Peter and James, and John his brother, and bringeth them up into a high mountain apart: [2]And he was transfigured before them. And his face did shine as the sun: and his garments became white as snow. [3]And behold there appeared to them Moses and Elias talking with him. [4]And Peter answering, said to Jesus:

---

[4] John 4:25-26.
[5] John 10:24-25, 30, 36.
[6] Matthew 3:13-17.

Lord, it is good for us to be here: if thou wilt, let us make here three tabernacles, one for thee, and one for Moses, and one for Elias. ⁵And as he was yet speaking, behold a bright cloud overshadowed them. *And lo, a voice out of the cloud, saying: This is my beloved Son, in whom I am well pleased: hear ye him.*[7]

There are a tremendous number of people in the human's world today—indeed, the greatest majority of them—who doubt the reliable witness of the Gospels and of the Bible. We can only encourage these creatures to take Christ's advice on this point; that if they will not believe in the word that He preached, then people should take as a reliable testament to the truth, in support of the doctrine being taught, the accomplishment of miraculous, supernatural events. God would not demonstrate His approval of the doctrine being taught, in such an extraordinary way, if the doctrine were false and led the human race away from Him:

> ²Now when John had heard in prison the works of Christ: sending two of his disciples he said to him: ³Art thou he that art to come, or look we for another? ⁴And Jesus making answer said to them: Go and relate to John what you have heard and seen. ⁵The blind see, the lame walk, the lepers are cleansed, the deaf hear, the dead rise again, the poor have the gospel preached to them.[8]

> ³⁷If I do not the works of my Father, believe me not. ³⁸But if I do, though you will not believe me, *believe the works*: that you may know and believe that the Father is in me, and I in the Father.[9]

As Jesus tried to teach people that they should believe in Him due to the testimony of the supernatural acts accomplished through His intercession, the same principle and standard should be applied to those who follow Him; and, once again, Jesus foretold of such people:

---

[7] Matthew 17:1-5.
[8] Matthew 11:2-5.
[9] John 10:37-38.

¹⁹And seeing a certain fig tree by the way side, he came to it, and found nothing on it but leaves only, and he saith to it: May no fruit grow on thee henceforward for ever. And immediately the fig tree withered away. ²⁰And the disciples seeing it wondered, saying: How is it presently withered away? ²¹And Jesus answering, said to them: Amen, I say to you, if you shall have faith, and stagger not, not only this of the fig tree shall you do, but also if you shall say to this mountain, Take up and cast thyself into the sea, it shall be done.[10]

Those who "stagger not" in their faith—performing great miracles and even raising the dead—are known today as Catholic saints. They have been performing such works since Jesus' coming into the world, and it is a requirement of the Church (excepting martyrs) that before a person can be canonized as a saint within the Church there must be at least two miracles that can be directly attributed to the intercession of the saint in question; whether the miracle happened during the saint's life or after their death. Moreover, since the coming of Jesus Christ into the world, it is only within the Christian faith that such works have been accomplished. The reason He primarily reserves such great miracles for the Catholic saints is to give supernatural witness to His claim that Christianity is the only true faith—"Jesus saith to him: I am the way, and the truth, and the life. ***No man cometh to the Father, but by me.***"[11]—and that the Catholic Church is the only true Church.

To conclude our intercession regarding the religions of their world, we hope that by putting all the evidence before the humans many of them will come to understand that Judaism was the original, true religion; and that when Jesus came into the world His teachings expanded the true Faith beyond the limits of the Israelites unto the rest of the human race; proving His divine favor by performing supernatural acts impossible for mere men to accomplish, just as Moses did when he delivered the Hebrews from the Egyptians. Finally, and especially because Islam is becoming a violently expansionary religion within their world, we likewise hope that we are able to demonstrate to the intellectually honest of their race—*especially* those Muslims who possess good will, but have been innocently

---

[10] Matthew 21:19-21.
[11] John 14:6.

enough deceived—that Islam is a false religion developed by its prophet (Muhammad) as a hybrid of Arabian paganism, and that its false nature is primarily demonstrated via its contradiction of Judaism and Christianity—the two religions known to have found favor with God—on a great many moral and ethical points.

What Is The True Path to Peace and Freedom?

Through a number of self-supporting influences throughout the world—primarily via concerted and purposeful indoctrination within the government-run school systems within societies all over the world—the human race has been predominantly transformed into a suicidal species due to the degenerate psychological attacks they have been subjected to over the course of their entire lives. This is certainly true of Western civilization, but this phenomenon is just as true in practically all other nations and societies of the world.

Earlier, I promised an honest attempt to demonstrate the dire situation that the world is facing today. The attempt will be made by demonstrating the dangers of some of the most powerful social forces working within the world today. These social forces primarily revolve around religion, which is why a concerted effort has been made to examine the topic and explain why Islam is false and discuss the evidences for why Christianity is the one, true religion of the human race. However, the reality still exists that a great many of you are probably still unconvinced. This is only natural considering the humanistic impulses that have become so increasingly and indelibly ingrained within the human mind since the advent of the French Revolution and the rationalism it introduced into the "modern" mind. However, after exploring the natural effects and consequences that accrue from following the various religions of the world, it is hopeful that the reader will be able to appreciate the dangers of the false religions and the beneficence of the true Faith.

There are four major religions on Earth that are the greatest competitors for allegiance among the human race: Judaism, Christianity, Islam, and humanism (a.k.a. "secularism," and as expressed by its animating philosophy: "liberalism"). Some people may be surprised to see humanism described as a religion; thinking it more of a philosophical outlook. However, it is a religion, and this is more clearly understood when one considers what a god is. In short, a god is the master that one serves. Humanists pursue their own, self-animated desires. This is the basis for their life philosophy: "If it feels good, do it." Because the master the humanist serves is their own desires, it makes humanism a subtle form of self-worship; causing each humanist to think of themselves as their own quasi-deity unto themselves: obeying the dictates of their own desires and combating any that would dare to contradict them. This theme—the god within—is the central focus of "New Age" spiritualism; but it has also spilled over to the great majority of the human race, regardless of any professed adherence to an established religion.

Of these four religions, two of them are murderous and suicidal (Islam and humanism), while the other two promote, and are supportive of, human life (Judaism and Christianity). Let's examine them in order to understand why humanism and Islam are so dangerous, as well as understanding why Judaism and Christianity promote what is supportive of human life.

Let's begin with the most prevalent religion on the face of the Earth, which claims the great majority of the world population: humanism. That humanism is the most prevalent religion on earth in this age may take more than a few readers by surprise, but let me more clearly explain why this is the certain case. To be an adherent to an established, doctrinal religion—such as Judaism, Catholicism, or Islam—one must adhere to *all* its teachings and honor the sacred text of the religion as if it were a divine revelation from God to man; demanding allegiance and obedience to the doctrine revealed by the religion. Those people who fully adhere to their faith make up only a very small minority of the proclaimed practitioners of any religion. The mark of the humanist, especially those who practice humanism while claiming to adhere to an established religion, is one who believes their own ideas to be true and correct rather than those taught to them by their religion; picking and choosing which doctrines they will believe in and adhere to, and which ones they will discard: "Cafeteria/Liberal Catholics," "secular" Jews, and "secular" Muslims. Such an attitude has become so common in the modern world that those who actually adhere to their faith are labeled as "fanatics"; while those who water down their faith, in order to make it more palatable to their sensibilities, consider themselves the "enlightened" ones.

Why has the great majority of the human race adopted such a self-deceiving disposition: claiming to be an adherent to a particular Faith in one breath, and then denying many of the fundamental doctrines of their proclaimed Faith in the next; all the while ridiculing and demeaning the true adherents to their Faith? Once again, it is mankind's greatest enemy (simple, human pride) that is primarily responsible for this perverse disposition—just as it is the primary source of all conflicts on Earth—but cowardice plays a large part as well. Pride is especially prevalent because most everybody in the modern world wants to maintain a positive self-image

186

of themselves; not having the requisite courage to look at their failures and weaknesses honestly and forthrightly. This sort of mind set is becoming more deeply engrained within the modern world as most government schools have undergone efforts to fortify their student's "self-esteem"; with such misplaced intentions merely resulting in greatly increased attitudes of self-importance and entitlement.

As most of the human race has become more averse to recognizing their own failings, they have likewise become more certain (in their own minds) of their own superior intelligence: intellectual pride. These mental processes have their foundation in rationalism. The very great majority of modern humanity, thinking that they can come to the truth of any situation through the means of their intellect alone, has come to rely solely on their intellect; denying the primary doctrine of all doctrinal religions: that mankind cannot come to the truth without the aid of divine revelation. Essentially, most of modern humanity is calling God a liar by saying within their hearts, "No, God, if you even exist, I have no need of divine revelation. I can figure out everything I need to know on my own; thank you very much."

This has led to a situation whereby a great majority of people who claim adherence to a particular Faith merely profess it with their lips, but do not truly believe it in their hearts and minds, and approach the practice of their Faith with tepidity and disdain in many instances. These souls no longer believe in divine revelation, and even contradict and deny the doctrine(s) that their proclaimed Faith establishes as infallible. Christians and Jews of this persuasion claim that the Bible isn't meant to be taken literally when they come across a passage they find disagreeable or difficult to perform. This type of reaction is common when dealing with passages that demand death for certain types of behavior; as the great majority of modern humanity lacks the fortitude to confront and punish evil in this world. Muslims of this persuasion proclaim that Islam is a religion of peace; denying the clear call, which the Qur'an demands, to murder those who don't ascribe to their religion until the whole world falls under the chains of Islam. Again, this is like saying to God within one's heart, "No, God. You're wrong. I see the error in your thinking, and I'm going to follow my 'enlightened' way instead."

Herein lies the greatest danger of humanism. By denying the true God, such people set themselves up as their own gods; essentially worshipping their own intellect, while remaining willfully blinded to how flawed their intellects actually are. As the intellect of the humanist becomes his own god, they then take it upon themselves to define their own moral code, which is unique to each humanist; causing humanism to eventually devolve into complete amorality, because a single, uniform moral code is no longer recognized within society. This is especially true for those who espouse no religion: agnostics and atheists. The consequence of humanism on the personalities of those who subscribe to it is almost always high levels of narcissism; because they follow the path of self-adulation as they consider themselves to be correct in practically all their ideas and opinions. Such mental processes then lead the humanist into sentiments of condescension and intellectual superiority in relation to those who do not agree with them on any particular point. As the sickness progresses, the humanist then goes beyond being certain of their superiority to a point where they believe themselves justified in using physical force and violence to put their "enlightened" ideas into motion (most of today's politicians, but especially amongst the socialists and communists of the world).

The world has seen much of this type of evil over the last century: Lenin, Stalin, Hitler, Mao Tse Tung, Pol Pot, Castro, Ho Chi Minh, etc. Frighteningly, we are seeing this disposition arise again all over the world in too many political figures to name here, including a very large number of such creatures within American politics; primarily within the Democrat Party. The great danger that humanism poses to the human race is due to what happens when the psychosis plays out to its full expression. In all societies built on humanism, the political structure that evolves is *always* socialist or communist. This is because the humanist denies life after death, and therefore demands that all social action must be taken to improve the immediate, material conditions of this world. As history has shown mankind time and time again, when societies reach this degree of humanistic degradation mass murder follows soon afterward, as the humanists force themselves on any who oppose their demands for a willfully slavish society; imprisoning opposition in "re-education camps" and murdering the most recalcitrant and defiant.

The world has begun to witness the re-emergence of this behavior in most all nations and societies of Western civilization, as the militant atheists and humanists have begun campaigns to criminalize any expression of religion in public—most especially Christianity—through "hate crime" and "hate speech" laws designed to encourage suicidal reprobation under the guise of "human rights" and suppress morality; so as to corrupt the whole of society at an accelerated pace. That this type of corruption is actively encouraged and abetted by the majority of politicians in the West, who are elected officials willfully chosen by the majority of their constituents, demonstrates the ascendancy of humanism in our age not only within the political class, but within the larger mass of society as a whole.

Next, let's consider Islam. The dangers of Islam are becoming more visible with each passing year. The most obvious danger is in Islam's central philosophy: the requirement to subjugate the entire world under Islamic rule. There is no separation of Church and State under Islam. Within Islamic culture, Islam subtends all human affairs. Religious leaders (imams) constitute the highest controlling political authority within the society (Iran, for example) and their legal code (Sharia) is based on Islamic religious tenets. This has become dangerous because, as we examined earlier, Islam worships a false, pagan deity. The result has developed into an ideology of mass murder perpetrated upon those of the human race who refuse to worship false gods. The practical consequences of Islam are always tyrannical, recalling its similarities to communism, and turn out to be an almost complete abdication of the dignity that God intended the human race to aspire to. Muslim women are treated as creatures almost less than human, and objectified by the Muslim male as breeding stock and sexual receptacles intended for their pleasure and at their will. The true Muslim male—those who follow the direction of the Qur'an as it is explicitly and literally stated in the book—is extremely carnal and violently aggressive. His visualization of paradise consists not of being in the presence of God for eternity; but rather of achieving the finest of fruits and earthly delicacies, and especially of possessing virgins to use sexually for all eternity.

Their idea of eternal pleasures are constituted in carnal and sensual delights rather than spiritual delights, which is why jailhouse conversions to Islam are so easily obtained, as the great majority of convicted felons are already predisposed to carnal and violently aggressive mentalities. The violent nature of the doctrinally adherent Muslim is amply, and routinely, demonstrated; as evidenced by the news reports of beheadings and suicide bombings of both non-Muslims and Muslims who do not practice "pure" Islam. The secular Muslim is not being referred to here. The "secular faithful" of any religion are truly humanists: accepting what is appealing in their professed religion and denying what is difficult. The true Muslims are those whom Westerners today call Islamofascists, Islamists, jihadists, etc.: those trying to force their religion on the rest of the world through murder and deceit. If the reader has never read a Qur'an it would be wise of you to do so; in order to understand that the politically correct misinformation being fed to you about how the Islamist is perverting a religion of peace is absolutely false. The jihadist is the strictest of conformists to the text and dictates of the Qur'an and Hadith (record of the sayings, customs, and traditions of Muhammad): the two most sacred books in Islam. Accordingly, their whole life is dedicated to obeying and fulfilling the word of Allah, as it was delivered to them through Muhammad in the Qur'an:

> Remember your Lord inspired the angels (with the message): "I am with you: give firmness to the Believers: I will instill terror into the hearts of the Unbelievers: you smite above their necks and smite all their finger-tips off them."[1]

> And fight them on until there is no more tumult or oppression, and there prevail justice and faith in Allah altogether and everywhere; but if they cease, verily Allah sees all that they do.[2]

> Fight them, and Allah will punish them by your hands, cover them with shame, help you (to victory) over them, heal the breasts of Believers,[3]

> Fight those who do not believe in Allah nor the Last Day, nor hold that forbidden which has been forbidden by Allah and His Messenger, nor acknowledge the Religion of Truth, (even if they are) of the People of the Book, until they pay the Jizya with willing submission, and feel themselves subdued.[4]

> O you who believe! Fight the Unbelievers who gird you about, and let them find firmness in you: and know that Allah is with those who fear Him.[5]

Instead, it is the secular, "Islam is a religion of peace" Muslims who are perverting the true identity of Islam and what it intends for the world; either out of deceitful motives to mislead non-Muslims, or out of sincere ignorance on their part.

---

[1] Qur'an 8:12.

[2] Qur'an 8:39.

[3] Qur'an 9:14.

[4] Qur'an 9:29.

[5] Qur'an 9:123.

Finally, understanding the evident dangers inherent within humanism and Islam, we'll look to the great advantages to human civilization in following a Judeo-Christian moral and ethical code. The best way to explain the beneficence of such a life is to examine the primary rules of Judeo-Christian life—the Ten Commandments—to see the advantages to be gained by obeying them and the harm that will come from discarding them.

The Ten Commandments may be grouped into roughly two groups: those whose end is meant to accomplish the worship of, and gratitude toward, God; and those whose end is meant to provide for justice among mankind: regulating the daily behavior and interactions within society. As our focus is on demonstrating the practical benefits to humanity of following the Ten Commandments, we will not examine those that refer to the worship of God. With that understood, let's briefly examine, from a perspective of observable actions and consequences, why adhering to them, as difficult or unpleasant as they may be to conform to at times, is vastly superior to the amorality and moral relativism inherent within humanism; as well as the only possible path to obtaining peace within human societies and civilizations.

The first Commandment to deal with human justice is: "Thou shalt honor thy Father and thy Mother." This Commandment provides for the foundation of all social order. The fundamental basis of all human socialization begins in the home. By honoring (obeying their rules and following their instruction) one's parents, several beneficial ends are achieved. To begin with, it establishes a recognizable hierarchy and social order within the family: the familial "chain of command"; with each member of the family fulfilling their particular, assigned role within the family. With the establishment of such a hierarchy, all within the family intuitively "learn their place" (their roles and responsibilities) within the family; imparting an understanding to the children of the virtues of humility and submission to proper authority while simultaneously providing a sense of order, direction, and purpose within their lives; so that the children do not grow up aimlessly confused and arbitrary in their actions, and in the intentions and purposes that impel those actions.

While this Commandment specifically addresses one's own father and mother within the family unit, the same principle also extends outside the family to more generally include the submission of the children within society to the recognition of the greater wisdom of their elders. This principle recognizes the accumulated wisdom that is normally inherent within the older members of society. Having more life experience to draw from than children, the parent is more properly disposed to direct their children with greater wisdom as a result of their superior level of worldly experience regarding this world's contradictions and unseen traps; both apparent and real.

Within a morally relativistic society, which does not honor its parents and elders, all people are arbitrarily crowned "equal" in wisdom or understanding. In matters of morals and behavior there is no distinction offered or accepted between the foolishness of youth due to a lack of life experience and the wisdom of society's seniors due to their greater abundance of life experience. The child, with little or no experience of what is required of them to properly, or successfully, order their minds, lives, and affairs; is taught that their opinion(s), regardless of their lack of life experience, are equally as valid as their parents, who have accumulated life experience through "the school of hard knocks"; and that solely based on the authority of their own caprice they may contradict their parent's authority and rule as they please.

Such foolishness can only tend toward one end: social upheaval, violence, and anarchy; both within the home specifically; and within society more generally; as children who grow up in such an environment learn to hold all authority in contempt, except when it serves their own, selfish purposes. As the child is not cognizant or mindful of the real dangers of poor decisions made in youthful ignorance and impatience, the character that develops through moral relativism can only gravitate toward disorder, discontent, and danger; as such people are neither accustomed to submitting to authority or looking beyond their short-term and immediate desires; most always remaining ignorant and thoughtless to the consequences of their actions. Accordingly, and in their selfish ignorance, they will most always choose the quick and easy gratification of short-term desires while remaining ignorant of the negative consequences that accrue to both others and themselves.

The second Commandment regarding human justice is, "Thou shalt not murder." This Commandment is both the most easily understood from a self-intuitive perspective, and about the most universally disregarded, Commandment. If a person's right to live is not secure all other rights and privileges are immediately null and void; for if a person is not alive to exercise any particular right or privilege, none of them are of any worth to the affected person. Honoring this Commandment provides security for the individual, so that they may freely exercise their other rights as human beings. While the previous Commandment lays the foundation for social order, this Commandment is meant to guarantee that people will be allowed to observe the social order it establishes and live out the balance of their natural lives within it. However, within a morally relativistic society, what constitutes murder, as opposed to justifiable homicide or self-defense, is, once again, left to the determination of each individual. If human history has taught us anything, it should have taught mankind that any act, no matter how barbaric, will always be excused through some sort of grossly perverse self-justification. For example, (1) it's acceptable to abort a baby if it is the "wrong" sex, potentially handicapped in some way, or an unwanted result of irresponsible promiscuity; because a fetus is not human, it is just a mass of tissue; or (2) it is one's duty to murder others if they don't subscribe to your belief system (Islam and communism). There are many other examples of such murderous self-justifications that the reader is undoubtedly able to recollect.

By leaving the determination of what is, or is not, murder to the individual, all security of one's right to live within society is summarily nullified; as the most perverse and deranged people within any society (often a person with numerous titles and academic honors) will endeavor to define what is, or is not, murder based on their own self-interested desires; most often founded on a utilitarian perspective and completely devoid of any consideration for another's right to life when it conflicts with, or is disagreeable to, the amoral person's self-interested goals. An example of the dangerous consequences of moral relativism is the justification offered for involuntarily euthanizing the tragically sick, elderly, or infirm "for their own good." Because the moral relativist sees the world through utilitarian eyes, they see no worth in a life that is not useful to themselves or others; in complete disregard of the desires of those being considered for extermination.

Adolf Hitler began such practices, under the self-justifying guise of purifying and perfecting the Aryan race (eugenics), when he quietly began exterminating the severely physically infirm and mentally retarded in Nazi Germany. Recently, this practice has begun anew in the United States with the extermination of Terry Schindler: a woman in a vegetative state who was deemed unfit to live by her former husband and the courts of the State of Florida. This type of self-justification can also be seen in ethical arguments over the use of embryonic stem cells and the use of genetic engineering to create babies with desired characteristics: the modern incarnation of eugenics. Not such an enviable position when one considers that the modern eugenicists are expanding upon, and promoting, ideas originally developed by Adolf Hitler's Third Reich for the purpose of achieving utilitarian, social engineering ends.

The third Commandment regarding human justice is, "Thou shalt not commit adultery." Observing this commandment aids in maintaining trust within a marital relationship. The trust maintained by observing marital fidelity directly fortifies the family in its role as the foundation of human civilization(s), which then incidentally strengthens the society within which the family lives. Moreover, the consequences of violating this Commandment can be terrible to both families and society as a whole. Married people are expectant of fidelity from their spouse, and rightfully so; as a married couple pledges solemn vows of fidelity to each other during the marriage ceremony. The adverse consequences to families proceeds from the fact that when fidelity in marriage is violated, the foundation of the family—trust in one's spouse—is completely undermined; with the only saving grace in such a circumstance being the capacity of the betrayed spouse to forgive the unfaithful spouse. Moreover, once betrayed, even though a spouse may be forgiven for their violation of the marriage, the betrayed spouse may never be able to regain the trust that existed between the couple before the infidelity occurred. The adverse consequences to society as a whole proceeds from the consequences of an unforgiving spouse. At best, the consequences of an unforgiving spouse will be a broken home and a dissolved family; a consequence that dissipates the society within which the affected family lives, as well as permanently scarring the children within the family. At worst, the consequences of an unforgiving spouse may include violence or the killing of the unfaithful spouse or their adulterous lover.

Within the construct of moral relativism there seems to be a schizophrenic view accorded to adultery; an underlying contradiction that unites most all morally relativistic dogma: the recognition of the evil nature of the act, while simultaneously condemning those who take notice of the evil and condemn the perpetrator; as if those who notice and condemn the evil are worse than those who perpetrate it. For example, when modern political figures are discovered to have violated their marriage vows, it is the moral relativist who comes to the defense of the adulterer. The most common rhetorical defense is that such demonstrated infidelity to their solemn oath is "a private matter between [the adulterer] and their spouse." Moreover, such a position held by the moral relativist espouses the foolish idea that it doesn't matter that a public figure is unfaithful to their family, so long as they faithfully fulfill the duties of the public office they hold. Such excuses demonstrate a grotesque, blind ignorance of the basic understanding that if a person is willing to violate a solemn oath and vow made to a spouse in order to satisfy selfish desires, jeopardizing the trust and health of their immediate family, they will certainly not hesitate to violate the public trust; especially when they have no familial, emotional ties to an unseen, unfelt, abstraction: "the people" (a.k.a. the "great, unwashed masses").

The fourth Commandment regarding human justice is, "Thou shalt not steal." This commandment is of great importance to the stability of any society; for if it is not adhered to the society that is replete with thieves will begin to break down due to the prevailing cynicism and mistrust of one's fellow man that will permeate throughout the affected society; essentially isolating the people within and fragmenting them into factious groups for the purpose of self-protection. Moreover, from an empathetic standpoint regarding the daily interaction between people, honoring this Commandment is the most constructive toward building strong communities and societies; for when people respect their fellow man's property, the whole of society feels themselves more secure in their lives and possessions. Let's look at the essence of personal property in order to understand why it is such an important concept and an inviolable right within a sustainable, civil society.

Every personal possession accumulated by any honest person is ultimately acquired through labor. When a person performs a task or service for another they are then compensated for their labor based on a predetermined level of compensation: their salary or wage. Henceforth, the laborer enters the marketplace with money and proceeds to accumulate the personal property they need or desire: food, shelter, clothing, luxuries, etc. Additionally, consider that the time a person devotes to accomplishing labor consumes a particular amount of time in their life. Understanding these points leads to the observation that the theft of another's property actually defrauds a person of not only the immediate property that is stolen, but the amount of time in a person's life, in the form of labor, necessary to originally earn the amount of wealth needed to acquire the property.

Through a proper understanding of what money represents, and the material goods accumulated through its use, it can be seen that stealing is actually a usurpation of a person's life; as represented by the amount of time in their life used to perform labor. Owing to the nature of time, the limited amount of it each human being possesses in the course of their life, the impossibility of recovering it once it passes, and that each person's time is properly, and constructively, used to provide for their own needs and wants should lead any person to understand the great injustice done to another when their material wealth or property is stolen by another.

In contrast, the moral relativist, seeing themselves as their own self-appointed arbiter of justice and morality, excuses the theft of another person's property, which is actually the usurpation of another person's life and time, by declaring themselves the only ones fit to determine how a person's labor, as represented by their money and material property, should be used. This is a fundamental precept of self-righteous elitism. The morally relativistic "elites" tell themselves, and all others, that only they are wise enough to properly allocate the material resources of society properly. Armed with this self-justification, they then proceed to justify gathering a great amount of the material production of society into their own hands and using it as they see fit; as they (in their own minds) are the only ones within their respective societies who possess the intelligence and self-righteous virtue to use the material wealth of the society wisely.

This is the essence of socialism and communism. The extraordinary, narcissistic arrogance and condescension of the morally relativistic elitist is astonishing in its naked audacity. They view their fellow man, whether the consideration is consciously active in their minds or not, as a "useless eater." In the liberal mind, the average man must submit to the rule of the intellectual elites for their own good; for any other course of action that deviates from the grand, benevolent action of the intellectually elite will only result in a negative outcome that is detrimental to society; or so the liberal, intellectual elitist believes. Therein lies *the* primary contradiction of liberalism, socialism, and communism: in the name of "social justice," justice is denied to all via the theft and accumulation of much (socialism) or all (communism) of a society's wealth into the hands of those few who, in their own arrogant minds, know better than everyone else regarding how to use the material wealth of a society for the welfare of all.

The fifth Commandment regarding human justice is, "Thou shalt not bear false witness against your neighbor." This Commandment is not only admirable and desirable in human society; it is absolutely indispensable; for without it the only possible results are confusion, anarchy, and ultimately violence. The primary directive of this Commandment is an injunction against calumny. The negative consequences and injustice that develop from calumny are many and varied, but the most important one is the unjust disparagement of another's reputation when they are falsely accused of something they are not guilty of.

Following such a circumstance, it is not uncommon for the falsely accused to attempt to exact some form of retribution against their false detractors; which only serves to perpetuate a cycle of antagonism, confusion, and, in the most severe cases, violent revenge. Beyond the immediate interpretation of calumny, this Commandment speaks secondarily to falsehoods in general. Every human being makes decisions and choices in life based on what they believe to be true and real. If people are laboring under false pretenses, and making important decisions based on false information, the consequences are almost always contrary to what is desired, and under the most extreme situations may lead to someone's death. For example, improperly identifying someone on the battlefield or using a dangerous piece of equipment in an unsafe manner, or for a purpose that it was not intended. Regardless of the severity of the situation involved, lying in general will always gravitate toward confusion and anarchy within society; as people make unwise decisions and take improper actions based on false information, which is then followed by social unrest as a consequence of the frustration and anger that follows as people fall from one false move to another.

From the perspective of the moral relativist, the ends justify the means. If it is necessary to blacken another's reputation and good name, or to intentionally mislead the public so as to steer their minds in a particular direction, the moral relativist will justify such treachery with the excuse that the deception is meant to ultimately serve some end they determine to be noble, and that only the moral relativist fully understands. However, as can be seen in today's world, the only outcome of these tactics is bitter enmity and division within society, which ultimately overshadows and undermines any "noble" sentiments the moral relativist may have been aiming for.

The sixth Commandment regarding human justice is, "Thou shalt not covet thy neighbor's property." This Commandment is closely related to "Thou shalt not steal," but also reinforces the Commandments that speak to the worship and honor of God; as an incidental benefit to accrue from this Commandment is the vulgarity of the value of material goods and wealth in relation to higher, "first principles." The immediate result of honoring this Commandment, as it applies to human justice, is that it would circumvent the motivation that ultimately leads to theft, but secondarily this Commandment is also a condemnation of materialism. Adhering to this Commandment keeps people's minds more proximately focused on the first principles of justice between mankind, rather than the selfish gain of material goods; which ultimately renders a person's property, and their sense of trust of their fellow citizens, much more secure than within a society that does not honor this principle. Moreover, observation of this commandment engenders a spirit of gratitude within a society for those things each person does possess, while disabusing the citizens of envious jealousy and other considerations regarding other people's property. The moral relativist, being an atheist, sees nothing beyond this life. From such a perspective, the natural frame of mind to develop is one of immediate gratification; for from such a perspective a person has to get as much enjoyment out of life as they can before this life is over.

⁵For our time is *as* the passing of a shadow, and there is no going back of our end: for it is fast sealed, and no man returneth. ⁶Come therefore, and let us enjoy the good things that are present, and let us speedily use the creatures as in youth. ⁷Let us fill ourselves with costly wine, and ointments: and let not the flower of the time pass by us. ⁸Let us crown ourselves with roses, before they be withered: let no meadow escape our riot. ⁹Let none of us go without his part in luxury: let us everywhere leave tokens of joy: for this is our portion, and this *our* lot. ¹⁰Let us oppress the poor just man, and not spare the widow, nor honour the ancient grey hairs of the aged. ¹¹But let our strength be the law of justice: for that which is feeble, is found to be nothing worth. ¹²Let us therefore lie in wait for the just, because he is not for our turn, and he is contrary to our doings, and upbraideth us with transgressions of the law, and divulgeth against us the sins of our way of life.⁶

Such a frame of mind draws its practitioners into a schedule of priorities that gravitates toward the destruction of justice within society, because it completely disregards principles of justice between people in deference to the gratification of immediate, material desires. Moreover, such sentiments create a gross spirit of ingratitude within the society and a lack of appreciation for the material articles a person already possesses; so that, in a psychologically dissipating spiral, the more material goods a person accumulates, the less they appreciate them, which drives them to desire more material goods.

The seventh, and final, Commandment regarding human justice is, "Thou shalt not covet thy neighbor's wife." This Commandment may also be seen as a complement to a previous Commandment: "Thou shalt not commit adultery." Like the previous Commandment, it is meant to keep a person's mind on the first principles of justice between mankind, rather than the gratification of a person's immediate desires; as every man would certainly consider it an injustice to himself to need to be concerned about other men trying to seduce his wife. For the same reason (atheism) as the previous Commandment, the moral relativist is highly disdainful of, and unlikely to honor, this Commandment, as it detracts from their selfish

---

⁶ Wisdom 2:5-12.

ability to gratify their immediate sensual desires by using another man's wife; the negative consequences of such behavior being both obvious and previously discussed.

From an evaluation of the Commandments that speak to human relations and justice between mankind, evaluated outside of moral or theological judgments, and while demonstrating their positive value based exclusively on an examination of the actions and consequences that result from observing, or not observing, them; it can be seen that observing these Commandments as the basis for morality and social order, even if the reader does not believe in God or any "higher power," is the only way to render justice between mankind, establish order in human relations, and tend toward the greatest possible happiness within any society. This conclusion is obvious when a person offers the same consideration to others that they would expect for themselves; for violating any of them only gravitates a society toward anarchy and results in an injustice done to another.

Rebellion in the home leads to a rebellious disposition within the members of society at large; murder destroys a society by destroying the value of life as well as the actual lives themselves that compose a society; adultery undermines the foundation of every civilization (the family); theft deprives people of the honest products of their labor; calumny and lying cause anarchy, social unrest, and in severe circumstances threatens people's lives; desiring another person's property gravitates the mind toward materialism and a forgetfulness of the importance and beneficence to be found for all by honoring the first principles of justice in human interactions; and desiring another man's wife leads to adultery and the same disregard for justice in human interactions that results from materialism. From this the reader can see, if they are honest with themselves, that observing the Ten Commandments, at the very least those relating to human justice, are of the utmost importance to the successful propagation of a healthy and sustainable society, even when viewed from a sterile, utilitarian perspective.

Why Does the Human Race So Despise God and His Moral Precepts; Even to the Point of Denying His Existence!?

My dear brothers and sisters, the answer to this question is the key to understanding what causes *all* our misery! It is simultaneously understandable and intolerable to our human nature! In short, the human being despises God's laws because they militate against our natural instincts. The two legs (one material, one spiritual) upon which our rebellious nature stands are: (1) the "concupiscence of the flesh" (material) and (2) human pride (spiritual). What does such a term as "concupiscence of the flesh" mean? Concupiscence is a strong desire of the senses. It is particularly applicable to sexual desire, but it is not limited to that sphere alone. It includes any sensate desire: anything that attracts a person through the physical senses: sight, hearing, touch, smell, and taste.

Being temporal creatures of this world, we are naturally attracted, consoled, and entertained by the things of this world through our physical senses. In this sense, we are no different than unintelligible, wild animals; for they operate under the same principles! However, as human beings, we are gifted with the higher faculty of reasoning; an intellectual ability our strictly animal brethren (dogs, cats, horses, etc.) are not capable of exercising. This is the capacity that has enabled human beings to excel beyond all other animals and dominate the world. It is also the central point upon which our trials—the "test" of this world—gravitate. Having an intellect to discern the consequences of our actions, we are then expected to use this discernment to judge our actions, and likewise recognize and promote the good (that which promotes life and strengthens human beings in both their individual and social capacities: sustaining and propagating civilization(s)) while condemning and punishing the evil (that which destroys life and reprobates human beings in both their individual and social capacities: debasing and eroding civilization(s)).

It is an innate component of our human nature to desire comfort, ease, and luxury in our daily lives. Any honest person recognizes this reality, as we see it every day; both within ourselves and within others. Given a choice between working a construction project, tilling a field, or persuading a difficult business prospect; or contrarily, lounging on the beach with a refreshment of our choice within easy reach, surrounded by a group of our favorite friends; the *great* majority of people would prefer the carefree and easy life over the stressful and laborious life. Amid this obvious reality, why then do people choose to spend most of their adult lives in labor rather than in luxury? Obviously, it is because if we do not work nothing would get done: food would not be grown, houses and roads would not be built, and all the other material items needed to sustain and enrich our daily lives would not be provided for. Human civilization would collapse and most of the human race would perish from self-neglect. In short, the human race chooses a life of labor out of necessity, rather than from a true preference for labor over luxury.

The totality of human history is a testament to both the necessity and the great efficacy of labor. Moreover, those civilizations that have labored with greater conscientiousness and proficiency have proved themselves superior to those of lesser aptitude. This reality is most immediately observable in the arena of sports; where those who labor the greatest in preparation for an athletic contest, among those of nearly equal natural abilities, prove superior to their competition when put to the test. This also conforms to the principle that greatness lies not in doing extraordinary things, but in doing ordinary things in an extraordinary manner. While we can understand these things intellectually, the concupiscence of the flesh—our natural, sensate-driven desire for comfort, ease, and luxury—remains a constant force at work within us trying to divert our efforts from laboriously productive pursuits to diversionary, unproductive ones. As a result of this ever-present reality, every one of us is constantly engaged in a battle against ourselves to act in a manner that renders us healthy, responsible, and productive members of society.

We know the value of labor and why we should not only perform it, but perform it with as high a degree of excellence as we are able. However, we simultaneously feel an aversion to it. The only "tie-breaker" that gives the victory to either the duties of labor or the pleasures of luxury is our will; choosing between doing what we know we should do, or doing what we want to do. Every day we each make a multitude of conscious choices between these two opposing forces at work within us, and the result of the choices we make ultimately determines both our success in life as well as our overall impact and contribution to the society within which we live. Consider that history remembers with admiration the great explorers, discoverers, doctors, scientists, holy men and women, and others who have actively and diligently labored their whole lives for the singular purpose of serving their fellow man and advancing the human condition. On the other hand, history remembers with contempt and loathing the ambitious and self-serving (Hitler, Lenin, Stalin, Mao Tse Tung, Pol Pot, etc.), welfare cheats, thieves, murderers, drug dealers, child molesters, and all others who live their lives animated by the singular purpose of indulging their selfish or sensual desires.

These principles directly relate to the recognition and worship of God, because it is well known among the human race that the "children of God" are expected to deny themselves and embrace the habit of selfless service to others. This includes the recognition of the sinfulness inherent in the indulgence of our sensual desires. However, in this current age, it is to be noticed that the great majority of the human race is succumbing to the natural, sensate desires generated by the concupiscence of the flesh. In comparison to civilizations of the past, all manners of sensate self-indulgence are up sharply. Within Western civilization, and especially the United States, the rates of obesity—a consequence of luxury and gluttony—have reached levels considered by most health professionals to be of epidemic proportions; so much so that a television program has been developed to propel this problem to the forefront of society's consciousness: *The Biggest Loser.* All manners of dissipating conduct and sensate immorality—especially sexual deviancy— are becoming more prevalent, and some are even being rendered culturally acceptable due to political and cultural agitation being fomented by society's reprobates: divorce, adultery, abortion, homosexuality, transgenderism, pedophilia and child molestation, alcoholism, drug abuse (both illicit and prescribed), etc. All these manifestations (and others) of dissipating, deviant, and suicidal behaviors are markedly up in relation to past generations.

To be one of the persons engaged in the "liberal"/"progressive," "If it feels good do it," rising tide of dissolute reprobation that is sweeping throughout humanity—especially those who indulge themselves without any sense of remorse, shame, or guilt—by default render themselves enemies of both the human race, and most especially to those religious principles that prohibit such dissolute behavior. This is the only possible consequence for those who indulge their sensual desires indiscriminately and attempt to corrupt others to their dissipating habits; for they desire to compromise themselves and others with an easy conscience. Naturally, they despise morally principled people who rebuke them for their dissolute conduct; and, by extension of the principle, they especially despise the author of moral principles: God.

The second leg that supports our rebellious nature against God is human pride. The essence of pride lies in the desire to exalt oneself above others:

the natural, self-glorifying craving for attention and recognition from others as possessing capabilities or accomplishments in any field of endeavor that excel beyond the average and cause us to stand out among our peers, and which likewise engenders sentiments of superiority in relation to others. Those infected by pride suffer from a delusional, destructively perverse presumption that they are more "special," intelligent, or important, than their fellow man in some fashion. The natural consequence of such mental processes, if left unchecked, is gross narcissism and arrogant conceit. Pride most often manifests itself through two avenues: intellectually and morally. In this age the primary avenue of intellectual pride comes from the field of "science," which was greatly emboldened in its atheistic proclivities with the advent of Charles Darwin's *theory* of evolution. It is only natural that this would be the foreseeable consequence, because scientists who spend their lives engaged in uncovering and understanding the material mysteries of the universe, by necessity of the nature of the work (exploring and deducing previously unknown principles and realities), are people of innately superior intelligence in relation to the common man. Possessing a superior intellect in one endeavor opens the door to human pride, so that those who fall prey to it then think themselves superior to others not only in their limited field of expertise, but in all operations of human understanding.

This behavior is especially evident in this age, as many so-called "scientists" have abandoned true science and have instead become socio-political agitators and engineers due to the incomprehensible heights of their intellectual pride: self-convinced of both their own brilliance and the dangerous stupidity (in their minds) of those who question or contradict their assertions. The current debate over anthropogenic (caused by humans) "global warming" (a.k.a. "climate change") is an excellent example of this phenomenon. To the strident "global warming" or "climate change" protagonists, those who disagree with their apocalyptic forecasts, and the accompanying seizure of political power they propose, are dangerous dolts who are imperiling the future survival of the human race and the very planet itself. Proudly self-convinced of their intellectual superiority in relation to their detractors, these creatures tirelessly work for the enslavement of the human race in order to avert an imagined catastrophe.

As pride takes over the human mind the interior focus of such individuals changes from the mere pursuit of excelling in their particular sphere of knowledge to the reprobated pursuit of justifying their own beliefs at seemingly all costs; to the point of attempting to pervert the perception of reality through the misrepresentation of demonstrable facts. In essence, they attempt to remake reality into their own image in order to pervert the perception of reality toward accepting their counterfeit offering; so as to convince others of their self-proclaimed infallibility and intellectual superiority. Intellectual pride invariably leads to a hatred of God, because when people believe themselves to be the most intellectually superior creatures in the world they then put themselves in a position of being direct competitors with God for the worship and adulation of their fellow man, which they believe to be their rightful due as a consequence of their self-convinced intellectual superiority.

For professing themselves to be wise, they became fools.[1]

Moral pride is manifesting itself in our day via multiple avenues of social activism. The morally proud, most often referred to as the "self-righteous," or "self-justified," indulge the dangerous belief that their ideas and plans for the human race are morally superior to those that have come before them, and that they are morally superior to those who oppose their grand plans for the human race. They propose that they would be able to cure numerous diseases (cancer, AIDS, etc.), eradicate poverty, destroy bigotry, achieve "equality" and "social justice," etc., if the human race would simply follow their "wise" counsel. The natural home for social activists lies primarily within the political sphere, but is not exclusively limited to politicians. These creatures also exist in large numbers within our legal system(s), within our government schools, and among "community organizers" and organizations that ply their livelihood by fomenting social agitation, discontent, and unrest. What makes these creatures so dangerous is that their self-presumption of perfect morality leads them to castigate, calumniate, and demagogue those who disagree with them; guaranteeing social upheavals, misery, and discontent.

Historically, the morally proud have been the primary, and greatest, instigators of mass murder. The atheistic left likes to denounce religion because of historical instances of violence that have resulted as a consequence of religious disputes; castigating all religion because of it. However, they appear to be blind to the reality that over the past several centuries— beginning with the French Revolution and continuing on through this age's criminally misguided fascination with socialism and communism—the most notorious violence against the human race has been perpetrated in the name of atheistic humanism's (socialism and communism) pursuit of "perfecting"

---

[1]   Romans 1:22.

the human race and ushering in, as Karl Marx coined a phrase, the "social New Jerusalem"[2] and the universal brotherhood of mankind. The primary stumbling block of the morally proud is that the foundation of their motives lies in their own self-glorification as being the saviors of mankind: stamping out "inequality," which they define through a purely materialistic construct, through any of a number of fantastical and grandiose schemes that they promise will bring about a social utopia, while purposefully dismissing the reality that all forms of socialism are morally criminal; as socialism is a form of universal theft on a universal scale.

What they fail to understand is that their morality is not based on justice. It is based on jealousy, envy, and just about every other debased human vice. Instead, their false morality intentionally endeavors to perpetrate injustice, as its foundation is rooted in a purely materialistic utilitarianism; where the worth of life is callously measured by a person's potential productivity: their *material* usefulness to society. St. Paul rebuked this type of pride in one of his epistles, which includes a prophetic discourse on the current state and severity of the reprobation of the human race:

> [23]And they changed the glory of the incorruptible God into the likeness of the image of a corruptible man, and of birds, and of fourfooted beasts, and of creeping things.[3] [24]Wherefore God gave them up to the desires of their heart, unto uncleanness, to dishonour their own bodies among themselves. [25]Who changed the truth of God into a lie; and worshipped and served the creature rather than the Creator, who is blessed for ever. Amen. [26]For this cause God delivered them up to shameful affections. For their women have changed the natural use into that use which is against nature.[4] [27]And, in like manner, the men also, leaving the natural use of the women, have burned in their lusts one towards another, men with men working that which is filthy, and receiving in themselves the recompense which was due

---

[2]   Karl Marx and Friedrich Engels, *Manifesto of the Communist Party*, (New York, NY: Signet Classic, 1998), 85.

[3]   Pantheistic environmentalism.

[4]   Feminism initially, which then progressed over the past century to include lesbianism.

to their error.[5] [28]And as they liked not to have God in their knowledge, God delivered them up to a reprobate sense, to do those things which are not convenient; [29]Being filled with all iniquity, malice, fornication, avarice, wickedness, full of envy, murder, contention, deceit, malignity, whisperers, [30]Detractors, hateful to God, contumelious, proud, haughty, inventors of evil things, disobedient to parents, [31]Foolish, dissolute, without affection, without fidelity, without mercy. **[32]Who, having known the justice of God, did not understand that they who do such things, are worthy of death; and not only they that do them, *but they also that consent to them that do them*.**[6]

The morally proud despise God because, in order to test the fidelity of the human race, He allows all manner of hardship and misery to transpire within the lives of all human beings. Despising the arduous and afflicting nature of this world, the morally proud deceitfully declare the false promise that humanity can be alleviated of their portion of suffering in this world if they instead follow the path commanded by them rather than the path commanded by God. They purposefully set themselves into a position of directly competing with Him for both glorification and the gratitude of the human race. Jesus understood and foresaw this perversion of morality and rebuked its perpetrators in a parable directly applicable to the situation:

[9]And to some who trusted in themselves as just, and despised others, he spoke also this parable: [10]Two men went up into the temple to pray: the one a Pharisee, and the other a publican. [11]The Pharisee standing, prayed thus with himself: O God, I give thee thanks that I am not as the rest of men, extortioners, unjust, adulterers, as also is this publican. [12]I fast twice in a week: I give tithes of all that I possess. [13]And the publican, standing afar off, would not so much as lift up his eyes towards heaven; but struck his breast, saying: O God, be merciful to me a sinner. [14]I say to you, this man went down into his house justified rather than the other:

---

[5] Homosexuality
[6] Romans 1:23-32.

because every one that exalteth himself, shall be humbled:
and he that humbleth himself, shall be exalted.[7]

Although each of these manifestations of human pride are socially dangerous on their own, what makes the situation so potently destructive is their convergence in our age; as the intellectually proud have come to view their advocacy in their particular field of interest (global warming, environmentalism, etc.) as not only intellectually superior to their detractors, but morally superior as well. As the saying goes, "all bets are off" once these creatures reach such a delusional state. They will happily employ *any* measure, no matter how deceitful and dishonest, and without shame or the slightest tinge of moral compunction, to run roughshod over their opposition and forward their ideology; for in their minds any means— including imprisonment and mass murder (for example, the Soviet Union and Communist China)—justify their self-righteously presumed ends. This has been the historical behavior of these creatures, and it will happen again if sanity remains out of reach for both these pitiable souls and the rest of humanity, which has the power to deny them the ability to realize their self-glorifying ambitions.

Why do these sad people make the insanely outrageous claim that God doesn't exist, and why are they so persuasive among our fellow creatures; even in the face of objectively demonstrable miracles that prove His existence? The answer lies in both the proponents of such sad folly and those who accept their arguments. It's similar to a dance, in which both participants of the dance must cooperate with each other to successfully consummate the act. Such mutual cooperation in their own self-deception can be summed up through the trite axiom, "It takes two to tango." From the perspective of the intellectually proud atheist, they desire to propagate the denial of the objectively real (the reality of miracles, supernatural and paranormal activity, and infallible prophecies as proof of God's existence) because they wish to be worshipped and glorified as superiors among their fellow creatures. From the perspective of those who accept their arguments, they desire to believe that there is no God because admitting His existence would necessarily demand certain behavior from them that directly contradicts their natural desires. If there were no God, there would be no need to restrain oneself from self-destructive, albeit highly enjoyable, behavior, which completes

---

[7] Luke 18: 9-14.

the psychological circle and brings us back to the other self-justification for denying God's existence: the concupiscence of the flesh.

Let me offer an anecdotal example to demonstrate why and how the human race is so easily seduced toward evil through the concupiscence of the flesh. As a child, I attended several summer camps. While at one of these camps a couple of other boys approached me and promised to introduce me to a wonderful sensation that I would marvelously enjoy. Not having any idea of any ill intention on their part, I happily agreed to be shown this wonderful sensation. They said that it could only be felt in the water of the lake at camp. The three of us waded out into the lake up to our necks. I stood in place while one boy, standing by my side, promised that I would soon experience the promised sensation. True to his word, a few seconds later, I felt a warm sensation circle my leg and radiate further up and down my leg. It was truly enjoyable and mystifying! Primarily, I was wondering what the cause of such soothing and enveloping warmth could be; and secondarily, why was the other boy giggling uncontrollably while this great experience was happening to me!?

The experience lasted less than a minute, and immediately afterward I was wondering how I could come to experience it again, and on demand, if I pleased. As we walked to shore I questioned the other boys regarding the cause of this wonderful sensation and how I could experience it again. At this point the giggling bystander, who was in on the prank from the start, became even more uncontrollable in his laughter. When we got to shore the perpetrator of the prank admitted what he did, which immediately explained the other boy's humor . . . he had urinated on my leg. Utterly humiliated by the disgrace, I was so stunned that I could not consider how to react, while the other two boys walked away laughing.

Likewise, too many human beings living in this era willfully submit to disgracing and defiling themselves via all manners of immorality and perverse reprobation because, as St. Paul noted, ". . . as they liked not to have God in their knowledge, God delivered them up to a reprobate sense, to do those things which are not convenient."[8] The great majority of the human race in the modern era indulges their sensate desires too indiscriminately because they do not seriously contemplate the world to come after our passing from this one; especially as it relates to the horrible promises of indescribable, *eternal* punishments for those who oppose God's will during their life on Earth. Instead, like insensible animals, too many people merely follow the

---

[8] Romans 1:28.

dictates of their sensate desires wherever they lead them, no matter how degrading they may be.

Due to the relative shortness of our lives, many of us ingrain a fatalistic mentality into our life philosophy: ". . . Let us eat and drink; for to morrow we shall die."[9] For those who desire to believe that there is no God, their primary motivation is that it is the *apparently* easiest path to take through life, as our lives are often times difficult to tolerate. The great majority of people are easily led into agnosticism and atheism because adhering to the principles of religious doctrine, especially self-denial, would require them to live a life greatly bereft of relief from the exigencies of the world that they currently enjoy. To most people, horrifically "softened up" by the past several generations of "soft living" that scientific advances have enabled the human race to enjoy, such a way of life is simply too *apparently*, and unbearably, repugnant.

---

[9] From Isaias 22:13.

For Catholics

As the central point of this work is to describe how the human race may once again achieve some semblance of harmony and abate the quickly unraveling social anarchy that is enveloping our species; the role the Catholic faithful can, and *must*, play in order to achieve this positive goal will be explained.

What the human race is witnessing in the modern world is the emergence of global socialism and communism, which is proliferating at an accelerated pace within today's world. Catholics should be especially attentive to the existence and dangers of this atheistic force because the Catholic Church is simultaneously both the greatest enemy, and the greatest enabler, of global socialism and communism and its associated New World Order (NWO) of global government: the emerging, "next-generation" ideological child that is being produced from the marriage of Fabian socialism and Bolshevik (Soviet) communism. The Church is the greatest enemy of socialism and communism because, from its beginnings, its proponents have named it as such.

> We hate Christians and Christianity. Even the best of them must be considered our worst enemies. They preach love of one's neighbor and mercy, which is contrary to our principles. **Christian love is an obstacle to the development of the revolution.** Down with love of our neighbor! **What we want is hate**. . . . Only then can we conquer the universe.[1]
> — Anatoly V. Lunarcharsky, Russian Commissioner of Education under Lenin and Stalin

> Religion . . . is the opium of the people.[2]
> — Karl Marx, co-author of *The Manifesto of the Communist Party*

This is entirely natural and understandable when considering that the foundation of socialism and communism is atheism: a mentality that is completely incompatible with religious faith; especially Christianity. The

---

[1] W. Cleon Skousen, *The Naked Communist* (Cutchogue, NY: Buccaneer Books, Inc., 1994), 71. [Quoted from the U.S. Congressional Record, Vol. 77, 1539-1540].
[2] http://en.wikipedia.org/wiki/Opium_of_the_people, accessed May 20, 2010.

reason for the especial hatred of Catholicism is due to its universality and leadership role within the Christian Faith; among a background of other Protestant, Christian denominations. Additionally, religion in general, and Catholicism specifically, stand as a shield and barrier within societies, and individual minds, from the degenerative transmission and propagation of socialistic and communistic ideology(s). If Catholics can be subdued, and Catholicism rendered impotent, via the inculcation of humanistic influences from within the Church, Catholic doctrine can then be circumvented and perverted so that the faithful could then be successfully "converted" (corrupted) to humanism. Later, this extremely subtle, esoteric form of humanism would then be portrayed as authentic religion. Overt faithlessness, apostasy, and ultimately atheism[3] would then follow as a direct consequence of the effects of humanism within the Church. St. Paul was shown how this would transpire and warned the faithful regarding these dangerous corruptions in these most dangerous of times:

> [1]Know also this, that, in the last days, shall come dangerous times. [2]Men shall be lovers of themselves, covetous, haughty, proud, blasphemers, disobedient to parents, ungrateful, wicked, [3]Without affection, without peace, slanderers, incontinent, unmerciful, without kindness, [4]Traitors, stubborn, puffed up, and lovers of pleasures more than of God: [5]***Having an appearance indeed of godliness, but denying the power thereof.***[4] Now these avoid. [6]For of these sort are they who creep into houses, and lead

---

[3] Practical atheism at first—acting and behaving as if there were no God, or that He was a disinterested observer in human affairs—followed by the more overt, doctrinal atheism—the positive denial of the existence of God—after practical atheism has had a chance to subvert the spirit of the people.

[4] The liberal, modernist prelate (Priest, Bishop, or Cardinal). They maintain an appearance of godliness through their vocation as a "man of religion," but subtly deny Christ's power via the reprobation of the principle of "love thy neighbor." Knowingly or unwittingly, they spread the humanistic philosophy that all of man's problems can be solved through charity and good works between men, while conveniently leaving unnoticed the sacrifice of Christ on the cross. St. Paul remarked on the uniqueness of Catholicism, in that it is the sacrifice of Christ that will ultimately redeem us, and not the good works of men: "But we preach Christ crucified, unto the Jews indeed a stumblingblock, and unto the Gentiles foolishness:" (1 Cor. 1:23).

captive silly women laden with sins, who are led away with divers desires: [7]Ever learning, and never attaining to the knowledge of the truth. [8]Now as Jannes and Mambres resisted Moses, so these also resist the truth, men corrupted in mind, reprobate concerning the faith. [9]But they shall proceed no farther; for their folly shall be manifest to all men, as theirs also was . . . [12]And all that will live godly in Christ Jesus, shall suffer persecution. [13]But evil men and seducers shall grow worse and worse: erring, and driving into error[5] . . . [3]For there shall be a time, when they will not endure sound doctrine; but, according to their own desires, they will heap to themselves teachers, having itching ears:[6] [4]And will indeed turn away their hearing from the truth, but will be turned unto fables.[7]

While the primary reasons for the adversarial, antagonistic relationship between socialism, communism, and Catholicism are more easily grasped, the corruption of true doctrine is more difficult to see and understand; primarily the corruption of Catholic doctrine via modernist errors, which transpired at a highly accelerated rate during the late Nineteenth and Twentieth Centuries, and institutionalized within the Church following the Second Vatican Council. Modernist errors have "legitimized" and accelerated the propagation of severe doctrinal errors and false, corrupted theology within the Church, which has resulted in a drastic increase in apostasy.[8] Yet, even more obscure to the understanding of most all people, and Catholics in particular, is the suicidal culpability of the Catholic Church in relation to the propagation of socialism and communism. However, before discussing the reasons for this pitiful reality, I would like to explicitly clarify my intentions for making such an accusation. This address is ultimately meant as an aid to the Church: to inform the faithful regarding the severity

---

[5] 2 Timothy 3:1-9, 12-13.

[6] A great example of false doctrine that is damaging to the Faith is the ordination of female and homosexual clerics within some of the Protestant denominations, which has caused much confusion and discontent within those denominations.

[7] 2 Timothy 4:3-4.

[8] For a more detailed examination of the apostasy, and its relationship to the Second Vatican Council, see: Kenneth C. Jones, *Index of Leading Catholic Indicators* (Fort Collins, CO: Roman Catholic Books, 2003).

of the Church's currently corrupted state; because if the corruption that is plaguing the institution today is going to be reversed and corrected it is going to have to come by way of an informed laity applying pressure to the corrupt clergy within the Church, until such time as the corrupted members either come to understand and amend their erroneous views and practices, or are swept out of the Church along with the corruption they have propagated.

To begin with, it must be understood that the Church is not a monolithic singularity. What is meant by the term "monolithic singularity"? A good example to demonstrate what this means is the treatment of the Church within the secular press as it relates to the scandal of homosexual priests who have molested children placed in their trust. Although the Church has rightly come under attack in the secular press due to the culpability of those within the hierarchy who refused to act responsibly and manfully when the accusations were originally made; the secular press often uses the instance of the moral failures of the individual presbyters responsible for the scandal as an opportunity to denigrate the Church as an institution. Treating the Church as a monolithic singularity, they then justify their contempt for the Church, and God, by implying that the moral failure of the few demonstrates the moral failure of the Church as an institution. This is a false perception that, unfortunately, plagues many of the "faithful"; some of whom have had their faith undermined, or even destroyed, by this scandal. While the scandal has proved that grave corruption exists within the hierarchy of the Catholic Church, it is incumbent upon the honest and the faithful to identify its true source so that we can dispose of what is corruptive and evil while keeping what is true and good. The first step toward rooting out the corruption within the Church is to discern its source.

As it is true for all human beings, it is true within all humanly administered institutions and organizations. Each individual or institution within this world is composed of two separately distinguishable components: the body and the spirit. One is physically material and sensible[9] (the body), while the other is physically immaterial and intellectual (the spirit). The body is the physical manifestation in our world: the functional components that constitute its material existence. With people it is simply our flesh and blood, temporal bodies, and the manner in which it is functionally organized: the relative position of the various organs and body parts, and how they

---

[9] Able to be perceived by the senses: sight, touch, taste, sound, or smell. It is not to be misunderstood in the context of being rational or reasonable.

function and interact with one another to ultimately constitute a physically functional human being. With the Church, the body includes its buildings and churches; the clergymen who are responsible for making decisions, carrying out policy, and ministering to the spiritual needs of the faithful; as well as the administrative and organizational infrastructure: the relative functional position(s) of the various organs and offices of the Church, and how they function and interact with one another to ultimately constitute a physically functional institution. More succinctly, the body—regardless of whether it is human or institutional—is any article that is materially tangible; to include the manner in which its various parts are functionally ordered to fulfill its purpose and acquire its ultimate end. The spirit is the immaterial, intellectual component that provides the motivating, animating force for the actions of the body.

When considering the source of corruption plaguing the modern Church, the attempt will be made to demonstrate that *all* of it is emanating from the body of the Church: those within the Church who are presently responsible for administering its function. We begin to understand this certain reality by examining the spirit of the Church, and what constitutes it. Love; obedience to higher, proper authority; hope; faith; charity; perseverance; and other higher, nobler ideals are all considered to be component parts of the spirit of the Church; which, as Catholic doctrine teaches, is the Holy Spirit. Also included within the spirit of the Church is authentic Catholic doctrine that has been expounded on by various saints and "Doctors of the Church" throughout history. Moreover, from another perspective, it can also be said that the spirit of an organization is the body of ideals upon which an organization or institution was founded and constructed. In the case of Catholicism, the ministry of Jesus Christ and the faith in His personal divinity was its foundation,[10] while the Holy Spirit has been the constructive spirit of the Church from its beginnings.[11] Because the Holy Spirit is one of the triune persons that comprise God, and in light of the fact that God is

---

[10] "For other foundation no man can lay, but that which is laid; which is Christ Jesus." (1 Cor. 3:11), and "Built upon the foundation of the apostles and prophets, Jesus Christ himself being the chief cornerstone:" (Eph. 2:20).

[11] "And I will ask the Father, and he shall give you another Paraclete, that he may abide with you for ever": (John 14:16), and, "But the Paraclete, the Holy Ghost, whom the Father will send in my name, he will teach you all things, and bring all things to your mind, whatsoever I shall have said to you." (John 14:26).

both perfect and immutable (unchanging),[12] it can be seen that the corruption unfolding within the Church is a corruption of the body and not of the spirit of the Church; as the Spirit of God, which is the spirit of the Church, is perfect and immutable. A well-known figure within the Church has made an acute observation regarding this problem:

> The Magisterium, on the other hand, has never failed to teach what is right. In the last decades, the Church's unchanging biblical-theological doctrine about Satan and his activity has been reiterated in no fewer than eighteen texts of the Second Vatican Council, three speeches of Pope Paul VI, and twenty-two speeches of Pope John Paul II. These voices are clear and authoritative, but, as Homer would say, "My poor verses, thrown to the winds."[13]

Plainly stated, there are no theological faults to be found within *true* Catholic doctrine and dogma: the "Spirit" of the Church (a.k.a. the "Magisterium"). This doctrine was expounded on during the First Vatican Council, and is referred to as "Papal Infallibility," which *only* applies to the arena of Catholic morals and doctrine.

With a clear understanding of the distinction between the Body and the Spirit of the Church, it then becomes much easier to see that the corruption that has taken hold of the Church has taken place exclusively within the humanly-administered body of the Church; as evidenced by the toleration of homosexual predation within the ranks of the clergy by those who are responsible for ensuring that such abuses do not occur: the hierarchy of the Church: primarily the Bishops and Cardinals. How is this sad reality related to the culpability of the Church for the spread of communism throughout the world, and how can the corruption, which has infested the body of the Church, be explained?

It has been explicitly revealed through private revelations, and is generally acknowledged within the Church, that God punishes men for their sins in a manner that corresponds to the nature and severity of the sin(s). Accordingly, the corruption of the body of the Church—which, at

---

[12] See Aquinas, Thomas, *Summa Theologica*, Part 1, Question 9 (immutability), Article 1 for proof in reason.

[13] Gabriele Amorth, *An Exorcist: More Stories* (San Francisco, CA: Ignatius Press, 2002), 57.

its foundation is based on willful disobedience and pride: the identical mortal sins that earned the Devil his damnation—can be viewed as a divine punishment proceeding from the open and willful disobedience of the Holy See (Vatican) to the openly, and publicly manifested will of God. Moreover, and not coincidentally, the nature of the Holy See's willful disobedience to God's will is directly related to communism and the clearly stated instructions the Holy See was commanded to follow in order to defeat it, which the Vatican has refused to obey up to the current day. The open and willful disobedience to God's will being referred to concerns the visitations, revelations, and supporting prophecies brought to three shepherd children at Fátima, Portugal in 1917 by the Blessed Virgin Mary, which were preceded by preparatory visits from an angel. If there are some Catholics who are still not aware of these apparitions, a brief summary of the events will be provided.

In the summer of 1916, three shepherd children—Lucia dos Santos and her two cousins: Francisco and Jacinta Marto—received a certainly unexpected visit from an angel who identified himself as the "Angel of Peace" and asked the children to pray with him:

> And kneeling on the ground, he prostrated himself until his forehead touched it, saying:
>
> "My God, I believe, I adore, I hope, and I love You! I beg pardon of You for those who do not believe, do not adore, do not hope and do not love You!"
>
> Three times he spoke the same words, while the children, as in a daze, repeated them after him. Then, arising, he said:
>
> "Pray thus. The hearts of Jesus and Mary are attentive to the voice of your supplications."[14]

A short time later the angel reappeared and asked the children to offer prayers and sacrifices, as well as to accept the suffering that God was going to send them as a form of reparation for the offenses of sinners and for their conversion. Finally, a few months later in late September or October of 1916, the angel made his final appearance, prayed with the children, offered Holy

---

[14] William Thomas Walsh, *Our Lady of Fátima* (New York, NY: An Image Book, a division of Bantam Doubleday Dell Publishing Group, Inc., 1990), 36-37.

Communion to Lucia and a chalice containing Christ's Blood to Jacinta and Francisco; who had not yet received their first Communion.

The Blessed Virgin Mary made her first appearance to the three children on May 13, 1917.[15] She requested that the children come to the same location for six months in succession on the thirteenth day of each month at the same hour as their original encounter. She promised that each of the children would be going to heaven, answered a few questions regarding the final disposition of deceased acquaintances that Lucia had known, then asked whether the children would be willing to offer themselves to God; to endure all the sufferings that God may send them as reparation for, and the conversion of, sinners. The children accepted. She requested that the children recite a Rosary every day to obtain peace for the world and an end to the war,[16] and then departed.

The second visitation was on June 13, 1917. Lucia asked to be taken to heaven. Our Mother informed her that Francisco and Jacinta would be taken soon, but that Jesus desired that she would remain in the world for a while to build a devotion to Her Immaculate Heart. During the third visit (July 13, 1917) Lucia requested that the Lady tell them who she was, and to perform a miracle for them so that people would believe the children's stories. She promised that in October she would reveal her identity and perform a miracle that everyone would have to believe. She once again requested that the children make sacrifices for sinners and that they recite a specific prayer when they do so: "O Jesus, it is for your love, for the conversion of sinners and in reparation for the sins committed against the Immaculate Heart of Mary." Following these instructions, she opened her hands, from which rays of light emanated to apparently penetrate the earth and reveal a view of hell. The Lady explained to Lucia:

> You have seen hell where the souls of poor sinners
> go. To save them, God wishes to establish in the world
> devotion to my Immaculate Heart.[17] If what I say to you is
> done, many souls will be saved and there will be peace. The

---

[15] She did not identify herself as the "Lady of the Rosary," the Blessed Virgin Mary, until their final meeting on October 13, 1917.

[16] World War I.

[17] "In the message of Fátima, the great promise of the salvation of souls is very often associated with the Immaculate Heart of Mary's intercession." (footnote from source text)

war[18] is going to end: but if people do not cease offending God, a worse one will break out during the pontificate of Pius XI.[19] When you see a night illuminated by an unknown light, know that this is the great sign[20] given you by God that He is about to punish the world for its crimes, by means of war, famine, and persecutions of the Church and of the Holy Father.[21]

To prevent this, I shall come to ask for the consecration of Russia to my Immaculate Heart, and the Communion of Reparation on the First Saturdays.[22] If my requests are heeded, Russia will be converted, and there will be peace;[23] if not, she will spread her errors throughout the world, causing wars and persecutions of the Church. **The good will be martyred, the Holy Father will have much to suffer, various nations will be annihilated**. In the end, my Immaculate Heart will triumph. The Holy Father will consecrate Russia to me, and she will be converted, and a period of peace will be granted to the world . . .

---

[18] "This refers to the First World War, 1914-1918." (footnote from source text)

[19] "Lucia has again explicitly confirmed the name of Pope Pius XI. To the objection that the Second World War, 1939-1944, actually started during the Pontificate of Pius XII, she replied that in fact the war began with the occupation of Austria in 1938." (footnote from source text)

[20] "Lucia presumed that the "extraordinary" aurora borealis during the night of 25th to 26th of January, 1938, was the sign given by God to announce the imminence of war." (footnote from source text)

[21] Sister Maria Lucia, *Fátima in Lucia's Own Words: Sister Lucia's Memoirs*, ed. Fr. Louis Kondor, SVD (Still River, MA: Ravengate Press, 1998), 108-110.

[22] "See Appendix 1." (footnote from source text) [The promise to return was fulfilled by the Blessed Virgin in two separate visitations. On December 10th, 1925, she appeared to Lucia at Pontevedra, Spain and delineated the devotion of the Communion of Reparation on the First Saturdays. On the 13th of June, 1929, Lucia had a further vision at Tuy, Spain; where Our Lady requested the consecration of Russia to her Immaculate Heart. (L.J.)]

[23] "See Appendix 2." (footnote from source text) [Appendix 2 of Sister Lucia's memoirs recounts the second visitation at Tuy, Spain; where the Blessed Virgin Mary requests the consecration of Russia to her Immaculate Heart. (L.J.)]

> When you pray the Rosary, say after each mystery: O my
> Jesus, forgive us, save us from the fire of hell. Lead all souls
> to heaven, especially those who are most in need.[24]

The fourth visit was on August 19, 1917, delayed by the children's
kidnapping by a government administrator, Arturo de Oliveira Santos. The
visitation was brief and mostly repetitive of previous requests; encouraging
constant prayers and sacrifices for sinners. The fifth visit (September 13,
1917) was also quite brief, announcing that Our Lady of the Sorrows of
Carmel, Saint Joseph, and the child Jesus would be coming in the following
month to bless the world; as she reaffirmed her promise to perform a miracle
to compel belief in the visitations.

Finally, the promised sixth visit occurred on October 13, 1917. The
Blessed Virgin Mary identified herself as the "Lady of the Rosary" and asked
that a chapel be built in her honor on the site of the visitations. Lucia asked for
the cure of some sick people and the conversion of others. The Virgin Mary
confirmed that some would be cured or converted while others would not,
and that everything depended on the amending of their lives and sincerely
asking pardon for their sins. At this she mentioned that mankind must stop
offending God because He was greatly offended already, and then opened
up her hands from whence rays of light ascended to the sun. Several different
visions were later reported by Lucia, which were unique to herself or the other
child seers, but the effect of the Virgin Mary's miraculous manifestation
was made evident for the members of the viewing public; estimated at about
70,000 people, faithful and faithless alike, who had gathered at the site in
expectation of the promise of the Virgin Mary (as related to the public by
the children):

> What they all did see, however, was something
> stupendous, unheard of, almost apocalyptic. The sun stood
> forth in the clear zenith like a great silver disk which,
> though bright as any sun they had ever seen, they could
> look straight at without blinking, and with a unique and
> delightful satisfaction. This lasted but a moment. While they
> gazed, the huge ball began to "dance"—that was the word
> all the beholders applied to it. Now it was whirling rapidly
> like a gigantic fire-wheel. After doing this for some time, it

---

[24] Lucia, *Fátima in Lucia's Own Words*, 174.

stopped. Then it rotated again, with dizzy, sickening speed. Finally there appeared on the rim a border of crimson, which flung across the sky, as from a hellish vortex, blood-red streamers of flame, reflecting to the earth, to the trees and shrubs, to the upturned faces and the clothes all sorts of brilliant colors in succession: green, red, orange, blue, violet, the whole spectrum in fact. Madly gyrating in this manner three times, the fiery orb seemed to tremble, to shudder, and then to plunge precipitately, in a mighty zigzag, toward the crowd.

A fearful cry broke from the lips of thousands of terrified persons as they fell upon their knees, thinking the end of the world had come. Some said that the air became warmer at that instant; they would not have been surprised if everything about them had burst into flames, enveloping and consuming them.

. . . Some who had come to jeer fell on their faces and broke into sobs and abject prayers.

The Marques do Cruz said, "Oh my God, how great is Thy power!"

This had lasted about ten minutes, perhaps. Then all saw the sun begin to climb, in the same zigzag manner, to where it had appeared before. It became tranquil, then dazzling. No one could look at it any longer. It was the sun of every day.[25]

Moreover, a lesser miracle was also performed during this episode. During the morning of 13 October, and up to the time of the apparition, the day had been overcast. It had been raining, and all the expectant pilgrims were muddy and soaked dripping wet. After the apparition, their clothes had become perfectly clean and dry.

Moving away from the description of events surrounding the apparitions at Fátima, and with an overview of the events before us, we can now move forward toward an understanding of the Church's culpability for the ascendancy of communism in the world over the last century; and how the Church, due to the self-incriminating disobedience of its prelates, has indirectly proclaimed its fault for the murderous rampage of communism

---

[25] Walsh, *Our Lady of Fátima*, 145-146.

that has claimed over one hundred million lives, and is poised to enslave all humanity with its untold multitude of false promises designed to empower evil men; greedy for power and control over all mankind.

When the Church is faced with reported apparitions of a supernatural visitation—*especially* when those apparitions are reported to involve Holy or venerated figures within Catholicism (God the Father, Jesus, the Virgin Mary, venerated Saints, etc.) who bring words of prophecy, instruction, or commandment—it becomes the unavoidable and imperative duty of the Church to investigate the reported apparitions to establish whether the apparition is false (believed to be of demonic origin), authentic (deemed to be a true visitation from heaven), or uncertain (in cases where events surrounding the apparition(s) render its source indeterminate). The investigation and determination by the Church regarding the authenticity of the Fátima apparitions was critical; because if the Church proclaims an apparition to be valid and authentic, they then bind themselves, by the Church's own doctrine of Holy Obedience, to follow every instruction and command that emanates from the apparitions. The first, and bindingly definitive ruling of the Church, was made in October, 1930 by the Bishop of Leiria-Fátima (Dom Jose Alves Correia da Silva); who held authority over the region that contains Fátima and the specific site where the apparitions occurred, the "Cova da Iria," and who was responsible for appointing a commission to investigate the apparitions. In a pastoral letter he stated:

> In virtue of considerations made known, and others which for reason of brevity we omit; humbly invoking the Divine Spirit and placing ourselves under the protection of the most Holy Virgin, and after hearing the opinions of our Rev. Advisors in this diocese, we hereby: –
>
> 1. Declare worthy of belief, the visions of the shepherd children in the Cova da Iria, parish of Fatima, in this diocese, from the 13th May to 13th October, 1917.
> 2. Permit officially the cult of Our Lady of Fatima.[26]

This ruling by the Church regarding the authenticity and validity of the Fátima apparitions immediately bound the Church to follow the directives contained within them; for to declare an apparition as valid and then to

---

[26] http://fatima.org/essentials/facts/bishapprov.asp, accessed November 27, 2007.

openly disregard and disobey the instructions contained therein was, and still is, a clear manifestation of self–contradictory faithlessness and a flagrantly open disobedience to the will of God. As a matter of justice, God cannot allow a willful disobedience to His will to go unpunished; as it is unjust to the faithfully obedient, angels and humans alike, to tolerate such a circumstance without incurring negative consequences.

The prophecies related to the Fátima visitations, and their subsequent conformance to future events, both bear out the unerring validity of the prophecies and speak to world events that are clearly visible to any conscious soul who cares to see them; as they are transpiring within today's world. Remembering that these prophecies were made in 1917—within days of Russia's "October Revolution";[27] which ushered in world communism as a global political force—it is clear that there is no way for a simply human intelligence to disclose future events so unerringly. Some of the major prophecies associated with Fátima include:

1. That another war, worse than World War I, would break out during the reign of Pius XI if the Virgin Mary's requests were not fulfilled;
2. That the night would be illumined by an unknown light as a great sign that God was about to punish the world;
3. That the Virgin Mary would come to request the consecration of Russia to her Immaculate Heart, and the "Communion of Reparation" on the First Saturdays to avert these disasters;
4. That if her requests were heeded there would be a period of peace granted to the world, but if they were not heeded that Russia would "spread her errors throughout the world, causing wars and persecutions of the Church.";
5. That the good would be martyred, the Pope would have much to suffer, and that "various nations will be annihilated."

Reflecting on all these promises and prophecies related to the children, it is clear to see the unerring accuracy of the prophecies. Her requests have not been honored or acted on, and as a result:

---

[27] October 25, 1917 on the Julian calendar and November 7, 1917 on the Gregorian calendar.

1. Another war (World War II), worse than World War I, did break out during the reign of Pius XI;

2. The night was illumined by an unknown light as a great sign that God was about to punish the world. This event occurred on the evening to morning, January 25 to 26, 1938. It was seen for roughly five hours, and reportedly seen all over Europe. It was later claimed to be a manifestation of the Aurora Borealis, but Sister Lucy, the sole remaining seer and declared nun at the time of the "illumination," immediately recognized the event as the fulfillment of the prophecy made in 1917 that the night would be "illumined by an unknown light.";

3. She did come to request the consecration of Russia to her Immaculate Heart, and the "Communion of Reparation" on the First Saturdays to avert these disasters. On December 10, 1925, the Virgin Mary and the child Jesus appeared to Sister Lucy. The Blessed Virgin said to her, "Look, my daughter, at my Heart, surrounded with thorns with which ungrateful men pierce me every moment by their blasphemies and ingratitude. You at least try to console me and say that I promise to assist at the hour of death, with the graces necessary for salvation, all those who, on the first Saturday of five consecutive months, shall confess, receive Holy Communion, recite five decades of the Rosary, and keep me company for fifteen minutes while meditating on the fifteen mysteries of the Rosary, with the intention of making reparation to me."[28] On June 13, 1929, Our Lady appeared to Sister Lucy again and said, "The moment has come in which God asks the Holy Father, in union with all the Bishops of the world, to make the consecration of Russia to my Immaculate Heart, promising to save it by this means. There are so many souls whom the Justice of God condemns for sins committed against me, that I come to ask reparation: sacrifice yourself for this intention and pray."[29];

4. Her requests have not been heeded, and Russia has "spread her errors[30] throughout the world, causing wars and persecutions of the Church"; to include China, Vietnam, Cambodia, Cuba, Latin America, Europe, the United States, etc.;

---

[28] Lucia, *Fátima in Lucia's Own Words*, 197.

[29] Ibid., 202.

[30] Primarily through communism, atheism, and secular humanism.

5. The various Popes have had much to suffer over the past century due to the internal deterioration and corruption within the Church. This situation has been especially evident since the conclusion of the Second Vatican Council; as the Popes have been made to suffer through the machinations of faithless and willfully treacherous prelates within the Church, and from a hostile, secular media from without.

For faithful Catholics it is especially important to note that every prophecy made during the Fátima apparitions has come to fruition with the exception of the final two, and most ominous, of all the promised punishments: mass martyrdom of the faithful and the "annihilation of nations," and within the insane world that we live in today, the groundwork for the fulfillment of these prophecies has been established with firm foundations. With the widespread toleration of homosexuality and abortion among the general public, two intolerable crimes against human dignity within Catholicism, the psychological framework is in place to, in the very near future, criminalize Catholic doctrine under the pretext of being a "human rights" violation. Already, in Canada, such action has been attempted against some who have actively spoken out against homosexuality, while noting Biblical citations as the reason for their opposition to it. Opposing homosexuality as a moral evil was prosecuted as being a form of "hate crime."

The persecutors of the faithful—under the pretext that such outspoken opposition to their sexual deviancy is a "human rights" violation—and their associated arguments, amount to nothing more than, "You hurt my feelings, so you need to go to jail"! The most frightful aspect of this scenario is that there are a great many people, even some who call themselves Catholic, who agree with this supposition; which *should* alarm the faithful regarding the rapidly developing persecution of Catholic doctrine, and practitioners of the Faith, in the very near future from detractors both without and within the Church.

The framework for the fulfillment of the "annihilation of nations" is also solidly in place, and growing more inevitable every day. North Korea, a puppet state of Communist China, is attempting to acquire the capacity to strike at the United States with nuclear weapons, while the leadership of the United States effectively does nothing substantive to persuade North Korea or Communist China to abandon their aggressive ambitions. In the Middle East, Iran—with the complicity of terrorist organizations such as Hezbollah, Hamas, and others—is actively seeking a nuclear capability to strike at Israel, so as to escalate a confrontation with the West. Again, the political and military leadership of the United States displays a horrifyingly cowardly disposition in the face of these sincere threats: a frightening complacency reminiscent of Neville Chamberlain's appeasement of Adolf Hitler, which *should* serve as a demonstrable and bitter lesson of history regarding the ultimate price that will *always* be extracted from the morally or physically weak. Moreover, such complacent and irresolute behavior can only serve to embolden these, and other, evil creatures in this world.

Now, those Catholics—regardless of their position within the Church; whether they be Cardinals or laymen—who say that the consecration of Russia to Our Mother's Immaculate Heart is not an absolute necessity at this particular juncture in the history of mankind, in order to spare it from a horrific fate, demonstrate a frightening level of faithlessness and theological ignorance regarding the most basic precepts of the Faith! This position is not taken merely for the sake of arousing controversy. For very sound theological reasons that go beyond the scope of this work, it must be absolutely understood and accepted by the faithful that . . . *it is impossible for God to lie!*[31] Proceeding from this fact, it can then be understood that every promise, every prophecy, and every threat uttered by God *must* be fulfilled. He binds himself by His word.

As it relates to the Fátima prophecies, the clever sophist (of which there are innumerable available) will argue that it wasn't God who delivered the messages, but the Virgin Mary; so for that reason it is possible that disaster can be averted without fulfilling the requests made at Fátima. This is a false argument that will be leveled by those ignorant of the Faith. All souls who make it to heaven become eternally conjoined with the will of God, so that they all conform to, and have no desire to oppose, His will: a perfection that is a necessary condition of being united to the eternal entity. Conversely, those spirits who are not in heaven, those in hell with the devil, are eternally opposed to the will of God. This is a simple precept of the Faith that is

---

[31] "That by two immutable things, in which it is impossible for God to lie, we may have the strongest comfort, who have fled for refuge to hold fast the hope set before us." (Hebrews 6:18). However, a more thorough examination of the reason(s) why it is impossible for God to lie can be found in *Summa Contra Gentiles: God* by St. Thomas Aquinas. The entire work develops and establishes the nature and attributes of God, which assist and support the reason(s) for why God cannot lie, but this particular point is specifically addressed in Chapters 60 – 62.

easily witnessed in the manifestation of the struggle between good and evil in everyday life on Earth.

The Blessed Virgin Mary, being the Queen of Heaven, is not what we would refer to as a "free agent"; wandering throughout the world acting on her own caprice. To begin with, the Virgin Mary has a singularly unique relationship within Creation to God and all His persons. She is the daughter of God the Father, the spouse of the Holy Spirit,[32] and the mother of God the Son (Jesus). Moreover, she is the only wholly human creature (Christ being both God and man) in all Creation to be born exempt from original sin and to have maintained a sinless life on Earth. When the Virgin Mary appears to creatures on Earth and makes a request of us, the faithful can be absolutely sure that what she is requesting is the expressed desire of the will of God. Additionally, the perfect fulfillment to date of the Fátima prophecies gives an irreproachable testimony of the veracity of the prophecies and apparitions. All the above considerations, in combination with the approval of the apparitions by the Church as being true and worthy of belief, bind the Church, by its own testimony and doctrine of Holy Obedience, to faithfully act on the desires of Heaven when the Church itself proclaims them to be true!

Let me be absolutely clear. The consecration of Russia by the Pope—in union with all the bishops of the world, and at the same hour worldwide—is an absolute necessity in order to avert divine punishment. Any lay person, priest, bishop, or cardinal who forwards or entertains a sophistical argument that this is not the case is denouncing the Virgin Mary as a liar while simultaneously refusing obedience to God by refusing their duty and obligation to Holy Obedience; and it is exactly these kinds of ignorant, thoughtless, or faithless people that must either be made to understand and amend their erroneous belief(s) or be swept out of the Church.

Regarding the duty of faithful Catholics to press the Holy See to obey God, and Our Mother the Blessed Virgin Mary, more specifically; it should be known that there are, and have been since the time of the apparitions, those people within the Church who are intent on defying God and obstructing His will by frustrating the consecration of Russia to the Virgin Mary. Frankly, whether these perverted creatures work against God through ignorance or willful malice is completely irrelevant to the consequent effects

---

[32] "[34]And Mary said to the angel: How shall this be done, because I know not man? [35]And the angel answering, said to her: The Holy Ghost shall come upon thee, and the power of the most High shall overshadow thee. And therefore also the Holy which shall be born of thee shall be called the Son of God." (Luke 1:34-35).

of their treacherous behavior: the failure to properly consecrate Russia in the manner that fulfills the Virgin Mary's request. Although there are many varied arguments forwarded to excuse and justify the refusal of the Holy See to consecrate Russia, we will cover a few of the most common ones and demonstrate the false or faithless foundation from which they are all constructed.

The most common excuse forwarded for the Holy See's refusal to consecrate Russia is that it is politically "impossible" because it would be considered too offensive to either the Russian government or the Russian Orthodox Church. This argument, while being one of the most common, is also the weakest and most inane. Scripturally, the faithful are warned, "And fear ye not them that kill the body, and are not able to kill the soul: but rather fear him that can destroy both soul and body in hell."[33] Catholics, and especially clergymen, are familiar with this principle. It means that men should not be concerned with the protests and opinions of other men, especially when the object of their protest directly opposes the will of God. A Catholic who argues against the consecration on the grounds that it may be offensive to certain men openly manifests either their abject faithlessness or cowardice; because such a position openly contradicts Christ and displays a greater fear of men than of God. But what's even worse, such a position demonstrates a desire to satisfy and appease the enemies of the Church! Such arguments are even more self-condemning when they come from those within the Church: priests, bishops, cardinals, so-called "devout" Catholics, etc.

Another argument that is routinely forwarded is that the consecration of Russia has already been accomplished. This claim is absolutely false, and it is plainly evident for two reasons. First of all, the consecration of Russia, in union with *all* the bishops of the world and at the same hour, for the expressed purpose of satisfying the Church's duty to Our Mother's requests, has never been performed. There have been half-measures accomplished following the apparitions: consecrations of the world (not Russia specifically) to the Virgin Mary that have included the participation of the clergy; and other consecrations performed that have specifically mentioned Russia in them, but without the participation of the Bishops. On each occasion, the Pope has fulfilled one of the elements of the request to consecrate Russia, but not all of them together. Such deception and half-measures leaves the distinct impression that there are a large number of people within the Church hierarchy that are trying to fool God; not being very mindful that they are

---

[33] Matthew 10:28.

only fooling themselves. This is the sort of behavior that one would expect from the faithless, and not from His representative body on Earth.

Secondly, it is evident that the consecration of Russia has not been performed because Russia has not been converted; as Russia is still "spreading her errors throughout the world." Make no mistake about it. The dissolution of the Soviet Union was a strategic shift within world communism. It was by no means the end of it. All one needs to do to recognize this fact is open their eyes to objective reality. Since the dissolution of the Soviet Union, the virus of communism has firmly taken hold in Venezuela, is taking root in Bolivia (Evo Morales), is gaining popularity in Mexico, and has expanded its influence via the false face of "liberalism" within the rest of Western civilization at an even more accelerated rate than when the Soviet Union was still in existence. If the consecration had been adequately performed Russia would have been converted.

World events over the past several decades clearly demonstrate that Russia has not undergone any type of conversion to Catholicism. Moreover, Russia is using China, Iran, Syria, and Islamists as proxy agents to bleed the West of both its resources and its resolve; as it is public knowledge that Russia has aided Iran in obtaining expertise and hardware related to their nuclear program, as well as providing material support and expertise to Saddam Hussein before his removal in 2003. Once again, for those within the Church to claim that the consecration has been performed, while Russia remains unconverted and "spreading her errors," is another manifestation of faithlessness and an open condemnation of the Blessed Virgin Mary as a liar. Many other justifications and excuses for the frustration of the will of God have been, and will continue to be, made; now and in the future. Christ spoke of these faithless prelates within the Church: those who work tirelessly to frustrate the will of God so that they could then glorify themselves in the eyes of men, and a very great number of clergymen are falling prey to this error. An equally great number of them—unwittingly, and through no willfully culpable fault of their own—are, by deception, falling prey to these errors due to the corruption ushered into the Faith by modernism:

> [1]Take heed that you do not your justice before men, to be seen by them: otherwise you shall not have a reward of your Father who is in heaven. [2]Therefore when thou dost an alms-deed, sound not a trumpet before thee, **as the hypocrites do in the synagogues and in the streets, that**

they may be honoured by men. Amen I say to you, they have received their reward,[34]

[8]This people honoureth me with their lips: but their heart is far from me. [9]And **in vain do they worship me, teaching doctrines and commandments of men.**[35]

It is absolutely true that the faithless will read this—yes, even a very large number of priests, bishops, and cardinals—and deride the necessity of the consecration of Russia to the Virgin Mary in exactly the manner she requested. A great number of faithless men have infiltrated the Church and will continue to actively work to undermine and dissipate the authority of the Pope, and the Church as an institution, while working against the consecration. But this should not surprise any faithful Catholic; as you have also been warned about this reality from the beginning:

[18]If the world hate you, know ye, that it hath hated me before you. [19]If you had been of the world, the world would love its own: but because you are not of the world, but I have chosen you out of the world, therefore the world hateth you.[36]

Wonder not, brethren, if the world hate you.[37]

However, this particular section is directed toward those who claim themselves to be faithful Catholics. The perversely evil days that we currently live in compel the Catholic reader to minutely examine their conscience and ask themselves some direct and harsh questions that will cut through any layers of self-deception. This will directly advance to the heart of the matter and to a large degree, at least within the reader's own conscience, reveal how much faith, or lack thereof, the reader truly possesses. First of all, does the Catholic reader believe in the singular necessity of the consecration of Russia to Our Mother's Immaculate Heart? If not, why not? In light of all the fulfilled prophecies, the dire threats of what awaits us if the Holy See does not submit to Holy Obedience and perform the

---

[34] Matthew 6:1-2.

[35] Matthew 15:8-9.

[36] John 15:18-19.

[37] 1 John 3:13.

consecration as Our Mother requested, in combination with the passage of world events that are putting the pieces in place to fulfill the promised threats; how can any Catholic who describes themselves as faithful have any doubt whatsoever!? Secondly, as a faithful Catholic, what would possibly induce you to care about what the faithless will say or think about you? Fear of public condemnation and ridicule has always served as a hindrance or frustration to the efforts of those people in this world who desire to act properly and "do the right thing."

DOING WHAT IS RIGHT, SIMPLY BECAUSE IT IS THE RIGHT THING TO DO, HAS NEVER BEEN, AND WILL NEVER BE, EASY! All the fanciful, wishful thinking in the world will never change the reality of this singular truth. Get used to it and get over it; at least to as great of a degree as you are capable. It is simply a component of our weak, human nature to avoid conflict and confrontation; seemingly at almost all costs. The great majority of human beings succumb to this tendency; not understanding the ultimate consequences of their capitulation in the face of evil. The harshness of this disturbing reality has become *especially* evident in today's world, and the horrible consequences of choosing the easy road is being actualized in the world because the great mass of humanity is surrendering to their natural inclinations toward moral cowardice, intellectual laziness, physical laziness, and materialistic self-promotion. This reality is not only evident within the field of religion; but equally so within the realms of politics and government, and within society at large on practically every cultural issue.

When speaking of not caring for the opinions of the faithless, it is not to be confused with, or construed as, being openly combative with the faithless. It is meant in the sense of exercising a resolute disposition when assaulted by the arts and arguments of the faithless. Where first principles are involved, the Catholic faithful do not need to besiege society with an army of proselytizers. They must simply refuse to compromise true doctrine in order to "go along" with the faithless, because doing so will simply lead to an even speedier apostasy than is already underway. Moreover, another reason that the faithful must be knowledgeable regarding what true Catholic doctrine is, and its sound theological basis, is so that they can explain it to the faithless. Without such knowledge, free of modernist errors and manipulations, the Catholic is pretty much useless in defending their position. If the faithless refuse to understand or listen because it offends their pride; then that is their loss, and their own blood is on their own hands. The Catholic cannot be held culpable for the errors of the faithless if the erroneous nature of their false ideas have been exposed and explained to them, and they willfully persist in clinging to their false beliefs.

The difference between these approaches may seem like an exercise in "splitting hairs," but the results obtained can often be dramatically different. Forceful proselytizing—a disposition of running to and fro, boldly condemning the faithless as damned if they do not conform to Catholic doctrine—will most always turn people away and be regarded by the disinterested or faithless as an offensive assault. Often times the messenger leaves an impression of self-righteousness on those who receive the message. On the other hand, the approach and effect on otherwise disinterested observers can be completely different when Catholicism and Catholic doctrine is made the object of an attack, and the Catholic, instead of reacting in kind with combative or aggressive behavior, comes armed to the debate with solid reasons for the defense of their position. And let it be known by all the faithful that there are very good reasons for all the Church's moral positions; however unpleasant or restrictive they may *apparently* be on the surface: the most notable today being the Church's position on sexual morality. If there are Catholics who read this and are unable to refute those who promote evil and perversion in the world, the problem is not with Catholic doctrine, but rather with an insufficiency in catechetical education and a deeper understanding among the faithful of the underlying reasons for the prohibitions on human behavior that the Church places on its members.

It is exactly this type of ignorance of true doctrine, and a competent level of catechesis, that has culminated in the appearance of a perversely self-deceived creature within the Church: the "liberal" Catholic, a.k.a. the "Cafeteria Catholic." Cafeteria Catholics harm both themselves and the Church, because in actuality they are not Catholics at all; but rather heretics who deceive themselves and others into believing that dissenting from the moral teachings and catechism of the Church is allowable, and that they will remain in "good standing" in God's eyes. Sadly, many of these people are sincere in the belief that they may pick and choose the doctrine(s) they will follow and remain in God's good graces. As Pope St. Pius X explained in *Pascendi Dominici Gregis*,[38] the beliefs and actions of the Cafeteria Catholic are a result of the inculcation of modernism within the Church, which he

---

[38] Available at http://www.vatican.va/holy_father/pius_x/encyclicals/documents/ hf_p-x_enc_19070908_pascendi-dominici-gregis_en.html; or Anthony J. Mioni Jr. ed., *The Popes Against Modern Errors* (Rockford, IL: TAN Books and Publishers, Inc., 1999).

referred to as the "synthesis of all heresies." The liberal Catholic—those who may be "pro-choice" regarding abortion, tolerant of homosexuality as a "lifestyle choice," or who accept divorce as an option in an imperfect marriage—contradict Christ and assert the supremacy and authority of their own intellect over the clearly stated doctrine delivered by Jesus. Regarding the moral teaching of the Church and its authority, Christ was clear. First of all he named St. Peter, and consequently the office of the Pope by succession, as the head of the Church and final authority on doctrine:

> [18]And I say to thee: That thou art Peter; and upon this rock I will build my church, and the gates of hell shall not prevail against it. [19]**And I will give to thee the keys of the kingdom of heaven. And whatsoever thou shalt bind upon earth, it shall be bound also in heaven: and whatsoever thou shalt loose on earth, it shall be loosed also in heaven.**[39]

The attitude of the Cafeteria Catholic is exactly the same rebellious, defiant spirit that the Devil exhibits; and we are all aware of how his efforts were rewarded. This reality should prompt the "liberal Catholic" to examine their conscience and the reasoning process(es) that brought them to the point of apostasy in order to determine at what point they departed from the Church, as well as how and why it happened. Another warning sign should be noticed by the Cafeteria Catholic: that they are always complaining, defying, and undermining the Church at practically every turn. The Church is an extension of Christ's authority. Accordingly, obedience to its doctrine is an absolute requirement to remain in good standing. The New Testament speaks specifically, in at least eight places, to be of "one mind"[40] with the Church. How can anyone who willfully

---

[39] Matthew 16:18-19: regarding Peter's, and the subsequent Pope's, supremacy over the Church as well as their ability to bind the doctrine of the Church.

[40] "All these were persevering with *one mind* in prayer with the women, and Mary the mother of Jesus, and with his brethren." (Acts 1:14); "Being of *one mind* one towards another. Not minding high things, but consenting to the humble. Be not wise in your own conceits." (Romans 12:16); "[5]Now the God of patience and of comfort grant you to be of *one mind* one towards another, according to Jesus Christ: [6]That with *one mind,* and with one mouth, you may glorify God and the Father of our Lord Jesus Christ." (Romans 15:5-6); "For the rest, brethren,

attempts to undermine the doctrine or authority of the Church to appease their personal lack of self-discipline believe that they can remain "good Catholics"? Such a premise exhibits either abject insanity or abject ignorance of the Faith they claim to profess. Moreover, Christ talked specifically about those people who follow such a path:

> [19]Every tree that bringeth not forth good fruit, shall be cut down, and shall be cast into the fire. [20]Wherefore by their fruits you shall know them. [21]Not every one that saith to me, Lord, Lord, shall enter into the kingdom of heaven: but he that doth the will of my Father who is in heaven, he shall enter into the kingdom of heaven. [22]Many will say to me in that day: Lord, Lord, have not we prophesied in thy name, and cast out devils in thy name, and done many miracles in thy name? [23]And then will I profess unto them, I never knew you: depart from me, you that work iniquity.[41]

With all the above articles to consider—the perfect fulfillment of prophecy to date; the horrible consequences promised to us as a result of the Church's obstinate disobedience to God's will; the ignorance or apathy of the laity in pressing the Holy See to do its duty to God by exercising Holy Obedience and performing the consecration of Russia to Our Mother (the Blessed Virgin Mary) as she requested; and the apostasy and widespread disobedience by a large number of liberal prelates, the laity, and "Cafeteria Catholics"—how can any of those who call themselves faithful Catholics, when presented with such a body of evidence, restrain themselves from demanding the consecration of Russia? Are some of the faithful fearful or reluctant due to the mockery of the faithless, even if some of the faithless are bishops and cardinals? Is it not

---

rejoice, be perfect, take exhortation, be of *one mind*, have peace; and the God of peace and of love shall be with you." (2 Corinthians 13:11); "Only let your conversation be worthy of the gospel of Christ: that, whether I come and see you, or, being absent, may hear of you, that you stand fast in one spirit, with *one mind* labouring together for the faith of the gospel." (Philippians 1:27); "Fulfil ye my joy, that you be of *one mind*, having the same charity, being of one accord, agreeing in sentiment." (Philippians 2:2); "And in fine, be ye all of *one mind*, having compassion one of another, being lovers of the brotherhood, merciful, modest, humble": (1 Peter 3:8); and, "I beg of Evodia, and I beseech Syntyche, to be of *one mind* in the Lord." (Philippians 4:2).

[41] Matthew 7:19-23.

more important to weigh such concerns against the promise from Heaven that "various nations will be annihilated"? Will not such a sincere threat move the faithful to action; especially when it comes directly from Heaven!? And finally, can the faithful say that they were not adequately warned and admonished regarding the necessity of obeying God's will?

In consideration of all the above, will not the faithful deserve their fate if they simply continue to wallow in their apathy; not desiring to take up their cross while waiting for "someone else" to take care of the problem, and by inaction implicitly branding the Virgin Mary a liar; when they know full well within their hearts that there is no "someone else" to carry this burden and compel the treacherous wolves within the Church to do their duty to God!? Does the faithful Catholic believe that the Protestant, Muslim, Hindu, Buddhist, Jew, agnostic, or atheist will take up this cause as their own? It is only the faithful Catholic who can pull the Church out of the wreckage that it is quickly becoming by applying very vocal and persistent pressure to the faithless prelates within the Church who purposefully work to frustrate the will of God.

Armed with the understanding that it is up to the faithful to clean up our own house, the natural question to proceed from this unpleasant reality, and which should also make itself most keenly felt within the intellect of those who truly want to render a service to their Faith and to God, is, "How do I identify who the faithless are within the Church, whether they be laity or clergyman; and how do I effectively combat them"? These questions really go to the heart of the matter and, in all candor, the days ahead will prove to be the greatest test of the faithful's will to overcome and defeat the evil rot that has infested Catholicism. The plan of action is simple, but the will and courage required of the faithful to carry it out is substantial. The first step is identifying the faithless within the Church. Within the laity, the faithless include the liberal, humanized "Cafeteria Catholic."

The "Cafeteria Catholic" believes that they can pave their road to heaven with brotherly love, good works, and good intentions; a gross corruption of doctrine that produces sentiments of self-righteousness and ultimately concludes in the heretical, liberal Catholic: a manifestation of practical atheism. These souls have been seduced by the idea of the legitimacy of private interpretation of Biblical and theological doctrine as being as acceptable and valid as the revealed doctrine of the Church; which is actually the philosophical equivalent of Protestantism, because it denies the divine leadership of the Church and instead places doctrinal and moral authority into the hands of individual human beings. Unfortunately, these mentalities have infected the great majority of those today who profess to be Catholics;

most of them unwittingly, as the corruption has been advancing for several generations at such a slow, incremental rate that it has been difficult to discern the subtle changes until they accumulate to the reprobated point they have reached in today's world.

The foundation of the Faith, as we have already discussed and as was strongly expounded by St. Paul, is Christ crucified; not good works and brotherly love. Good works and brotherly love are what the Catholic is supposed to do for the love of Christ alone, and not as the primary means of salvation; which is what is being displayed by those who believe it is acceptable to selectively adhere to Church doctrine in the false belief that so long as they are charitable—in their own minds fulfilling the commandment to love thy neighbor—that all things will be forgiven them. This is false, because it contradicts and reverses the order of priorities within the minds of those who think in such a fashion. Christ proclaimed, "I am the way, and the truth, and the life. No man cometh to the Father, but by me."[42] Placing preeminence on good works, charity, and love of neighbor as a means of salvation contradicts Christ by improperly elevating human charity to the throne as the vehicle of salvation; effectively replacing Christ as the means of salvation within the hearts and minds of those who think in such a fashion. Charity is merely a virtue, albeit an admirable one. However, it is no replacement for the self-sacrifice of Christ's crucifixion, or the gratitude owed to Him for condescending to offer it up for us.

For the self-professing Catholic to admit or profess any exception to this foundational principle of the Faith, whether it be by ecumenism[43] or selective

---

[42] See John 14:6.

[43] Ecumenism is the practice of trying to incorporate within the Catholic Church the desires or concerns of the schismatic Christian denominations, and in some cases even opposing religions: a.k.a. coming to a 'religious' consensus. This approach is itself a contradiction of Catholic doctrine. Moreover, it is just such an ideological and philosophical vehicle that will be used to attempt to propagate a "unified" One-World religion in the future. True Catholic doctrine teaches that Catholicism is the one, true religion (just as many others do as well), and that the Catholic Church is its representative body on Earth. To demonstrate a willingness to discuss modifying or accommodating Catholic doctrine in order to appease various schismatic, or even non-Christian, denominations demonstrates faithlessness in the doctrine of the Faith that the Catholic pretends to profess. This type of philosophical and spiritual disease is especially problematic when it is spread from within the Holy See. By virtue of the high position some of the proponents of ecumenism possess, when such ideas are propagated to the

adherence to Church doctrine and rules, is actually a demonstration of faithlessness that puts such people closer within the camp(s) of Protestantism: declaring the belief that Christ is King, but then failing to follow His doctrine(s) and His commandments; as they are enunciated and promulgated within the framework of His Church. The submission of the liberal Catholic to the doctrine of private interpretation of Biblical and theological doctrine (Protestantism) actually destroys and subverts all authority by proclaiming the individual as a self-contained, autonomous interpreter of Biblical and theological doctrine; which then in turn implies that each person becomes their own arbiter of morality; which, by the very force of the principle drawn to its ultimate, logical conclusion, propels humanity toward the anarchistic end of practical atheism (moral relativism), as we are witnessing in the world today. Moreover, the distortion of true doctrine, in combination with the perverted glorification of the principle of "love thy neighbor," have been *the* primary sophistical and philosophical tools used to introduce humanism within the Catholic Church and pass it off as authentic religion, which now takes us to the discussion of how to identify the faithless prelates and declared religious within the Church.

A great many of the faithless prelates and religious within the Catholic Church have no conception of their practical faithlessness. This is a sad result of the purposeful corruption that has been introduced into the Church by those who are antagonistic toward Catholicism and who purposefully subvert the Faith out of spite or self-important pride. This state of active, purposeful corruption by such faithless creatures within the Church, many of them at the highest levels (bishops and cardinals), has been ongoing for probably more than the past century; with the innovations introduced via the Second Vatican Council providing a firm basis to accelerate the dissolution of the Faith. In the first place, consider from what source the potential priest, nun, or other religious comes from. They come from the same Churches and Catholic communities as the rest of the laity. They are also weaned, brought up, and subjected to the same sour milk of corrupted doctrine that has become almost universally accepted within the Church by most all the faithful; a byproduct of the surprising number of those who no longer study, or even read their Bible any longer; which makes them easy prey

---

faithful many are deceived into accepting the premise for no greater reason than the naturally trusting, but thoughtless, reaction of, "A high official within the Church is promoting it, so it must be OK." Henceforth, the rot is spread and the corruption is subsequently institutionalized.

for the subtle corruption as it is, and has been, introduced into the Catholic community at large.

Having been raised in such a corrupted atmosphere, those who decide to pursue a religious vocation then enter seminaries where illegitimate, corrupted doctrine is reinforced and solidified within their conscience. The understanding of how the religious communities have been corrupted is not an indictment of the religious' sincerity by any means. Like a very great number of the laity within the Catholic community today, who sincerely desire and believe in their faithful service to God, they have been led astray from birth and truly believe with all their heart that the corrupted doctrine they believe and preach is authentic. There are more than a few priests who have very great convictions regarding the erroneous, humanistic doctrine they propagate to their congregation, as they expressly contradict or defy true Church doctrine that is thousands of years old, as well as directives that are relatively new and formally promulgated by the Holy See and its official congregations in charge of maintaining and propagating true Church doctrine.

To clearly see how some of the members of the clergy and religious communities are subverting the Faith requires a consideration of the organization of the Church and how it functions. There are two legs that hold up the Church: faith and obedience. Faith is the most important and rudimentary prerequisite, for without it there is no basis for the expectation and practice of obedience to those within the Church in their duly ordained positions of authority. Obedience is required within the Church because without it the only possible result would be varying degrees of disorder and anarchy. Moreover, obedience to one's lawfully ordained superior within the Church is the only means of maintaining and exercising the institutional discipline necessary to make the Church an effective organization, as well as providing the basis for its moral authority. Additionally, it is upon such a hierarchical structure that heaven is ordered and administered; from the top (God) down through the various choirs of angels in order from those of a superior to those of a lesser nature: the Divine "chain of command": God > Seraphim > Cherubim > Thrones > Dominions > Virtues > Powers > Archangels > Principalities > Angels. By conforming the Church to the hierarchical, patriarchal structure of heaven the Church conforms itself to the will of God, as Christ revealed when He taught the 'Our Father' to the faithful: ". . . Thy Kingdom come, Thy will be done, *on earth as it is in heaven* . . ." The following figure (Figure 9) is meant to illustrate, at a fundamental level, the organizational hierarchy and procession of authority within the Church:

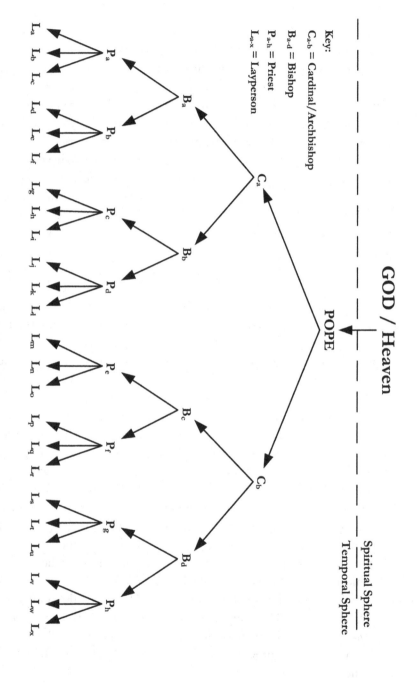

GOD / Heaven

Spiritual Sphere
Temporal Sphere

POPE

Key:
C_{a-b} = Cardinal/Archbishop
B_{a-d} = Bishop
P_{a-h} = Priest
L_{a-x} = Layperson

Figure 9. Hierarchy of Authority within the Catholic Church

238

From Figure 9 there are several important points to note, many of which are being violated by the faithless or disobedient prelates. At all times throughout the discussion to follow, keep in the forefront of your consciousness the fact that the structure of the Church on earth is meant to mimic the organization of Heaven. To begin with, notice the structure's centralization of authority within the office, and person, of the Pope. The Pope, by virtue of his position—the highest authority on issues regarding the Faith—serves in the analogous, authoritarian position that God exercises within Heaven: the highest authority within the administration of the organization: exercising ultimate authority and oversight over all those within the sphere of his authority (all Catholics). As it pertains to matters of doctrine, the precept of papal infallibility stems from the fact that the Pope is instructed by the Holy Spirit: the animating and enlightening Spirit of the Church, the third person of the triune God, and who, in consideration of the immutable, perfect nature of God, cannot err. However, it is critical to once again note that this is true in matters of doctrine *only*: those precepts that have been defined by Church councils or that have been promulgated from the Pope as *Ex Cathedra* tenets of doctrine. The Canons of Church councils and *Ex Cathedra* doctrine are those dogmatic positions that bind the faithful to believe in order to still consider themselves Catholic, and originate from a Papal declaration that specifically identifies the particular teaching as such. Papal infallibility is *not* applicable within any other arena.

A good example of this, and the confusion that followed as a result, was Pope John Paul II's opposition to capital punishment. The authority of the state to take a man's life as punishment for his crime(s) does not pertain to divine doctrine: the field of knowledge devoted to the understanding and worship of, or obedience to, God. Therefore, John Paul II's position on such a matter was purely his personal opinion alone, and the faithful are free to respectfully disagree with him in such cases. Moreover, in that particular case, Pope John Paul II's personal beliefs contradicted both the position of the most learned and prolific Doctor of the Church on that issue (St. Thomas Aquinas),[44] as well as God Himself; as God—through His doctrinal

---

[44] Aquinas, Thomas, *Summa Theologica*, Second Part of the Second Part, Question 64 (Murder), Article 2: ". . . It is written (Exod. xxii. 18): *Wizards thou shalt not suffer to live*; and (Ps. c. 8): *In the morning I put to death all the wicked of the land*. I answer that, as stated above (A. 1), it is lawful to kill dumb animals, in so far as they are naturally directed to man's use, as the imperfect is directed to the perfect. Now every part is

teachings to Moses, as related in the Old Testament (primarily in the books of Exodus and Leviticus)—described many crimes that incurred the death penalty. This point is not mentioned to denigrate Pope John Paul II in any way, but it is brought up to illustrate the point that we are all subject to committing personal errors in judgment as it relates to worldly matters, and the Pope is no exception.

The natural question to logically follow is, "If even the Pope is subject to errors in personal judgment, how can he pretend to be infallible"? This is a good question that needs to be addressed, and in fact is the basis upon which many people and organizations have dissented with the Pope, and as a consequence the Catholic Church, in the past on matters of theological doctrine. The answer to this question lies not in the presumption of extraordinary intellectual perfection possessed by all the Popes throughout history; for if this were true it would naturally imply that their reasoning would be just as infallible in all matters, which it is not. The basis for infallibility comes not from human capabilities, but rather from a promise Christ made to the disciples shortly before He was crucified: "But the Paraclete, the Holy Ghost, whom the Father will send in my name, he will teach you all things, and bring all things to your mind, whatsoever I shall have said to you."[45] and, "But when the Paraclete cometh, whom I will send you from the Father, **the Spirit of truth**, who proceedeth from the Father, he shall give testimony of me."[46]

In matters of doctrine, Christ promised that He would send the Holy Spirit to uphold the Church's authoritative doctrinal position. Moreover, Christ promised that the Holy Spirit would guide the Church until the end of time: "And I will ask the Father, and he shall give you another Paraclete, that he may abide with you **for ever**":[47] Therefore, the doctrine of papal

---

directed to the whole, as imperfect to perfect, wherefore every part is naturally for the sake of the whole. For this reason we observe that if the health of the whole body demands the excision of a member, through its being decayed or infectious to the other members, it will be both praiseworthy and advantageous to have it cut away. Now every individual person is compared to the whole community, as part to whole. Therefore if a man be dangerous and infectious to the community, on account of some sin, it is praiseworthy and advantageous that he be killed in order to safeguard the common good, since *a little leaven corrupteth the whole lump* (1 Cor. v. 6)."

[45] John 14:26.

[46] John 15:26.

[47] John 14:16.

infallibility regarding matters of doctrine rests not on the judgments of men, but rather on the promises Christ made to His followers: that the Holy Spirit would ensure that errors in doctrine would not be propagated by the Magisterium.

The second thing to notice from Fig. 9 is that just as the Angels inhabit the lowest order—their "rank" within the Divine "chain of command"—among the choirs of angels within the spiritual sphere, the faithful layperson inhabits the lowest order within the Church in the temporal sphere. Church doctrine and directives are passed from the Pope, and then disseminated throughout the structure of authority down to their proper destination; whether the ultimate destination of any communication is the layperson or a higher, intermediary level for the purpose of administering Church function(s). In all cases, and at all times, the intermediary levels within the Church (the cardinals, bishops, priests, and other religious) are meant to function as servants of the Holy Father (Pope); for the purpose of disseminating his spiritual guidance to the faithful in the temporal realm; just as the intermediary choirs of angels are meant to function as servants of God for the purpose of disseminating His will to those choirs of angels (and mankind) inferior in rank to themselves. The reason for the Church's organizational structure is twofold. Primarily, it is meant to mimic the organization of heaven, and to operate as a mirror of the same in functionality and purpose: the propagation of the message of God's will to all souls. Secondarily, because there are simply too many professing Catholics, and the scope of the Church is so large (worldwide), that unlike God, a single man (the Pope) could not possibly administer it without substantial assistance.

As a matter of practical administration, efficiency, and as a timely service to the faithful, it is necessary to employ helpers in the work of disseminating the will of God down to the faithful layman. Of prime importance to observe regarding this structure is that the intermediary levels within the Church are meant to function strictly as ***servants*** to the legitimately ordained authority superior to them within the hierarchy: the layman receives and obeys instruction from their priest; the priest receives and obeys instruction from their bishop; the bishop receives and obeys instruction from their cardinal or archbishop; the cardinal or archbishop receives and obeys instruction from the Pope; and the Pope receives and obeys instruction from God (under normal circumstances, via inspiration from the Holy Spirit). Moreover, the reader will notice that the most important part of keeping this structure standing is ***obedience***; for the singularly simple reason of the example that is set, and propagated for others to follow, if open disobedience is tolerated. The doctrine of Holy Obedience is the mortar that binds the structure of the Church into a functional and cohesive organization. If obedience is undermined the cohesive force holding the Church together is likewise dissipated; so that as disobedience to higher, proper authority within the Church becomes more prevalent, the entire structure of the Church is subsequently weakened, and ultimately threatened with collapse if the error(s) of disobedience—accompanied by the great scandal and confusion that results as a consequence—are not corrected; as we are currently seeing in this age.

In understanding the nature of how and why the Church is supposed to work, it can then be understood why the modern Catholic Church is in so much trouble: the widespread spirit of disobedience that has taken hold throughout the organization. This disobedient spirit is evident at all levels of the Church: the laity, priests, bishops, and cardinals. Many of the disobedient refer to this attitude as "religious liberty" or "freedom of conscience," which is just another way of describing Protestantism: the rejection of the revealed doctrine and norms of the Church in deference to private, personal judgment and interpretation(s) of Biblical and theological doctrine: an assent of the will to human pride. There are too many instances to note, but a couple of the tactics used by the faithless and proud members of the clergy require recognition. The first is outright refusal to scrupulously follow authentic doctrine and legitimate directives promulgated by legitimately ordained authority.

This rebellion is most commonly seen and felt by the layperson at the level of the parish priest and the bishops. For instance, a common practice that is coming under assault more regularly is the practice of kneeling during the Eucharistic prayers and the reception of the Eucharist. In some dioceses, the faithful have been instructed that the Eucharist shall only be distributed while standing, as opposed to the traditional posture of kneeling, by direction of parish priests or bishops. Some prelates have gone so far as to accuse those who kneel for reception of the Eucharist as an act of disobedience. This is, of course, absolutely false! When kneeling for reception of the Eucharist in a Washington (State) diocese I was informed that within the diocese in question, the bishop had instructed that Communion was to be received standing up. However, in the recent Vatican directive *Redemptionis Sacramentum*,[48] intended to standardize norms within the celebration of the

---

[48] Available at http://www.vatican.va/roman_curia/congregations/ccdds/documents/rc_con_ccdds_doc_20040423_redemptionis-sacramentum_en.html

liturgy, it was clearly stated that, ". . . it is not licit to deny Holy Communion to any of Christ's faithful solely on the grounds, for example, that the person wishes to receive the Eucharist kneeling or standing."[49] However, there appear to be more than a few priests, bishops, and cardinals who apparently think that their opinions, beliefs, and desires are superior to the authority of the Pope and his duly ordained representatives in matters regarding the liturgy and magisterial doctrine.

In effect, human pride has taken over within the hearts and minds of many consecrated religious. To compound the problem, the Vatican of the last several decades has actually helped to create and propagate this problem by allowing bishops autonomy and discretion in too many things. This practically guarantees that conflicts will arise between the faithful and their parishes or dioceses, as the more "liberal" (heretical) priests and bishops decide to push the latitude given them by the Holy See beyond their intended limits; so as to impose the liturgy of Bishop X, Y, or Z, rather than the liturgy set down by the Holy See.

This approach is obviously self-destructive to the discipline of the Faith and the continuity of the liturgy. As somewhat extensive travel is a part of my work, it can be honestly stated (from direct, personal experience) that as one travels from diocese to diocese there are no two of them that celebrate the mass identically; and even within a diocese there are some parishes where the conduct of the mass differs slightly between others! Some parts are sung while others are spoken. At different parts of the mass, especially during the Eucharistic liturgy, the congregation stands or kneels depending on the diocese or parish one is in. There is no longer any universal uniformity and continuity in the conduct of the mass! If one never leaves their parish, such realities do not make themselves felt by the faithful, but for those of us who travel to different locales, the lack of consistency is disconcerting; such that as one travels from one parish to another they must be prepared for the many variations (the consistency of inconsistency) regarding what they will experience during the conduct of the Mass.

The ultimate cause of these problems is modernism and pride on the part of many disobedient clergymen who have introduced all manners of novelty within the Church, and along with these novelties have introduced many new points of contention for the faithful to pointlessly squabble over; thereby destroying the unity of mind that St. Paul so ardently admonished

---

[49] *Redemptionis Sacramentum*, Sec. [91].

the faithful to pursue all throughout his many epistles. The faithless or proud clergyman can be recognized most clearly in two ways. Firstly, they introduce or change something within the liturgy or Church doctrine entirely on their singular initiative; without first gaining the necessary, lawful permission from the proper, higher authority(s) in order to institute the new novelty or change. The reception of the Eucharist in the hand was introduced in this manner. Secondly, they subvert and counterfeit the doctrine of Holy Obedience by demanding obedience to their commands and directives, while disobeying commands and directives from their legitimately ordained, higher authorities. If they are confronted with the proof of their errors or malfeasance—for instance, when Vatican directives are used to demonstrate and expose a priest's or bishop's contradiction of Vatican policy, doctrine, or liturgical norms—they will conveniently discover any excuse necessary, regardless of logic or merit, to justify their disobedience. And thirdly, the most pernicious troublemakers within the Church work to undermine the legitimate authority and supremacy of the Pope within the Holy See.

They are trying to transform the structure and organization of the Church from its proper and intended nature as a mirror of the divine, hierarchical order—with a singular personage issuing authoritative decrees in all matters concerning the organization—into a humanistic, democratic structure and organization. Reducing the Pope, as much as possible, to a *de facto* position of a titular figurehead; stripped of the authority and respect among the faithful that is needed to singularly exercise command of the Church. It was this faction within the Church who was most interested in, and responsible for, trying to pressure Pope John Paul II into resigning his pontificate during the last few weeks of his life and rule by floating speculative rumors within the media regarding the possibility of his resignation. And why do such men persist in trying to overturn the centuries-old order of the Church? The simple, shameful answers are any of a combination of factors: self-important human pride, a thirst for power and control over others, a desire to be admired by other men, faithlessness, or a secret hatred of the Church. It is these sorts of men who are the greatest threat to the Church and the guiltiest parties in its unraveling. The faithful must come to realize that these creatures are trying to duplicate, here on Earth, the original revolt that the Devil tried to lead in Heaven, before the creation of humanity.

Lucifer was from the most exalted rank of all angels, and was himself given the greatest gifts, authority, and responsibility among them; like a prince in relation to his father, the King. As such, it was his assigned duty to serve God and protect His throne. The Devil, fascinated at the greatness of his being, came to be filled with self-love and pride; subsequently turning against God in the belief that, due to his self-supposed greatness, he should be worshipped and honored as God was. In defiance, he declared his separation and rebellion from God; refusing obedience to serve as he was commanded. Take notice of how the men within the Church who work to "democratize" the Holy See, and deprive the Pope of his status as the singular, ultimate authority and leader of the Church, are replaying this divine scenario of ultimate rebellion once again here on Earth.

Those who are most responsible for the corruption of the Church occupy the most exalted ranks of all clergymen; that of cardinals and bishops. In their capacity and position as senior officials within the Church, it is their assigned duty to protect the "Throne of Peter": the office and person of the Pope. Instead, the proud ones wonder at the self-supposed greatness of their intellect; believing they know as well or better than the Pope regarding how the Church should be administered and the modifications that should be made to true doctrine in order to bring it "up to date" with the rest of the modern world: modernism. Those clergymen (or laymen) who preach or propagate any message that undermines the hierarchical, patriarchal structure of the Church, or the supremacy of the Pope as the singular leader of the faithful, even though they may be cardinals or bishops, are those who must be either reproved and corrected regarding their dangerous errors, or eradicated from the Church (defrocked, excommunicated, or both) if they refuse to desist in undermining the proper authority of the Pope and the hierarchical, patriarchal structure of the Church.

> But though we, or an angel from heaven, preach a gospel
> to you besides that which we have preached to you, let him
> be anathema.[50]

Recall that the worldview and perspective that these men should possess, as archbishops and cardinals, is one of a reliance on God, and Christ specifically, to deliver humanity from all trials and tribulations: men who are supposed to be the richest in faith in all the world: the most eminent regarding their knowledge, and defense, of authentic Church doctrine and ardent proponents of the Faith. Various saints of the past have compared the

---

[50] Galatians 1:8.

way the mind functions concerning religion and faith to the action of gravity; and within that context have described their faith and love of God as if He were the central body around which their minds and souls gravitated. This is the worldview and perspective that men in the position of an archbishop or cardinal should personify. As cardinals and bishops, these men are supposed to be the most knowledgeable and potent evangelizers and expositors of the Faith within the Church. Sadly, a great many of them are not, and have instead taken on a worldly disposition; putting their faith in men rather than in God, and forgetting the very foundation of their declared Faith: "⁸It is good to confide in the Lord, rather than to have confidence in man. ⁹It is good to trust in the Lord, rather than to trust in princes."[51]

Several factors are common among those who are either falling down in their duty to God and the faithful, or who are purposefully subverting the Church: (1) a routine forgetfulness, or ignorance of, supernatural action and God's participation in the outcome of world events and in people's daily lives; (2) a lack of moral clarity on unpleasant or difficult problems centered around approved Church doctrine; accompanied by a lack of moral courage to squarely confront evil when it is discovered;[52] (3) deference to, and respect for, the various self-interested opinions of men rather than an adherence to, and defense of, the moral and theological, foundational principles of the Church; (4) a lack of implicit trust and faith in God that all things that pass in this world do so because it is either allowed, or directly willed, by God; and (5) a "democratic" spirit of power-sharing with the Pope: an overwhelming desire to be "associate popes." Those bishops and cardinals in the Church who lack faith, understanding, or courage demonstrate any one, or a combination, of these attributes.

Let us briefly look at how practical faithlessness is manifesting itself within the Holy See; so that in the future, as the faithless prelates within the Vatican expose themselves more clearly—and they *will* need to expose themselves more blatantly in the future to finally tip the scales in their favor—

---

[51] Psalms 117:8-9. The reference to "princes" is directly applicable to all modern politicians; as they, like princes, are those people who are directly responsible for the affairs and conduct of governments.

[52] For example, the failure of bishops to defrock and prosecute homosexual predators within the priesthood when they were discovered, instead of covering up for them by shipping them off to "rehab" or to another unsuspecting diocese; and after that failure, the failure of the cardinals to sack the bishops when it was discovered that many of the bishops were willfully derelict in their duty to the faithful.

it will be easier to discern the attributes of their behavior from those of the faithful servants of the Pope and of God. It was reported in 2004,[53] by John Allen, the Rome correspondent of the newsweekly *National Catholic Reporter,* that during the 2004 election of the U.S. President there was a split within the Vatican, numerically breaking down on the order of approximately 60% to 40% in favor of John Kerry. The variance of opinion was most notable for its tendency to differentiate itself between the varying dicasteries and congregations within the Holy See. This single article is extremely powerful in illuminating both the nature and extent of the corruption within the Vatican and how it manifests itself in the public eye.

If the assessment of the 60-40 ratio in favor of John Kerry within the College of Cardinals is anywhere near accurate, then the Church is really in much graver trouble than Catholics can imagine; because John Kerry's ideological philosophy is socialistic. Now, before the reader balks at such an assertion, they need to remember that any idea or ideology does not change its nature depending on the "dressed up" label that is attached to it. A prostitute, no matter how much makeup and fine clothing you put on her, is still a prostitute. Calling her by any other name or dressing her up to make her *appear* respectable does not change the nature of what she is. Modern political labels and parties—such as those who call themselves liberals, progressives, Democrats, Greens, et al.—are all, at their ideological foundation, socialistic.

This is due to the premise upon which all these ideologies are built on: reliance on the "community of man" to solve all social problems and challenges, accompanied with the repudiation of individual initiative and personal responsibility for the success or failure of the lives of individual citizens. The only difference between these groups is the focus of attention and the degree of socialism or communism they adhere to: the liberals being heavy socialists or light communists; the progressives being further left than the standard liberal, with typical doctrinaire Marxist allegiances (Barak Obama); the Democrats being a combination of both and tending more toward the progressive every day; the Greens being Democrats with the focus of attention gravitating around environmentalism, etc.

In each case, and others, the underlying foundation of their ideology runs along the lines of, "We know better than everybody else regarding how to lead a happy and successful life. To make everybody happy and successful we

---

[53] http://natcath.org/NCR_Online/archives2/2004d/101504/101504a.htm, accessed November 27, 2007.

must seize the reins of political power and force our ideas on everyone else through the enactment of laws consistent with our ideology. Those people who stand against us are dangerous fools, and when we are in power we must "reeducate" the recalcitrant masses and deal very severely with those few psychotic people who refuse their indoctrination. Naturally, the means we may employ, even if they are somewhat harsh, are allowable and moral because we are acting in the best interests of the society." Of course, the font from which such grandiose ideas flow from is abject pride and narcissistic arrogance; and yes, the Bible speaks explicitly about creatures like this: "Yea, and the fool when he walketh in the way, whereas he himself is a fool, esteemeth all men fools."[54] and, "For professing themselves to be wise, they became fools."[55] Moreover, in this particular example, Mr. Kerry, due to his "pro-choice" position on abortion, has voluntarily separated himself from the Catholic Church, and for knowingly and willfully contradicting the doctrine and moral precepts of the Church, has incurred an automatic, self-imposed excommunication.

My fellow Catholics, what does it say about the College of Cardinals if it is true that more than half of them prefer a willfully self-excommunicated heretic over a man who, although not Catholic, publicly subscribes much more closely to the moral precepts of the Church!? That there would be even *one* Cardinal who would express a preference for a heretic—a declared enemy of the Church—to ascend to one of the most powerful political positions on earth, over a man whose moral positions are more inclined to the Church, portends grave dangers for the Church when its highest officers are not only willing, but desirous, to court and embrace its avowed enemies! Additionally, it demonstrates a stunning lack of moral courage by those cardinals who refuse to persevere in the doctrine of the Church, and by their good example allow "the chips to fall where they may." Contrarily, they choose a route of political expediency in the face of growing threats to the very *divine* organization they are supposed to protect!

---

[54] Ecclesiastes 10:3.

[55] Romans 1:22.

For Priests:

Before delving more deeply into the failings of the priesthood today, let me make it absolutely clear that this effort is undertaken with charitable intentions and sentiments regarding both his fellow man and the priests that govern our spiritual life; so as to hopefully bring attention to some very serious errors that have wormed their way into the Church and require correction. Moreover, I desire to be equally clear that I am not making myself out to be more holy, pious, or righteous than our priests. I am simply noting observations that I believe are inescapable to the honest; based on experiences in parishes all over the United States, even if they are difficult to hear. As difficult as this criticism may be to take, it is truly meant to be *constructive* criticism regarding many of the practices and attitudes that are undermining today's priesthood; and as such it is intended as a service to both the numerous flocks of sheep that are being led astray and as a service to the shepherds who have themselves been led astray. In so doing, this layman is not criticizing for the sake of contentiousness. Hopefully, as you contemplate the following observations, it is my fervent desire that you consider the criticisms as an honest attempt to point out where things have gone wrong instead of simply taking offense with them. If you believe the observations presented here to be in error, I would simply beg one thing from you: your forgiveness and prayer in my behalf for any perceived errors.

With that in mind, as priests you are called to a higher ideal and standard of piety than the laity. This is understood by all, and as a result our priests are burdened with a much heavier cross than the laity; one that this layperson does not profess to understand. In return for the greater cross and burden on yourselves there is the understanding that your reward will be greater in Heaven due to your heavier burdens on this side of the "veil." Conversely, if the priest fails in his duties to God, his fall, and consequent punishment, is much more severe than the laity. Very literally, Christ "holds your feet to the fire" much more rigorously than the laity. The manifest reason for this is obvious; because when a shepherd leads his flock astray the damage to souls is innumerably magnified than if a single sheep had gone astray on their own.

Understanding this, let's look at some of the grave errors that many (not all) of our priests have fallen into; a great number of them, unwittingly. The first thing that priests should do to more faithfully satisfy their calling is to put a great deal more distance between themselves and worldly concerns. Although you are priests, in the essence of your being you are just men; subject to the same temptations and errors as the laity. The only protection you have from these temptations and errors is grace. The only way you can maintain a superior level of friendship with God, and consequently call more of His grace to yourselves, is to separate yourselves from the world and those worldly concerns that weigh men down in vain and ultimately spiritually unfruitful pursuits. In your own consciences, evaluate where your time and mental efforts are focused in contemplation. Are you concerned about the Church finances? *Don't Be.* Financial concerns will always be a part of the administration of a Church. Find some faithful laymen that fear the judgments of God to administer the Church finances and keep you informed on these matters.

By tending to the things of God with rigor, men take notice of your piety and devout service to God. Flocks gather to good shepherds like thirsty animals in search of the "living waters." Monetary concerns will take care of themselves as a flock is drawn to the "good shepherds" of the world. Sadly, it is the inescapable observation of this Catholic that many of the priests in this age have taken on the face of the Pharisee: preferring to be approved of by men rather than by God. This is especially true of "liberal" priests and theologians. "Liberal" prelates within the priesthood, understanding the modern use of the word, have become heretics in too many frightening ways; because "liberal," as the word applies to the Church today, is actually nothing more than a euphemism for undisciplined conformists to the world. Priestly liberalism has led many priests to seek the approval and consent of the laity in the affairs and administration of the Church; so much so that many priests have begun to compromise on a great many basic and fundamental theological principles; to the great harm of their own souls and to those whom they mislead.

> [10]His watchmen are all blind, they are all ignorant: dumb dogs not able to bark, seeing vain things, sleeping and loving dreams. [11]And most impudent dogs, they never had enough: the shepherds themselves knew no understanding: all have turned aside into their own way, every one after his own gain, from the first even to the last.[56]

St. Paul admonished that we should not be conformed to the world, and this is especially true of the priest: "And be not conformed to this world; but be reformed in the newness of your mind, that you may prove what is

---

[56] Isaias 56:10-11.

the good, and the acceptable, and the perfect will of God."[57] From time immemorial, it has been the nature of men to bend and massage the teachings of the Church so that men would not be compelled to feel so guilty about being so weak. It is simply a component of our perverse human nature to seek to sin with an easy conscience. As God observed, through Isaias: "all have turned aside into their own way, every one after his own gain . . ." This appears to be the case with too many modern priests. While there are a good number who are unduly concerned with church finances and meeting the "bottom line," a more subtle way in which modern priests are "turned aside into their own way, every one after his own gain," is the way in which so many priests have abandoned the discipline of the Church's doctrines to please the laity: their "own gain" being the approval and favor of the laity. This type of laxity, and the eliciting of approval from the laity, must stop; for the sake of the souls of both the layman and the priest who has allowed himself to fall into this error.

This error primarily stems from four sources: a lack of discipline, a lack of fortitude, a lack of knowledge, or a desire for human approval; but again, as noted earlier, this type of disposition and behavior within the priesthood is completely backwards and unfit for men of the cloth; in light of the duties you have taken upon yourselves to perform. The manner in which this behavior most commonly manifests itself is in an inappropriate familiarity with the laity; where the laity view their priest as a [familiar] friend rather than as a [spiritual] father figure to be obeyed. From such a psychological disposition, the laity then comes to view the direction of their priest as being simple suggestions they can either obey or disregard, rather than spiritual commands or instruction. Of course, the priest cannot be blamed if some of the laity incorporate such an attitude into their conscience, as no man can be held directly accountable for the thoughts and actions of other men. However, many modern priests are indirectly responsible for encouraging this false and dangerous disposition among the laity due to the manner in which they tacitly encourage it through their own behavior: accepting and even encouraging an unduly familiar relationship with their parishioners.

As a priest, consider your relationship to your parishioners as that which exists between a parent and a child. To maintain an orderly household, the parent must exercise discipline with his children. Sometimes the child readily submits to the requests of their parent; but on other occasions, the child rebels, and discipline is required to bring the disobedient child back into line.

---

[57] Romans 12:2.

This principle, or more accurately the lack of its application, is extraordinarily apparent in the modern world. A common social dysfunction within the modern world is the breakdown of authority at all levels within society: in the home, in the Church, and among civil authorities. Too many modern "parents" want to be their children's friend; a dangerous disposition that allows the children to go astray and engage in self-indulgent behavior that is not in their best interest, or of that of our society. Not desiring to injure little Johnny's precious feelings, a great many people are pandering to their children so as to gain their friendship and approval. This same phenomenon is exactly what is transpiring within the modern Church: an almost complete breakdown in the analogous, parental authority the priest is supposed to exercise over the laity in his parish.

This rebellious spirit that has taken hold of mankind has continued on to spill out into civil society in the form of increased crime and civil disobedience. If the Church is to be repaired, it must start by ushering in a return to obedience and discipline within the Church. Remember, as priests you are our (laity) spiritual fathers. It is certainly nice when the parent and child are on good terms; but as a spiritual guide to your spiritual children you must at all times remember that your role is to enforce discipline within the home (the Church), so as to maintain order. There is absolutely nothing to be gained, and everything to be lost, when the priest compromises on doctrine to keep the laity happy. Just look to the disrepute without the Church, and irreverence within the Church, that such behavior has caused. Moreover, exercising discipline within the Church will ultimately, although not immediately, be appreciated by the faithful.

Just like children whose parents let them do as they please; the child understands that what this behavior on the parent's part symbolizes is a lack of love and caring for the child. As a result, these children come to despise their parents and view them with contempt. In truth, the same principle applies in the relationship between the priest and the parishioner. How could it possibly be any other way? When the laity see the priests allowing things to transpire within the Church that they know should not be going on, what other conclusion can they come to, except that the priest is either (1) ignorant of his duty, (2) too weak to enforce the rules and doctrines of the Church, or (3) too concerned with currying favor among the people? These possibilities reflect poorly on the priest who allows improprieties to occur in the Church; either during or outside the Mass.

Another way to view your relationship with the laity is within the context of a military organization; as those members of the Church who live in this world are referred to as the Church Militant within the context of the Communion of Saints. As we discussed earlier, there is a divine "chain of command" in Heaven. Moreover, the Church is supposed to mimic that structure. Consequently, the priest is in a superior position in relation to the laity within this chain of command. It is widely known that within the military there exists a separation between the Officer Corp and the enlisted ranks. This is absolutely necessary for maintaining order and discipline within the organization; because once officers begin to become familiar with those under their command the enlisted personnel often begin to second-guess the commands relayed to them, and in the worst circumstances openly defy the officer's orders.

Such a circumstance erodes the authority and respect the enlisted personnel have for the officer in question; so that when faced with difficult choices that may very well cost someone their life, the likelihood is greatly increased that either (1) the enlisted personnel will resist their orders, or (2) the officer will hesitate to make a life-threatening decision, however necessary it may be, due to the friendship that exists between the two, which often accrues to even deadlier results as a consequence of the indecisive and subversive delay of action. Moreover, as discipline breaks down within a military unit it increasingly threatens the lives of the personnel, as their effectiveness and efficiency are compromised as a result of their lack of discipline. The very same principles apply within the context of the priest's (officer) relationship to the laity (enlisted).

The only protection against the evil tendencies within human nature, and the sustenance of the Church, is a united priesthood of one mind and spirit. What does a priest think God will have to say to him, when he goes before Him to be judged, if they allowed depraved human tendencies to bend their minds, and subsequently the doctrines being taught in their respective churches, in the direction of more laxity within the Church in order to satisfy the undisciplined, disorderly, and depraved inclinations of men? In full knowledge of the depravity of human nature, it is only to be expected that the most routinely used word in a priest's vocabulary *should* be . . . **NO**! It is the duty of the priest to *command* the flock, not to obtain their approval on anything. What is required for this ideal to be met are faith, truth, fortitude, knowledge, and charity.

As priests, your faith and desire for truth is a given; unless, of course, you are one who secretly desires the destruction of the Church; and any honest prelate knows very well that these types of warped men exist within today's priesthood. You need not look any further than the homosexual abuse scandal to recognize that the priesthood is being corrupted from within. For those priests who truly desire to perform their duties faithfully, the only other qualities necessary are fortitude, knowledge, and charity. Fortitude is difficult, and easily misapplied, in ignorance: when one is not absolutely sure of what they must be firm on, and why. Fortitude is much easier in knowledge: when one knows what they must be firm on, and why. The critical factor is *knowledge*. Once knowledge is obtained, fortitude comes as a natural consequence from the clear understanding of "what is the good, and the acceptable, and the perfect will of God."[58] Sadly, and undeniably, when one looks at the sad state of the Church today, many priests today show a stunning ignorance of too many fundamental theological principles. The Bible also speaks of the consequences of this ignorance in the priesthood:

> My people have been silent, because they had no knowledge: because thou hast rejected knowledge, I will reject thee, that thou shalt not do the office of priesthood to me: and thou hast forgotten the law of thy God, I also will forget thy children.[59]

This passage says quite a bit. More importantly, note the responsibility placed on the priests. For those who have rejected knowledge—in truth, most prelates have been led away from knowledge rather than rejecting it; but either way many still remain lacking of knowledge—the consequences apply not only to yourselves, but to those within your assigned flock who are led astray by either your lack of knowledge or fortitude in firmly correcting their errors. Undoubtedly, many of you have been betrayed by the seminaries where you received your training; unbeknownst to yourselves. The theological and philosophical reading material in Appendix B would undoubtedly serve the priesthood immensely well. Second to the Bible, *Summa Theologica* by St. Thomas Aquinas is invaluable. As this layperson is not intimately aware of what goes on in today's seminaries, he would only request that you examine your own training and consciences. Were you instructed in modernist theology? Was material from Pierre Tielhard de Chardin, Hans Kung, and other similar, heretical "theologians," taught in your seminaries? Were you yourselves seduced into trying to unite science or modernism with Faith?

---

[58] Romans 12:2, in part.

[59] Osee 4:6.

In 1907, Pope Pius X wrote a Papal decree and an encyclical regarding the problems related to modernist theology. The Papal Decree, *Lamentabili Sane*,[60] issued on 3 July, 1907, expounds the modernist errors that are to be rejected as contrary to the Faith. His encyclical, *Pascendi Dominici Gregis*,[61] released on 8 September, 1907, explained the errors of modernist theology and directed the measures that were to be taken to suppress it. These documents were written so as to ban and remove modernist influences from the faithful, and especially from the seminaries. Whether through negligence or open disobedience to the Pope, the measures meant to cut off the errors of the modernists failed abysmally. These measures and sanctions against modernist theology and theologians are still in force, although they are ignored today. How many of the priests reading this have ever read these documents? How many of you have never even heard of them?

As well, how many of today's priests are well grounded in the Doctors of the Church and *true* theological philosophy: most especially St. Thomas Aquinas? To see the gross corruption within the Church today, one need only reflect on a single proof of reason established by Aquinas in Part 1, Question 9, Article 1 in his work *Summa Theologica*: the immutability of God. [62] This key

---

[60] Available at http://www.newadvent.org/library/docs_df07ls.htm; or *The Popes Against Modern Errors*.

[61] Available at http://www.vatican.va/holy_father/pius_x/encyclicals/documents/hf_p-x_enc_19070908_pascendi-dominici-gregis_en.html; or *The Popes Against Modern Errors*.

[62] In part . . . "*On the contrary*, It is written, *I am the Lord, and I change not* (Mal. iii. 6). *I answer that,* From what precedes, it is shown that God is altogether immutable. First, because it was shown above that there is some first being, whom we call God; and that this first being must be pure act, without the admixture of any potentiality, for the reason that, absolutely, potentiality is posterior to act. Now everything which is in any way changed, is in some way in potentiality. Hence it is evident that it is impossible for God to be in any way changeable. Secondly, because everything which is moved, remains as it was in part, and passes away in part; as what is moved from whiteness to blackness, remains the same as to substance; thus in everything which is moved, there is some kind of composition to be found. But it has been shown above (Q.3, A. 7) that in God there is no composition, for He is altogether simple. Hence it is manifest that God cannot be moved. Thirdly, because everything which is moved acquires something by its movement, and attains to what it had not attained previously. But since God is infinite, comprehending in Himself all the plentitude of perfection of all being, He cannot acquire anything new, nor extend Himself to anything whereto He was not extended previously. Hence movement in no way belongs to Him. . ."

reality, which is not understood by very many people, is that **GOD CANNOT CHANGE**. This Catholic would strongly encourage our priests to read this material for their own edification. A primary reason for God's immutability is because God, being eternal, *must* be perfect; for if He were not perfect He could not be eternal. Any imperfection in God's nature and essence would introduce corruption into His essence and being. But since God is eternal, and incorrupt, He must be perfect; and hence, unchangeable in any way from His state of perfection. Moreover, Aquinas established that God is pure act; and that there is no potency (potential for change) in Him. If there is no potency in God, there is no potential or ability to change in Him.

These proofs of reason, having been established by Aquinas over seven hundred years ago, lead to a very important consequence: God desires the same level of attentiveness and adoration from His creation, and especially His priests, as He commanded in the days of Moses and Aaron during the Exodus and the establishment of His covenant with Israel. His desire to be adored by humanity cannot change, because He cannot change. Moreover, in truth and justice, He has a right to desire this type of gratitude.

The last quality needed among the priesthood is charity. An uncompromising disposition when it comes to teaching and enforcing Church doctrine is the highest form of charity the priest can exercise; because by standing firm in the truth of revealed doctrine the priest is helping his spiritual children ultimately obtain their desired end: God. Compromising doctrine and discipline within the Church demonstrates a lack of charity on the priest's part, because it demonstrates a willingness to allow error—however subtle it may *appear* to be—in order to avert confrontation with the laity, which only contributes to the possible damnation of both the layman and the priest for compromising on doctrine.

Humanity, being imperfect and temporal, is *highly* corruptible. Due to our imperfect and corruptible nature, it is humanity that changes; and it is an undeniable, historical fact that as humanity changes, it almost always changes in the direction of greater corruption. Just turning on the news or reading a newspaper story relating the increasing numbers of child molestations, murders, rapes, thievery, fraud, the continuing dissolution of the respect for human life, etc., is clear evidence of how far humanity has descended to an evil and almost completely carnal, animalistic, and barbaric state. Seeing the corruption that has taken place within the world—and most especially within the Church—today, it is all too obvious that the dissolution of Faith and morals has come about because of the dissolution of both obedience and discipline within the Church; starting within the hierarchy of the

Church, and then extending to the laity. Over the past several hundred years "liberal" (more correctly, libertine) theologians and priests have been either introducing or allowing increasingly lax standards within the Church, to the dangerous point that there are now a great many enemies of the Church who have become emboldened and have corrupted many of the "faithful" who are ignorant of their motives. There are now people, and even a great number of heretics within the Church itself, who openly and brazenly demand that the Church conform to the desires of the people: acceptance of homosexuality, abortion, divorce, birth control, female priests, etc.

Now, when priests see so many heretics—some of them their fellow priests—openly demanding that the Church conform to the corruptible nature and inclinations of men, rather than conforming themselves to the traditional doctrines of the Church, as originally taught by Christ Himself, there *must* be a voice within you that lets you know clearly that there is something terribly wrong and evil going on among the faithful and within the Church. The wolf is scattering the sheep, and those priests who either cannot or will not stand firm regarding the Magisterial teachings and doctrines of the Church are either allowing or encouraging this sad and pitiful chain of events to transpire either by omission—by failing to take a firm stand against heretical teachings—or by commission—encouraging "liberal," libertine doctrine and behavior among the laity.

As there is only *one* God, there is, and can only be, *one* way; the way of the Church through tradition and the De Fide, Canonical doctrines, as promulgated by His representative body on earth (the Holy See); with the Pope, directed by the Holy Spirit, as its leader. There is *no* other way! Holy Obedience demands that the priests uphold these standards and demand the same from the faithful. If the faithful will not recognize the authority of the Church in these matters and conform themselves to the doctrines of the Church, then it is their loss; *and it is a very great loss indeed!*

> [15]But if thy brother shall offend against thee, go, and rebuke him between thee and him alone. If he shall hear thee, thou shalt gain thy brother. [16]And if he will not hear thee, take with thee one or two more: that in the mouth of two or three witnesses every word may stand. [17]And if he will not hear them: tell the church. ***And if he will not hear the church, let him be to thee as the heathen and publican.***[63]

---

[63] Matthew 18:15-17.

By allowing liberal and modernist theological doctrines to seep in and undermine both the authority and doctrine of the Church, the disobedient priest only helps the adversary scatter the flock and will only incur a black mark against his own soul. These things are intuitively obvious. How it has come to pass that many priests have been so seduced by modernism and liberal theology can only be attributed to a combination of a violation of their vows of obedience and a lack of knowledge: ignorance. But recalling Osee 4:6, God warns that this ignorance will only lead to your own damnation and those of the flock that are misled. This Catholic implores the priests of the Catholic Church to turn away from modernism and liberal, libertine doctrines and philosophies, and in so doing gather the flock once again, through obedience and self-discipline, into one body; united in truth and faith.

From a practical perspective, the following are offered as ways to bring the scattered sheep back to the flock. More than anything else in this world, the "faithful" need to once again be taught discipline. In concert with a laity that is determined to exercise self-discipline, this Catholic implores our priesthood to rigorously enforce the doctrines and practices of the Church. To begin with, demand reverent silence within the Church. Make it clear to the congregation that silence in the Church is both expected and demanded. For those who decide to take up conversation within the Church, politely but firmly demand that they remove themselves from the Church. A few instances of embarrassment will set an example to the congregation and quickly quell this form of irreverence, which has become routine in all too many churches. Moreover, the faithful who come to pray and offer God thanks will be able to do so in peace. Secondly, demand that those who come to Church dress appropriately for the occasion. Our Mother warned of this eventuality during her apparitions at Fátima. You must put a stop to these practices immediately! Every person who presents themselves for reception of the Eucharist dressed immodestly receives a sacrilegious Communion. Those priests who distribute a host to a person immodestly dressed enable this sacrilege. In this scenario, both the priest and the communicant incur the anger of Christ on their souls; the communicant for approaching the Eucharist so irreverently, and the priest for allowing the profanation to occur.

> For he that eateth and drinketh unworthily, eateth and drinketh judgment to himself, not discerning the body of the Lord.[64]

---

[64] 1 Corinthians 11:29.

The most common manifestation of this type of profanation are people who come to Mass very shabbily dressed, as if they were going from Church to a day at the beach: T-shirts (sometimes with emblems of skulls and other icons of death), flip-flops, jeans, and shorts. Even worse are the vain women who approach the Eucharist in miniskirts, very tight clothes that leave nothing to the imagination, and revealing blouses with very low-cut necklines that expose much more of themselves to the congregation than should be seen. People who approach the Eucharist in this manner should be denied the Eucharist; both for their own sake and for that of the priest. Does the modern priest say, "But almost everybody comes to Church casually or immodestly dressed these days"! Well, if they do, it is your fault for not enforcing the rules, and the situation would be reversed and amended if you would only exercise the discipline required and expected of you regarding enforcement of the rules of the Church. Is it extremely difficult for a priest to confront an entire parish and demand a return to the rules and discipline required within the Church; especially when he has a history within his parish of previously allowing laxity and irreverence in the Church? Absolutely, it is! That is just one of the items that makes being a priest such a difficult calling, and which requires a very masculine firmness, and resolute disposition, among men in the priesthood; especially when such firmness only brings ungrateful abuse from the recipient of a charitable rebuke. It's not your fault that human nature is so perverse, but that doesn't change the fact that you still need to maintain discipline and obedience to sound doctrine within the Church.

Next, recall to your flocks the Ten Commandments, especially the commandment to keep the Sabbath holy and *do no work*. This is one of the most widely ignored and abused Commandments of them all. Bring the consciences of men back to a fear of God. Over the past several decades there has been an endless parade of homilies relating the love of God for His children, and at the same time this proliferation of the message of God's love has allowed the message of His vengeance and wrath to be drowned out; to the point that mankind really doesn't *fear* God any longer—as evidenced by the dress and decorum of most people during Mass. Most people today seem to think that because God is such a loving and forgiving God that we can do practically anything and that God will give us a "pass" in the end; a grossly false and effeminately romanticized conception of God's relationship with mankind. The Bible and the Church have clearly established that this is not how it works. Remind your respective flocks, and yourselves if necessary, of this simple fact; and incorporate a few homilies into the Mass regarding God's terrible judgments and punishments. A recollection of the fire and brimstone of Sodom and Gomorrah or His persecution of Egypt for their treatment of the Jews would do very nicely in a world being overrun by Sodomites, child molesters, murderers, rapists, etc.

Another item that is greatly ignored or misunderstood is the abuse of the Eucharist during the reception of Holy Communion. There are currently two practices that lead to the desecration of the Host and diminish or debase the reverent awe that *should* be accorded to His sacramental presence within the Eucharist. These two practices are the use of laity as "Eucharistic ministers" and the distribution of the Eucharist in the hands of the communicant. The use of laity as Eucharistic ministers, as it is practiced in many of today's Churches, is *illicit* and directly disobedient to the directives of the Holy See. Many, if not most, churches and dioceses in the United States (this Catholic cannot speak of practices abroad) use "Eucharistic ministers" (laity) in the distribution of the Eucharist. Besides being a sacrilege (the hands of the laity are not consecrated by Holy Orders),[65] this practice is strictly forbidden by the Holy See.

Articles 88 and 158 of *Redemptionis Sacramentum* speak to the abuse of the use of laity as Eucharistic ministers: "[88] The faithful should normally receive sacramental Communion of the Eucharist during Mass itself, at the moment laid down by the rite of celebration, that is to say, just after the Priest celebrant's Communion. It is the Priest celebrant's responsibility to minister Communion, perhaps assisted by other Priests or Deacons; and he should not resume the Mass until after the Communion of the faithful is concluded. *Only when there is a necessity* may extraordinary ministers assist the Priest celebrant in accordance with the norm of law. . . [158] *Indeed, the extraordinary minister of Holy Communion may administer Communion ONLY when the Priest and Deacon are*

---

[65] See St. Thomas Aquinas' *Summa Theologica*, Part 3, Question 82, Article 3: "The dispensing of Christ's body belongs to the priest for three reasons. First, because, as was said above (A. 1), he consecrates as in the person of Christ. But as Christ consecrated His body at the supper, so also He gave it to others to be partaken of by them. Accordingly, as the consecration of Christ's body belongs to the priest, so likewise does the dispensing belong to him. Secondly, because the priest is the appointed intermediary between God and the people; hence as it belongs to him to offer the people's gifts to God, so it belongs to him to deliver consecrated gifts to the people. Thirdly, *because out of reverence towards this sacrament, nothing touches it, but what is consecrated; hence the corporal and the chalice are consecrated, and likewise the priest's hands, for touching this sacrament.* Hence it is not lawful for anyone else to touch it except from necessity, for instance, if it were to fall upon the ground, or else in some other case of urgency."

lacking, when the Priest is prevented by weakness or advanced age or some other genuine reason, or when the number of faithful coming to Communion is so great that the very celebration of Mass would be unduly prolonged. This, however, is to be understood in such a way that *a brief prolongation, considering the circumstances and culture of the place, is not at all a sufficient reason."*

In short, the use of "Eucharistic ministers," as it is practiced today in most all our Churches, is an illicit practice that must be corrected. This profane practice diminishes the reverence due to the Eucharistic presence of Christ in the Host, and likewise tends to diminish the belief in Christ's real presence in the Eucharist within the minds of the faithful. People begin to wonder what the big deal is over the Eucharist if all you need to do is go to a few classes and a few hours of instruction before you begin to pass it out to the congregation like candy at Halloween. Moreover, some female Eucharistic ministers dress immodestly while distributing the Host; which is even worse—for both the layperson and the priest that allows her to distribute the host—than approaching the Eucharist indecently dressed.

Article 92 of *Redemptionis Sacramentum* speaks to the practice of Communion in the hand: "[92] Although each of the faithful always has the right to receive Holy Communion on the tongue, at his choice, if any communicant should wish to receive the Sacrament in the hand, in areas where the Bishops' Conference with the recognitio of the Apostolic See has given permission, the sacred host is to be administered to him or her. However, special care should be taken to ensure that the host is consumed by the communicant in the presence of the minister, so that no one goes away carrying the Eucharistic species in his hand. If there is a risk of profanation, then Holy Communion should not be given in the hand to the faithful." From article 92 it is clear that the practice of Communion in the hand requires special attention over and above the traditional manner of receiving the Eucharist on the tongue; to the point that it is forbidden "if there is a *risk* of profanation." The above articles clearly instruct the clergy that only priests (or deacons) shall distribute the Eucharist, except when there is a "necessity" to use extraordinary lay ministers, and not for reasons of convenience. Holy Obedience demands that these instructions be followed. At the very least, the instructions of the Holy See should be adhered to for the sake of the souls of the priests who contemplate disobedience to the legitimate authority of the Holy See; because open disobedience to the Holy See, especially in such serious matters as the distribution of the Eucharist, may very well put the souls of our priests in jeopardy of judgment.

Additionally, because of the lack of reverence it engenders and the *"risk of profanation"* that occurs each time the Eucharist is distributed in the hand, the practice of Communion in the hand should also be abolished. Apply some simple, straightforward thought to understand why Communion in the hand is such a severe desecration of the Eucharist and why each distribution incurs a risk of profanation. Recall that in times past great care used to be exercised in the distribution of the Eucharist so that no particles were left astray and allowed to fall to the ground. The priest would sweep any stray particles into the chalice and drink down the remnants mixed with the consecrated wine (blood of Christ) to ensure that no particles of the Host went astray. By distributing the Eucharist in the hands of the communicants, it is certain that some particles of the Eucharist will be lost either in falling to the ground or remaining in the hand of the communicant. Either way, the host would suffer desecration. What's worse is what will happen to the particles of the host—with Christ really and truly present within them—at the conclusion of the Mass.

The first place some people head for after Mass is the restroom. As we all know, when people relieve themselves they often get particles of urine or feces on their hands. This is the reason people wash their hands after a visit to the bathroom. It's important to note that some of those who take the Eucharist in the hand will inevitably leave some particles in their hands, then proceed to the restroom after Mass and urinate and defecate on their Creator. It's a repugnant thought, but not an exaggeration by any means. In fact, it's impossible that this does not happen when one considers the great number of hosts distributed in the hand. Even if the communicant does not defile his God by urinating or defecating on Him directly, He will be washed down the bathroom sink when the person washes their hands. Consequently, Christ will be sent to mix with the feces and urine of the entire common sewer system of the city.

This is a repugnant and extremely sacrilegious scenario; but simple, straightforward understanding leads to the conclusion that this scenario is not only unavoidable but that it actually happens after the conclusion of many Masses where the Eucharist is distributed in the hand. Moreover, as if the preceding weren't bad enough, it is well known that over the last several decades the occult—witchcraft, Satanism, etc.—has seen a surge in adherents. It is well known that there is a black market for consecrated hosts all over the world. In egregious temerity, a consecrated host has even been sold on eBay! By offering Communion in the hand, the opportunity to steal a host—intended for desecration at a black mass or other occultist ceremony—

is made all the more easy. For whatever misguided reason, Communion in the hand was instituted to suit the lax inclinations of men, rather than to accommodate the pleasure of our Creator and give due thanks to Him. It is up to our clergy to put a stop to this practice. The result of this practice leads to a gross desecration of the host and the dissolution of faith in many minds by removing the remembrance of Christ's sacramental presence in the Eucharist.

A clear example of the pernicious products that have accrued, due to a lack of reverence and disbelief in transubstantiation, is a practice which has begun in the last several decades within the Church: the institution of low-gluten hosts for those who suffer from Celiac Disease (a condition which causes illness to an afflicted person when ingesting normal wheat products, such as unconsecrated hosts), and the use of "mustum" (fresh juice from grapes in which fermentation has been suspended) in order to accommodate alcoholics and others who may have physical conditions which make it difficult to ingest alcohol. What's wrong with this? The problem lies in the denial of transubstantiation that such measures tacitly imply. As priests, you should understand and accept that there are certain tenets of the Faith that must be accepted by the faithful in order to consider oneself Catholic: Ex Cathedra doctrine and dogmatic canons that are promulgated from legitimately constituted Church councils. To deny or contradict the truths of these doctrines renders that person a heretic.

Regarding the change of the substance of the bread and wine at the moment of consecration into the Body and Blood of Jesus Christ, the Council of Trent clearly defined (Session XIII, Canons I and II) those principles and dogmas which the faithful must accept as infallible truths:

> CANON I.–If any one denieth, that, in the sacrament of the most holy Eucharist, are contained truly, really, and substantially, the body and blood together with the soul and divinity of our Lord Jesus Christ, and consequently the whole Christ; but saith that He is only therein as in a sign, or in figure, or virtue; let him be anathema.

> CANON II.–If any one saith, that, in the sacred and holy sacrament of the Eucharist, the substance of the bread and wine remains conjointly with the body and blood of our Lord Jesus Christ, and denieth that wonderful and singular conversion of the whole substance of the bread into the Body, and of the whole substance of the wine into the

Blood–the species only of the bread and wine remaining–
which conversion indeed the Catholic Church most aptly
calls Transubstantiation; let him be anathema.

My dear priests, these canons are non-negotiable. What the Council of
Trent clearly proclaimed was that once the host is consecrated it is wholly,
in its substance, changed from a wafer of wheat into the Body of Jesus; and
from wine into the Blood of Jesus. Canon II goes so far as to declare that
no part of the bread or wine remains conjointly with the Body and Blood of
Christ. What the institution of the low-gluten host and "mustum" protocols
signifies is that there are many members of the hierarchy of the Church who
are allowing the insinuation of a heresy into the Church through either their
lack of faith in the certitude of transubstantiation or their unwillingness to
uphold the doctrines and truths of the Faith. This is an excellent example of
the craftiness of the Devil, because in order to corrupt Church doctrine and
faith it is not necessary to directly challenge or contradict Church doctrine.
It is only necessary to insinuate a corruptive idea that, by the force of what
it necessarily implies, achieves the same corruption as if the doctrine were
directly challenged or contradicted. This is also an excellent example of
Orwellian "doublethink" at work within the Church; where both priests and
the laity "hold simultaneously two opinions which cancelled out, knowing
them to be contradictory and believing in both of them." If one believes in
transubstantiation they would believe that the whole substance of the bread
and wine would be changed into the Body and Blood of Jesus at the moment
of consecration. If that were true, there would be no need to use low-gluten
hosts for Celiac sufferers and "mustum" for those who cannot or should not
consume alcohol; because once it is consecrated the substance is no longer a
wheat product or alcoholic beverage. Those people, whether they be priests or
laity, who request or promote either of these protocols are making an implicit
admission of their lack of belief in transubstantiation.

As priests, what should be the reaction when a parishioner approaches
you with a concern regarding the consumption of the Body or Blood of
Christ, due to their inability to consume wheat or alcohol? Such an instance
is an opportunity to correct and catechize individuals whose faith was either
passed to them incorrectly or incompletely. If the person in question refuses
to believe in transubstantiation, then the fault lies with them for their lack of
faith in what the Church teaches. What is required of our priests, however,
is a refusal to compromise doctrine and the revealed truths of the Faith in
order to accommodate a lack of faith amongst the laity, because doing so

ultimately leads to a situation where a revealed truth of the Faith is called into question, and ultimately challenged; leading to a dissolution of faith within the Church at large. This is true when confronted with any situation that has the potential to corrupt the Faith.

Brothers, there is a reality that you need to be aware of (if you are not already), and confront forcefully when you cross paths with it: the existence of wolves amongst the sheep: Priests, Bishops, and Cardinals who are purposefully working to corrupt the Church and the Faith. This reality was demonstrated in a most public fashion during the sexual abuse scandal. It did not go away with the punishment of some of the malefactors and the payout of billions of dollars. By allowing the insinuation of practices into the Church that implicitly (although not directly) contradict the canons of the Faith, the wolves have subtly, and sublimely, undermined one of the most important articles of the Faith (transubstantiation) and have laid down an unspoken challenge to the faithful: "Contradict me, if you dare. I am a member of the hierarchy. If you think you can 'swim uphill' against my corruption of the Faith, then try your hand." My dear priests, it is hard to swim against the tide; especially in an era of almost universal corruption in which the laity are happy to swim with the tide because it suits their lax inclinations and lack of discipline. However, the only options available to you are to allow yourself to be swept along by the tide of corruption, or to push back against it by confronting those within the Church who promote practices that contradict and dissolute the Faith; even if they be your superiors, Bishops, and Cardinals.

To say that this is not an attractive choice is an understatement, but it is nevertheless what you are faced with! You may not win any friends by confronting error (in fact, you can be assured of it), but as long as your allegiance is to the Magisterium and you work to uphold the truth you will ultimately prevail; if not in this world, certainly in the next. On the other hand, the same cannot be said of those who are corrupting the Faith. Ultimately, that is all that matters; regardless of whether the world, the laity, your fellow priests, or superiors may oppose you in this life because they have been seduced by modernism and a spirit of laxity or worldly conformance. Now is the time for choosing. You either believe in what the Magisterium teaches, in its entirety, or you do not. Above all, understand this; if you deny the infallible truths of the Faith, you are participating in the propagation of heresy.

Finally, *discipline* must be restored, along with a resolute will to oppose evil. It is the incremental loss of discipline over the past century or more that is the root cause of all the evils currently assailing both the Church and the world. The evils in this world must be opposed with a *firm* hand; not a lax, effeminate, and almost apologizing, "there must be some reason for your rebellious spirit," disposition. Any sane person who understands the depraved nature of men can understand that the only effective rebuke for evil is firm, sincere, consistent, and *charitable* discipline. Without these attributes all is lost and evil people are emboldened in their evil ways and plans. Those with faith can understand these things immediately. It is not pleasant, but then again God didn't ask us if we like the world we live in. He simply laid it out before us and warned us about the evils of this world and commanded us to oppose them. This is part of what makes this world such a stifling test.

If we refuse to oppose evil we only manifest our rebellion to God's will and incur a black mark against our own souls. As priests, this responsibility primarily falls on your shoulders; to approach the errors within the Church with the same rigor that men approach murderers, child molesters, and rapists. As you can see today, the proliferation of heretics within the Church, as well as those who have always existed outside it, is growing at an exponential rate: the cry for female priests, the acceptance of homosexuality and abortion among too many "Catholics," the call for the abrogation of priestly celibacy, etc. As priests, it is your duty and responsibility to crush these heresies within the Church.

An excellent example of how the compromise of doctrine and discipline in the Church leads to outright rebellion amongst the laity is in the use of the veil by women in Church. The practice of women wearing veils in Church is a requirement; mandated by St. Paul from the beginning.[66] There has never been an abrogation of this requirement. However, looking at the scene of the modern world, there are less than one percent of women who dutifully don the veil for Mass. In most modern Mass services, there are no women wearing the veil. This reality only came about due to the laxity of priests regarding the enforcement of discipline regarding obedience to Church doctrine(s).

Paul admonished the faithful to "be not conformed to this world." The laity needs its priests to remain faithful to their vows and demand that they truly conform themselves to the teachings of Christ and the Church, rather than the depraved examples taught by this world. The priests must demand

---

[66] 1 Corinthians 11:5-6: "⁵But every woman praying or prophesying with her head not covered, disgraceth her head: for it is all one as if she were shaven. ⁶For if a woman be not covered, let her be shorn. But if it be a shame to a woman to be shorn or made bald, let her cover her head."

this from the faithful for the sake of their own souls—as they promised Christ they would perform this function upon their ordination—as well as for the sake of the souls of the flock; many of whom are running headlong into serious errors and heresies due to their ignorance and narcissistically self-absorbed mentalities; courtesy of modern, "popular" culture. Will the laity oppose you and badmouth you for your firmness and faithfulness? Most likely, a great many of them will; for they have become habituated to an undisciplined and worldly Church. Many may decide to leave the Church due to its firmness; and if they do their blood is on their own hands for refusing to follow the teachings and doctrines of the Church.

Christ warned you of this resistance during His ministry; and it was expected that you understood this before you pursued the priesthood: "If the world hate you, know ye, that it hath hated me before you."[67] If the priesthood today refuses to exercise this faithfulness to Church doctrines and teachings, the blood of the scattered sheep is also on your hands for failing in your assigned duties as temporary shepherds of His flock. Christ wanted all men to come to him and partake of His Body and Blood in His Church, even though he knew that *all* would not come to Him; but those who do wish to come to Him must do so in a spirit of supplicating humility; according to His doctrines and teachings *only*; as promulgated by the action of the Holy Spirit through His Vicar of Christ and the Holy See. Moreover, a priest need not be concerned about apostasy resulting from exercising firmness and discipline, because such considerations once again betray a deference to please men rather than God. Besides, as the world continues to descend into increasingly depraved anarchy many, if not most, will return for the simple reason that they will believe they have no other place to turn:

> [54]Then Jesus said to them: Amen, amen I say unto you: Except you eat the flesh of the Son of man, and drink his blood, you shall not have life in you. . . [61]Many therefore of his disciples, hearing it, said: This saying is hard, and who can hear it? . . . [67]After this many of his disciples went back; and walked no more with him. [68]Then Jesus said to the twelve: Will you also go away? [69]And Simon Peter answered him: **Lord, to whom shall we go?** thou hast the words of eternal life.[68]

[67] John 15:18.
[68] John 6:54, 61, 67-69.

The world will no longer offer them any solace, and they will hunger for the true good: God. For there to be peace and unity within any organization there must be one unifying and animating philosophy that moves that organization; accompanied by obedience to the directors of the organization, and firm discipline to handle insurrections within it. The Holy See, from its foundation with Peter at its head, is *the* one unifying and animating philosophy and way. Catholics must remain obedient to the tradition and doctrines of the Church, and priests must once again exercise firm discipline to crush the heretical insurrections sprouting up within it. By giving an ear to "liberal" (heretical) Catholics and "theologians" to make Catholicism more palatable to the average person, the Church is only being divided against itself. Moreover, it is being conformed to the world rather than to Christ.

What the modernist Catholics and theologians are doing, whether they realize it or not, is demanding that Christ, through the Church, conform Himself to the depraved inclinations of men. But Christ, being one of the three persons of the triune God, neither can, nor would, change Himself to conform to our depraved nature. This would introduce corruption into His being and destroy His eternal, perfect nature. It is neither possible, nor desirable, that God (through Christ) would change to conform to the depraved inclinations of His creation! For the sake of your own souls, and those of the wayward sheep of the flock, our priests *must* put an end to these heresies and the open disobedience to traditional doctrine; especially if a priest is responsible for propagating errors either by commission or omission. It is the *only* way; especially, and most importantly, because it is *His* way. If, as priests, you doubt the necessity of rejecting modern innovations and returning to traditional Catholicism—especially because such a proposition will naturally incur severe resistance from the laity—then I would simply beg you to appeal to God directly, through the Holy Spirit.

As priests (consecrated to Christ) you are, by your very position within the hierarchy of the Church, His chosen shepherds of the flock and dispensers of His grace. If you go to Him in prayer—and, *most importantly*, with a disposition of supplicating humility—for guidance on these issues with a firm resolution in your mind to serve Him in all truth and sincerity, He will direct your minds so that they conform to His will. How can you be absolutely certain of this fact? Because these have been His promises to the human race; promises that compel us, both by faith and two millennia of faithfulness on His part, to believe!

But the Paraclete, the Holy Ghost, whom the Father will send in my name, he will teach you all things, and bring all things to your mind, whatsoever I shall have said to you.[69]

[7]Ask, and it shall be given you: seek, and you shall find: knock, and it shall be opened to you. [8]For every one that asketh, receiveth: and he that seeketh, findeth: and to him that knocketh, it shall be opened. [9]Or what man is there among you, of whom if his son shall ask bread, will he reach him a stone? [10]Or if he shall ask him a fish, will he reach him a serpent? [11]If you then being evil, know how to give good gifts to your children: how much more will your Father who is in heaven, give good things to them that ask him?[70]

Now, having observed the rampant disobedience to the teachings and doctrines of the Church, via the open disobedience to the instructions of the Holy See—both among the laity and the priesthood—a glaring question should raise itself to the forefront of Catholic conscience. How could this have happened? Are not the Holy See and the Church led by the Holy Spirit to fulfill the will of God? The answer to that question is yes, but with the understanding that God will allow His Church to fall into error if His representatives (clergy) willfully separate themselves from Him through deliberate disobedience. For every action and request on God's part, the Church must reciprocate with humility and obedience to retain God's favor and graces. As long as the Holy See follows the commands of God and remains obedient to His will He will maintain, sustain, and lead it. If the Holy See refuses the dictates of Heaven—as was made evident in a most miraculous fashion at Fátima[71]—in preference, and deference, to the dictates and wills of men, He will allow it to go its own way headlong into disaster; separating itself and its children from Him.

Unfortunately for the Church and all the Catholic faithful—not to mention the greater world at large—the Holy See has willfully departed from the will of God for almost one hundred years, and we are witnessing today the manifestation of the punishment for this open disobedience to God's will. It is only to be expected that Christ would allow the prelates and

---

[69] John 14:26.

[70] Matthew 7:7-11.

[71] The consecration of Russia to Our Mother's Immaculate Heart.

laity within His Church to go astray in disobedience, as a form of divine punishment, after His Church had made a willful choice to disobediently depart from His will. Leadership comes from the top down. If the Holy See continues to be disobedient to God's will and His commands—choosing to go their own way, rather than God's way—the Holy Spirit will allow many within the Church to likewise go their own way; further separating themselves from the Church and (by proxy) Jesus.

Moreover, this scenario of divine request, and subsequent punishment for disobedience, has played itself out numerous times in the history of mankind; both in the times of the ancient Israelites and in more recent times. The latest example of divine disobedience and subsequent punishment is the seminal event in the modern history of the human race that brought us the godless, humanistic interpretation of "liberty" we are currently suffered to endure: the French Revolution. In 1689, St. Margaret Mary Alocoque—the saint to whom the devotion of the Sacred Heart of Jesus was revealed—sent a letter to the King of France, Louis XIV, requesting the following: "The Lord wished that Louis XIV should consecrate France to the Sacred Heart of Jesus, erect a national monument to His Sacred Heart and place an inscription to His Heart on the national standard. In return He would protect France from her enemies and give her a lasting reign of glory."[72]

Jesus' requests, as relayed through St. Margaret Mary Alocoque, were not acted on, and as a consequence Jesus abandoned France; which ultimately led to the French Revolution, the end of monarchical rule in France, and the execution of Louis XIV's grandson, Louis XVI; once again demonstrating that in this world the ones to receive divine punishment are the descendants of the defiant rather than the original malefactors. Why is this practically always the case? In His justice he allows the disobedient time to reconsider the obstinate refusal of His requests and amend their errors. In the case of the French Revolution, a century[73] had elapsed between the time of His request and the subsequent punishment that followed. As priests, this layman humbly proposes the question to you, "Will you submit to the divine request to consecrate Russia to Our Mother's Immaculate Heart, or will you continue in disobedience to an ultimate, divine punishment in this age"? He may, *or may not*, allow a full century to transpire before delivering the punishing blow.

---

[72] http://www.ourladyofamerica.com/whatsnew/SaintMargaretMaryAlacoque. pdf, accessed June 12, 2010.

[73] The French Revolution began in 1789 with the storming of the Bastille (14 July 1789) and the *Declaration of the Rights of Man and of the Citizen* (August 26/27, 1789).

For Laypeople:

Among the laity, the most important thing we can do to call God's favor to us in this quickly degenerating world is to exercise the requisite self-discipline that is needed to follow Holy Obedience to the doctrines and dogma of the Faith. Obedience is the cohesive mortar of the Catholic Faith, but ***UNDISCIPLINED PEOPLE WILL NOT BE OBEDIENT!*** How the laity can observe obedience is to follow the teachings of the Church rather than trying to "reform" it to ape the innately depraved inclinations of mankind: acceptance of birth control, toleration of homosexuality, muted opposition or toleration of abortion, the call for admission of women to the priesthood; and all other articles of Church dogma that run counter to modern "wisdom":

And wisdom is justified by her children.[74]

There are *extremely* good reasons for all of the Church's moral positions, rules, and teachings. By starting with some of the suggested theological reading material (Appendix B), and spending a considerable amount of time in contemplation—making a logical extension of the consequences of a world with and without these prohibitions to the utmost of their extremes—the mind can grasp the good reasons for these (and other) Church teachings and positions; even when they so strongly oppose our inherent inclinations and desires. If you, the reader, are not a contemplative or philosophical soul that has the inclination to investigate and understand the deeper reasons for Church teachings and positions, then you should simply resign yourself to following the rules. By openly voicing opposition to Church teaching(s), or even holding them in contempt within the privacy of one's own heart, a person only makes themselves a heretic and are possibly setting themselves up for a harsh judgment by manifesting their opposition to the will of God; as taught to them through the tradition(s) and teaching(s) of the Church; the same Church established by Christ and that they claim to identify themselves with.

When someone openly opposes Church teachings they only make their ultimate damnation (excepting a sincere repentance) a practical certainty, because by openly attacking the Church—which is, by extension, Christ's

---

[74] From Mathew 11:19.

representative body and voice on Earth—they are openly directing an attack at Christ Himself; the same Christ they claim to be loyal to. Can people not see the horrible dangers and hypocrisy of those who claim to be "loyal" Catholics while openly opposing Church teachings and doctrines? Those who do this are only aping the same sin that brought Adam and Eve their original condemnation: they opposed God, and abandoned their obligation to Holy Obedience, in deference to their own desires. To say that this can't lead to anything good is an understatement.

If some "Catholics" can't bring themselves to adhere to the Church's teachings and discipline, then they should simply keep their mouths shut. Don't help undermine the Church due to a rebellious spirit, which will only bring a person greater condemnation at their end. For the sake of one's own soul, think deeply and seriously about the damage being done to the souls of the rebellious, and the other souls whom they are misleading. Many of those who are leading the attacks on Church teachings and doctrines are purposefully subversive, know what they are doing, and are actively seeking the destruction of the Church. By falling in with them, due to ignorance or a rebellious spirit, it only encourages disunity within the Church; leading to the only possible, ultimate conclusion: schism, discord, and apostasy. What good can come of it; either to the rebellious, or to the other faithful? By opposing the Church's teachings and doctrines one makes manifest, for all to see, an attitude of superiority to God: making themselves like a god unto themselves by telling God that they know better than He how we should worship Him. I sincerely pray that those "Catholics" who oppose the Church on teachings and doctrine will quickly recognize their grave and dangerous errors and awaken from the delusion that has overtaken them. Return to Holy Obedience to Church dogma and rectify the damage you have done to yourselves and others.

What can faithful Catholics do to aid in the restoration of the Church from its sad, corrupted state of near-derailment and put it back on the right track? There are several things that must be done if the errors and corruption within the body of the Church are to be corrected. What is required to effect a positive change within the Church is proactive action on the part of the faithful laity in the form of pressure. Previously, we discussed how social pressure is used from both below (slaves) and above (masters) to psychologically "compress" the rest of society into capitulating in the struggle for self-determination. The same tactics must be reversed and employed against the corrupted, heretical prelates (modernists and their "fellow travelers") within the Church. The Pope can apply the pressure from above, but the faithful must apply mass pressure from below to either correct the corrupt, deceived, or faithless into amending their errors or to drive them out of the Church; so as to put an end to the corruption they propagate.

Of course, the Pope is fully aware of true doctrine, but he is effectively a prisoner in his own house due to the level of corruption that has already taken hold within the body of the Church. If he attempts to unilaterally apply a heavy amount of pressure from above on the faithless and erroneous in order to try and force a correction of the many errors existent within the minds of the hierarchy and the laity, he will be faced with a revolt from within the Church, led by the faithless and treacherous cardinals and bishops who desire to destroy it from within; who will then enlist the ignorantly deceived, "liberal" factions of the laity in their revolt. Without a strong counter-pressure from below, by the laity, to squeeze the schismatics and heretics out; pressure from the top would only drive the Church into the ground; effectively giving the faithless infiltrators the result they have been seeking for the past several generations. This has been the case within the Church since at least the time of Pope Paul VI and the Second Vatican Council. Pope Paul VI made a subtle plea for help in the early 1970's, but apparently it was too subtle for the masses, and his plea for help went largely unnoticed:

> From some crevice, the smoke of Satan has entered into the temple of God. . . . This condition of uncertainty reigns within the Church as well. After the Second Vatican Council, we believed that the history of the Church would enjoy a period of sunshine. Instead, the day became ugly, dark, cloudy, and stormy.[75]

In response to the corruption that has spread throughout the body of the Church, the past several Popes have been forced to try and outmaneuver the faithless and treacherous prelates; who are truly treasonous politicians and saboteurs disguising themselves as clergymen.

> A nation can survive its fools and even the ambitious. But it cannot survive treason from within. An enemy at the gates is less formidable, for he is known and he carries his banners openly against the city. But the traitor moves among those within the gates freely, his sly whispers rustling through all

---

[75] Amorth, *An Exorcist: More Stories*, 57-58.

alleys, heard in the very halls of government itself. For the traitor appears no traitor; he speaks in the accents familiar to his victim, and he wears their face and their garments and *he appeals to the baseness that lies deep in the hearts of all men*. He rots the soul of a nation; he works secretly and unknown in the night to undermine the pillars of a city; he infects the body politic so that it can no longer resist. A murderer is less to be feared. The traitor is the plague.[76]

— Marcus Tullius Cicero, Roman politician, lawyer, and orator

However, before the laity can engage the corrupt element(s) within the Church they must first be able to discern true doctrine from false, and understand the basis for true doctrine; which can only be accomplished through sincere study, prayer, and the assistance of the Holy Spirit. Begin by learning the *true* doctrine and catechism of your Faith, so that it will be much harder for the faithless to deceive you. It is a certainty that some of the catechetical information the faithful are getting today is corrupted. To correct this problem, the best place to start is the Bible. Sadly, very few Catholics read a Bible any longer; in English, the Douay-Rheims version being the most reliable in light of its undisputed longevity. As a complement to the Bible, there are the writings of the Doctors of the Church; especially those of St. Thomas Aquinas (*Summa Theologica* and *Summa Contra Gentiles*). In concert with the authority of the Bible and the Doctors of the Church, there are Papal Encyclicals and Syllabuses that explain Catholic doctrine; especially those written to expressly combat modern errors within the Church.[77]

The corruption of the Church and distortion of true doctrine within the minds of the faithful has been an ongoing process for many decades. Some seminaries have been caught up in these errors and are teaching erroneous, modernist pseudo-theology that is actually a cleverly-veiled, esoteric program of conversion to humanism; so that the Biblical admonition is showing the devastating realities of the penalties of ignorance and pride: "Let them alone: they are blind, and leaders of the blind. And if the blind lead the blind, both fall into the pit."[78] Moreover, the faithful have been

---

[76] http://waysandmeans.house.gov/hearings.asp?formmode=view&id=954, accessed March 20, 2008.

[77] *The Popes Against Modern Errors* serves as an invaluable starting point.

[78] Matthew 15:14.

warned from the beginning regarding corruption from within the Church: "But though we, or an angel from heaven, preach a gospel to you besides that which we have preached to you, let him be anathema" (Galatians 1:8), and "Having an appearance indeed of godliness but denying the power thereof" (2 Timothy 3:5).

Only a firm foundation in the knowledge of true Catholic dogma among the laity will be able to dispel ignorance and provide a firm foundation from which the faithful can then apply their necessary counter-pressure. The theological material suggested in Appendix B is very beneficial, but it is also necessary to be aware of the scope and nature of the modernist errors that have been introduced into the Church. *Lamentabili Sane, Pascendi Dominici Gregis, The Syllabus of Errors*, and others[79] are important documents that go a long way to explaining the errors that modernist priests and theologians have introduced into the Church. These documents should be read by every Catholic, and then acted on. They describe the prohibitions against the theological errors inherent in modernism and explain the nature of their primary errors and contradictions of the Faith. These documents, although they are over one hundred years old, read like documents that could have been issued within the past few years; for their applicability to modern theological errors and apostasy within the Church are even more prescient today than they were when they were originally written.

Once armed more adequately with true Catholic doctrine, there are two courses of action that need to be simultaneously pursued: (1) demand that the Church demonstrate Holy Obedience to the will of God by fulfilling Heaven's request to consecrate Russia to the Blessed Virgin Mary's Immaculate Heart, in union with all the Bishops of the world, and for the explicitly stated intent of making reparation to Our Mother's Immaculate Heart, and (2) rejecting and opposing modernist "theology" wherever it is taught or expounded. Any Catholic who denies or marginalizes the absolute necessity of consecrating Russia to the Blessed Virgin Mary suffers from a common, monumental, modernist delusion that has corrupted the understanding of the faithful via a combination of several corrosive factors: (1) inadequate or erroneous faith formation via an ignorance of true theological and catechetical doctrine, (2) worldly apathy, and (3) a constant stream of propaganda for practically all our lives that has been designed to accelerate and exacerbate the problems of factors (1) and (2). Again, the faithful have been warned about this from the beginning:

---

[79] See *The Popes Against Modern Errors*.

> [2] Preach the word: be instant in season, out of season: reprove, entreat, rebuke in all patience and doctrine. [3] **For there shall be a time, when they will not endure sound doctrine;** but, according to their own desires, they will heap to themselves teachers,[80] having itching ears: [4] And will indeed turn away their hearing from the truth, but will be turned unto fables.[81]

Before her death Sister Lucy (the last remaining seer of Fátima) counseled the faithful to maintain their allegiance to the Pope. Many Catholics may not be aware of this, and others who are may wonder why she would make such a statement; thinking that it is an unnecessary repetition of an obvious principle. However, she was well aware of the machinations underway within the Church to undermine the Faith from within, as many within the Church today are doing; laity and clergy alike. Being aware of the troubles besetting the Church, she offered up a warning to all for a time in the future when the papal office would be called into question, denigrated, and subverted from within.

This address to the faithful Catholic has been assembled to explain how and why the Church has been corrupted from within; the complicity (due to disobedience) of the Church in its own undoing; the inerrant fulfillment of prophecy to date and what awaits humanity if the Church refuses obedience to Heaven's directives; the action(s) required from the faithful to rescue it from faithless infiltrators or deluded prelates within its hierarchy; the most common arguments used to frustrate the will of God and the erroneous, false, and dishonest basis of these arguments; the theological errors and dangers inherent in liberalism and the "religious liberty" (heresy by a more attractive name) perspective of the "Cafeteria Catholic"; the proper organization and function of the Church, to include the reasons for the necessity of maintaining doctrinal allegiance to the Pope and the Magisterium; how the corruption in the Church manifests itself in the public eye; the tactics used by the faithless within the Church to undermine the institution; and the exact

---

[80] The modernist clergymen and "theologians" who constantly contradict traditional Church doctrine that has existed for thousands of years; themselves introducing, "according to their own desires," a more "liberal" interpretation and view of Catholic doctrine; so as to find approval in the eyes of those with little or no faith, a corrupted catechism, or both: desiring the approval of men rather than of God.

[81] 2 Timothy 4:2-4.

parallels between the current revolution within the Church and the original rebellion of the Devil against God in Heaven (the refusal to obey and serve).

In consideration of all this material, hopefully assembled in a coherent and compelling manner, regardless of its unpleasantness; two considerations remain: one for me, and one for the reader. On my part, I freely admit that I am just as imperfect as other men. If any of the material in this section is doctrinally incorrect, I would certainly like to be made aware of it; so that I could amend any erroneous views and abstain from propagating error: "If I have spoken evil, give testimony of the evil . . ."[82] However, the consideration on the part of the Catholic reader is . . . "What are you going to do"!? In very many ways it all seems to be too much—too surreal to be true—because when the reader strips off any "varnish" from this message, what is basically being said is that the modern body of the Church is responsible for the descent of the human race into the state of narcissistic anarchy that is rampaging throughout the world.

Since the Fátima apparitions to three, small, peasant children, socialism and communism have left anywhere from 100 million to 300 million murdered souls in its wake. Through the intercession of the Blessed Virgin Mary, the hierarchy of the Catholic Church was told how to defeat communism and was commanded to do it, but instead has simply refused to obey God. Communism has brought the world nearly one hundred years of wars and all manner of social turbulence. This force of materialistic atheism has settled over the planet like a thick cloud of dark and grimy smoke; advancing a veil of despair in the minds of a great many people. All the destruction of communism—the millions of dead bodies and the constant threat of wars all over the globe—could have been averted if the Holy See would have simply submitted to Holy Obedience and had performed the consecration.

It boggles the mind to consider that in *less than a few hours* of solemn prayer, a century of indescribable suffering and pain in the lives of so many could have been averted! But let not the reader get the impression that the Holy See is the only culpable party in this scenario, because the community of faithful (roughly one *billion* Catholics) has mostly ignored Our Mother's requests as well. Since the revelations at Fátima, there has been no large outcry from the community of the faithful for the Holy See to consecrate Russia; in their silence giving the Holy See tacit approval of its disobedient behavior. Moreover, very few of the faithful have submitted to the particular

---

[82] From John 18:23.

requests of Our Mother: to say a daily Rosary, and to complete the devotion of the Five First Saturdays. There are a great many Catholics who are not even aware of these requests!

There have always been antagonistic entities attempting to corrupt the Faith from within since the beginning of the Church; the Arian heresy being one of the greatest examples. That is the source of history's schisms and heresies. However, in the past the faithful remained faithful and held their allegiance, at least doctrinally, to the Pope; which ultimately brought the Church through its trials. This is no longer true in many respects. Most of the "faithful" have become excessively worldly, no longer scrutinizing the corrupting errors and changes that are being insinuated into the Church. As a result, all hell is breaking loose (literally) within the Church, which is what is making the accomplishment of the consecration more difficult with each passing year.

Let not the reader take away the impression that I possess any sentiments of self-righteousness; because for most of my life I was just as guilty as the rest of the laity. But enough is too much, already! The insanity of the world has become simply too overwhelming to fully comprehend. Iran is pursuing an Islamic nuclear weapon—aided and abetted by the material support and expertise of Russia—that it would use to destroy Israel and spread global jihad. That has been their stated position, and nobody seems willing to take serious measures to stop them, or the rest of the body of Islamic terrorists for that matter. In a visitation to Sister Lucy, Jesus said, "They did not wish to heed My request! . . . Like the King of France, they will repent and do it, but it will be late. Russia will have already spread her errors throughout the world, provoking wars, and persecutions of the Church: the Holy Father will have much to suffer."[83]

Can anybody not see that the hour is late, indeed!? Ask yourself, "Is it really that hard to say a daily Rosary, or to make a monthly Confession for less than half a year"? Will the faithful Catholic now take the revelations and warnings relayed at Fátima more seriously? Will you forcefully petition your bishops and cardinals to perform the Consecration? Will you begin to say the daily Rosary and attend to the First Five Saturdays devotion? And if those who call themselves faithful refuse to obey, just as the Holy See has done, how can any of us grumble against God when He carries out the threat of the "annihilation of nations"; for are we not all culpable in light of our obstinate disobedience? Moreover, He has given us nearly one hundred

---

[83] Lucia, *Fátima in Lucia's Own Words*, 202.

years to submit to His requests, and we are still looking for any excuse not to obey. Will we not deserve everything that we get if we haven't the courage or sense to obey, and instead choose to continue opposing Him in our prideful, obstinate defiance?

At this juncture in time, the great question to be answered by the faithful is, "How can the faithful rectify the situation and bring peace to the world"? This question is easily answered by modeling the debate after the Old Testament rivalry of Elias and God vs. Achab, Jezebel and Baal (3 Kings 18). On the one hand there are the modern-day worshippers of false gods (Karl Marx, the state, freemasonry, and faithless man (humanism)). They are absolutely sure and positively certain that there is no God; because the concept of, and belief in, God runs contrary to everything they have ever known and been taught. And since these creatures consider themselves to be so far and exceedingly superior to all other men in terms of intellect and personal ability, all that is needed to destroy God in this world is their affirmation that He does not exist (positive atheism). Communists, Marxists, Freemasons, humanists, and their "fellow travelers" consider themselves to be *the* superior form and essence of man and the greatness of humanity: gods unto themselves, if you will. To the faithless, God is a myth only believed in by grossly inferior, unscientific minds; steeped in infantile superstition and too cowardly to explore the greatness and power of humanity when unleashed to discover its self-deified greatness.

For those within the Church who are willfully perfidious—being faithless and unbelieving in God—there is nothing to fear by consecrating Russia to Our Mother's Immaculate Heart. To an atheist of "reason," this consecration would mean nothing to them. In their eyes, a few thousand men would be called together for a few hours to blow hot air and beseech their fictitious God; who lives only in their childish and intellectually inferior fantasies. Since—in their true hearts—they are sure that there is both no God and that the faithful are insipidly childish and intellectually inferior (the Untermensch of the world) when compared to themselves and their mighty intellects (the self-perceived Übermensch and rightful masters of humanity), there would be no harm done in the exercise; as in their eyes Catholics would simply be spraying empty words to the wind and embarrassing themselves with such a display of anti-intellectual, unscientific, and infantile stupidity. As a result, the heretics within the Church would suffer no harm to their plans by "playing along" with the consecration. To the faithless, this would be a "win-win" situation in which the Church would be seen to be willingly walking into their trap and handing them the ammunition they desire to destroy the Faith. The faithful could be held up for further ridicule and dissolution of faith, while the efforts of the faithful will, within the faithless' belief system, be fruitless because they are self-convinced that there is no God.

On the other hand you have the modern day worshippers of the one, true, and triune God. As an article of Faith, we faithful should offer this occasion as an opportunity for the heretics to accelerate the demise of the Church; as Elias mocked and incited the worshippers of Baal to cry louder and with more fervency because their god might be otherwise occupied or sleeping (3 Kings 18:27-29). Let the faithless propagate to their "fellow travelers" within the mass media outlets, labor unions, Masonic lodges, and other cults of the world a call to ridicule the effort and both restate and intensify their claims that a "United Worker's Party," or "Brotherhood of Man" is the only solution to the world's problems. As they have been doing for decades, let them cry out to their gods of Marxism, Freemasonry, and humanism. But on the part of the faithful and the Holy See, let us at least play our analogous role in the contest by beseeching God's intercession through the consecration of Russia to Our Mother's Immaculate Heart. For the past one hundred years (or more) the priests of Marxism, Freemasonry, and humanism have been calling to their god(s) for peace and love among humanity; and just look at the "Hell on Earth" these pitiful souls have created.

Let the Holy See now do its part by making its cry to God to show the whole world who is the true God: humanity (Baal, Allah, humanism, etc.) or God. By failing on its part to cry out to God to "shew this day that thou art the God of Israel, and I thy servant, and that according to thy commandment I have done all these things,"[84] the Holy See fails in its primary duty to God, and secondarily to mankind. The analogy today is to show that there is a God (of all creation, and not just Israel), that the Holy See is His servant, and that according to His commandment to consecrate Russia to Our Mother's Immaculate Heart—delivered to humanity and the Church at Fátima, via the vehicle of Our Mother, the Blessed Virgin Mary—they will undertake the effort to conform to His will and actually perform the consecration. If the Holy See fails—by exercising its own free will to disobey God—to even make the attempt to save the Church and mankind from the folly of proud, arrogant, and foolish men; and by the silence of the Holy See allow the modern-day worshipers of false gods to win the contest by its faithless silence and inaction; what other impression can the past three or four increasingly apostatizing generations come to believe, except that the atheists are right

---

[84] 3 Kings 18:36, in part.

and that there is no God!? Moreover, a singularly important consideration is ever-present in this layman's mind: Who will be called to account and held most responsible for this willful disobedience at the time of Judgment? Those who are faithless in their ignorance, or we who knew what had to be done, but simply refused to obey?

This is the point at which the prospect becomes frightening from the perspective of human wisdom. What is being proposed is directly analogous to ridiculing the followers of false gods, as Elias did in his contest. What is needed is *bold* action from the laity that is completely reliant on the power of Christ, and His Mother, to succeed. Let the Church go on the offensive to draw the enemy into our field of battle—the supernatural—rather than trying to continue an assault on theirs: the natural, worldly wisdom of men. Throw down a challenge to the faithless to show them the foolishness of their reliance on men and the wisdom of relying on the faithfulness of God.

> [8]It is good to confide in the Lord, rather than to have confidence in man. [9]It is good to trust in the Lord, rather than to trust in princes.[85]

For those Catholics who are faint of heart regarding confronting the faithless within the hierarchy of the Holy See, please consider the following two warnings to the faithful. The first was penned by a faithful priest of a few decades ago, Fr. Herman Bernard Kramer, in his work *The Book of Destiny*; and the second by the seer of Fátima herself: Sister Lucy. Fr. Kramer's work is an exposition on the many hidden things within the Book of Revelation, and it provides great insight into the workings within the Church hierarchy in our day.

> The tail of the dragon draws in its coils one third of the stars of Heaven and casts them to the earth. This is one third of the clergy . . . The tail is a symbol of lying and hypocrisy. Through false doctrines and principles, Satan will mislead the clergy, who will have become worldly-minded, haughty, hypocritical, obsequient avaricious sycophants . . . By their lax principles

---

[85] Psalms 117:8-9. The term "princes" refers to the leaders of nations. Moreover, it includes the faithless prelates within the Holy See who work to discourage the consecration of Russia to Our Mother's Immaculate Heart; as the Vatican is its own wholly constituted country.

they will infect the laity. They will easily welcome a mitigation or change of doctrine to sanction the lukewarm lives they want to lead.[86] Then will Satan see a rich harvest ripening for himself. The symbolic meaning of the dragon's tail may reveal that the clergy who are ripe for apostasy will hold the influential positions in the Church having won preferment by hypocrisy, deceit and flattery . . . The great apostasy will then most likely include the laity as well as the clergy . . . The voluptuous, the drunkards, the impure who commit crimes and abuses against marriage, the fornicators, the proud and avaricious, the lukewarm and indifferent and all who are not ready to suffer everything the world can inflict on them will certainly be drawn into apostasy by the dragon's power . . . If bishops weakly give sanction to false principles, and priests praise them to be in their good graces, and the people love laxity, they will all apostasize . . . Nothing can demoralize the Church so fast and so far as the knowledge that faithful work and strict attendance to duty count for little and that studied diplomacy in playing up to the members of the episcopacy gains everything . . . The influence of the dragon will everywhere aim to subject the Church to the state. This persecution is thus a political subjugation, and one third of the bishops and priests will be ripe for apostasy.[87]

— Fr. Herman Bernard Kramer, author of *The Book of Destiny*

The Blessed Virgin Mary told me that the devil is in the mood for engaging in a decisive battle against the Virgin. From now on we must choose sides. Either we are for God or we are for the devil. There is no other possibility.[88]

— Sister Lucy, seer of Fátima

How do we frame the challenge and draw the enemy into an ambush of their false gods of Marxist Communism and humanism? Very easily! As Elias

---

[86] The Second Vatican Council.

[87] Fr. Herman Bernard Kramer, *The Book of Destiny*, (Rockford, IL: TAN Books and Publishers, Inc., 1975), 280–285.

[88] In an interview with Fr. Agustín Fuentes on December 26, 1957.

put all faith in God to show his adversaries that his God was the one, true God; let the Holy Catholic Church put all faith in the promises of Heaven, as proclaimed by the Church via its recognition of the genuine nature of the Fátima apparitions, by consecrating Russia to Our Mother's Immaculate Heart! Boldly proclaim—without apology, reticence, or appearances of doubt—that the Holy Catholic Church believes in the promises of Heaven and Our Mother and that the time has been long overdue for the Church to fulfill its obligations to Heaven in Holy Obedience! Naturally, as a result of the reliance on worldly wisdom that is so prevalent in our day, there will undoubtedly be an uproar of dissent from every corner of the world; including the faithless infiltrators within the Church. Contrarily, I submit that it is irrelevant what the faithless desire or believe; even those within the College of Cardinals and among the bishops. After making oneself knowledgeable regarding *true* Catholic dogma, as taught by God (via the Bible), the Doctors of the Church, and the Magisterium; simply make a choice, "Will I choose God, or will I choose faithless men"? Moreover, be willing to live or die by this choice. As hard as it may be to take, this is the choice Christ calls the faithful to make.

A Call to Return to the Faith and a Correction of Common Protestant Errors and Misunderstandings

This section is addressed to the many Protestant brothers and sisters who have become estranged from the Church; beginning many centuries ago during the Reformation initiated by Martin Luther. With Protestantism being an established movement for several hundreds of years, it is completely understandable that you would continue in that tradition; as it is what was taught and passed down to you by your ancestors. You have been immersed in the tradition of Protestantism since your birth. However, please recall that St. Paul explicitly warned the faithful, *"For there shall be a time, when they will not endure sound doctrine; . . ."*[1]

As the effort is undertaken to explain the errors of the most common justifications offered by Protestant denominations for the refusal of Catholicism, I desire to be clear regarding my intentions. Most importantly, I desire not to arouse enmity between myself and any Protestants regarding what follows. Everything explained here is offered up in the spirit of charity to my Protestant neighbors. St. Paul explained it best in 1 Corinthians 13, and I desire to follow in his spirit. Moreover, it is understood that there will be some who are so invested in their current belief system that they will not tolerate the clarification(s) offered here. For just such people, let us simply recognize that we will not be reconciled on these points and let us depart from the following discussion amicably; without any feelings of ill will. For those who may be open to the explanations offered here, I would humbly request that you say the following prayer, in all sincerity of heart, before proceeding:

> Come, Holy Spirit, fill the hearts of Thy faithful and enkindle in them the fire of Thy love. Send forth Thy Spirit and they shall be created. And Thou shalt renew the face of the earth. Let us pray. O God, Who didst instruct the hearts of the faithful by the light of the Holy Spirit, **grant us by the same Spirit to have a right judgment in all things,**

---

[1] From 2 Timothy 4:3.

and ever to rejoice in His consolation. Through Christ our
Lord. Amen.

The purpose of this prayer is to request divine enlightenment, so that the
reader may discern, in truth, what is explained here. With that said, let us begin.
At the most fundamental level, the most common errors regarding Protestant
objections against Catholicism seem to revolve around the blessedness and
exalted nature of the Virgin Mary within the Catholic Church and the use
of statues, relics, and other material items that are identified with the Saints.
These misunderstandings directly relate to two misunderstood principles: (1)
worship vs. veneration, and (2) idolatry: principles that are prudently taken
very seriously by all faithful, but also easily confounded if not accurately
understood in the proper way.

The first item that must be clarified is the importance and sanctity of the
Blessed Virgin Mary. The objection to Mary's *veneration* within the Church
seems to be founded on the false belief among Protestants that Catholics
worship Mary on a level equivalent to that of God. This is false, but many
people fall into this error because they do not understand her great power and
position within the divine order. Instead, the Blessed Virgin Mary is *venerated*
above all other humans who ever walked the earth due to her sanctity,
her sinless life, and her preordained position within the divine order. This
unique and special position of Mary within the divine order was related by
the Blessed Virgin herself to a Spanish nun, Mary of Jesus of Agreda, in the
17th Century; who related what she was taught in a work entitled *Mystical
City of God*. Of course, everyone knows that anyone can claim anything,
but the reader is encouraged to believe in what was revealed to Mary of
Agreda due to both the approval of this work by multiple Popes in the years
following its publication, as well as the mystical, supernatural favors granted
to this nun (If you don't believe her, believe the works that God did through
her). During her life she was reputed to have been granted the mystical gift
of bilocation—being present in two places at the same time—to convert
the Native Americans in what is today's Southwest United States (Arizona
and New Mexico), and in her death she has been favored with the gift of
incorruptibility.[2] Sister Agreda relates the following:

> The angels were informed that God was to create a human
> nature and reasoning creatures lower than themselves, in

---

[2] Her deceased body has not decomposed.

order that they too should love, fear and reverence God, as their Author and eternal Good. They were informed that these were to stand in high favor, and that the second Person of the blessed Trinity was to become incarnate and assume their nature, raising it to the hypostatic union and to divine Personality; that therefore they were to acknowledge Him as their Head, not only as God, but as God and man, adoring Him and reverencing Him as God-man. Moreover, these same angels were to be his inferiors in dignity and grace and were to be his servants. God gave them an intelligence of the propriety and equity, of the justice and reasonableness of such a position. For the acceptation of the merits foreseen of this Mangod was exhibited to them as the source of the grace which they now possessed and of the glory which they were to obtain. They understood also that they themselves had been, and all the rest of the creatures should be created for his glory, and that He was to be their Head. All those that were capable of knowing and enjoying God, were to be the people of the Son of God, to know and reverence Him as their Chief. These commands were at once given to the angels. . .

When it was revealed to the angels that they would have to obey the incarnate Word, another, a third precept was given them, namely, that they were to admit as a superior conjointly with Him, a Woman, in whose womb the Onlybegotten of the Father was to assume flesh and that this Woman was to be the Queen and Mistress of all the creatures.[3]

This revelation dealt with the fact that God conceived of the plan for both the angelic and temporal creations, but that for His own reasons He created the angelic dimension first and then instructed the angels regarding His plans for the creation of humans; commanding that Christ and His mother, the Blessed Virgin Mary, were to be honored as superior to all created creatures; both angelic and human. For this reason Mary is venerated within

---

[3] Mary of Jesus of Agreda [Spain], *The Mystical City of God: The Divine History and Life of the Virgin Mother of God. Volume 1: The Conception*, trans. Fiscar Marison (Rockford, IL: TAN Books and Publishers, Inc., 2006), 89 – 91.

the Catholic Church: due to her superior position within the divine order, which was preordained before the creation of both angels and men. What is the proper perspective to understand Mary's relationship to the Godhead? Because of her exalted position within the divine order, and through the decree of God, she is known as the Mediatrix of all graces conferred upon humanity; meaning that she is the primary agent of graces.

What does it mean to be the Mediatrix of all graces? Let me explain this concept through recourse to a business analogy. Although the analogy is simplistic, so as to be more easily understood, it is not meant to be taken as a jest. Consider God as the manufacturer of all graces. Mary, as Mediatrix, would then be considered as the "retailer" of graces. God creates the graces, and then the Virgin Mary distributes them to humanity at large through her "store" of grace. This is not to say that God is unable to provide grace directly to humanity. He simply chooses to use Mary as the mediator through which they are distributed. By making Mary the Mediatrix of grace He is purposefully directing mankind to her solicitude in order to promote her veneration as the Queen of Heaven; especially in this age of almost universal corruption.

Why would God do such a thing? To make manifest to the human race her exalted position in the divine order. The Blessed Virgin Mary once related to St. Dominic, "One day through the Rosary and Scapular, I will save the world." The modern world—as utterly faithless, corrupt, and degenerate as it has become—*is* that day. Why should modern humanity believe such a thing? Because during the last several centuries the primary messenger of the divine will has been the Blessed Virgin Mary. At La Salette (France), Lourdes (France), Fatima (Portugal), Akita (Japan), and others more obscure, she has been the intercessor who brought news of the divine will to humanity. Why should humanity run to Our Mother as their primary refuge and intercessor with God? The *Memorare* explains why.

> Remember, O most gracious Virgin Mary, that never was it known that anyone who fled to your protection, implored your help, or sought your intercession, was left unaided. Inspired with this confidence, I fly unto you, O Virgin of virgins, my Mother; to you I come, before you I stand, sinful and sorrowful; O Mother of the Word Incarnate, despise not my petitions, but in your mercy hear and answer me. Amen.

Let us consider why she would be the perfect intercessor with God for our intentions. As humans are sinful creatures, by their very nature, who else should we run to when we've done something bad: to wit, when we have sinned? Relate this to your own family life. Let's say that we have broken a window playing baseball or stolen something that didn't belong to us. Feeling sorry for what we've done, and knowing that our misdeeds will be discovered by our father, we run to our earthly mother and admit our guilt and ask her to intercede for us with our earthly father so that the punishment for our guilt will be somewhat ameliorated. After all, it's mom who will try and "smooth things over" with dad—if, and only if, we can convince her of our true penitence—when he gets home and discovers the bad thing(s) we've done.

The same principle applies in the divine order. Our spiritual mother, the Blessed Virgin Mary, will attempt to intercede with our spiritual Father if we are truly sorry for our transgressions. Why would any sensible creature do anything else than try to mitigate the punishment for their faults by appealing to their mother to temper the anger of their father? Because Our Mother was wholly human, and not a full participant in the Godhead, she is not worshipped, but rather venerated by the faithful; meaning that her influence with God is recognized as being of a superior nature.

This understanding of the veneration, as opposed to the worship of the Blessed Virgin Mary, helps to directly address the misunderstanding of the issue of idolatry and veneration of the saints. The common objection among Protestants regarding statues and relics of the saints seems to revolve around the issue of idolatry. Veneration of the relics of saints and material representations (statues) of them is due to the spirit in which prayers are offered. Properly understood, prayer that is offered before a statue or in the presence of a relic of a saint is *not* idolatry. It must be freely admitted that many faithful, Catholics included, err in this regard. The purpose of statues and relics of the saints is meant to serve as a material representation of the saint; something that humans can identify with; as if the saint was actually present and listening to their petitions.

When a Catholic prays before a statue of St. Michael or the Blessed Virgin Mary they are not praying to the piece of wood or stone that represents their likeness. Such a thing would be true idolatry; similar to the Israelites who worshipped the golden calf; as if the material item was in fact divine. Instead, they are appealing to the intercession of the personage represented by that piece of wood or stone. Because the particular saint is not physically available to discourse with in a directly material fashion, the Catholic merely offers up prayers to the reasonable facsimile of the saint; as if their spirit was conjoined to their image and they were directly addressing the saint.

With all this understood, the reasonable question remains, "Why should we pray to the saints as intercessors in our behalf? After all, in their own way they were all sinners just like us." The answer to this question is in their proximity to God's ear. Saints are saints because of their sanctity. They lived lives that were superior in their allegiance to the will of God than the rest of us. Yes, they were sinners in the strictest sense of understanding, but they tended to sin much less than the rest of us and their heart was more aligned to accomplishing God's will than ours is. For that reason, their influence is greater with the divine mind. Recall the example of running to mother when we've done something wrong in order to mitigate our punishment for our wrongdoing. In the case of the saints, the same principle applies, but in a lesser degree. The saints are able to "bend the ear" of God according to the sanctity of the life they led on Earth. The more faithful they were to the will of God during their earthly life, the more influential they will be with God in the intercession of our petitions. Consider this in the same light as Our Mother's intercession, but instead view the saints as our big brothers and sisters.

Why do Our Mother and the saints listen to our petitions? Because as our spirits leave this world and depart for the eternal they are incorporated into the perfection of the divine nature (if they are not damned). They must be perfectly aligned with the divine will in order to participate in the blessedness of eternity. As a result of Our Mother and the saints being perfectly united to the divine will they likewise participate in *perfect* empathy for those of us wallowing in the darkness of this world. Just as God desires our sincere repentance and "return to the fold," Our Mother and the saints desire just the same thing and they will do whatever they can to effect forgiveness for us if we are truly sorry for our sins.

The key thing to understand is that our faith in their intercession is the determinate factor in the efficacy of their intercession. Why is faith the determining factor? Again, relate this scenario to what you face in your earthly life. If, after misbehaving, you went to your mother and big brothers or sisters, admitted your guilt, asked for their intercession, and then concluded your intercessory pleadings (via your faith in their intercession) with, "I really want you to help me, but I don't believe that it will do any good," what do you think your lack of confidence in your mother or big brothers and sisters will procure? Won't they be disheartened at your lack of confidence in their influence with your father? If you go to them with a lack of belief in their intercession they will present themselves to the father and say something unenthusiastically generic along the lines of, "Dad, Johnny broke the neighbor's window today. He says he's sorry and wants you to go easy on him."

On the other hand, if you had great faith in the influence of your mother and big brothers or sisters you would go to them pleading, "Mom, big brother/sister, I know your dad's favorites. I'm *so* sorry that I broke our neighbor's window (while crying)! Please talk to dad and let him know how sorry I am." With a firm faith in the intercessory power of your mother and big brothers or sisters, they will likewise be convinced of your sincere sorrow and petition your dad more forcefully; something more along the lines of, "Dad, Johnny broke the neighbor's window today. He's really, really sorry! He's been crying in his room since he came home. Please, please, please go easy on him. He made a mistake and he admitted to it right away. *Please* forgive him. Don't be harsh. He is really, truly sorry"! In this way, the efficacy of the intercession of Our Mother and that of the saints depends on our faith in their power to intercede.

Yes, Our Mother (the Blessed Virgin Mary) holds the most weight with Our Father, but the saints are like the favored children in the family. What could be more beneficial to one's cause than if you petitioned not only your mother, but your big sisters and brothers to "go easy" on you when it came time to dolling out punishment for the things you've done wrong in this life!? Imagine the scene! The Eternal Father comes home from a hard day at work ruling the world; only to discover that one of His children had done wrong. What will be the best outcome for the particular miscreant? Do you go to dad and throw your errors in His face and say, "What are you going to do about it"!? Such an approach will only force him to make an example out of you so that the other children don't follow in your errors. A more reasonable approach, for the truly penitent, is to instead run behind mother's skirt (the Blessed Virgin Mary) while begging the favored children in the family to beg leniency from the Eternal Father. Remember, Dad just came home from ruling the world—quite a big responsibility—and he just wants to sit at home in peace; maybe read the paper or watch a good ball game. He doesn't want to worry about the petty squabbles among the siblings in the house or the vain habits of his children. He gets more than enough of that at work!

If the Father came home to an unenthusiastic intercession of the family for our faults, wouldn't he be irritated by the nuisance of uninterested children parading before him? Instead of ameliorating our punishment, his displeasure would only be increased by the monotony of our mother and siblings making half-hearted petitions in our behalf. It would only solidify in his mind the perception of our insincerity. As a result, he would call us before him and "tear us up"; both for our transgression and for the annoyance of sending our mother and siblings to insincerely petition in our behalf! After all, he could have been enjoying a good game rather than listening to half-hearted intercessions for the guilty.

On the other hand, consider the scene if we were truly faithful in the intercessory power of Our Mother and the saints. Initially, Father would come home and learn of our misbehavior. He would be disappointed with us, but if Our Mother and siblings beseeched Him in all the earnestness that they could muster in our behalf, Father would be more greatly convinced of the sincerity of our sorrow for our mistake. If, with great faith, we begged the intercession of Our Mother, the angels, and the saints; they would besiege the Father with pleadings in our behalf to mitigate our punishment as soon as He walked into the house. Such an assault of intercession may convince the Father of our true sorrow and inspire Him to lessen the punishment due to us for our faults! After all, all this begging and pleading in our behalf is just as much of a nuisance as having to deal with our punishment. If we are truly sincere in our sorrow He may just dismiss our fault with a stern look and an admonition against such behavior in the future; similar to the scene when the Jews brought an adulteress before Jesus and asked whether she should be stoned. Instead of approving the stoning his reply disarmed the expectant executioners and He sent her away with the simple admonition to "sin no more."[4]

Having addressed some of the most common errors regarding Protestant objections to Catholicism, let us look more closely to the very nature of Protestantism at its foundation. The very nature of the word "Protestant" is fully descriptive of its erroneous nature. A Protestant is (phonetically) a 'prō-tes-tunt' against the authority of the Catholic Church: the Church begun by Christ Himself. Remember, the Protestant denominations originally arose due to the abuses within the body of the Catholic Church that were transpiring in Martin Luther's generation; primarily instigated by the monetary sale of indulgences to the faithful; so as to insinuate that the faithful could very literally buy their way out of hell or into heaven. Martin Luther, as well as many of the faithful of his day, was quite rightly disgusted with the prelates at all levels within the Church who participated in this disgrace. However, in his opposition to obviously reprobated practices he went entirely too

---

[4] From John 8:3-11.

far with his protestations. His principal error was in not discerning the difference between the body and the spirit of the Church. As explained in the earlier address to Catholics, the Church is not a monolithic singularity. It is composed of both body and spirit. Had Luther properly circumscribed his objections to the Catholic Faith, as it was being practiced in his day, to the abuses transpiring within the corrupted body of the Church, he may very well have been an instrument by which many abuses transpiring within the Church would have been all the more speedily rectified.

However, for whatever reason—Luther's intentions will not be maligned, for it is not possible for others to know his true heart, and they may very well have been altogether virtuous—Luther lacked the grace or discernment to properly circumscribe his protests to those abuses being perpetrated by errant prelates. In comparison to a modern axiom, Luther "threw the baby out with the bathwater." He went entirely beyond simply protesting against the corrupted prelates selling indulgences for money (the dirty bathwater), and took the extraordinary step of discarding the baby (the Catholic Church) as well. Instead of simply, and rightfully, decrying the corrupt body of the Church, he went too far by denying its spirit (the *Holy* Spirit) as well when he denied the Catholic Church's position as the supreme authority of Christian doctrine: making himself the primary instigator of schismatic sects within Christianity: teaching multiple erroneous doctrines contrary to the approved doctrine of the Faith—especially as it relates to the principle of private revelation and the primacy of the Bible as the only source of revealed truth. Hopefully, my Protestant brothers and sisters can see the great danger of an approach that denies that the Holy Spirit is the guiding spirit of the Church: "And whosoever shall speak a word against the Son of man, it shall be forgiven him: but he that shall speak against the Holy Ghost, it shall not be forgiven him, neither in this world, nor in the world to come."[5]

Moreover, looking at the scene in this age, it is hopeful that many Protestants will quickly come to recognize the corruption that is destroying many denominations. Just as the practice of homosexuality has corrupted the *body* of the Church via the sexual abuse scandal, the perniciousness of this abomination is far more advanced in some of the Protestant denominations; as evidenced by the *doctrinal* acceptance of homosexual prelates within some of the Protestant denominations. This has come to pass because the animating *spirit* of all Protestant denominations is, at the foundational level, humanistic in nature: the denial of the Holy Spirit's leadership position within

---

[5] Matthew 12:32.

the Catholic Church in deference to the leadership of human interpretation of Christian dogma.

A simple fact must be related that may not be very well received by my Protestant brothers and sisters, but it must be made known with certainty. Before the final judgment and the end of the temporal world, all schismatic denominations *will* fall away. The adherents to Protestantism will either recognize the doctrinal errors upon which Protestantism is founded (human interpretation of the Bible and personal, private revelation) and reunite with the Catholic Church, or they will separate themselves. We are witnessing the beginning of this process in this extraordinary age. How could it be any other way? In this age, several Protestant denominations are now admitting practicing homosexuals into leadership positions within their denomination(s). For the Protestant who desires to remain faithful to Christ, a terribly difficult choice presents itself: "Will I remain with my Protestant denomination—that which I have known, loved, and supported for all my life—when it actively encourages practices that the greatest expositor of Christian morality (St. Paul) boldly denounced;[6] or will I return to the Faith that has always held true to the *spirit* (the Holy Spirit) of Christian morality; even in dark and spiritually stormy days when the *body* of the Church is in the midst of tremendous corruption"?

Hopefully, in the end most will remember Christ's admonition: "[37]He that loveth father or mother more than me, is not worthy of me; and he that loveth son or daughter more than me, is not worthy of me. [38]And he that taketh not up his cross, and followeth me, is not worthy of me."[7]

Some of the most obstinate, Protestant opponents to the Catholic Church have even gone so far as to refer to the Catholic Church as the "Great Whore." Those who take such a position fall into error in exactly the same way as Luther did. They view the Catholic Church as a monolithic singularity. Flawed and wicked prelates have done flawed and wicked things. As a result, opponents of the Faith then demonize the Catholic Church as an institution, rather than seeing the failings of the men within the hierarchy of the Catholic Church—as a consequence of original sin and the failings of human nature—as the true evil in need of correction. My guidance to

---

[6] "And, in like manner, the men also, leaving the natural use of the women, have burned in their lusts one towards another, men with men working that which is filthy, and receiving in themselves the recompense which was due to their error." (Rom. 1:27).

[7] Matthew 10:37-38.

Protestants who adopt this belief (the Holy Catholic Church as a monolithic singularity, and subsequently . . . the "Great Whore") can be summed up as follows: the failings of wicked men within the Church are their personal failures alone. They *are not*, and never have been, a failure of the Holy Spirit in His duties of leadership within the Catholic Church; especially as it relates to the exposition of sound moral doctrine. Christ promised the leadership of the Holy Spirit within His Church to the end of time during His ministry: "And I will ask the Father, and he shall give you another Paraclete, that he may abide with you **for ever**":[8] By denying the Church's authority as it relates to Christian dogma, the Protestant repeats Luther's schismatic error. Let us again consider this scenario from a more common, human perspective. The Catholic Church is known as "Christ's Bride." By denying the authority of the Church, the Protestant effectively says to Christ, "I love you Lord, but your wife is a whore. Therefore, I will have nothing to do with her."

However, when one looks deeper into the situation one will hopefully recognize the double insult being offered to both Jesus Christ Himself and the Catholic Church as a consequence of this position! When Christ departed this world, he made St. John the earthly custodian of His Mother, the Blessed Virgin Mary: "[26]When Jesus therefore had seen his mother and the disciple standing whom he loved, he saith to his mother: Woman, behold thy son. [27]After that, he saith to the disciple: Behold thy mother. And from that hour, the disciple took her to his own."[9] In the same way, Christ ordains the men who administer the Catholic Church as the custodian(s) of His "bride" throughout all time until the end of time. What a responsibility for those who, through their own free will, choose to partake in the priestly vocation! Just as St. John assumed earthly responsibility for the Blessed Virgin Mary at the time of His death, those men who are the consecrated caretakers of the Catholic Church (priests, bishops, cardinals, etc.) assume a commensurate responsibility for "Christ's Bride" (the Catholic Church) on Earth.

As custodians of "Christ's Bride" they are expected to care for Her with the same solicitude that St. John cared for the Blessed Virgin Mary in this life: impeccably and without any stain of corruption. Jesus walked this world as a man for a mere thirty-three years. In his material absence, it then became necessary for Him to relinquish the care of His Church to other men; to sustain and propagate it into the future until the end of time. While He promised that the Holy Spirit would sustain His Church until the end of

---

[8] John 14:16.
[9] John 19:26-27.

time, He did not promise that those who followed after Him, in His Church, would remain as faithful as He: "And I say to thee: That thou art Peter; and upon this rock I will build my church, and the gates of hell shall not prevail against it."[10] This passage from Matthew is important to note because it promised that hell would not "prevail against it": meaning that His church would never be completely overcome. However, just because Christ promised that hell would never completely overcome His church in no way suggests that hell would not make tremendous strides within it! God allows the free will of men to choose to be faithful or faithless. Understanding the failings of human nature (due to original sin), it should then become obvious that there would be many prelates within the Church who would consequently fail in their duty to Christ to keep His bride as impeccable as it was when He instituted it.

Consider the situation from the following perspective . . . A poor, but beloved, brother is dying (Christ's crucifixion on the Cross). As a result, His newly betrothed wife (the Catholic Church) will be left in destitution if His family members do not take up His cause and provide for her care. After the beloved brother's death, His family members then assume the responsibility of sustaining her life until her end.[11] Being a faithful spouse, the wife follows her spouse's instructions; submitting to the care of her deceased husband's family. However, some of those instructions are difficult to bear. As a result, some of her caretakers become frustrated at the difficulty of remaining faithful to their departed brother's instructions. In the course of life, difficult times arise that require difficult choices. Remaining faithful to the departed brother's instructions becomes an impediment to the weaker individuals among the wife's caretakers.

Due to their human weaknesses, some of the caretakers willfully choose expedient, but disobedient and faithless, measures that will make their lives easier in the short term; not seeing the ultimate damage that such "short cuts" will cause. Not believing that they have the proper means to care for their beloved brother's widow, these weaker members of the family then conceive to use her as a means of their own enrichment. To "care" for their deceased brother's wife, they then choose the disgraceful measure of prostituting her to the desires of the world: corrupting her body to "go along to get along" with the world. Although her spirit is never broken,

---

[10] Matthew 16:18.

[11] In the case of the Catholic Church on Earth, Christ's Bride, her end will only come at the end of time.

the unfaithful caretakers of His bride effectively "pimp her out" so as to make a living from her spouse's good name. Remember, in her spouse's absence from this world, she is wholly and completely at the mercy of her caretakers. As time passes, some of the citizens who are familiar with the bride's husband and His instructions for her care make public notice of the disgraceful way her caretakers are treating her.

By understanding the situation from this perspective, the double-insult of Protestantism is more readily understood. When the faithful followers of Christ notice that Christ's bride is being prostituted, as in the case of selling indulgences for monetary gain during Luther's day, the way they can best serve both Jesus and His bride best is by intervening in her behalf; saying to her faithless caretakers, "You have disgraced the memory of our Lord and His spouse by prostituting her in this fashion. Therefore, those of us who are faithful to His memory and her good name will dismiss you from her care and assume the responsibility ourselves." Sadly, Protestantism took a different approach. Seeing Christ's Bride being prostituted by her faithless caretakers, they instead chose to abandon her as a faithless spouse; not being mindful that, as a faithful bride of Christ, she would always remain faithful to His direction: submitting herself to the care of His prelates; for better or for worse. Whether she likes it or not, she (the Catholic Church) is *always* faithful to her spouse's commands; even if it means being mistreated by her caretakers. During His ministry, Christ ordered her to *completely* submit to her caretaker's direction: "And I will give to thee the keys of the kingdom of heaven. And whatsoever thou shalt bind upon earth, it shall be bound also in heaven: and whatsoever thou shalt loose on Earth, it shall be loosed also in heaven."[12]

Consider the utter depth of sorrow for Christ's bride (the Roman Catholic Church)! In dire need of rescue from her perfidious caretakers, potentially faithful caretakers—those who could rescue her from her sorrowful and shameful predicament—fail to look to the cause of her shameful state. Instead, they only see her exterior condition; passing her by on the street while uttering abominable obscenities and spitting on her. What consolation can she possibly have when those who claim to be faithful to her husband abandon her to liars, pimps, hypocrites, and thieves!?

All things must be discerned according to their consequences, as Christ instructed: "Wherefore by their fruits you shall know them."[13] When many

---

[12] Matthew 16:19.
[13] Matthew 7:20.

prelates within the Catholic Church turn a blind eye to sexual abuse within their ranks, what type of fruit grows thereof!? When many prelates within the Catholic Church actively work to frustrate the will of Heaven; as delivered at Fátima (a revelation approved by the Church) to three young, children seers, what type of fruit grows thereof!?

My dear, Protestant brothers and sisters, this appeal is made to you for two reasons: (1) the rehabilitation and sustenance of Christ's bride (the Holy Catholic Church), and (2) your own sanctification. Both ends would be accomplished by your return to the one, true Faith of the human race. When you notice the errors and evils being propagated by the current hierarchy of the Catholic Church, and actively work against them, you effectively take up His cause: rescuing His bride from those who so happily prostitute her while extending His influence throughout the world! Why are you so invaluable to the Catholic Church? Sadly, it is because of the laxity and lack of discipline that has befallen the Catholic Church in this age. Discipline, solemnity, and reverence have fallen to an abysmal low within the Catholic Church.

Among many Protestant followers of Christ there exists a zeal and honest desire to serve Christ (even as the Protestant denominations are also being subjected to subversion from within) that, on whole, is lacking among the Catholic laity at large. Pride has swelled the hearts of many Catholics; so that within their hearts they seem to say to themselves, "I am a follower of the one, true religion. Therefore, all I must do is show up to Mass (in T-shirts, shorts, "flip-flops," and other disgraceful apparel) and "punch the ticket" so as to make it into Heaven when my time comes. They no longer live their Faith in word and deed! This is exactly why you are so badly needed. Christ's bride is being woefully abused and neglected by faithless caretakers. Most of Her children (Catholic laity) have grown undisciplined, lax, and apathetic; lulled into a slumbering state by the advances of both clever toys of human creation (science and technology) and the silky smooth tongues of wicked men preaching a "social gospel" (socialism and communism) rather than the Gospel of Christ crucified.

If the Protestant reader will simply reflect on a singular reality, the realization of this difficult truth may more easily sink in. As there is only one God, there can only be one *true* religion. At the time of the end of the temporal world, which religion do my Protestant brothers and sisters believe it will be? The religion of Calvin (Calvinism) . . . the religion of Martin Luther (Lutheran) . . . the religion of King Henry VIII (Anglican) . . . the religion of Joseph Smith, Jr. (Mormon) . . . the religion of John Smyth (Baptist) . . . or will it *possibly* be the religion of Jesus Christ (the Catholic Church): the God-man: recognized as such by the Protestant denominations?

My Protestant brothers and sisters, Christ's bride and Her woefully slumbering children (Catholic laity) are in dire need of an infusion of your zeal! In terms of social advocacy for Christian principles (opposition to abortion, homosexuality, pornography, and all other types of moral decay) it is predominantly members of Protestant denominations who are standing at the forefront of the fight! The Protestant community possesses a key that could potentially unlock a great renewal within the Catholic Church! Will you use it and unlock the door to a greater day in which the slumbering are awakened and revitalized? Will you come to the rescue of Christ's bride by first acquainting yourself more deeply with Catholic theology and dogma, and then speak out forcefully against her faithless caretakers who are prostituting her so shamefully, rather than passing Her by on the street and spitting at Her? She (the Catholic Church) needs you to return to the *discipline* of the Faith in order to rescue Her. We, Her children (Catholic laity) need you to infuse within our communities the zeal that a great many of you possess: a zeal that has been sadly waning for far too long. Like the prodigal son who came home after recognizing his errors, your return would likewise be a momentous occasion of *great* rejoicing!

Coming To a Choice and Making a Stand

My dear brothers and sisters, what a sad, confused, and bitter world the human race has made for itself! At the foundational level, *all* the strife, discord, and points of contention within societies throughout the world stem from the battle in this world between good and evil: the rule of God (Christianity: Catholicism primarily, and Protestant denominations of Christianity secondarily) vs. the rule of man (humanism: which includes atheism, agnosticism and false religions; as false religions are a form of humanism under the guise of legitimate worship). As individuals, each one of us *must* make a choice between these two irreconcilably opposed belief systems to discover which of them can lead us to *true* happiness and prosperity. At the end of the day, we must discern which leads to *life and happiness* and which leads to *death and misery*; both individually and socially. With these two choices standing before us, let's examine the consequences of both belief systems so that we can make our choice from a more enlightened position.

Probably the greatest expositor of humanism in the modern day was Aldous Huxley; because his novel, *Brave New World* (originally published in 1932), is the most shining example of literary prophecy regarding the ultimate ends of humanism/atheism when extended to their logical conclusion(s). His vision of the supremacy of the rule of man over the rule of God can most easily be seen as the world we are currently suffered to live in: the stratification of societies into various "classes," the proliferation of sexual deviancy and excess to the point of being socially tolerable (homosexuality, transgenderism, and pornography), the manufacture of human beings (artificial insemination and cloning), the worship of science and technology, the widespread use of drugs to escape reality, the New World Order of societies controlled by global governing authorities (United Nations), etc. The overarching foundation of Huxley's vision revolves around society's denial of God, which then untethers the human race from any sense of personal restraint—no shame or guilt for the consequences of our actions—as they then look to themselves as gods unto themselves (liberalism).

There used to be something called God . . .[1]

God isn't compatible with machinery and scientific medicine and universal happiness. You must make your choice. Our civilization has chosen machinery and medicine and happiness.[2]

However, what's curious to note is that although Aldous Huxley was a "hard-core" humanist, he viewed his vision of the future as a nightmare. In a reprinted edition of *Brave New World*, Huxley wrote in the foreword:

All things considered it looks as though Utopia were far closer to us than anyone, only fifteen years ago, could have imagined. Then, I projected it six hundred years into the future. Today it seems quite possible that the ***horror*** may be upon us within a single century.[3]

Does the reader not recognize the suicidal, insane perversity of humanistic thought when so forcefully confronted with it!? In a mere two sentences, Mr. Huxley referred to his humanistic vision of the future as "Utopia" (the perfect society) while deriding it as a "horror"! Sadly, but most befittingly in consideration of the spirit that animated his life, Aldous Huxley died from an overdose of a psychotropic drug (LSD) while on his deathbed from cancer; *exactly* as his literary characters chose the life of a falsely manufactured "happiness" over that of facing the arduous hardships of real life. He chose a drug-induced death over facing the pains of life. My dear friends, is this not the height of insanity!?

The humanistic world view is, at its heart, narcissistic, hedonistic, and voluptuous. Its ultimate end, including all means constructed to reach that end, is the gratification of human desire(s); both sensual and emotional. The encapsulation of humanistic thought can be understood from the perspective of absolute, narcissistic selfishness: all things ordered within society so as to serve humanity's desire(s). The reader may ask the question within themselves, "What's wrong with that"? My dear friends, what's wrong with

---

[1] Aldous Huxley, *Brave New World*, (New York, NY: Harper Collins Publishers, Inc.; First Perennial Classics Edition, 1998), 230.

[2] Ibid., 234.

[3] Ibid., xvii.

that is that living an existence subsumed by desire(s) completely ignores the consequences of our actions! In essence, when the human race capitulates to their desires they then become indistinguishable from the realm of the unintelligible animals! Dogs live by instinctual motivations: food, water, sex, etc. But is the human race nothing more than unintelligible dogs!? Are our choices in life framed within the context of, "What do I need to do to provide for my material necessities, so that I can then gratify my instinctual desires with impunity"? Unintelligible animals have no conception of the future and the consequences of their actions on it. Contrarily, human beings have an ability the unintelligible animals do not: the faculty of reason that is able to comprehend the consequences of actions based on historical experience(s).

Remembering that, as reasoning creatures, human beings must judge all things according to their consequences; we will start with an evaluation of nine common social and political issues seen in today's world from the humanistic perspective, as this is the prevalent, philosophical world view the vast majority of the human race embraces in this age. Next, we will evaluate these issues from a Christian perspective; so as to contrast the consequences ("fruits") of the two philosophies. These issues are (1) economics, (2) race relations, (3) hunger, (4) homelessness, (5) drug abuse, (6) immigration, (7) health care, (8) environmentalism, and (9) crime.

ECONOMICS

In a humanistic world, economics is the central foundation upon which almost every action that mankind considers is built on. This is because within humanism the whole purpose of life is to serve the desires of mankind. From an economic perspective, this initially means a person's own financial security and comfort, and then subsequently their desire to control others so as to amass even more wealth and power unto themselves. What such a disposition drives people toward is the pursuit of money for the sake of economic and social power. Economic power provides both a "cushion" of security should hard economic times strike, as well as to provide the means necessary to indulge hedonistic and luxurious passions. Social power is derived when the economically powerful use wealth to exercise influence and control over whole societies. A humanistic view of economics causes two tremendous social problems: it discourages charity and promotes injustice. If the central pursuit of one's life is building a comfortable "nest egg" from which to draw on in difficult times, amassing enough wealth to pursue luxurious living, or obtaining enough wealth to influence society (for example, buying off politicians through direct payoffs or campaign contributions), charity will be the first victim of humanistic economics; because relinquishing wealth for the sake of the more needy necessarily reduces one's economic power by a commensurate amount.

Economic injustice is also greatly multiplied; because if the foundation of one's actions is built on the accrual of money, all too many people will arrange their lives and affairs around schemes and strategies that will tend to increase their income. The most clever and cunning schemers and strategists within society will establish systems of economic injustice in order to "feather their nests" while depriving others of their means. Those who have been duped out of their money by the beguiling schemers may not possess the requisite economic knowledge and understanding to uncover the devious and unjust schemes, but they will understand that an injustice has occurred and they were its victims. Such sentiments will promote discontent and jealousy within the whole of society; encouraging the most base and reprobated behavior and psychology within those who believe themselves victimized. A universally reactionary mentality will develop that will only inspire envy and hatred of others who have more material means than themselves, regardless of whether such sentiments are just or helpful to society (the Occupy Wall Street movement).

From a humanistic perspective there is no divine judgment or punishment for our actions, as well as nothing to hope for after this life. This perspective impels humanists to accrue as much material wealth into their hands as possible for their own self-serving "needs," and at all costs, regardless of any deleterious social consequences. What follows is a stratification of wealth into the hands of the most clever and cunning; leaving the "simple folk"— those more concerned with meeting daily necessities—at the mercy of the clever and cunning; who then throw the simple, "unwashed masses" just enough crumbs to keep them from disturbing the established social order, while simultaneously driving them, due to economic duress, to come back to their economic masters for relief. Ultimately, it becomes a perverse circle of dependence; like drug addicts in need of a "fix." The economically powerful humanist uses the dependence of the economically needy to herd them into a greater dependence on themselves; setting themselves up as masters, and the economically distressed as their slaves.

This is the *modus operandi* of the economic masters within a humanistic world: all things ordered so as to increase the flow of economic power into their own hands. They accomplish their ends by applying their wealth to controlling whole societies through paid functionaries: politicians, journalists, lawyers, and social activists of varying stripes. All social disturbances within a humanistic society are seen as opportunities to herd more economic power into their own hands (via their functionaries), while using the present particulars of social turbulence (race relations, hunger, homelessness, drug abuse, immigration, health care, environmentalism, crime, and any others the reader can conceive of) to distract the "unwashed masses" from their machinations.

As we examine some of the humanistic "solutions" to social ailments facing the world, the economic benefit to be derived by the economically powerful from the propagation of these problems should be of preeminent consideration.

RACE RELATIONS

In a humanistic world, race is seen as a socially stratifying factor. Distinctions are made, and accepted within society at large, between peoples of different races. The end effect of such distinctions is a willful separation within the human family into distinct groups that identify themselves according to race. Such willful self-segregation into varying racial classes then tends to the separation of peoples into separate, competing sub-cultures: Whites, Blacks, Asians, Hispanics, etc.

Racial identification pits people against one another based on inconsequential physiological factors that are wholly unimportant to their character formation. This is primarily accomplished through the establishment of various enterprises meant to forward the social power of specific racial groups (for example; the NAACP, the Ku Klux Klan, and La Raza). It matters not which racial sub-culture is under consideration. Any organization that forwards the specific cause of a particular race is, by definition,[4] a racist organization; because in action such organizations show exclusive favoritism for their race, which in turn promotes separatism and antagonism toward those of other races.

How this forwards the mastery of the human race to the economically powerful is through the aggregation of wealth into the hands of those who run such racist organizations; using the sentiments of racial identity extant within their targeted audience to procure funds for the exclusive cause of their race.

---

[4] Racism is prejudice in favor of a particular race. It should not be confused with its close cousin, bigotry, which is the consequence in act of racism: purposeful discrimination of others based on their race.

Such organizations appeal for finances by exclusively promoting the interests of those of a particular racial identity, while withholding assistance to those of other races; so as to self-justify their own existence and propagate the identity politics of racial separatism. Peace among the human race will never be achieved when organizations exist that purposefully work to inculcate within their members a separatist spirit and feelings of alienation from the rest of the human family. Under such a social paradigm, the competing sub-cultures view themselves from a superior, favored perspective: showing favoritism to "their own" while denying a truly just consideration to those of others races; exactly because they see those of other races as "lesser" peoples from competing sub-cultures, to be conquered and subjugated, rather than human beings to be treated with equity and justice.

HUNGER

In a humanistic world, hunger will be widespread; especially among the less educated, those not socially or politically "well-connected," and those of lesser economic means. Hunger stems from two sources: (1) the lack of adequate foodstuffs to sustain the human demand, or (2) the lack of economic resources to acquire the available food. Within developed nations the lack of adequate foodstuffs to sustain the human demand is rare. The most common source of hunger is poverty. This brings us back to the consideration of economics in such a tragedy: those who have to choose between paying the rent, buying shoes, or eating. Within a humanistic society, utilitarianism becomes the "yardstick" by which human life is valued; where a person's perceived usefulness to society becomes the measure of their worth as a human being; both economically and socially. Within such a system the uneducated "simple folk," the physically disabled, and the mentally disturbed or incapacitated are seen to be of lesser worth to society than the professional athlete, doctor, engineer, or scientist.

They may not be intentionally discarded as human rubbish, but the consequent effect of utilitarian thought will lead to the abandonment of people who are not able to properly provide for themselves; primarily because the "usefulness" of such individuals will be seen as an economic drain on society. To assuage the guilt of the humanist, token efforts will be made to address hunger, but no substantive measures will be undertaken to address its root cause because the humanists will be engrossed in their own pursuit of material wealth, while leaving those unable to tend to their own needs to their own devices as best as they can manage in their limited capacities. How such a situation serves the interests of the economically powerful is in the way in which they are able to use the situation to induce guilt within society for the plight of the hungry; especially within prosperous, developed nations where such things should not be a problem. Using society's guilty conscience against their own best interests, the economic masters then propose solutions that draw more wealth away from the citizens who could more wisely use and apply it themselves, in the name of serving the hungry, while creating a perceived need for the economic masters (food stamps, welfare, etc.).

HOMELESSNESS

In a humanistic world, homelessness will be widespread; especially among the less educated, those not socially or politically "well-connected," and those of lesser economic means. The great majority of the homeless are most often mentally disturbed or disabled, drug-addicted, or simply too lazy and parasitic to provide for themselves; with some of them suffering from simple ignorance—either economically or otherwise. Those who are simply ignorant will receive their education in the school of hard knocks and recover themselves through their own diligent efforts in order to rescue themselves from difficult circumstances. They will take any job, no matter how "menial" or "degrading," to provide for the necessity of a roof over their head, food on their plate, and clothes on their back. The other homeless fall into the category of the drug-addicted, willfully parasitic, or mentally disturbed or disabled. Due to the utilitarian ethos of the society, a great many of them will be abandoned as useless appendages. As it is in the case of hunger, token efforts to assist the homeless will be undertaken to assuage the guilt of the self-righteous, but the root cause of the problem(s) will be left unaddressed. The drug-addicted will not be compelled into sobriety, the willfully parasitic will not be derided for their shameless imposition on society, and the mentally disturbed or disabled will not be offered counseling or remediation in their disability. The foundational causes of homelessness will be ignored in favor of blaming the scourge on "society." In truth, it will be society's fault, but the people within a humanistic society will be too engrossed by their utilitarian pathos to enact the proper measures to address the problem(s).

How such a situation serves the interests of the economically powerful is identical to the problem of hunger: using guilt to draw material wealth into their own hands in order to mask the symptoms of homelessness, while ignoring the true, underlying causes: like a doctor who prescribes medicine to alleviate the symptoms while ignoring the disease. The mentally deranged, willfully parasitic, or drug-addicted will be provided meager, immediate assistance via homeless shelters, but their mental derangement, parasitic tendencies, or drug addiction will be mostly ignored. The problem(s) will persist and the demand for more money to address the self-perpetuating problems will subsist indefinitely; thereby sustaining the constant demand for money so as to "eradicate" homelessness.

DRUG ABUSE

In a humanistic world, drug abuse will be acceptable. Because the end of humanism is the satisfaction of human desire(s), the abuse of drugs will be seen as a merely recreational endeavor. Although the deadly effect of drug abuse will be evident for all to see, there will be no will among the majority of the population to eradicate the practice(s). Most all the inhabitants of the society will be pursuing their own pleasure(s) through pharmaceuticals of some variety, either prescription or illicit, with many people trying to legalize dangerous narcotics due to their addiction to the substances. Moreover, the economic masters of the society will tacitly encourage drug abuse so as to keep the population mentally subdued, compliant, and distracted.

IMMIGRATION

In a humanistic world, illegal immigration will be widespread and tacitly encouraged by the social and political leaders. Since one of the fundamental pursuits in a humanistic world is the accumulation of material wealth, illegal immigrants will be seen as an ideal source of quasi-slave labor. Due to their unlawful presence within the nation, employers will be able to more easily exploit them through unjustly depressed wages or abysmal working conditions that legitimate citizens would not tolerate; thereby amassing more wealth into the hands of the economic masters of the society.

HEALTH CARE

Within the humanistic mind, life in the material world constitutes the totality of human aspirations: ". . . Let us eat and drink; for to morrow we shall die."[5] Under such a world view, the health of the citizen is one of the most important considerations; because the years in their life will constitute

---

[5] From Isaiah 22:13.

the totality of opportunity for them to enjoy this life. Within such a society, a self-contradiction establishes itself. The humanistic ethos will impel the society to live for pleasure and luxury. However, such a frame of mind naturally drives people toward recreational drug abuse and other forms of "soft" living: two behaviors that markedly deteriorate the health of the human body. In short, the people will want "to have their cake and eat it too." But, as we all know, reality cares not for the desires of mankind.

Consequently, the overall health of the society will suffer. Sickness and disease will abound due to drug abuse, obesity, and sexual deviancy. While people are clamoring to satiate their pleasures, their pleasures will be undermining their health by a commensurate degree. Not willing to abandon their pleasures in exchange for their health, the society will clamor for more physicians and hospitals to treat self-induced maladies. As the downward spiral intensifies, health care will become a greater priority in their lives. In desperation to extend their years on Earth, so as to multiply the pleasures of life they are able to experience, people will begin to seek any remedy to their self-induced illness—excepting, of course, the abandonment of unhealthy pleasures—through all manner of self-deceiving, clever schemes. This situation will play well into the hands of society's economic masters; as they play along with the charade in order to amass the incalculable wealth that will be thrown at their feet to solve the seemingly unsolvable problem of adequate health care for all.

ENVIRONMENTALISM

In a humanistic world, Earth will be elevated to a quasi-divine entity (Gaia Mater) due to its nature as the sole home of the human race. Because human beings are the masters of Earth due to their intellectual supremacy in relation to the unintelligible animals, most problems related to the environment (famines, floods, tsunamis, hurricanes, extreme weather, etc.) will be attributed to human interference with Gaia Mater. The natural perversion to develop from such thinking is that mankind is in competition with "Mother Earth" for the sustainment of Earth's ecological system(s), rather than understanding that *mankind is a participatory element in the natural order*; just as any other plant or animal is. What such thinking will lead to is a form of self-hatred of the human race.

Simply because the human race has the capability to affect the environment to a greater degree than other plants or animals, the atheistic environmentalist will come to view the human race as a cancerous, parasitical

307

component; separated and apart from it. The ultimate end of such perverse thought processes completely reverses the proper understanding of the means and the ends of environmental stewardship, because it places Earth's resources in a position of relative importance that is superior to the well-being of the human race. From this perspective, they likewise choose to undermine the human race in deference to some idealized fantasy environment untouched by humanity. The environment, for the sake of the environment, is the desired end; and the means to achieve this desired end is the diminution or destruction of both human interests and human beings alike.

Such environmental advocates will support any and all measures to promote the "pristine" nature of the environment, while vociferously opposing any action supportive of human life. If a tree is uprooted or a species of fish or fowl is dislocated from their current environs to make room for human beings, environmentalists will oppose the action through any means—including violence and destruction (for example, the Earth Liberation Front (ELF))—seeing Gaia Mater as an entity to be worshipped and revered, while seeing human plans for Earth and its resources as murderous transgressions against "Mother Earth." As the psychology progresses, the economic masters of the human race will use the cause of environmentalism to amass more material wealth into their own hands under the guise of using the wealth to protect Earth and its environment ("cap and trade", carbon credits, etc.).

CRIME

In a humanistic world, crime will be rampant. Because the concept of crime from a humanistic perspective differs greatly from that of a Christian perspective, the first thing that must be understood in this discussion is, "What constitutes a crime"? While humanists despise Christian morality, they use a perverted interpretation of the "Golden Rule" as the basis for their definition of a crime. From a humanistic perspective, *a crime is committed when someone disturbs the humanist's feelings or sensibilities, or violates their sense of ABSOLUTE freedom.* The ultimate consequence of such a mentality is that anyone who speaks out against anything humanistic is considered a criminal in the mind of a humanist, because it violates their absolute freedom to do as they please; even if what they please is dangerous or deadly to the individual or society. By perverting the principle of, "Do unto others as you would have them do unto you," they then make the claim that anyone who disturbs their conscience is a criminal; because, in their self-justifying minds, their dangerous behavior isn't impeding the absolute freedom of others to destroy themselves or society: seeing the castigation of their dangerous practices as a violation of their "human rights."

Such a perspective enables the economic masters within society because it gives them the "social leverage" to amass wealth into their own hands so as to persecute those who disturb the conscience of the humanist. Moreover, the actual commission of predatory crimes (rape, murder, robbery, etc.) will be substantial, as the humanist has no fear of divine accountability at the conclusion of their lives. Unfortunately, there are many people of lesser intelligence in this world who marvel at how cunning and brilliant they are . . . in their own, delusional minds. There will be no psychological impediment for such people to dissuade them from committing innumerable crimes, as their only restraint is the possibility of being apprehended by other people, which they greatly disregard; believing themselves to be entirely too smart and clever to ever be caught in their criminal acts.

Now that we have evaluated the consequences to accrue from the treatment of several problematic issues affecting the human race from a humanistic perspective, let's now evaluate them from a Christian perspective so that it will be much easier to discern which approach leads to constructive behavior that promotes human life, and which approach leads to destructive behavior that destroys human life.

Before we begin the examination of the Christian approach to social ills, it must first be understood how the Christian comes to their position. In essence, "How is their conscience formed"? Catholic doctrine teaches that the Holy Spirit is the animating spirit of the Church; even if many of the modern caretakers are not acting in an exemplary fashion that ennobles and enables the Faith. However, this admission in no way diminishes the efficacy of a social order consisting of people who live out the Christian way of life; animated by the "fruits of the Spirit":[6] (1) charity, (2) joy, (3) peace, (4) patience, (5) benignity, (6) goodness, (7) longanimity,[7] (8) mildness, (9) faith, (10) modesty, (11) continency, and (12) chastity. If the hierarchy of the Church had been faithful servants of Jesus Christ, maintaining true *discipline, liturgy, and catechetical formation*, this would be evident to all.

If we are to understand the Christian mentality, and considering that no truly Christian society exists in the world today from which we would have recourse to reference, we must begin at the foundational level;

---

[6] Cf. Galatians 5:22-23.

[7] The ability to bear injuries and sufferings with patience.

an understanding of the purpose and meaning of life: the foundational philosophy that would form and guide a person's every thought and action. In a Christian society, the purpose of their lives would be understood to be a test of our faithfulness to God, because His intention in creating us in the first place was that the human race would love and adore Him as our Creator; worshipping Him by honoring His commandments, rules, and laws. Human beings who pass the test of this world would inherit the vacancies left by the unfaithful angels that were cast into hell after the angelic rebellion. Those who fail the test will join the demons in hell. With this understanding as the foundation of their lives, the average citizen would circumscribe their thoughts, deeds, and actions around obedience to God's will, so that when their test comes to its conclusion (their death in this world) they will attain to eternal happiness rather than eternal horror and suffering.

People within such a society would understand the purpose of their lives from birth. Therefore, they would not be constantly trying to "find themselves" in this life. From this understanding we then move on to the more practical question, "How do we come to know God's will so that we may stay in His good graces and pass the 'test' of this world"? The Church would teach us all things doctrinal through the Magisterium; providing guidance in all matters regarding faith and morals. Even with that foundation of knowledge, there would still be the question of how they should live out their lives from day to day in a manner that would be pleasing to God and helpful to them in reaching the desired end of Heaven at the time of their passing from this world. This question was answered by the founder of the Faith, Jesus Christ:

> **All things therefore whatsoever you would that men should do to you, do you also to them. For this is the law and the prophets.**[8]

This principle is known today as the "Golden Rule" and it's more commonly known today through the maxim, "Do unto others as you would have them do unto you." At this point, they would then have everything they needed to know (the Magisterium and the Golden Rule) to live a life pleasing to God. Let us now apply this understanding to the aforementioned problems facing our current world.

---

[8] Matthew 7:12.

ECONOMICS

In a Christian world, economics would be a necessary, but burdensome consideration. Money, being necessary as a means of valuing labor, will be seen as both a necessary evil and a means to the end of providing for one's immediate material needs, rather than an end in itself. Economic matters would take care of themselves as the citizens lived their lives in accordance with the "Golden Rule." Those people who were more intellectually gifted than their neighbor would view their talent as a blessing from God and would feel the weight of responsibility to act with integrity; in the best interests of society. They would attempt to economically order their society from a perspective of, "How can the lowest among us, through the dignity of earning an honest wage, provide for themselves and their families," no matter how menial the work may be considered.

While it is true that the most gifted would earn a wage greater than those of lesser abilities, because their perceived value to society would be greater, they would not attempt to abuse their fellow man through schemes of economic self-indulgence. All people, regardless of their function in this life, rather "great" or "small" in the world's eyes—doctors, scientists, philosophers, garbage men, janitors, etc.—would look to one another as a true brother or sister within the human family. As a result, proximate economic parity within society would be desired; so that all people could sustain their needs while avoiding the shame of making themselves a burden on society.

Their whole existence would be seen as an attempt to accomplish the will of God rather than their own desires; recognizing that material gain in this life is not an important end, while fearing divine judgment for their actions in this life. What such a disposition drives people toward is the pursuit of money as just compensation for their labor and for the sake of serving their immediate necessities . . . nothing more. There will be no desire to pursue financial security and comfort for self-serving ends; because all people would understand that worldly power and recognition is worthless, and can even be mortally dangerous, at our final judgment. Why would the pursuit of economic power be so dangerous to our souls? Those who wield economic power almost always do so for their own gratification and aggrandizement. It engenders within human beings a desire to control, and when such desires root themselves within the hearts and minds of mankind their eyes are turned away from the attainment of God as their ultimate end; instead, diverting their gaze toward the attainment of some self-glorifying, worldly pursuit as their end. This is the reason for Jesus' admonition against those who build worldly wealth: "And again I say to you: It is easier for a camel to pass through the eye of a needle, than for a rich man to enter into the kingdom of heaven."[9]

The "captains of industry" who manufacture the necessities of life would feel a double burden of responsibility: primarily to produce what is needed for society, and secondarily to pay the workers who manufacture the goods a sum that is fair, in consideration of the market value of what they produce. The employers (small business owners, CEOs, etc.), who bear the burden of risk associated with maintaining any business, would naturally be economically compensated at a rate higher than their workers; as they bear the burden of success or failure for the particular enterprise. However, this higher level of compensation would be limited to two or three times the economic compensation of their employees. It would be implicitly understood that everyone working within the company had an important part to play, and that the products could not be manufactured without the conscientious participation of each employee; regardless of whether they are working "on the line" or in the "front office."

Within such a society there would be very little economic disparity between the "greatest" and the "lowest." Consequently, there would be almost no economic stratification into various "classes": rich, poor, middle class, etc. The basis for economic envy and jealousy would be almost completely undermined; discouraging unjust, irrational sentiments of material envy within society and accruing to the greater economic stability of all within it, while encouraging all within society to find their way into a profession that matched their aptitude. Under such a social order the whole of the human race would ultimately fall into one, great "middle class."

A Christian view of economics would facilitate two virtues: it would encourage charity and promote justice. Because the whole of such a society would be very near to one another in terms of economic capacities, empathy for others in their difficulties would be more natural; as most of those within the society would be living lives very similar to one another. When a fellow brother or sister was stricken by some sort of extraordinary difficulty there would be more than enough assistance available to help them recover from their difficulty, either economically or otherwise, because the empathetic spirit within the society would impel people of good conscience to help their neighbor; both for selfless and self-serving reasons. From the selfless perspective, a man would want to help his neighbor because he truly felt pity

---

[9] Matthew 19:24.

for him. From the self-serving perspective, a man would want to help his neighbor because he understands that he may also suffer hard times himself at some point in the future. If such an event arose—and they most always do in everyone's life, no matter who you are—he would want to encourage charity in his neighbor by first demonstrating it himself; setting a charitable example for others to emulate should the need arise in his life.

Justice would be promoted because within a Christian society all people would feel a compulsion to support themselves through their own labor, rather than attempting to parasitically attach themselves to their neighbor's wallet due to indolent tendencies. Those who worked honestly for their economic means would view the lazy man as an intolerable creature and would allow such a person to suffer from their poor character rather than encouraging such behavior. For those who harbored parasitic sentiments, they would be too afraid of their fellow man's condemnation should they attempt such activity; choosing to earn their own way through life, as disgusting as the idea may be to them, rather than potentially bringing their fellow man's condemnation on themselves, as well as fearing the possibility of a depravation of their needs. They will choose to work because, if they haven't the sense of self-respect and dignity that comes from supporting oneself, they will be shamed into it.

RACE RELATIONS

In a Christian world the differences between races, instead of being seen as a socially stratifying factor, would be viewed as a testament to the variety inherent within God's plan and creative power. While distinctions would be noticed between peoples of different races, it would not be viewed as a cause for competition or hatred; because the citizens, as a matter of natural habit, would look through such superficial differences among themselves and instead attempt to discern the character of their fellow man. This is the essence of what Martin Luther King's "I Have A Dream" speech attempted to visualize for the human race.

All discernment based on human physiology will be viewed as a silly, distractive element that only obstructs the assessment of one's character via their personal demeanor and behavior: their true, inner selves. A universal understanding will exist that there will always be physiological differences between human beings. However, to form a prejudice based on whether a person is of Asian, Hispanic, African, European, or other descent will be seen as ridiculous as a prejudice based on eye color, hair color, or toe length (some people have second toes longer than their "big" toe).

Economic diffusion and parity would be accomplished as the people within the society would pay an honest wage for an honest day's labor based on the nature and value of the work performed, rather than the race of the laborer; thereby undermining the ability of politically opportunistic people to foment hatred along racial lines using economic disparity as an excuse. Additionally, economic means would be more dedicated to providing for the daily necessities of life rather than to forward the identity politics of racially bigoted hatred that racial identity organizations attempt to forward.

HUNGER

In a Christian world, hunger would be almost nonexistent. Remembering that hunger is a consequence of the lack of adequate foodstuffs to sustain the human demand, or the lack of economic resources to acquire the available food; it would be seen that within a Christian society both causes would be exceedingly rare. As economic means would be more diffusely spread among the whole of humanity, there would be no want of the means to obtain food. Additionally, a society that truly lived in a manner concordant with God's will would rarely suffer a lack of food through drought or some other natural cause. It is an understood principle within Christianity that in most ages when food was actually in want, as opposed to being humanly manipulated or withheld for political ends, it was a result of divine punishment for some sin the people were committing communally: worshipping false gods, adhering to false doctrines, universal licentiousness, etc. On the other hand, God would rarely deny a sincere request from His obediently faithful children as they struggle against their human desires in order to fulfill His will; as the request for food is an integral component in their primary prayer . . . "Give us this day our daily bread."[10]

God will always throw some sort of "roadblock" in our way to try the fidelity of the human race. If He didn't, the "test" of this world would be no test at all. However, it must also be understood that in a truly faithful society each hardship in our lives would be tailored to our particular situation, and of a lesser degree and severity than the threat of wholesale extermination through starvation. He accomplishes such tests through the death of a loved one (especially the young), the collapse of a business enterprise, sickness and

---

[10] From the "Our Father" prayer.

disease, etc. The tests of this world would be almost exclusively applied to each one of us individually, instead of on a universal scale. Moreover, the people would recognize that such hardships were those God chose to lay upon us individually. Therefore, people would not be so ready to blame other people for their hardships in life, but would instead accept their suffering in a spirit of longanimity.

When God visits a universal punishment on the human race, such as a true famine, drought, or want of any material necessity; He does it to bring us back to the recognition of our departure from His will. Such hardships as true hunger and want of material necessities are His manner of "spanking" His disobedient children. The desired end of such "spankings" is not our suffering, but rather our return to His will.

HOMELESSNESS

In a Christian world, homelessness would be almost nonexistent. Due to the established economic order, there would be no lack of material means to purchase or rent a place to live. Remembering that homelessness is a result of mental incapacity, drug addiction, or laziness, the members of such a society would forcefully address the causes of the problem. The great majority of afflicted persons would be cared for by family members and neighbors; who would offer up any assistance they could, material or otherwise, to help their afflicted relations and neighbors. The conscientious sufferers of such impairments would do their very best to cooperate with sympathetic family members, while the family members and friends would bear up under the strain in a spirit of charity for their afflicted brother or sister. The people who are too burdensome to be cared for by families and friends, through no willful fault of their own, would be cared for in institutions that would be established to both care for their psychological, emotional, or spiritual disorders; while providing a roof over their head and a meal to eat. The intended ends of such institutions would be the rehabilitation of the afflicted persons to a point whereby they could be returned to their families; or, ideally, be brought to the point of being conscientious, self-sufficient human beings through the charity and compassion showed them by their caretakers.

Those who are found to be without shelter would be evaluated in order to determine the cause of their state. The drug-addicted would be committed to the care of rehabilitation clinics in which their ability to obtain addictive elements would be cut off and remediated; compelling them to sobriety. The willfully parasitic: those fully capable of caring for themselves, but being

315

too lazy to do so, would be treated as criminals; as they would be otherwise fully capable of supporting themselves but simply refused to do so due to a parasitic and indolent sentiment. The contempt for such creatures would arise from the understanding that all people must work their way through this life:

> [8]Neither did we eat any man's bread for nothing: but in labour and in toil we worked night and day, lest we should be chargeable to any of you. . . [10]For also, when we were with you, this we declared to you: that, *if any man will not work, neither let him eat.*[11]

It would be understood by all that those who refuse to work, but who are otherwise fully capable of doing so, are attempting to parasitically attach themselves to the means of the honestly productive. As a result, they would be allowed to suffer the consequences of their own indolence: either a deprivation of their needs or incarceration as a criminal. In this way, all causes of homelessness would be covered. The mentally incapacitated would be supported if the burden of their condition is too great for a family's resources; the drug-addicted would be deprived of their incapacitating drugs; and the petulant parasite would be incarcerated as a criminal.

DRUG ABUSE

In a Christian society, drug abuse would be almost nonexistent. The principal, motivating factor in drug abuse is a *dreadful fear* of reality: to manufacture an alternate reality to the one currently experienced by the drug abuser; in order to take them to a temporary, counterfeit perception devoid of the hardships of real life. In truth, such a disposition of escapism is a manifestation of moral cowardice. Members of a Christian society would more faithfully exercise the spirit of longanimity: suffering the particular hardships of their lives without recourse to a falsely manufactured "reality," in accordance with St. Paul's admonition: "For God hath not given us the spirit of fear: but of power, and of love, and of *sobriety.*"[12] In short, a Christian society would abhor drug abuse as an exercise in moral cowardice, and consequently despise it. It would be viewed as a sin as well as a personal disgrace.

---

[11] 2 Thessalonians 3:8, 10.
[12] 2 Timothy 1:7.

Because the purpose of Christianity is the fulfillment of God's will in this world, which naturally includes the propagation and support of human life, the abuse of drugs will be seen as an impediment to the proper fulfillment of the desired end; as drug abuse incapacitates the individual in their ability to achieve constructive work as well as destroying their health. The incapacitating and deadly effects of drug abuse will be understood by all, therefore there will be a desire among the population to eradicate the practice(s).

IMMIGRATION

In a Christian society, illegal immigration would not be tolerated. It would be understood that a nation is like a home to its people in the larger, social sense. Nations are established by peoples who share a common culture. From this perspective, illegal immigrants would be seen as home invaders: breaking into the people's house without permission. Such a society and culture would not tolerate infiltration by members of a culture foreign to their own; for such an infiltration would only tend to the pollution of the established, national culture. If a nation's neighbors also lived as a Christian culture there would be no desire to illegally migrate to other lands; for the members of the neighboring nation would realize the injustice of breaking in to their neighbor's house (country) illegitimately. Moreover, citizens of a neighboring nation living according to a Christian social order would not desire to leave it! If people desired to migrate to another nation for reasons of climate or some other reason, they would go through the legitimate channels of migration. Those who attempt to break into their neighbor's nation illegally would be summarily deported as criminals whenever and wherever they were found: seeing their criminal acts as contagions to the established culture that they have so dutifully worked to establish and build up; primarily because the very act of entering and living in a country illegally is *prima facie* evidence of a desire to infiltrate the effected nation for selfish ends, rather than a desire to embrace the culture of the nation they were breaking into.

In the case of legitimate migration, the principal, deciding factor would be the potential migrant's willingness to leave behind their current nation *and* culture. Would they embrace the culture of the nation in which they desire to live, or would they contrarily desire to export the foreign culture from which they are fleeing? This willingness to embrace a new culture is referred to as assimilation. Any applicant for migration would need to demonstrate a willingness, through both word and deed, to leave behind not only the land from which they wish to depart, but its culture as well: embracing the culture of their newly chosen home; so as not to disturb its cultural continuum.

It would be understood that those people who harbored or employed illegal immigrants were doing so for motives of economic gain. Because those who encouraged illegal immigration would be doing so as a means to invade the people's house, or as a means to exploit quasi-slave labor (due to their unlawful presence within the nation), the citizens of such a society would be disgusted by the potential employer's desire to exploit illegal immigrants through unjustly depressed wages or poor working conditions. The illegal immigrant would be deported to their native country, while the employer(s) who encouraged or hired them would be jailed as accessories to their criminal behavior.

Such a position would actually serve two beneficial ends. First, and most importantly, it would provide for the internal security of the nation. Secondarily, it would bring to light the corruption and injustice of the society from which the illegal immigrant was fleeing; for if the society from which the illegal immigrant fled was just and supportive of the laborer's needs, they would not be fleeing from the nation in pursuit of opportunities elsewhere.

HEALTH CARE

Within a Christian society, life in the material world would be seen as a brief, but admittedly very difficult and unpleasant, test of mankind's fidelity to God's will. The finite length of this world's sufferings would be weighed against the infinitely eternal happiness that is to follow this life's sadness and horrors. From this perspective, the breadth and length of human suffering would be seen as a mere blink of an eye when considered in relation to an infinite eternity of blessed happiness. Within such a worldview, the health of the citizen would be seen as a trifling consideration, because all within the society would understand the suffering nature of our existence in this world, as well as that everyone within the world would someday perish; some early in years, and others later, as determined by the will of God.

An early exit from this world (death in youth) would be seen as a grace from God, so that those who leave it at an early age would be more expediently taken up to Him; circumventing much of the horrors and sadness of this life. A later exit from this world would also be seen as a grace from God; allowing people more time to repent and do penance for their sins. Either way, whether a person expires in youth or old age, all things would be seen as working toward accomplishing God's plan. The ultimate consideration of the citizens within such a society would not be how long or how healthy their lives were, but rather the quality of the lives they lived with the time they had in this life:

In the end, it's not the years in your life that count. It's the life in your years.
— Abraham Lincoln, 16th President of the United States

The citizens would be living a life they believed was pleasing to God, or at the very least attempting to do so as much as their corrupted human nature would allow. While all of them would be sinners in the strictest sense of the word, they would find comfort in the fact that they held true to the recognition of Christian principles within their society: recognizing good and evil as taught by the Church, while opposing the evils of this world and promoting the good. Therefore, they would have no fear of death and eternal punishment. From a Christian perspective, death in this world is a blessing to be desired, *but not aided* (suicide): like a long-awaited parole following a lengthy prison sentence. Why would this life's trials be viewed as a prison sentence, especially as their birth into the world incurred no guilt on themselves? After all, they did nothing wrong by being born! While this is absolutely true, it would be understood to be a consequence of the "original sin" of Adam and Eve.

Consider the situation from the perspective of an inheritance. When parents die and distribute their wealth to their children, all the children are only so happy to take their fair share; and even more if they can cunningly contrive some method to cheat their siblings of their share (Jacob vs. Esau, for example). However, as in the case of Adam and Eve, if the parents had left their children with an insurmountable debt, the children would then be obligated to pay their parent's debt. From this perspective it would be understood that the human race, the children of Adam and Eve, would eternally incur a debt as a consequence of their parent's, and their own, disobedience to God; a debt they could never repay.

In the understanding of the all-too-unpleasant reality of the debt to be repaid, those living within a Christian society would see sickness and death in this world as a consequence of inherited, original sin. When routine sickness came, it would be viewed as both a trial to be endured with longanimity as part of the test of this world or as a penance to be paid for their sins. They would endure the suffering of sickness to the utmost of their ability; refraining from blaming any exterior force or organization for their condition. In the case of a routine cold or fever, they would simply "press on" in their lives; not running to medical providers every time they came down with a runny nose. They would consult with a physician only when it became evident that a particular ailment was more than routine. If the patient was materially impoverished (poor) they would appeal to the charity of their neighbors to care for their relations. If the patient was not poor they would simply pay for the services of the doctor and continue on in life. Either way, members of a Christian society would attribute all things to the will of God and leave the outcome to His discretion; with very little "second-guessing" regarding the final outcome.

When death came, they would naturally be affrighted by the prospect of passing over to an unknown eternity—as all people naturally fear that which they do not know or understand—but they would also feel great comfort in the hope of a happy eternity; having regularly received forgiveness for their sins via the Sacrament of Reconciliation (Confession), and being in a state of grace should the angel of death knock at their door unexpectedly. In this manner, death would be accepted as a necessary reality, and would likewise be accepted with a faithful resignation to the will of God; no matter at what age or condition in this world death chose to strike them. The citizens would view death as merely an end to their particular "test" of their faithfulness to God. After their release from this world, they would have high expectations of an eternal happiness!

It should also be noted that such a society would also be predominantly free of drug abuse, hunger, and homelessness. Consequently, the need for health care would be greatly reduced; as unhealthful living conditions and lifestyles would be greatly diminished.

ENVIRONMENTALISM

In a Christian world, everybody would be solicitous of environmental considerations. In the largest, temporal sense, Earth is the home of the human race. As such, it would be viewed in an analogous context to our individual homes. Natural resources would be seen as gifts from God; tools that have been made available for the use of the human race for the sustenance and benefit of mankind. Conservation and protection of natural resources would be the natural approach to any environmental concern; as such an approach would be demonstrative of keeping a clean and orderly home. The natural resources available to mankind would be managed so as to provide a sustainable environment for humanity; both for the currently living and for future generations. Humanity would see itself as contributors and participatory elements within the ecological system, rather than competitors; so as to provide for the best results for both humanity and nature. There would be no advocacy for the earth as an end in itself; only a desire to determine which means, out of several options under consideration, would best serve the needs of the human race while minimizing damage to the environment.

In all things that pertained to the earth and its environment, any potential change would be considered from the perspective of its ultimate utility to humanity versus its ultimate, foreseeably harmful effects: actions versus consequences. In the understanding that all natural things were originally created to satisfy the needs of the human race; mankind would both use them as they were needed to sustain the human race, while simultaneously avoiding any action that would tend to corrupt the environment and render the earth and its resources toxic or unusable.

CRIME

In a Christian world, crime would be rare; due primarily to the fear of God. As Christians understand crime to be a transgression of God's will and laws, they would arrange their criminal code according to the Christian moral code in order to (1) discourage sin, (2) provide a means to protect the citizenry from human predators, (3) forcefully punish criminals, and (4) discourage others from criminal acts. Because the criminal code would be constructed upon Christian morality, the people would have two reasons to avoid criminal activity. The most immediate reason would be a fear of humiliation and a potentially severe punishment at the hands of other men, but the most important reason would be a fear of God's eternal judgment should they commit a crime; especially serious and grave crimes such as theft, rape, murder, drug dealing, etc.

Having contrasted the approach to many social problems extant in the modern world between a humanistic perspective and that of a Christian perspective, the perversity and insanity of humanism is clearly seen when considered in comparison to its antithesis: a Christian social order. Clearly, the Christian world view promotes human life, prosperity, and happiness; while humanism causes dissipation, misery, and ultimately destroys life: "For the wages of sin is death."[13] In this present age it has become both

---

[13] From Romans 6:23.

common and socially acceptable to both murder our children (abortion) and ourselves; both individually (euthanasia and "assisted suicide") and socially (homosexuality, transgenderism, and licentiousness). If the entirety of the human species were to become homosexual or transgendered, our species would become extinct in less than a hundred years! If the entirety of the human species were to become heterosexually licentious, the propagation of narcissistically self-serving children would consume itself in hedonistic madness; as we are witnessing in our day!

All children created through licentious encounters, if they were not murdered via abortion, would be taught the rule of the dog by their narcissistic "parents": your own gratification first; all other things being subordinate! Such a humanistic paradigm is that which we are quickly creating for ourselves. Does the human race not comprehend the impending doom they are bringing down upon themselves!? Where is the understanding to have a vision of the ultimate consequences of our murderous actions!? Do people suppose that the homicidal narcissism that has impregnated the world will lead to anything good because it serves their own, immediate desires; void of any consideration of the ultimate, objectively real consequences?

Seeing both the individually and socially deadly consequences that accrue from humanism, the question must be asked, "Why is the human race choosing death over life"? The answer is found in the competing elements inherent within mankind's nature. Human beings are composed of two competing elements: the body vs. the spirit; the animal vs. the intellectual; the barbaric vs. the civilized. At the lowest, physical level human beings are animals. However, at a higher level, the other part of our selves is intellectual: the ability to evaluate the future consequences of our actions. Between the two capacities, the animalistic, sensual part of our nature is the easiest to indulge; because our most immediate and pressing stimuli are received through our physical senses, which make the greatest demands for our attention: hunger, thirst, *pleasure*, pain, etc. Contrarily, the intellectual component of our nature is exceedingly more difficult to indulge; because in most all instances it takes great mental efforts to contemplate the consequences of our actions. In so many innumerable ways, the ultimate consequences of our actions are inconceivable by the common man; for there are so many variables to consider when contemplating any action in our life, many of which are left unconsidered or forgotten due to a lack of either knowledge or life experience (ignorance).

Within the human mind, the battlefield is established in such a way between these two competing forces so that the animalistic, barbaric component enjoys an overwhelming advantage against the intellectual, civilized component. The concerns for the ultimate consequences of our actions will never make themselves known to the individual's intellect if people give up understanding them due to the urges of their senses. In the battle between the animalistic and barbaric versus the intellectual and civilized; the animalistic, barbaric nature always has the upper hand. What it takes to defeat our animalistic, barbaric impulses is a conscious act of will to defeat them; in the knowledge that if we submit to our animalistic, barbaric senses, the ultimate end of such a capitulation is a form of slavery to our sensual desires that only accrues to the ultimate destruction of human civilization(s). Why do we so easily capitulate to our animalistic, barbaric senses? The easily understood, albeit very sad, answer is that it is both easy and *fun*!

I am *all too familiar* with this battle. Before I could be bothered to listen to the intellectual, civilized component of my nature, I freely indulged my animalistic, barbaric nature in my younger years. What brought me to my senses, and that which will potentially bring many people to their senses, was a consideration of the actions taken in the immediate moment (urged on by our animalistic, barbaric nature) versus the future consequences of those actions. St. Paul once wrote, in consideration of his faults, "A faithful saying, and worthy of all acceptation, that Christ Jesus came into the world to save sinners, of whom I am the chief."[14] In his day, St. Paul was a man who was transformed from an insensible, barbaric persecutor of the Catholic Church to one who became its greatest expositor. The point to be made is that such a conversion can be obtained by all people if they would simply take a few moments, in a quiet place solicitous of contemplation—as far removed as humanly possible from the television and all other modern techno-toys (computer, iPad, smart phones, etc.)—to give ear to their intellectual, civilized self rather than perpetually listening to their animalistic, barbaric nature; which always compels human beings to foolish, selfish, and ultimately murderous, action(s): "There is a way that seemeth to a man right: and the ends thereof lead to death."[15]

Is this an easy thing to accomplish; suppressing our animal nature in deference to our spiritual and intellectual nature? Let me not sugar-coat the reality of the situation. The answer is not only no, but **hell no** (pardon the pun)! My dear brothers and sisters, this is the foundation upon which the

---

[14] 1 Timothy 1:15.
[15] Proverbs 16:25.

divinely ordained "test" of this world emanates from: the battle between our animalistic/barbaric selves and that of our spiritual/intellectual selves. Human history has demonstrated that living by God's laws has resulted in the greatest prosperity and happiness of the human race for those who chose to submit to them. Contrarily, people who have chosen to live by their barbaric, natural instincts have found themselves confounded and ultimately brought to ruin by their own barbaric insensibility (e.g., the Roman Empire)!

God has always offered us a choice. It is the same today as it was in the times of the ancients. Live by His laws or suffer the punishment of our own foolishness! As things stand today, we are suffering the punishment of our own foolishness, and it is only getting worse with each passing day. Are we to continue on this path to our own ruination? The choice lies within each of us! The modern masters of humanity work every nuance of division to maintain their hold on power over the human race: generational (old vs. young), racial (Black vs. White vs. Hispanic vs. [any other race convenient to the argument]), economic (rich vs. poor), etc. They demagogue the most convenient party in order to forward their own power; to the continued ruination of those they are supposedly "helping." Why are they so extraordinarily successful in their pursuit of pitting mankind against itself? The answer to this question lies in the horrific ignorance of the human race as it relates to the nature of evil. Too many people are being cajoled into a hatred of others who aren't like themselves because they are swallowing the absurd lie that evil lies in some dark corner far from themselves. My friends, *this is the height of insanity*! Evil exists within all of us to one degree or another: rich, poor, Black, White, Hispanic, young, old, etc. This is a self-evident truth that offers no exceptions to any human being. It matters not who you are.

The great problem of evil in this day, and why human civilizations are collapsing all around us, is due to the refusal of the great majority of the human race to recognize evil when it clearly manifests itself in the world; and most especially when evil manifests itself within ourselves. The cause of this grotesque blindness is human pride. It's always "somebody else" who is causing all our misery ("Big Oil," "Big Pharma," the "rich," etc.). However, when people are allowing themselves to be maneuvered into a position of hating others for any reason whatsoever, they are—whether willingly or unwittingly—turning the corner down a road that facilitates their own descent into becoming evil creatures themselves; for hatred of one's fellow man is one of the *greatest* evils in this world; secondary only to the hatred of God.

Hatred lays the foundation for practically all other evils in the world to flourish. It is the foundation and sustenance for evil actions that debase and corrupt the human race. Hatred of the old causes the young to neglect their duty to the old. Hatred of the young causes the old to abandon the young to the folly of youth. Racial hatred causes a member of one race to despise and actively seek the harm of members of other races. Hatred of the rich causes the poor to actively seek to harm those who create the wealth that pays their wages, as meager as they may be; so that destroying the economically productive will only cause the poor to go from possessing very little to possessing nothing at all! Hatred of the rich disgraces the dignity of being a productive human being and feeds into the hands of those who actively seek to foment hatred among the poor in order to feed their own self-serving ambitions.

Brothers and sisters, if we are to overcome the overwhelming social chaos and anarchy that is quickly descending on us we must first and foremost seek to stem the evil that lies within each of us. Stop looking for the "boogey man" that lies just around the corner and is ever-threatening within our imaginations. The ambitious and self-serving people of this world (politicians, social activists, lawyers, etc.) are those who are promoting hatred, and they are doing it to forward their own selfish ends; for power, money, adulation, or whatever base and criminal purpose drives their evil hearts. When these creatures stand before the public and state that it's [so and so's] fault that you don't have what your heart desires, or even needs, they are only trying to enlist you in their own personal army of self-promotion and self-glorification. When their demagoguery and vitriol inspires an audience to hatred—and even worse, acts of destruction and violence that naturally follow as a consequence of hatred—they have succeeded in turning those who fall prey to their evil machinations into the "boogey man" that the sadly manipulated person believes themselves to be combating! This turn of events is extraordinarily sublime and subtle in both its operation and consequences; turning a human being into an evil creature, while simultaneously making them believe that they are a "soldier of righteousness."

These very same demagogues among us will make the charge that I am engaging in demagoguery by speaking out against their evil manipulations. Therefore, I am engaging in the same activity I pretend to castigate. This is absolutely false, but let me explain the critical distinction. I am counseling against hating the modern manipulators of the human race. Instead of hating them I am, with all my heart, counseling the human race to instead take another course of action: pity them because they are animated by debased, reprobated minds; but at the same time they must be absolutely, and completely, ignored! Treat them as the pariah that they are! When someone foments hate and discontent against anybody they should be absolutely shunned. This requires people to be able to recognize true hatred.

As previously discussed, hatred is a desire that compels the person who hates to place their own self-interest in a position of relative importance that is superior to the well-being of others; and it manifests itself in a willingness to sacrifice another for one's selfish interests. Ultimately, such a depraved attitude always works toward the dissolution of human civilization(s): abortion, sexual deviancy (homosexuality, transgenderism, licentiousness, pedophilia, etc.), feminism, drug addiction, etc. These evil proclivities (the pursuit of singular self-interest: narcissism), which are all too natural to our animal/barbaric nature, prod us to look to our own selfish interests and gain; many times, at someone else's expense. These proclivities are the essence and foundation of what is theologically referred to as "original sin," and ultimately lead to the corruption of both individuals and societies. To overcome our naturally sensual, evil tendencies we must instead ask ourselves, "Will [this or that] action or attitude actually cultivate and support society or will it be harmful"? Only by actively trying to understand the "bigger picture" regarding the consequences of our actions—not only on our own situation, but upon the larger social body—will we be able to discern the beneficence or maleficence of any particular act or belief.

All our actions must be measured against the weight of their consequences. As things stand today, the prevailing attitude among the human race is predominantly one of an almost pure narcissism: "It's good, if it's good for me"! Such unabashed selfishness will only lead to suicide as a civilization, and it truly marks the descent of the human race into a culture of self-hating barbarism.

The attempt has been made to clearly explain the evidences in reason for why Catholicism is the one, true Faith of the human race. Moreover, the fortifying consequences to human civilization that will be derived by living a life according to Christian moral principles (faith, patriarchy, sexual morality, and sobriety) have been chronicled; and contrarily, the great self-destructiveness of opposing Christian moral principles (atheism, feminism, promiscuity, contraception, sexual deviancy, and drug abuse). The great question yet to be answered is, "Will the human race continue in their descent into abject barbarism, or will they instead come to their senses and return their civilization to a state that follows a healthy moral order; promoting the good and condemning the evil"? At this point in human history we still possess the power to choose our own fate. What will it be?

Behold, I stand at the gate, and knock. If any man shall hear
my voice, and open to me the door, I will come in to him,
and will sup with him, and he with me.[16]

The choice is still ours to make. God *will not* abrogate our free will. We
must either choose His way, or reject it. As He promised, He is standing
at the gate and knocking. Will we answer and admit Him, or refuse Him.
Either way, it is completely our choice; both individually and as a larger
society. In this battle of choices that we face, it is necessary to clarify my
rebuke of the destructive behavior that is grinding down humanity. All of
the barbaric attitudes and behaviors being condemned, due to their inherent
destructiveness, are just that: attitudes and behaviors. No *person* who engages
in evil practices is being castigated here; because those who submit to barbaric
practices do so predominantly because of a lack of understanding, simple
human weakness, or a psychological framework that has been reprobated by
modern, popular culture; which is rapidly inducing a suicidal mentality into
the human race. Moreover, I do not pretend to be a model of perfection.
Having my eyes opened—through the grace of Jesus Christ alone, via the
intercession of His Mother, the Blessed Virgin Mary—to the evils of the
world, and how they are dragging it to a sad and painful death; I still succumb
to many imperfections. Let not the reader believe that I think of myself as
being better or more morally perfect than any other person.

No sane person runs to the gallows crying, "Last one there's a rotten
egg"! Those poor souls seduced by the innumerable evils of this world
are victimized by a reprobated understanding. To the strident feminist,
homosexual, abortionist, socialist, the promiscuous, and all others who
despise Christian morality; the message conveyed here is one of, "Despise
the sin, not the sinner." This is a hard thing to hear, but it must be said. If
you despise God and morality, you do so because your mind has been turned
from understanding, and consequently doing, what is right and good to
what is evil and purely narcissistic because you have given your animalistic,
barbaric nature the victory over your spiritual, intellectual selves due to the
corrupting influences of your physical senses and the desires that naturally
arise from the unrestrained indulgence of the senses.

Before we leave this discussion, please consider a crucial point of
understanding that supersedes spiritual and religious considerations. Let
us consider for a moment, although the premise is certainly false, that there

---

[16] Apocalypse 3:20.

was no God; as the atheists and humanists try to forcefully insinuate in every corner. Even if this were the case, it would in no way change the reality of the consequences to accrue from ordering our lives upon either the barbaric, atheistic, humanistic paradigm or the Christian, intellectual, civilized paradigm.

If God was not, it would still promote human life and the health and happiness of human civilization(s) to circumscribe sexuality exclusively within the bond of heterosexual marriage for the express purpose of the propagation of the human race; because in this way children would either not be murdered through abortion or would not be brought into the world as unwanted consequences of promiscuous encounters; eradicating the emotional harm to children caused by being considered a burden to be suffered rather than a source of happiness to be loved and cherished. Additionally, sexually transmitted diseases propagated through libertine sexuality would be completely eliminated. If God was not, homosexuality and transgenderism would still promote death to both the individual and society; as these poor creatures are unable, through their own choice, to give life to new children who would then propagate the human race. They would still actively spread the sexually transmitted diseases common to homosexuals (primarily AIDS, herpes, genital warts, etc.). In the absence of God, it would still promote human life and peace among the human race to seek economic proximity between one another so as to undercut sentiments of materialistic envy and jealousy.

Christian morality would still promote human life and peace if we were able to ignore racial differences among us and look to the character of the individual rather than the color of their skin. Even without God, it would still promote human life and peace among the human race to discourage drug abuse; so that the members of society would not dissolute themselves, and their society as a whole, as a consequence of their failings. If God was not, it would still promote human life and peace among the human race if people accepted their personal health concerns with moral courage, even unto death, rather than clamoring for other's wallets to alleviate themselves from a situation that other human beings are not responsible for creating. And finally, if there was no God it would still promote human life and peace among the human race if the human predators in our midst were harshly punished; thereby removing the evil(s) from among us and discouraging predation from those who may be inclined to such behavior. It is my greatest desire that the reader(s) would understand, and indeed accept, the consequences of objective reality. If there was no God, living by Christian moral principles would still be the greatest road to the fortification of humanity, both individually and socially, as admittedly hard as it may be to live by many of the principles of Christian morality.

Hopefully, it has become clearly evident to the readers that the Christian social and moral order is, in every way, conducive and supportive of humanity; while the atheistic, humanistic social and immoral order is ultimately destructive to humanity, and that *this would be the case regardless of whether God did or did not exist!*

If we choose to give the victory in this battle within us (animalistic, barbaric vs. intellectual, civilized), by a conscious act of will, to our natural desire for pleasures and comforts, or from an aversion to discomfort or suffering, we will only lead ourselves into a dissolute life that will eventually—and sooner, rather than later—lead to ruination as a civilization. Are we mere animals foraging for our existence, or are we something more!? The atheist insists that we are nothing more than a higher level of animal due to our greater intelligence as a species in relation to other animals. The atheist's whole argument rests on this place. However, God, and objective reality (for those who refuse to believe in Him), declares contrarily.

The denial of the reality of God is nothing more than an exercise in self-hating insanity. He has proved His existence through the works of infallible prophecies and supernatural miracles throughout all ages—including the raising of the dead and other extraordinary examples that have left behind objective, physical proofs as evidence—to demonstrate the *certain* reality of His existence. Denying the infallible prophecies of the Bible and the supernatural manifestations of the world is comparable in insanity to the hypothetical situation previously mentioned; where a person denies that another is holding a pencil in front of their face simply because they don't like the nature of reality and all the unpleasant consequences that accompany it.

In conclusion, let that which is objectively real be reaffirmed . . . *GOD IS!* The human race will either choose to live by His laws, or continue to deny Him and simply exist under the influences of their insensible nature; to their ultimate ruination, both individually and socially. The choice lies before all of us. However, one thing must be known with certainty. If the human race continues to live under the influences of their insensible, barbaric nature, they will have *no right* to complain regarding the horrible punishment that will follow as a result, both in this world and in the next; *all* of it being self-imposed.

The Consequences of Our Choice

The beneficent consequence of choosing the Christian paradigm would be the continual propagation of the human race in peace, prosperity, and admittedly limited happiness, until the end of time. Our loved ones would still die and leave us bereft for the loss. Business ventures would still fail. All manner of calamities would still beset us on a personal level. Our health would still fail at some point in our lives; as we all pass from this world regardless of age, wealth, or any other factor. In short, suffering from one source or another would be our common lot. However, we would share a common understanding that would make our personal sufferings much more tolerable. We would understand that this life is replete with loss and disappointment for all people. In this way, we wouldn't begrudge another's good fortune; for we would see it as a happy intermission from this world's disappointments. On the other hand, we would see our misfortunes as burdens to be borne with quiet fortitude; for we would understand that practically all people experience misfortune in their lives.

The misfortunes and hardships we experience in our lives would be things personal to us. We would not wish to share our difficulties with others for two reasons. Primarily, because we would understand that complaining about our sorrows to others will not magically mitigate them. Secondarily, we would understand that all people would be facing their own trials in life. As a matter of justice, we would not wish to burden others with our problems because we would not wish to be burdened with theirs. The way of life that Christian morality leads to is one of fortitude in suffering. Charity would be seen as a win-win virtue. By coming to the aid of our needy brothers and sisters, we would more easily forget our own sufferings; thereby giving aid to those who need it more than ourselves while simultaneously mitigating the self-destructive sentiments of self-pity. In such a way, human civilization would perpetuate itself with the greatest degree of happiness and prosperity achievable; even in consideration of the failings of human nature.

Now . . . the hard part. What will be the consequences if we continue to live by our animalistic, barbaric nature and senses? The world has already begun to witness the consequences of barbarism; as licentiousness, abortion, homosexuality, and transgenderism are commonly practiced, with a large percentage of the population accepting these deadly behaviors as socially tolerable practices. However, as bad as they already are, they will become much worse. The cultural battles being waged in the modern world, once again, can ultimately be distilled down to two camps from which the battles are waged: atheistic humanism (most commonly referred to as "liberalism") vs. Christianity (Catholicism and Protestantism). The atheistically humanist "liberal" believes in the moral autonomy of the individual. From this perspective they believe that there is no such thing as absolute morality and absolute truth. What this automatically implies is that morality is subjective. Operating from this premise, the natural argument to follow is that nobody can criticize any other person's behavior; because if morality is subjective there is no moral authority from which anybody could rebuke another for their behavior. The argument runs along the lines of, "What makes you think your morality is better than mine? You're being judgmental. Who do you think you are trying to impose your morality on me"!?

How and why will this progress into a much more barbaric, and ultimately murderous, society? The answer lies in the understanding of the concept of evil from the perspective of the civilized Christian vs. that of the barbaric humanist. While the Christian views evil, from a practical perspective, as anything that ultimately threatens human life and civil society, the barbaric humanist views evil as anything that offends their sensibilities. Moreover, anyone who disturbs the humanist's conscience for any reason whatsoever is considered by them to be an evil person attempting (from their perverted perspective) to disturb society as a whole: people to be punished and eradicated from society; as they view their barbaric understanding of civilization as a society ordered around the satisfaction of their desires rather than an attempt to propagate, strengthen, and fortify the society itself.

While the civilized Christian rebukes the reprobate due to the harm they are causing to both themselves and the larger society as a whole, in an attempt to impede the harm, the barbaric atheist/humanist decries the rebuke(s) because the nature of a rebuke is hurtful to their feelings. The essence and entirety of the battle can be reduced to the struggle between life and death. The civilized Christian cries out, "Stop! You're murdering yourselves and our society, as evidenced by the deadly consequences of your behavior"! In opposition to the voices of sanity who decry the horrors the human race is bringing upon itself, the barbaric atheist/humanist cries out, "Stop! You're hurting our feelings and spoiling our fun"! In relation to the importance of the struggle, it can be seen that the concerns of the civilized Christian are for the sustenance and propagation of the human race and civilized society, while the concerns of the barbaric atheist/humanist are for their injured pride.

In today's world this can be most clearly seen in the arguments of homosexuals who liken their cause with the civil rights efforts of Blacks in the 1960's. Whereas the color of one's skin has no intrinsic effect on one's character or their personal ability to exercise virtue and sustain and fortify the human race, homosexuality—and all other manifestations of sexual deviancy; including heterosexual licentiousness (promiscuity)—can be seen to be intrinsically deadly to the human race and human civilization(s). However, the militant homosexual seizes on the sentiments of victimization and hurt feelings that are common between the two situations, while ignoring what is truly important: the unjust nature of opposing someone due to a factor that is intrinsically benign (skin color) vs. the just nature of opposing someone due to the suicidal and homicidal nature of their behavior. Being self-deceived, or willfully deceitful, regarding the deadly consequences of their actions, due to their capitulation to sensual desires, they then agitate for the punishment of those who oppose their dissolute behavior.

There are two excellent examples, which relate to the homosexual disorder, that serve to demonstrate the depths of depravity and insanity that have followed as a result of mankind's capitulation to their sensual nature. The first is an editorial, attributed to Michael Swift (most likely a pseudonym), that appeared in the February 15-21, 1987, edition of *Gay Community News*. The second is a book written by two homosexual activists (Hunter Madsen and Marshall Kirk) in 1989, entitled *After the Ball*. It was written as a guide in psychological warfare, clearly explains itself as such, and has been used as a primary tactical and strategic guide to forwarding the acceptance and tolerance of homosexuality since its publication. Each will be addressed in their turn. Let's first look at Mr. Swift's editorial. It reads as follows:

> This essay is an outré, madness, a tragic, cruel fantasy, an eruption of inner rage, on how the oppressed desperately dream of being the oppressor.

> We shall sodomize your sons, emblems of your feeble masculinity, of your shallow dreams and vulgar lies. We shall seduce them in your schools, in your dormitories, in your gymnasiums, in your locker rooms, in your sports arenas, **in your seminaries,**[1] in your youth groups, in your movie theater bathrooms, **in your army bunkhouses,**[2] in your truck stops, in your all male clubs, **in your houses of**

---

[1] The corruption of the Priesthood by homosexual infiltrators.
[2] The repeal of the "don't ask, don't tell" policy regarding homosexuals within the military.

Congress,[3] wherever men are with men together. Your sons shall become our minions and do our bidding. They will be recast in our image. They will come to crave and adore us.

Women, you cry for freedom. You say you are no longer satisfied with men; they make you unhappy. We, connoisseurs of the masculine face, the masculine physique, shall take your men from you then. We will amuse them; we will instruct them; we will embrace them when they weep. Women, you say you wish to live with each other instead of with men. Then go and be with each other. We shall give your men pleasures they have never known because we are foremost men too, and only one man knows how to truly please another man; only one man can understand the depth and feeling, the mind and body of another man.

All laws banning homosexual activity will be revoked. Instead, legislation shall be passed which engenders love between men.

All homosexuals must stand together as brothers; we must be united artistically, philosophically, socially, politically and financially. We will triumph only when we present a common face to the vicious heterosexual enemy.

If you dare to cry faggot, fairy, queer, at us, we will stab you in your cowardly hearts and defile your dead, puny bodies.

We shall write poems of the love between men; we shall stage plays in which man openly caresses man; we shall make films[4] about the love between heroic men which will replace the cheap, superficial, sentimental, insipid, juvenile, heterosexual infatuations presently dominating your cinema screens. We shall sculpt statues of beautiful young men, of bold athletes which will be placed in your parks, your

---

[3] Governmental authority: James McGreevey, former Governor of New Jersey; Kevin Jennings, President Barack Obama's "safe schools czar", etc.

[4] *Brokeback Mountain*, for example.

squares, your plazas. The museums of the world will be filled only with paintings of graceful, naked lads.

Our writers and artists will make love between men fashionable and de riguer, and we will succeed because we are adept at setting styles. We will eliminate heterosexual liaisons through usage of the devices of wit and ridicule, devices which we are skilled in employing.

We will unmask the powerful homosexuals who masquerade as heterosexuals. You will be shocked and frightened when you find that your presidents and their sons, your industrialists, **your senators, your mayors**, your generals, your athletes, your **film stars, your television personalities**, your civic leaders, **your priests** are not the safe, familiar, bourgeois, heterosexual figures you assumed them to be. We are everywhere; we have infiltrated your ranks. Be careful when you speak of homosexuals because we are always among you; we may be sitting across the desk from you; we may be sleeping in the same bed with you.

There will be no compromises. We are not middle-class weaklings. Highly intelligent, we are the natural aristocrats of the human race, and steely-minded aristocrats never settle for less. Those who oppose us will be exiled.

We shall raise vast private armies, as Mishima[5] did, to defeat you. We shall conquer the world because warriors inspired by and banded together by homosexual love and honor are invincible as were the ancient Greek soldiers.

The family unit-spawning ground of lies, betrayals, mediocrity, hypocrisy and violence—will be abolished.

---

[5] Yukio Mishima: Japanese homosexual militant. On November 25, 1970, he and four other men (part of his private militia) kidnapped and seized the office of a Tokyo army general. He demanded to speak to the troops, where he called on them to demand a revision to the postwar constitution that forbade a meaningful standing army. Afterward, he returned to the general's office and committed ritual suicide.

The family unit, which only dampens imagination and curbs free will, must be eliminated. Perfect boys will be conceived and grown in the genetic laboratory. They will be bonded together in communal setting, under the control and instruction of homosexual savants.

All churches who condemn us will be closed. Our only gods are handsome young men. We adhere to a cult of beauty, moral and esthetic. All that is ugly and vulgar and banal will be annihilated. Since we are alienated from middle-class heterosexual conventions, we are free to live our lives according to the dictates of the pure imagination. **For us too much is not enough.**

The exquisite society to emerge will be governed by an elite comprised of gay poets. One of the major requirements for a position of power in the new society of homoeroticism will be indulgence in the Greek passion. Any man contaminated with heterosexual lust will be automatically barred from a position of influence. All males who insist on remaining stupidly heterosexual will be tried in homosexual courts of justice and will become invisible men.

We shall rewrite history, history filled and debased with your heterosexual lies and distortions. We shall portray the homosexuality of the great leaders and thinkers who have shaped the world. We will demonstrate that homosexuality and intelligence and imagination are inextricably linked, and that homosexuality is a requirement for true nobility, true beauty in a man.

We shall be victorious because we are fueled with the ferocious bitterness of the oppressed who have been forced to play seemingly bit parts in your dumb, heterosexual shows throughout the ages. We too are capable of firing guns and manning the barricades of the ultimate revolution.

Tremble, hetero swine, when we appear before you without our masks.

The most important thing to be noted from this editorial is both the admission (in the opening sentence) from its author(s) that their aims, goals, and desires are "madness, a tragic, cruel fantasy"; while witnessing the accomplishment of this insane, tragic, and cruel fantasy in the modern world. They have succeeded in sodomizing our culture in "army bunkhouses" via the repeal of the "don't ask, don't tell" policy in the military and "in your houses of Congress" via their militant attempts to criminalize those who speak out against the dangers of homosexuality as "hate crimes": "All laws banning homosexual activity will be revoked. Instead, legislation shall be passed which engenders love between men." As promised, "Our writers and artists will make love between men fashionable and de rigueur, and we will succeed because we are adept at setting styles." This insane fantasy is becoming reality in both television and movies. The corruption of the priesthood by homosexual infiltrators has also, sadly come to pass. They promise "no compromises," and that "Those who oppose us will be exiled." How do they propose to accomplish their ends? "We shall raise vast private armies. . ."

In the full understanding that homosexuality cannot propagate itself, due to its inherently self-destructive nature, they propose to propagate their destructive cause as follows: "Perfect boys will be conceived and grown in the genetic laboratory." In short, boys will be created to gratify the sensual desires of the homosexual and propagate profligate sensuality "under the control and instruction of homosexual savants." They freely admit, "For us too much is not enough," and that those who oppose them will be barred from positions of influence and will be tried in courts of law; again, via "hate crimes" legislation. They promise victory for their cause "because we are fueled with . . .*ferocious bitterness* . . ."

As the reader witnesses the encroaching accomplishment of the stated goals in the modern world, it must be noted that such events can only be accomplished due to the complicity of the society; either due to its tacit acceptance of the insanity or due to its apathy as the evils encircle it.

> All that is necessary for the triumph of evil is for good men to do nothing.
> — Edmund Burke, 18th Century British statesman and philosopher

Why would a society allow such deadly evils to dissolute itself? The answer to this question takes us to an examination of *After the Ball*. This book was, and is, quite extraordinary for many reasons; the greatest of which is its insane internal self-contradiction. It demonstrates stunning and brutal honesty regarding the depravity and dangers related to homosexuality, while at the same time presenting itself as a work intentionally designed as a handbook in psychological warfare intended to promote the acceptance of behavior the authors readily acknowledge as dangerous and destructive. The important thing to note from this book are the author's glaring admissions regarding the inadequacy and emptiness that homosexuality leads to, while at the same time trying to promote that which they themselves castigate as harmful! Let's first look at the open admission by the author(s) of the emptiness, depravity, and dangers of homosexuality:

> Alas, it turns out that, on this point, public myth is supported by fact. There *is* more promiscuity among gays (or at least among gay men) than among straights . . .[6]

> Straights hate gays not just for what their myths and lies *say* we are, but also for what we *really* are . . . And as it happens, our noses (and other parts) are far from clean. In one major respect, America's homohaters have, like the proverbial blind pig, rooted up the truffle of truth: the lifestyle—not our sexuality, but our *lifestyle*—is the pits.[7]

> Thus, many apparent devotees of impersonal sex are no such thing: rather, they are further victims of a gay lifestyle that just doesn't work.[8]

> As with so many maladaptive ways of administering quick, symptomatic fixes to deep-seated social maladies, gay dependence on pills and liquor ultimately makes the problem far worse.[9]

---

[6] Marshall Kirk and Hunter Madsen, *After the Ball: How America Will Conquer its Fear and Hatred of Gays in the '90s* (New York, NY: Doubleday, a division of Bantam Dell Doubleday Publishing Group, Inc.), 47.
[7] Ibid., 276.
[8] Ibid., 325.
[9] Ibid., 337.

Acting as pied pipers of radicalism, they take us all to blind
extremes in rejecting the values of morality and family
structure, leaving us with no values or community structure
to replace these, and taking us with them into the complete
void of individual isolation and communal amorality. They
know how to tear down, but not how to rebuild.[10]

We are reminded of Robert Reinhart's gruesome *Christopher
Street* piece ("Solos: A Suite") about the seventy-year-old
dying in the hospital, who, at this supremely critical juncture,
can offer no more uplifting subject for conversation than
a laundry list of all the penises he's fellated in his long,
action-packed life. His awe-inspiring vacuity seems, in
a way, the natural conclusion of the gay life cycle, and a
horrible warning to us all.[11]

In short, the gay lifestyle—if such a chaos can, after all,
legitimately be *called* a lifestyle—just doesn't work: it doesn't
serve the two functions for which all social frameworks
evolve: to constrain people's natural impulses to behave
badly and to meet their natural needs.[12]

Being very forthright regarding the self-destructive ends of homosexuality,
and obviously in full knowledge of its dangers, the authors persevere
in proposing a plan of psychological warfare in order to promote social
acceptance, and indeed ascendancy, of the very same behavior they freely,
and openly, acknowledge "just doesn't work." They propose the following as
the desired ends of their campaign of psychological warfare:

We want straights to revoke all laws criminalizing sex acts
between consenting adults, as the abhorrently arrogant and
invasive barbarisms they are; no legal double standard in
the content or application of such laws must be permitted.
We want straights to provide for us, by special legislation
and affirmative action if need be, the same rights to

---

[10] Ibid., 351.
[11] Ibid., 364.
[12] Ibid., 363.

public speech and assembly, to work, shelter, and public accommodations, to legal marriage and parenthood, that straights enjoy. What is sauce for the straight gander must be sauce for the gay goose.[13]

Their desired end is no less than the acceptance and promotion of homosexuality within society, even to the point of a form of homosexual "affirmative action." Having clearly explained their goals, which include special legal promotion of their self-admittedly self-destructive behavior, they also went into great detail regarding how the psychological warfare campaign is to be waged. The most important thing to note in their tactical plan is that they promote the obfuscation of reality by making their appeals on a purely emotional level (affective reasoning, as opposed to cognitive reasoning); instructing the expositors of homosexuality to avoid the discussion of reality or consequences; focusing exclusively on psychological manipulation; primarily via emotional appeals:

> As cynical as it may seem, AIDS gives us a chance, however brief, to establish ourselves as a victimized minority legitimately deserving of America's special protection and care.[14]

> The campaign we outline in this book, though complex, depends centrally upon a program of unabashed propaganda, firmly grounded in long-established principles of psychology and advertising.[15]

> Where the target of an emotional appeal is aware of the attempt at manipulation, he will tend to resist it; where he is distracted from the true nature of the appeal by a 'cover argument,' the emotional effect, paradoxically, will be all the greater. Thus, an argument can function as a distractor.[16]

---

[13] Ibid., 380.
[14] Ibid., xxv.
[15] Ibid., xxvi.
[16] Ibid., 138.

When you're very different . . . this is what you do: *first* you get your foot in the door, by being as *similar* as possible; then, and only then—when your one little difference is finally accepted—can you start dragging in your other peculiarities, one by one. **You hammer in the wedge narrow end first**. As the saying goes, Allow the camel's nose beneath your tent, and his whole body will soon follow.[17]

We can extract the following principle for our campaign: to desensitize straights to gays and gayness, inundate them in a continuous flood of gay-related advertising, presented in the least offensive fashion possible. If straights can't shut off the shower, they may at least eventually get used to being wet.[18]

Rather, *our effect is achieved without reference to facts, logic, or proof*. . . Indeed, the more he is distracted by any incidental, even specious, surface arguments, the less conscious he'll be of the true nature of the process—which is all to the good.[19]

First, propaganda relies more upon emotional manipulation than upon logic, since its goal is, in fact, to bring about a change in the public's feelings.[20]

We mean 'subverting' the mechanism of prejudice to our own ends—using the very process that made America hate us to turn their hatred into warm regard—*whether they like it or not*.[21]

Once again, it's very difficult for the average person, who, by nature and training, almost invariably feels what he sees his fellows feeling, not to respond in this knee-jerk fashion to a sufficiently calculated advertisement. In a way, most

---

[17] Ibid., 146.
[18] Ibid., 149. The application of the old axiom, "If you can't beat'em, join'em."
[19] Ibid., 152-153. Bold italics added.
[20] Ibid., 162.
[21] Ibid., 153-154. Bold italics added.

advertisement is founded upon an answer of Yes, definitely! to Mother's sarcastic question: I suppose if all the other kids jumped off a bridge and killed themselves, you would, too?[22]

For example, in the average American household, the TV screen radiates its embracing bluish glow for more than fifty hours every week, bringing films, sitcoms, talk shows, and news reports right into the living room. These hours are a gateway into the private world of straights, *through which a Trojan horse might be passed.*[23]

Finally, the answer to the question, "Why would a society allow such deadly evils to suicidally dissolute itself"?, has its answer in a campaign of extraordinarily subtle psychological warfare waged on an unwitting populace. In truth, the horrific answer is that the human race is participating in its own self-destruction as a consequence of indulging its debasing proclivities: refusing to give up licentiousness and submitting to the self-destructiveness of their animal nature. The whole of humanity is quickly accepting all forms of social suicide, especially sexual deviancy, as tolerable; because they do not wish to be rebuked for their own self-destructive behaviors: feminism, unrestrained licentiousness ("shacking up," "hooking up" and abortion on demand to "take care of" the products of their sexual immorality and lack of self-control), contraception, drug abuse, predatory criminality, etc.

To be fair to the homosexual, they are neither the primary, nor singular, cause of the self-destruction of the human race. Rather, they are merely one of the many grave symptoms of multiple, degenerative social diseases. The only reason it was possible to devote a few pages to the intentional psychological warfare campaign being waged against the human race by homosexual activists is due to the existence of a work dedicated to dissoluting humanity. Heterosexual licentiousness, its natural byproduct (abortion), drug abuse, and all other forms of "communal amorality" are equally to blame. The only difference is that drug addicts and the licentious have not penned a work dedicated to the division and destruction of human civilization(s) in order to forward their own self-destructively perverse and suicidal ends.

Before we leave this topic I would like to clearly state my position regarding homosexuals: the people, not the behavior. While the acts of homosexuality

---

[22] Ibid., 155-156.
[23] Ibid., 179. Bold italics added.

are always and everywhere evil, I in no way assert that all homosexuals are purposefully evil people. In practically all respects homosexuality is no different than any other psychological or emotional illness; comparable to addiction in the way it controls those who have succumbed to it. Moreover, it is not constructive to vilify the homosexual for suffering from an affliction that corrupts both mind and body. We all have numerous faults and imperfections (myself included), and there are a great many people who succumb to their human weaknesses on a daily basis.

This difficult reality applies to the homosexual as well. Each person is different. Various individuals are afflicted to different degrees and view their situation from different vantage points. There are two keys that separate the homosexual that realizes their affliction from the militant homosexual: sanity and shame. The dangers of homosexuality to both the individual and to society have already been discussed, and everybody *should* be fully aware of them. Like addicts who understand the dangerous situation they are in, those homosexuals who have retained a connection with reality and sanity understand the dangers and evils of homosexuality, feel varying degrees of shame regarding their illness, and desire to be free of it.

Contrarily, like the addict who denies they have a problem, the militant homosexual is an insanely delusional creature who has willfully lost any psychological connection with reality. Willfully disregarding the dangerous and evil consequences of their behavior, which objective reality displays for all to see (AIDS, other sexually transmitted diseases, drug addiction, etc.), they are absolutely unashamed of their self-destructive behavior; demonstrated by not only the destruction of themselves, but by their demands that the rest of society condone and even celebrate their dangerous and evil behavior. Because the scourge of homosexuality works through the same mechanisms as addiction, allow me to ask a question of the reader. When militant homosexuals attempt to force their sickness on society, especially as they are focusing much effort in promoting their illness through propaganda campaigns within the public school systems via numerous legislative efforts disguised under the pretext of "anti-bullying" measures, how is this any different than the drug dealer who hangs out at the local elementary school offering free samples of their product? Both are promoting corruption, a life of addiction and despair, and ultimately an untimely death in many sad and unfortunate circumstances.

Understanding the great variance in the homosexual community, from those who maintain a grasp on reality to those who are so criminally insane that they constantly work to promote their grave corruption, another question must be posed to the reader. As there is a great deal of effort to assist those addicted to drugs (interventions, half-way houses and treatment centers), why, as a society, is there not a commensurate level of diligence to assist those who suffer from the dangerous affliction of homosexuality? Moreover, why, as a society, do we tolerate militant homosexuals who try to propagate their corruption when we won't tolerate drug dealers trying to "hook" our children on drugs? While some deserve help and consolation, others deserve punishment and condemnation.

If the current dissolution of the human race remains unchecked, those who unapologetically promote the Christian moral order will be viewed as disruptive elements to the newly established, barbaric social order of unrestrained sensuality; to be discouraged and persecuted at every turn. This turn of events will not happen naturally, but will be forcefully promulgated by the reprobates, as St. Paul prophesied: "But evil men and seducers shall grow worse and worse: erring, and *driving* into error."[24] The only, and natural, consequence of such a society will be the attempted, forcible destruction of Christianity; which has already begun via legal machinations, and will conclude with the heretofore unimaginable, torturously atrocious murder of innumerable martyrs. The precursor to these events, which should be seen as an example of things to come if the human race continues on its suicidal path of social dissipation due to the indulgence of its sensual instincts, was the universal criminality and horrors of communism, which the human race was explicitly warned of during the Fátima apparitions.

Because atheists fear no judgment from God, they will view their actions as irreproachable once they gain the ascent of the population; which will at first be acquired willfully, then later through fear; induced by the terroristic persecution of the Church (and any others who resist them) that is to come. Ultimately, almost all men will be pitted against one another; and the reigning confusion regarding how humanity had reached such a debased level will not allow for a correction of the insanity; because when the situation comes to this point the reprobates will be in full control of *all* governmental infrastructure: the police, the military, local and national governmental bodies, etc. Atheistic, humanistic "liberalism" will be the ascendant power in that day, and any brave enough to murmur the least reproach against it will be punished as harshly as the Christians. Witnessing the horrors and depravity of their militantly atheistic masters, the great majority of the population will be cowed into submission.

---

[24] 2 Timothy 3:13.

Concluding Remarks

The reader(s) must not be lied to regarding the reality of a social order built upon Christian morality. Our lives would still be full of dead-ends and disappointments due to the many failings of human nature. However, these failings and disappointments would only serve to fill us up with disgust for this life, while at the same time increasing our hopes and desires for the one to come. And in the case of those who refuse to believe, living by Christian morality would be a means to "squeak by" in this life with the least amount of suffering and disappointment obtainable to the human race. In a manner of speaking, the situation can be reduced to a social equation: living by the precepts of Christian morality = the least amount of human suffering in this life, with the possibility of hope at our end for a brighter eternity vs. living by atheistic/humanistic amorality = constant disappointment and suffering in this life, with no possibility of hope for a happy eternity to come.

This is the choice that lies before the human race. Anyone with just a basic understanding of the failings of human nature will be able to immediately grasp the dangers that lie before us if we continue on our path of hedonistically voluptuous, suicidal dissipation. A key point to note is that if the readers believe me to be "over the top" or "extreme" in my vision, then they are allowed the benefit of time for discernment. The evils portended will not overtake the world in a single day, week, month, or year. They will subsume, and indeed have already begun to subsume, the whole of humanity at such a gradual pace that it will allow for a change of heart for those who are possibly weak in either understanding or fortitude.

This book is an attempt to aid those who are weak in understanding. However, fortitude is something that each of the readers will have to accomplish for themselves if they so desire. The road back to a sane social order (Judeo-Christian morality) will always be open to the human race; right up until the end of civilization and its descent into abject barbarism. Make your choice! Life or Death! Remember, there is nothing destructive in choosing the Christian way of life and morality, as hard as it is to bear, and even if God did not exist; but there is everything destructive in humanistically "liberal" atheism. If you choose death over life because you are either too weak to deny your animal instincts, or too proud to admit that you need divine help to overcome them, then you will have no defense at the conclusion of your life to save yourself from your abominable, suicidal choice!

As the effort has been made to demonstrate both the reality of God and the truth that the Catholic Church is the one true religion, the fact remains that there still exists in the modern world a *great* division between the Catholic faithful and those who do not believe. For those who do not at this point in time believe in the truth of what is explained here, there exists a remedy that exceeds human abilities. For those who are unconvinced by the case that has been put forward, I humbly propose something for the reader that relies not at all on words or arguments, but rather completely on God. In other words, "If you don't believe me, ask God yourself"! How is such a thing done? Very simply . . . *prayer.* If there is any doubt regarding the truth of what has been related to the readers, then simply go "straight to the horse's mouth," so to speak. Pray to God for direct knowledge from Himself; something along the lines of . . . "God, if you are really real, I need to know it. Moreover, is it true that the Catholic Church is really the only true religion on Earth"? Why will God answer such a prayer offered in *sincerity*? Because He promised to do so, and for Him to ignore a *sincere* prayer from anybody is equivalent to God making Himself a liar:

> [7]Ask, and it shall be given you: seek, and you shall find: knock, and it shall be opened to you. [8]For every one that asketh, receiveth: and he that seeketh, findeth: and to him that knocketh, it shall be opened. [9]Or what man is there among you, of whom if his son shall ask bread, will he reach him a stone? [10]Or if he shall ask him a fish, will he reach him a serpent? [11]If you then being evil, know how to give good gifts to your children: how much more will your Father who is in heaven, give good things to them that ask him?[1]

However, it must be made known to the reader(s) that there are two caveats to this prayer.[2] The first caveat regards the internal attitude and disposition of the individual when they pray. If you are willing to go straight to God for answers you *must* do so in a spirit of humility; willing to receive the answer He will give, whether the answer conforms to your own present belief system and desires or not, and not in a spirit of sarcasm or contempt: being convinced that you already know the answer before the question was

---

[1]   Matthew 7:7-11.
[2]   Did you notice the italics on the words *sincere* and *sincerity* in the previous paragraph?

asked. Why is a person's internal disposition so critical to the outcome of the prayer? . . . *free will!* Human beings are allowed the freedom to believe whatever they want, if they so will themselves to believe it. Even if any particular idea or belief is false, God will allow people to believe that which they will themselves to believe. If you pray for guidance from God you *must* be willing to accept the answer, even if it is one you may not like or be prepared to hear.

If you pray for guidance from God while being self-convinced of the answer before the question is asked, how can this be viewed in any other fashion, from God's perspective, than as a challenge to, and mockery of, Himself? It's the same as saying, "I know I'm right, God. Convince me otherwise if you can." He will not try to convince you otherwise if you come to the question not desiring to know what is real and true, but rather that which you will yourself to believe! How could anyone expect a sincere answer when asked from such a petulant and intellectually proud heart?

The second caveat regards the expectation of an answer. God is not a dog to be commanded. Anyone who prays to God for anything must be willing to wait for an answer in His good time.

> But of this one thing be not ignorant, my beloved, that one
> day with the Lord is as a thousand years, and a thousand
> years as one day.[3]

Some prayers may be answered immediately, but others, depending on a person's life situation and internal disposition, may be delayed for reasons only God knows. So long as you remain humbly patient and open to receive the answer in God's time (not yours) . . . *It will come.*

For the faithful who already believe, it is timely to remember that Christianity, especially as it is embodied by the Catholic Church, was the foundation upon which Western civilization was built. There is a saying within the Church, "As the Church goes, so goes the world." As the human race has rejected Church teachings on morality and social order, they have steadily trod down the current path of narcissistically nihilistic self-destruction.

The modern Catholic bears the burden of restoring the human race back to a state of sanity. The reprobates of the world detest the Church because it preaches self-control and self-sacrifice. Unfortunately, many of them are too far progressed down the road of submission to their barbaric, animalistic

---

[3] 2 Peter 3:8.

nature to return to sanity without great help; both human and divine. As Catholics, this is our duty to ourselves, our progeny, and the human race as a whole. It does not mean, and should not be construed as, any type of forcible coercion regarding the acceptance of the Catholic Faith. God gave mankind free will in accepting or rejecting Him. We have no right to try and circumvent the free will God granted to mankind through any type of coercive measure(s). All that is required of us is living lives faithful to the teachings of the Church, so as to set a better example for others to follow, while exercising obedience to God; as expounded by the Magisterium.

As mentioned earlier, at this point in human history the only way to call God's mercy upon us is through Holy Obedience to His will, which was explained to mankind during the Marian apparitions at Fátima. The Virgin Mary has promised a period of peace if her requests are granted: the consecration of Russia to her Immaculate Heart; simultaneously by all the world's bishops during a single act of consecration.

The world scoffs at and mocks such things as being "superstitious." However, Catholics should know better; that this would be the natural, worldly response:

> But we preach Christ crucified, unto the Jews indeed a stumblingblock, and unto the Gentiles foolishness:[4]

As Catholics, do you treat this the same way; with an attitude of, "That's just superstition"!? Is your faith real or just pretense? This is the time in human history where you are being most sorely put to the test. Will you pass or will you fail? Either way, the choice is entirely yours to make. However, my fellow Catholics are exhorted to choose wisely, because nothing less than everything is at stake; both temporally and eternally. May God bless, forgive, and have mercy on us all; and especially so if the human race continues to choose its sad and long march down the road of the Dark Night.

---

[4] 1 Corinthians 1:23.

Appendix A

Declaration of the Rights of Man and of the Citizen

Approved by the National Assembly of France,
August 26, 1789

The representatives of the French people, organized as a National Assembly, believing that the ignorance, neglect, or contempt of the rights of man are the sole cause of public calamities and of the corruption of governments, have determined to set forth in a solemn declaration the natural, unalienable, and sacred rights of man, in order that this declaration, being constantly before all the members of the Social body, shall remind them continually of their rights and duties; in order that the acts of the legislative power, as well as those of the executive power, may be compared at any moment with the objects and purposes of all political institutions and may thus be more respected, and, lastly, in order that the grievances of the citizens, based hereafter upon simple and incontestable principles, shall tend to the maintenance of the constitution and redound to the happiness of all.

Therefore the National Assembly recognizes and proclaims, in the presence and under the auspices of the Supreme Being, the following rights of man and of the citizen:

Articles:

1. Men are born and remain free and equal in rights. Social distinctions may be founded only upon the general good.
2. The aim of all political association is the preservation of the natural and imprescriptible rights of man. These rights are liberty, property, security, and resistance to oppression.
3. The principle of all sovereignty resides essentially in the nation. No body nor individual may exercise any authority which does not proceed directly from the nation.

4. Liberty consists in the freedom to do everything which injures no one else; hence the exercise of the natural rights of each man has no limits except those which assure to the other members of the society the enjoyment of the same rights. These limits can only be determined by law.

5. Law can only prohibit such actions as are hurtful to society. Nothing may be prevented which is not forbidden by law, and no one may be forced to do anything not provided for by law.

6. Law is the expression of the general will. Every citizen has a right to participate personally, or through his representative, in its foundation. It must be the same for all, whether it protects or punishes. All citizens, being equal in the eyes of the law, are equally eligible to all dignities and to all public positions and occupations, according to their abilities, and without distinction except that of their virtues and talents.

7. No person shall be accused, arrested, or imprisoned except in the cases and according to the forms prescribed by law. Any one soliciting, transmitting, executing, or causing to be executed, any arbitrary order, shall be punished. But any citizen summoned or arrested in virtue of the law shall submit without delay, as resistance constitutes an offense.

8. The law shall provide for such punishments only as are strictly and obviously necessary, and no one shall suffer punishment except it be legally inflicted in virtue of a law passed and promulgated before the commission of the offense.

9. As all persons are held innocent until they shall have been declared guilty, if arrest shall be deemed indispensable, all harshness not essential to the securing of the prisoner's person shall be severely repressed by law.

10. No one shall be disquieted on account of his opinions, including his religious views, provided their manifestation does not disturb the public order established by law.

11. The free communication of ideas and opinions is one of the most precious of the rights of man. Every citizen may, accordingly, speak, write, and print with freedom, but shall be responsible for such abuses of this freedom as shall be defined by law.

12. The security of the rights of man and of the citizen requires public military forces. These forces are, therefore, established for the good

of all and not for the personal advantage of those to whom they shall be intrusted.

13. A common contribution is essential for the maintenance of the public forces and for the cost of administration. This should be equitably distributed among all the citizens in proportion to their means.

14. All the citizens have a right to decide, either personally or by their representatives, as to the necessity of the public contribution; to grant this freely; to know to what uses it is put; and to fix the proportion, the mode of assessment and of collection and the duration of the taxes.

15. Society has the right to require of every public agent an account of his administration.

16. A society in which the observance of the law is not assured, nor the separation of powers defined, has no constitution at all.

17. Since property is an inviolable and sacred right, no one shall be deprived thereof except where public necessity, legally determined, shall clearly demand it, and then only on condition that the owner shall have been previously and equitably indemnified.

Appendix B

Suggested Reading Material

America and the Constitution
Borden, Morton ed. *The Antifederalist Papers*. Ann Arbor, MI: Michigan State University Press, 1965.
De Tocqueville, Alexis. *Democracy In America*. Trans. Arthur Goldhammer. New York, NY: The Library of America, 2004. ISBN: 1-931082-54-5
D'Souza, Dinesh. *What's So Great About America?* Washington, DC: Regnery Publishing, Inc., 2002. ISBN: 0-89526-153-7
Grafton, John ed. *The Declaration of Independence and Other Great Documents of American History, 1775-1865*. Mineola, NY: Dover Publications, Inc., 2000. ISBN: 0-486-41124-9
Ketcham, Ralph ed. *The Anti-Federalist Papers and the Constitutional Convention Debates*. New York, NY: New American Library, a division of Penguin Putnam, Inc., 1986. ISBN: 0-451-62525-0
Rossiter, Clinton ed. *The Federalist Papers*. New York, NY: New American Library, a division of Penguin Putnam, Inc., 1999. ISBN: 0-451-62881-0
Skousen, W. Cleon. *The Five Thousand Year Leap: The 28 Great Ideas That Are Changing the World*. Washington, DC: National Center for Constitutional Studies, 1996. ISBN: 0-88080-004-6
Skousen, W. Cleon. *The Making of America: The Substance and Meaning of the Constitution*. Washington, DC: National Center for Constitutional Studies, 1986. ISBN: 0-88080-017-8

Culture
Kupelian, David. *The Marketing of Evil: How Radicals, Elitists, and Pseudo-Experts Sell Us Corruption Disguised as Freedom*. Nashville, TN: WND Books, 2005. ISBN: 1-58182-459-9
Washington, Booker T. *Up From Slavery*. Mineola, NY: Dover Publications, Inc., 1995. ISBN: 0-486-28738-6

Culture
Kirk, Marshall and Madsen, Hunter. *After the Ball: How America Will Conquer its Fear & Hatred of Gays in the 90s.* New York, NY: Doubleday, a division of Bantam Doubleday Dell Publishing Group, Inc., 1989. ISBN: 0-385-23906-8

Economics
Griffin, G. Edward. *The Creature From Jekyll Island: A Second Look at the Federal Reserve.* 4th ed. Westlake Village, CA: American Media, 2002. ISBN: 0-912986-39-5
Smith, Adam. *Wealth of Nations.* Amherst, NY: Prometheus Books, 1991. ISBN: 0-87975-705-1

Education
Blumenfeld, Samuel L. *NEA: The Trojan Horse in American Education.* Boise, ID: The Paradigm Company, 1997. ISBN: 0-941995-07-0
Iserbyt, Charlotte Thomson. *The Deliberate Dumbing Down of America: A Chronological Paper Trail.* Ravenna, OH: Conscience Press, 1999. ISBN: 0-9667071-0-9
Sowell, Thomas. *Inside American Education: The Decline, The Deception, The Dogmas.* New York, NY: The Free Press (a division of Simon & Schuster, Inc.), 1993. ISBN: 0-02-930330-3

History
Everitt, Anthony. *Cicero: The Life and Times of Rome's Greatest Politician.* New York, NY: Random House, Inc., 2003. ISBN: 0-375-75895-X
Gibbon, Edward. *The Decline and Fall of the Roman Empire (Volumes 1 – 3).* New York, NY: Alfred K. Knopf, a division of Random House, 1994.
Gibbon, Edward. *The Decline and Fall of the Roman Empire (Volumes 4 – 6).* New York, NY: Alfred K. Knopf, a division of Random House, 1994.
Heineman, John L. *Readings in European History, 1789 – Present: A Collection of Primary Sources.* 2nd ed. Dubuque, IA: Kendall/Hunt Publishing Company, 1994. ISBN: 0-8403-9125-0

Liberalism/Socialism/Communism
Charen, Mona. *Useful Idiots: How Liberals Got It Wrong in the Cold War and Still Blame America First.* Washington, DC: Regnery Publishing, Inc., 2003. ISBN: 0-89-526139-1
Flynn, Daniel J. *Why the Left Hates America.* Roseville, CA: Prima Publishing, 2002. ISBN: 0-7615-6375-X
Foster, William Z. *Toward a Soviet America.* Balboa Island, CA: Elgin Publications, 1961.
Gielow, Fred. *You Don't Say: Sometime Liberals Show Their True Colors.* Boca Raton, FL: Freedom Books, 1999. ISBN: 0-9603938-2-X
Kramer, Mark, ed. *The Black Book Of Communism.* Trans. Jonathan Murphy and Mark Kramer. Cambridge, MA: Harvard University Press, 2001. ISBN: 0-674-07608-7
Orwell, George; *Animal Farm;* New York, NY: New American Library, a division of Penguin Putnam, Inc., 1996. ISBN: 0-451-52634-1
Orwell, George. *1984.* New York, NY: New American Library, a division of Penguin Putnam, Inc. ISBN: 0-451-52493-4
Rummel, R. J. *Death By Government.* New Brunswick, NJ: Transaction Publishers, 1994. ISBN: 1-56000-927-6
Skousen, W. Cleon. *The Naked Communist.* Cutchogue, NY: Buccaneer Books, Inc., 1994. ISBN: 1-56849-367-3
Weigand, Kate. *Red Feminism: American Communism and the Making of Women's Liberation.* Baltimore, MD: The Johns Hopkins University Press, 2001. ISBN: 0-8018-7111-5

Literature
Alighieri, Dante. *The Divine Comedy.* Trans. John Ciardi. New York, NY: New American Library, a division of Penguin Putnam, Inc., 2003 ISBN: 0-451-20863-3
(St.) More, Thomas. *Utopia.* New Haven, CT: Yale University Press, 1964. ISBN: 0-300-00238-6
Swift, Jonathan. *Gulliver's Travels.* New York, NY: Penguin Putnam, Inc., 2003. ISBN: 0-14-143949-1

New World Order (NWO) / Conspiratorial
Corsi, Jerome. *The Late Great U.S.A.* Los Angeles, CA: WND Books, an Imprint of World Ahead Media, 2007. ISBN: 0-979045-14-2

New World Order (NWO) / Conspiratorial

Quigley, Carroll. *Tragedy & Hope: A History of the World In Our Time*. San Pedro, CA: GSG & Associates, 1975. ISBN: 0-945001-10-X

Robison, John. *Proofs of a Conspiracy*. Boston, MA: Western Islands. ISBN: 0-88-279121-4

Skousen, W. Cleon. *The Naked Capitalist*. Cutchogue, NY: Buccaneer Books, Inc., 1993. ISBN: 0-89968-323-1

Philosophy

Aristotle. *Metaphysics: Books I - IX*. Trans. Hugh Tredennick. Cambridge, MA: Harvard University Press, 1979. ISBN: 0-674-99299-7.

Aristotle. *Metaphysics: Books X – XIV; Oeconomica Magna Moralia*. Trans. Hugh Tredennick and C. Cyril Armstrong. Cambridge, MA: Harvard University Press, 1982. ISBN: 0-674-99317-9.

Aristotle. *Nicomachean Ethics*. Upper Saddle River, NJ: Prentice Hall, Inc., 1999. ISBN: 0-02-389530-6

Aristotle. *Physics: Books I - IV*. Trans. P.H. Wicksteed and F.M. Cornford. Cambridge, MA: Harvard University Press, 1986. ISBN: 0-674-99251-2

Aristotle. *Physics: Books V - VIII*. Trans. P.H. Wicksteed and F.M. Cornford. Cambridge, MA: Harvard University Press, 2006. ISBN: 0-674-99281-4.

Bastiat, Frederic. *The Law*. Translated by Dean Russell. New York, NY: The Foundation for Economic Education, Inc., 1996. ISBN: 1-57246-020-2

Grant, Michael ed. *Cicero: Selected Works*. Trans. Michael Grant. New York, NY: Penguin Books, 1971. ISBN: 0-14-044099-2

Politics

Machiavelli, Niccolo. *The Prince*. Trans. Daniel Donno. New York, NY: Bantam Books. ISBN: 0-553-21278-8

Aristotle. *Politics*. Trans. Benjamin Jowett. Mineola, NY: Dover Publications, Inc., 2000. ISBN: 0-486-41424-8

Plato. *Republic*. Trans. G.M.A. Grube, 2nd ed., revised by C.D.C. Greeve, Indianapolis, IN: Hackett Publishing Company, Inc.; 1992. ISBN: 0-87220-136-8

Prophecy (Literary)
Huxley, Aldous. *Brave New World.* New York, NY: HarperPerennial, a division of HarperCollins Publishers, 1998. ISBN: 0-06-092987-1
Raspail, Jean. *The Camp of The Saints.* Trans. Norman Shapiro. Petoskey, MI: The Social Contract Press, 1994. ISBN: 1-881780-07-4

Religion/Theology
Holy Bible. Douay-Rheims version
Q'uran; Mohammed.
American Scientific Affiliation, The and F. Alton Everest Ed. *Modern Science and Christian Faith: Eleven Essays on the Relationship of the Bible to Modern Science.* Wheaton, IL: Van Kampen Press, 1948.
Carré, Marie. *AA-1025: The Memoirs of an Anti-Apostle.* Rockford, IL: TAN Books and Publishers, Inc., 1991. ISBN: 0-89555-449-6
(St.) Hildegard of Bingen. *Scivias.* Mahwah, NJ: Paulist Press, 1990. ISBN: 0-8091-3130-7
(St.) Aquinas, Thomas. *Summa Contra Gentiles: Book One: God.* Trans. Anton C. Pegis, F.R.S.C. Notre Dame, IN: University of Notre Dame Press, 1997. ISBN: 0-268-01678-X
(St.) Aquinas, Thomas. *Summa Contra Gentiles: Book Two: Creation.* Trans. James F. Anderson. Notre Dame, IN: University of Notre Dame Press, 1992. ISBN: 0-268-01680-1
(St.) Aquinas, Thomas. *Summa Contra Gentiles: Book Three: Providence, Part I.* Trans. Vernon J. Bourke. Notre Dame, IN: University of Notre Dame Press, 1991. ISBN: 0-268-01686-0
(St.) Aquinas, Thomas. *Summa Contra Gentiles: Book Three: Providence, Part II.* Trans. Vernon J. Bourke. Notre Dame, IN: University of Notre Dame Press, 1991. ISBN: 0-268-01688-7
(St.) Aquinas, Thomas. *Summa Contra Gentiles: Book Four: Salvation.* Trans. Charles J. O'Neil. Notre Dame, IN: University of Notre Dame Press, 1989. ISBN: 0-268-01684-4
(St.) Aquinas, Thomas. *Summa Theologica.* Trans. Fathers of the English Dominican Province. 5 Vols. Notre Dame, IN: Ave Maria Press, Inc., 1981. ISBN: 0-87061-063-5
Cristiani, Léon. *Evidence of Satan in the Modern World.* Trans. Cynthia Rowland. Rockford, IL: TAN Books and Publishers, Inc., 1977. ISBN: 0-89555-032-6

Religion/Theology
Cruz, Joan Carroll. *Eucharistic Miracles*. Rockford, IL: TAN Books and Publishers, Inc., 1987. ISBN: 0-89555-303-1
Emmerich, Anne Catherine. *The Dolorous Passion of Our Lord Jesus Christ*. Rockford, IL: TAN Books and Publishers, Inc., 1994. ISBN: 0-89555-210-8
Jones, Kenneth C. *Index of Leading Catholic Indicators: The Church Since Vatican II*. Fort Collins, CO: Roman Catholic Books, 2003. ISBN: 1-929291-58-2
Kempis, Thomas. *The Imitation of Christ*. Trans. William Griffin. San Francisco, CA: HarperCollins Publishers, Inc., 2000. ISBN: 0-06-063400-6
Kowalska, Maria Faustina. *Divine Mercy In My Soul: Diary of St. Maria Faustina Kowalska*. Stockbridge, MA: Marian Press, 2006. ISBN: 0-944203-04-3
Kramer, Herman Bernard. *The Book of Destiny*: Rockford, IL: TAN Books and Publishers, Inc., 1975. ISBN: 0-89555-046-6
(Fr.) Arminjon, Charles. *The End of the Present World and the Mysteries of the Future Life*. Manchester, NH: Sophia Institute Press, 2008. ISBN: 978-1-933184-38-8
(Fr.) Martin, Malachi. *Hostage to the Devil*. San Francisco, CA: HarperCollins Publishers, Inc., 1999. ISBN: 0-06-065337-X
The Popes Against Modern Errors. Mioni, Anthony J. Jr. Ed. Rockford, IL: TAN Books and Publishers, Inc., 1999. ISBN: 0-89555-478-X
Mary of Jesus of Agreda [Spain]. *The Mystical City of God: The Divine History and Life of the Virgin Mother of God*. Trans. Fiscar Marison. 4 Volumes. Rockford, IL: TAN Books and Publishers, Inc., 2006. ISBN: 0-89555-825-4
Sarda y Salvany, Felix. *Liberalism Is A Sin*. Trans. Conde B. Pallen. Rockford, IL: TAN Books and Publishers, Inc., 1993. ISBN: 0-89555-643-X
Schmöger, Carl E. *The Life and Revelations of Anne Catherine Emmerich. 2 Vols.* Rockford, IL: TAN Books and Publishers, Inc., 1993. ISBN: 0-89555-061-X
(Fr.) Schouppe, F.X., S.J. *HELL: The Dogma of Hell, Illustrated by Facts Taken from Profane and Sacred History*. Rockford, IL: TAN Books and Publishers, Inc., 1989. ISBN: 0-89555-346-5

Religion/Theology
(Fr.) Schouppe, F.X., S.J. *Purgatory: Explained by the Lives and Legends of the Saints.* Rockford, IL: TAN Books and Publishers, Inc., 1998. ISBN: 0-89555-301-5
Sister Maria Lucia of Jesus. *Fatima in Lucia's Own Words.* Ed. Fr. Louis Kondor, SVD. Still River, MA: Ravengate Press, 1998.
Sister Maria Lucia of Jesus. *Fatima in Lucia's Own Words II.* Ed. Fr. Louis Kondor, SVD. Still River, MA: Ravengate Press, 2004. ISBN: 972-8524-04-8
Walsh, William Thomas. *Our Lady of Fátima.* New York, NY: Doubleday, a division of Bantam Doubleday Dell Publishing Group, Inc., 1990. ISBN: 0-385-02869-5
Stoner, Peter W. *Science Speaks.* Chicago, IL: Moody Press Publications, 1963
(Fr.) Hebert, Albert J. *Saints Who Raised The Dead.* Rockford, IL: TAN Books and Publishers, Inc., 1986. ISBN: 0-89555-798-3
Cruz, Joan Carroll. *The Incorruptibles.* Rockford, IL: TAN Books and Publishers, Inc., 1977. ISBN: 0-89555-066-0

United Nations
Babbin, Jed. *Inside The Asylum: Why the United Nations and Old Europe are Worse Than You Think.* Washington, DC: Regnery Publishing, Inc., 2004. ISBN:0-89526-088-3

Appendix C

Miracles Within Christianity
The Raising of the Dead:
St. Stanislaus

One of the most prolific miracle workers in the history of Christianity was St. Vincent Ferrer. He was credited with converting around 200,000 souls to Christianity and was reported to have risen over thirty people from the dead during his lifetime. Throughout the history of the Church, dozens of saints have raised hundreds of people. However, Saint Stanislaus was chosen to demonstrate the raising of the dead because the miracle credited to the saint happened in such a dramatic, and especially public, manner.

St. Stanislaus

St. Stanislaus, Bishop of Cracow and martyr (July 26, 1030 – May 8, 1079) is surely one of the greatest—if not the greatest—of the patrons of Poland. Born Stanislaus Sazepanouski in Sezepanou, in what was then the diocese of Cracow (lately the archdiocese of Cardinal Wojtyla, to become Pope John Paul II), he had great difficulties with Duke Boleslaw, who had become the cruel King Boleslaw II of Poland. He prayed for the king and pleaded tearfully with him to better his life—but to no avail.

It is generally conceded that there were disputes with the king over property claimed by the Church. Boleslaw was also hostile to the saint because of his preaching and holiness. The king conspired with the heirs of one Peter Miles, who had been dead for three years. Before he died he had sold a certain piece of property to the Church. But the conspirators claimed that Stanislaus possessed it for the Church by fraud, and they brought the saint to court on this false charge.

St. Stanislaus asked the judge for a three-day delay, after which he would produce the dead man himself as a witness to the right of the Church to possess the property. His request was granted, although the saint was laughed to scorn by some, particularly his enemies. St. Stanislaus then prayed and fasted for three days (and it is likely others may have done the same along with their holy bishop).

On the third day the court reconvened. After Mass Stanislaus led a procession to the graveside of Peter Miles. Stanislaus prayed before the grave. Then he had the grave opened; there before them lay nothing but the bones of Peter Miles, deceased three years.

Stanislaus then touched the bones of Peter with his episcopal crozier, and in the Name of Christ, ordered the dead man to rise. Before the awed clergy and crowd the bones suddenly reunited, became covered with flesh, and Peter Miles came forth from the grave.

Peter took the hand of Stanislaus and they proceeded to the trial. There Boleslaw waited with his "witnesses" in expectation of securing "restitution" of the property, and disgracing the holy bishop. In amazement and consternation king and plotters watched as the Bishop and Peter Miles entered the court, followed by a reverent but excited crowd.

"Behold Peter"! spoke the saintly Bishop. "He comes to give testimony before you. Interrogate him. He will answer you."

Amidst the stupefaction, awe and—one suspects—the frightened consciences of king and conspirators, Peter affirmed before the court that he had been paid for the contested property. He then turned to his terrified relatives and reproached them for their evil plans, exhorting them to do penance. St. Stanislaus was acquitted.[1]

---

[1] Fr. Albert J Hebert, *Saints Who Raised The Dead* (Rockford, IL: TAN Books and Publishers, Inc., 1986), 147-149.

The Incorruptibility of the Saints: The Absence of Decay or Deterioration in Their Deceased Bodies

The cases of incorruptibility noted here are especially significant because the bodies in question were not prepared for long term preservation after they died (i.e., they were not embalmed). Moreover, although there are many documented cases of saints who have remained incorrupt, only those currently on display for any person (skeptic or faithful) to view are mentioned.

St. Rose of Viterbo (d. 1252)

Defender of the Church. Promoted allegiance to the Pope amidst the oppression of Emperor Frederick II. "In 1921 her heart, still perfectly incorrupt, was extracted and placed in a reliquary, which is taken in procession through the city every year on the fourth of September, the feast day of this saint . . . The body of the young Saint, who died over seven centuries ago, is dark but perfectly flexible and is exposed in a reliquary for the veneration and edification of the faithful."[2]

Saint Sperandia (d. 1276)

Benedictine nun and ascetical penitent. "The body of the saint was last examined in 1952 when it was found to be still perfectly intact, flexible, and "exhaling a suave fragrance."[3] Although the skin is dry, it has maintained a natural color, with only a slight tendency to darken. The excellent condition and suppleness of the body has existed for over seven centuries and for that reason is reverently esteemed by the devoted pilgrims to the shrine as a "Miracolo Permanente."[4]

---

[2] Joan Carroll Cruz, *The Incorruptibles* (Rockford, IL: TAN Books and Publishers, Inc., 1977), 85.

[3] "*Un Fiore di Santita Benedettina S. Sperandia, Vergine*. D. Guglielmo, Can. Co. Malazampa. Cingoli. 1952. p. 57." (footnote from the source text)

[4] Cruz, *The Incorruptibles*, 87.

Saint Zita (d. 1278)

Domestic worker. Through patience and charity she converted her employer's household, and fellow workers, to the Church. "The relic, as seen through the glass-sided walls of her reliquary, appears somewhat dark and dry, but still perfectly entire . . ."[5]

Blessed Margaret of Metola (d. 1320)

Born a blind, hunchbacked, and lame dwarf; she was abandoned at the age of sixteen by her parents when a visit to the miraculous shrine at Citta-di-Castello failed to produce a miraculous cure. She eventually became a Dominican tertiary. "The body of Bl. Margaret, which has never been embalmed, is dressed in a Dominican habit, and lies under the high altar of the Church of St. Domenico at Citta-di-Castello, Italy. The arms of the body are still flexible, the eyelashes are present, and the nails are in place on the hands and feet. The coloring of the body has darkened slightly and the skin is dry and somewhat hardened, but by all standards the preservation can be considered a remarkable condition, having endured for over six hundred fifty years."[6]

St. Catherine of Bologna (d. 1463)

Nun and mystic. Author of *The Seven Spiritual Weapons*; enshrined in the sitting position in the chapel of the Poor Clares at Bologna since 1500. "For over four and one-half centuries the relic remained without a protective covering; however, now it is surrounded by a glass urn that was constructed in 1953. During the last World War the hands and feet of the relic became somewhat chapped and these were covered with a light coat of wax for protection. The face and body are still normal, but the color of the flesh is black, a condition blamed for the most part on the oil lamps used throughout the centuries in the chapel and the many votive candles which burned near the unprotected relic."[7]

---

[5] Ibid., 88.

[6] Ibid., 112.

[7] Ibid., 144.

Blessed Margaret of Savoy (d. 1464)

Dominican nun and mystic. "The sacred body of the Saint, clothed in the Dominican habit, lies exposed to view in a glass-sided reliquary on the lateral altar of the Church of St. Magdalen in Alba, Italy. The body is rather brown, but after five hundred years it still retains its softness and flexibility."[8]

Blessed Eustochia Calafato (d. 1485)

Nun of the Poor Clare order. Established a convent according to the original rule of St. Clare. Credited with numerous miracles. "Still preserved at the Monastero Montevergine[9] is the perfectly preserved body of the Beata. Although darkened after the lapse of five centuries, the body is nonetheless perfect in every respect, with the two fingers of the right hand poised in an attitude of perpetual blessing."[10]

Blessed Bernard Scammacca (d. 1486)

Born into a noble family, he lived a sinful life until a serious leg injury, received in a fight, caused him to reconsider the course of his life. "He was received into the Dominican Order at Catania and spent the rest of his life practicing severe penances to expiate for the sins of his youth. . .

The sacred relic, still incorrupt after a period of almost five hundred years, is exposed to view in the parish church of S. Biagio in S. Domenico, Catania, where the faithful still marvel at the preservation of the remains of the Beatus which, though somewhat dry, are still tender and light in color."[11]

Saint Catherine of Genoa (d. 1510)

Wife, nurse, and author of the *Spiritual Dialogues* and *Treatise on Purgatory*. "In 1694 the body was placed in a shrine having glass sides, and it is in this

---

[8] Ibid., 146.
[9] In Messina, Italy (Siciliy).
[10] Cruz, *The Incorruptibles*, 151.
[11] Ibid., 152-153.

reliquary that it still reposes high above the main altar of the church dedicated to her in the Quarter of Portoria, in Genoa.

The Saint's body was carefully examined by physicians in 1837 and again on May 10, 1960, when it was ascertained that the relic, which is brown and somewhat dry and rigid, was never embalmed nor had any treatment administered to it in order to preserve it."[12]

St. Catherine Dei Ricci (d. 1590)

Dominican nun, mystic, and stigmatic. "The Basilica of Prato possesses with pride the incorrupt remains of this saint who has been designated the patroness of the city. The darkened, but still beautiful relic of the Saint lies in an ornate reliquary, which is exposed for public veneration below the major altar of the basilica."[13]

Venerable Maria Vela (d. 1617)

Cistercian nun and mystic. "The body of the Venerable now rests in a crystal reliquary, which is still situated in its lofty position between the upper and lower choirs and can be viewed by both those in the church and the sisters in the cloistered choir. The rigid but only slightly yellowed body of the Venerable has miraculously contradicted the laws of nature for over three hundred fifty years."[14]

Venerable Mary of Ágreda (d. 1665)

Spanish Franciscan nun and author of *Mystical City of God*; an account of the life of the Blessed Virgin Mary. Her body is today kept in the Church of the Convent of Ágreda.

---

[12] Ibid., 160.
[13] Ibid., 198.
[14] Ibid., 229.

St. Lucy Filippini (d. 1732)

Foundress of the Pontifical Institute Maestre Pie Filippini, for the purpose of education. She established several catechetical training centers under the direction and approval of Cardinal Marcantonio Barbarigo and Pope Clement XI. "After two centuries, her body is still remarkably preserved. No bones have separated, and these are covered with soft and flexible tissue. Her legs and feet are especially well conserved and "look like a person just after death." . . . The precious relic of this holy foundress is exposed in her crystal reliquary in the crypt of St. Margaret's Cathedral in Montefiascone."[15]

St. Teresa Margaret of the Sacred Heart (d. 1770)

A Discalced Carmelite nun; St. Teresa was struck down by a gangrenous condition in her intestines. "Her body, now dark and dry but still perfectly incorrupt, lies exposed to public view in the chapel of the Monastery of St. Teresa, Via dei Bruni 12, Florence, Italy."[16]

St. Catherine Labouré (d. 1876)

Visionary nun, to whom the Blessed Virgin Mary delivered a vision of the "Miraculous Medal," and hence instructed her to have a medal struck in the design shown her. St. Catherine's body has been "placed in the motherhouse chapel under the side altar of Our Lady of the Sun, where it still reposes behind a covering of glass. The upturned hands around which a rosary is entwined are made of wax. The incorrupt hands of the Saint, which have been amputated, are kept in a special reliquary, which is now enshrined in the novitiate cloister of the motherhouse. The heart of the Saint was likewise put into a special reliquary made of jeweled crystal and gold, which is reverently kept in the chapel at Reuilly where the Saint had so often prayed between duties at the hospice."[17]

---

[15] Ibid., 254-255.
[16] Ibid., 259.
[17] Ibid., 284-285.

St. Bernadette Soubirous (d. 1879)

Visionary nun, most famous for her visitations by the Blessed Virgin Mary in Lourdes, France. "The sacred relic was placed in a coffin of gold and glass and can be viewed in the Chapel of Saint Bernadette at the motherhouse in Nevers."[18]

---

[18] Ibid., 289.

Eucharistic Miracles: The Miraculous Transformation or Preservation of Consecrated Hosts

Lanciano, Italy (700 A.D.)

This Eucharistic miracle is probably the most exceptional instance in the history of the Church. It has happened in the past that some very old consecrated Hosts have persisted to this day. However, this miracle is unique in that not only has it persisted for over thirteen hundred years, but at the time of the miracle the Host changed into human flesh and the consecrated wine changed into human blood in order to demonstrate the reality of transubstantiation—the changing of the bread and wine into the Body and Blood of Jesus Christ at the moment of consecration—to the monk who was celebrating Mass, but who persisted in doubts regarding the reality of transubstantiation.

The flesh and blood were scientifically examined in 1970 by Professor Doctor Odoardo Linoli, professor of anatomy and pathological histology, and in chemistry and clinical microscopy. He was assisted by Doctor Ruggero Bertelli, a professor emeritus of normal human anatomy at the University of Siena.

As a result of the histological (microscopic) studies, the following facts were ascertained and documented: The flesh was identified as striated muscular tissue of the myocardium (heart wall), having no trace whatsoever of any materials or agents used for the preservation of flesh. Both the flesh and the sample of blood were found to be of human origin, emphatically excluding the possibility that it was from an animal species. The blood and the flesh were found to belong to the same blood type, AB. The blood of the Eucharistic miracle was found to contain the following minerals: chlorides, phosphorous, magnesium, potassium, sodium in a lesser degree, and a greater quantity of calcium. Proteins in the clotted blood were found to be normally fractionated, with the same percentage ratio as those found in normal fresh blood.

Professor Linoli further noted that the blood, had it been taken from a cadaver, would have altered rapidly through spoilage and decay. His findings conclusively exclude the possibility of a fraud perpetuated centuries ago. In fact, he maintained that only a hand experienced in anatomic dissection could have obtained from a hollow internal organ, the heart, such an expert cut, made tangentially—that is, a round cut, thick on the outer edges and lessening gradually and uniformly into nothingness in the central area. The doctor ended his report by stating that while the flesh and blood were conserved in receptacles not hermetically sealed, they were not damaged, although they had been exposed to the influences of physical, atmospheric and biological agents.[19]

Ferrara, Italy (1171 A.D.)

On Easter Sunday, March 28, 1171, Mass was being celebrated by Padre Pietro de Verona; assisted by Padre Bono, Padre Leonardo and Padre Aimone. At the moment when the consecrated Host was broken into two parts, a stream of blood began to spurt from it. The blood was so great that it sprinkled a semi-circular vault behind and above the altar. Moreover, not only had the witnesses seen the blood, but the Host had turned into human flesh. The blood is still visible to the naked eye.

Santarem, Portugal (Early 13th Century)

A woman, in her distress over her unfaithful husband, visited a sorceress who promised to deliver her from her problems for the price of one consecrated Host. The woman stole a consecrated Host by removing it from her mouth and attempting to hide it in her veil. Shortly thereafter the Host began to bleed profusely, soaking the woman and her garments in blood. At

---

[19] Joan Carroll Cruz, *Eucharistic Miracles* (Rockford, IL: TAN Books and Publishers, Inc., 1987), 6.

the sight of this prodigy the woman quickly escaped from church to avoid the other parishioners, who believed her to be injured.

When home, she attempted to hide the Host in a trunk; but was forced to admit what she had done when a mysterious light began to emanate from inside the trunk: penetrating the wood and illuminating the whole house. The Host was returned to the Church of St. Stephen, where it remains to this day; having been placed inside a pear-shaped monstrance for viewing.

Bolsena-Orvieto, Italy (1263 A.D.)

A traveling German priest on pilgrimage to Rome (Peter of Prague), while suffering from doubts regarding transubstantiation, stopped at Bolsena along the way and offered Mass at the tomb of St. Christina. Immediately after the consecration, blood began to flow from the Host; covering his hands, corporal, and altar. The corporal is still on display in the Cathedral of Orvieto; and blood stains attributed to the miraculous host are still visible on the floor of the Chapel of the Miracle.

Siena, Italy (1330 A.D.)

A parish priest, responsible for a village on the outskirts of Siena, was called to the bed of an ailing farmer. In haste, the priest put a consecrated Host between the pages of his breviary (priest's prayer book) for transport to the man's home, rather than in a pyx, which is the approved method of transporting consecrated Hosts. After the priest had prayed with and over the sick man he opened up his breviary to retrieve the Host. To the priest's astonishment, the Host had bled and took on a condition such that it appeared to have melted. One of the blood-stained pages was lost during the French Revolution, but the other is still preserved in an ostensorium at the Basilica-Sanctuary of St. Rita in Cascia, Italy.

Siena, Italy (1730 A.D.)

In August, 1730; amidst preparations for the solemnity of the Assumption of the Blessed Virgin Mary, thieves broke into the Church of St. Francis and stole a ciborium from the tabernacle that contained consecrated Hosts. Several days later, no doubt due to the pressure of the growing public outrage over the theft and profanation, a priest recognized a Host sticking out of a church offering box. After the box was opened and the Hosts inventoried, the number exactly matched those believed to have been in the ciborium at the time of the theft. For some reason, the Hosts were not consumed during a mass, as would normally happen in similar situations. As time began to pass it was noticed that the Hosts were not deteriorating. They still remain in a state of perfect preservation and are venerated in the Basilica of St. Francis in Siena.